TELEVISION NEWS

TELEVISION NEWS

Revised and Enlarged Edition

BY

I. E. FANG, PH. D.

School of Journalism and Mass Communication
University of Minnesota

A COMMUNICATION ARTS BOOK

Hastings House, Publishers   New York

To Rachel, Ingrid and Daisy

First published, September 1968
Second printing, July 1970
Third printing, July 1971
Second Edition, Revised and Enlarged, August 1972
Second Edition, Reprinted, February 1974

Library of Congress Cataloging in Publication Data

Fang, Irving E.
  Television news.

  (A Communication arts book)
  Bibliography: p.
  1. Television broadcasting of news. I. Title.
PN4784.T4F3 1972   070'.43   72-10726
ISBN 0-8038-7117-1
ISBN 0-8038-7125-2 (pbk.)

Published simultaneously in Canada by Saunders, of Toronto, Ltd., Don Mills, Ontario

Printed in the United States of America

CONTENTS

PREFACE TO THE
SECOND EDITION

ONCE UPON A TIME, in early 1968, when the moon and China were far away, I wrote a preface which argued the point that television news was a vital force in our society. Now, as this preface to the second edition is being written, that point is a cliché. Who doubts it?

Critics of present television news practices—and there are many—seem to imply that television news is *too* vital a force in American life. TV newscasts are being blamed for the nation's ills, for prolonging the war, for preventing victory, for the defeat of needed bills as well as for the passage of bad laws, and for misdirecting Americans, especially the young. After Vice President Spiro T. Agnew flew to Des Moines to give a speech attacking network television news,[1] tens of thousands of letters, mostly angry, clogged the mailrooms at ABC, CBS and NBC. The Vice President had declared, "Nowhere are there fewer checks on vast power. . . ." and writers of some of those letters wanted that "vast power" to support *their* opinions, or be checked.

In 1971 a CBS documentary, *The Selling of the Pentagon,* infuriated enough men of power so that battle lines formed for a test of freedom of the press. Revoke the licenses of CBS owned-and-operated stations, some said. A congressman introduced a "truth in news broadcasting" bill. The president of CBS News called for an academic convention to consider how broadcast journalism may operate freely in the context of licensing.

[1] Notes for each chapter are grouped for convenience in one section at the end of this book (see pages 457-461).

11

The documentary won a Peabody Award and an Emmy, despite question-able editing of two interviews.

All this raises fundamental questions, troubling questions:

Can a licensed press be free? If so, how do we insure freedom? If things stay as they are, can government forever resist the temptation to use the lever of licensing to "improve" journalism?

Some other questions:

While we all pay lip service to the concepts of freedom and fairness, what should happen in broadcast journalism if the two concepts conflict? Should broadcast journalism be free even if it is biased, or should it be fair even if this means outside control which can be applied subtly, skirting the First Amendment? Is it wrong for television journalism to follow in the vigorous tradition of investigative print journalism, although that tradition does not include too nice a concern for balance? Despite the disclaimers from the profession, is it possible that Tuesday's accurate report of a college disturbance, followed by Wednesday's accurate report, followed by Thursday's accurate report, add up to an inaccurate understanding by viewers of what life at that college is like?

And yet more questions:

Should television journalism get the hands-off treatment accorded by the First Amendment to newspaper and magazine journalism? Would America be better served by a multiplicity of television news voices through CATV or through common carrier broadcast channels? And where do we go from here?

Faced with the present anger, television and radio newsmen might like to retreat to the wishful thought that they are hearing only a tempest in a teacup, a political tempest which will expend itself, leaving broadcast journalism none the worse. But that desire to be left alone to get on with the job ignores the power of television news to shape social and political attitudes, a power which the Vice President of the United States publicly and forcefully recognized, a power which behavioral scientists report, a power which Roper and other pollsters rediscover annually, a power which now lies out of reach of the men who run the government.

If television news were ineffectual, it would be let alone.

It is not.

A study to learn which news medium most influenced the undecided and split-ticket voters of Michigan in 1970 put television newscasts first, followed by television documentaries, newspaper editorials, newspaper stories, television editorials, television talk shows, and radio newscasts. Ads (including television political commercials), billboards and telephone campaigns trailed badly.[2]

A national study asked this question: "If you got conflicting or dif-ferent reports of the same story from radio, television, the magazines and the newspapers, which of the four versions would you be most inclined to

Most believable news source

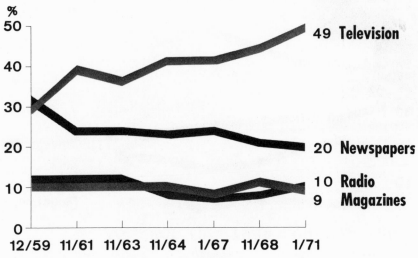

Source: The Roper Organization, Inc., March 1971

Source of most news

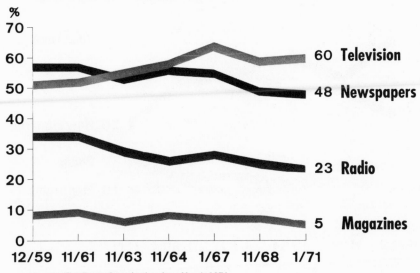

Source: The Roper Organization, Inc., March 1971

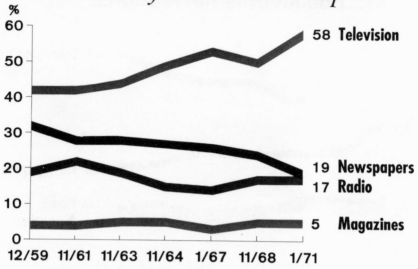

The medium you most want to keep

Source: The Roper Organization, Inc., March 1971

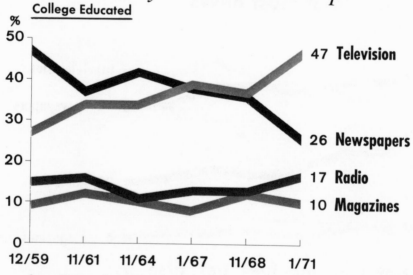

The medium you most want to keep
College Educated

Source: The Roper Organization, Inc., March 1971

believe—the one on radio or television or magazines or newspapers?" Results: television, 49%; newspapers, 20%; radio, 10%; magazines, 9%; don't know or no answer, 12%.[3]

Had *The Selling of the Pentagon* been a newspaper story or a magazine article, the outcry might have been all but inaudible. What was really remarkable about this documentary was its impact upon everyone: those who agreed with it, those who disagreed with it, those who heard and saw things they never heard and saw before, those who said it told the truth, and those who said it told lies.

Another question intrudes. Why do people watch television news? The obvious answer is: to become informed about the day's events. Yet a study of San Francisco Bay Area residents reported that 51% of network newscast viewers could not recall even one story afterward.[4] Perhaps for many viewers, television news is only a kind of early warning radar telling them the world won't blow up today and their taxes won't go up. Or perhaps it's a kind of entertainment. Perhaps it's both, or neither. Answers can only come from research, but little if any research is being done here, although tens of millions of dollars are spent annually to funnel news by television to tens of millions of nightly viewers.

Television news left its childhood a long time ago. Memory now dims of newspapermen who brought clackers to news conferences in order to ruin film sound tracks. We saw television news help to hold this nation together when a president fell in Dallas. Through television news we felt a war across 10,000 miles. Through television news we watched men walk upon the moon and another president visit China, and we saw these events at the moment they were happening.

Speaking about all journalism, Howard K. Smith said, "I would guess that, after formal schooling is over for the average citizen, at least four-fifths of what he continues to learn about his community, about his state and city, and about his nation and the world, come filtered through the observations of the journalist." [5]

Speaking about television news, former NBC president Robert Kintner, said: [6]

> On the day when those of us who have given our lives to the medium are called to account for our time, the heaviest weight on our side of the balance will be this expansion of reality for tens of millions of people. Today many people of relatively little formal education, who read slowly and without pleasure, have met with and probably understood more of the world around them than any but a handful of sophisticated and curious minds understood fifty years ago. They have watched the British bury the greatest of their modern heroes; seen a Russian premier bang his shoe on the table at the UN; looked on while South American students threw tomatoes at a Vice President of the United States; visited classic and modern

Greece; observed the savagery of guerrilla warfare in Vietnam, Yemen, the Congo, Algeria. New Englanders have seen for themselves how Mexican braceros live in California's Imperial Valley; people on the banks of Puget Sound have been plunged into the cauldron of a Harlem riot.

The world day by day moves closer to that peculiar place which Marshall McLuhan calls the global village. The United States already is a section of that village, with television sets in more than 60 million homes. Like it or not, electronic information involves everyone with everyone else, North with South, white with black, old with young. That this involvement stems from accurate information which is understood in its true perspective is, in part, the responsibility of the television journalist. That many people, not just a few people, willingly choose involvement is also, in part, the responsibility of the television journalist.

Go to any corner of this nation, walk through any neighborhood, and you will find television aerials poking up. The roof may leak, but those skinny sticks of metal protrude from it. The television screen is now Everyman's window to both fantasy and reality. In our profession we leave fantasy to others and concentrate on reality.

Or at least we try.

But because reality is not always serious, television news is not always serious. The human comedy is not a misnomer for much of what we see either with camera lens or naked eye, and television newsmen with whom I worked for years can hardly be described as a somber lot. Words of thanks belong here, and they might as well be whimsical. To confront the Seven Deadly Sins of television news—Awkwardness, Bias, Confusion, Dullness, Error, Fear, Grossness—I have drawn upon the working experience of people both in and out of television news. My thanks to film editor Lou Buchignani, reporter Ed Arnow, cameramen Tom Dunnahoo and Joe Longo, soundman Roy Gardener, videotape engineer Nick Pantelakis and video engineer Earl Ross. Professors Donald Gillmor and A.Stuart Bay offered valuable criticism. ABC News provided most of the photographs. My research assistants, Susan Alnes and Nancy Locke, caught many errors. I want to express my deepest gratitude to Ann Noble Bateson for the index, the suggestions which provided the basis of the FOR THE STUDENT questions and exercises, and the fresh eye she brought to these pages. The dedicated men and women, some of whom are quoted in these pages, who regard television news as a profession which needs the best that is in them deserve more thanks than I can convey.

Irving E. Fang
Minneapolis, May 1972

Television cameramen are a visible and vulnerable target for the frustrated. Above, KPIX-TV cameraman Stephen Paszty is beaten to the ground by angry blacks in San Francisco after a police raid on Black Panther headquarters. He was badly hurt and had to be hospitalized. Below, a patrolman in Americus, Ga., shoves an out-of-town television cameraman who was filming a civil rights demonstration. The governor of Georgia had asked civil rights leaders to halt their demonstrations and keep "outside agitators" away. (*UPI Photos*)

1

THE TROUBLES
WE'VE SEEN

BECAUSE MOST OF THE attacks on network television news in recent years have come from political conservatives, we may forget that they are not alone in alleging network news bias. Their concern is shared— and it is a deeply felt concern all around. Cynics who regard the attacks as merely an effort to mute disagreement with conservative policies are shortsighted, wrong and unfair.

Clearly, genuine concern exists about the political and social effects of television news. What is less clearly understood is that if you argue that television news presents a warped image of events, you can find some unlikely allies. For example:

Some liberals claim that television reporters and camera crews, overwhelmingly white, present a superficial and twisted picture of ghetto life, showing the looting and rioting, but never the cause of Negro bitterness.

Some conservatives claim that television newscasts dwell too much on the black man and his problems, that they encourage rioters by putting them on the television, and that newscasts give black and white extremists stature by giving them a platform.

The political left claims that television newscasts show only the bearded hippies and the flareups of violence in covering demonstrations, that they ignore the problems of our society, that they brutalized Americans by turning a bloody war into living room entertainment, and that newscasts give the President and members of his Administration far more air time than they give to political leaders of the opposition.

The political right claims that television newscasts showed American and allied troop atrocities, but never the atrocities committed by the other side, that they show police in a poor light by filming their response to provocation, but not filming the provocation, that network newsmen are hostile to a conservative administration, and that negativism suffuses the newscasts.

In summary, a lot of Americans with strong political convictions believe that this powerful medium of television news puts the causes in which they believe—the good, decent causes—in the worst possible light, while glorifying the wrong-headed, malicious, evil causes of men they detest. And even those Americans without burning convictions on major issues have been heard to tell television journalists, "Why do you always report things going wrong? Why don't you ever talk about the good things that happen?" Public irritation with television news flared after that speech in Des Moines by Vice President Spiro Agnew blistering network television news practices. He concluded by asking the journalists he attacked "to turn their critical powers on themselves" and by asking the public "to let the networks know."

Criticism tends to fall into three broad categories. They can be phrased as questions:

1. *"Why do you want to show that stuff?"*
2. *"Why can't you be objective?"*
3. *"Why don't you put on some good news for a change?"*

Television journalists get these questions frequently. Let us examine them one by one, because they are the sources of hostility and we cannot afford this hostility, which may not be limited forever to speeches and grumbling. Those who work in television news, and also those who do not, cannot afford to let suspicion grow about the honesty and soundness of our best means of giving people the news. Charles Evans Hughes said:

We have in this Country but one security. You may think that the Constitution is your security—it is nothing but a piece of paper. You may think that the statutes are your security—they are nothing but words in a book. You may think that an elaborate mechanism of government is your security—it is nothing at all, unless you have sound and uncorrupted public opinion to give life to your Constitution, to give vitality to your statutes, to make efficient your government machinery.

... "As a public service we are not reporting the news tonight ... "

From *Saturday Review*

"Why Do You Want to Show That Stuff?"

Somebody once said it may take a page of the finest print to convey the effect of one piercing scream. One hundred pages will not do it.

When recalling television news reports which one feels distorted reality, what comes to mind is film, very dramatic film which leaves a lasting impression. Examples in recent years: Marines setting a South Vietnamese village afire with cigarette lighters, armed blacks leaving a Cornell University building, the Saigon police chief shooting a bound Vietcong prisoner through the head, starving Bengali children dying of cholera, ghetto looters, the high-pressure water hoses and police dogs of Birmingham, casual cruelty by Cambodian soldiers, the Chicago police during the Democratic National Convention. The list runs longer.

The television cameraman who sees drama in front of his lens films it. He would be dishonest to do less. The news reporter or writer who screens the dramatic film will choose to use it. He, too, would be dishonest to do less. But he tries to put what the viewer sees into perspective. Herein lies one of the dilemmas imposed by the medium of television: *the impact of strong film is not neutralized by words.* (In the context used here, "dilemma" means only that a solution has not appeared, not that a solution is impossible.)

No matter what the television journalist tries to say or do to put his exciting film into perspective, its impact may outweigh and outlast everything. Equal impact may not be possible, but if 95% of the students at a university did not riot, if 95% of the strikers did not throw bricks, if 95% of the ghetto residents did not loot, the reporter should emphasize this, and the cameraman should shoot film of these people behaving peacefully, for these TV journalists have a responsibility to give perspective to the violence that took place. However, journalists will and should show the violence, too. Otherwise, they are guilty of censorship. A newscaster cannot paraphrase the thwack of a policeman's billy club on the head of a rioter. He cannot quote glass shattering. No substitute exists for exciting actuality film. And no television journalist worthy of his profession would refuse to show civil unrest erupting into violence.

These pictures touch the emotions more than the intellect. They rub nerves raw as nothing else can. They *move* us. Yet by choosing the exciting over the unexciting, the dramatic over the dull, the moving picture over the "talking head," the television journalist often is also choosing the action over the thought, the event over the issue, the effect over the cause, the personality over the idea.

BBC-TV commentator Robin Day put it this way:[1]

Man's supreme gift is seen in terms of what the eye sees on that wretched little screen: "a talking head" . . .

Words on television tend to have their own limitation. They tend to be put into the background by the pictures, especially if these are extremely dramatic . . . The vivid impact of the picture remains in the consciousness longer than the words of interpretation or qualification. The sight on a TV screen of a person being brutally injured will linger in the emotions far longer than the accompanying words.

The insatiable appetite of television for vivid, action-packed pictures has wide and profound implications. It means that television has a built-in tendency to present issues solely or mainly in terms of their immediately visible results. Wars on television are seen almost exclusively in terms of casualties and combat, as in the case of Vietnam, the first television war. Or as in the Biafran rebellion, in terms of the starving children who were seen with sickening regularity on our television screens . . . Television does not always take sufficient trouble to ask "who is responsible," "why is it happening," or "what is the alternative."

Television's proud motto is "see it happen," but seeing is not necessarily understanding and the sights selected to be seen may not be the whole picture.

When people are horrified by the sight of bloodshed and mutilation they are not easily convinced that a cause may be at stake. The sight of a dead child, a burning home, a dying citizen-soldier—all these may have a much more powerful impact than abstract concepts like "liberty" or "collective security."

"You can pass by a headline, even if dramatic, but you cannot close your eyes to a dramatic picture that appears on TV," Walter Cronkite said. "We take the troubles of the world and we transfer them to their (the American people's) homes, nightly, and we oblige them to watch. But they don't want to watch. They want to escape such troubles, they want to hide their heads in the sand. And they are brought up to agree with politicians who would like us to shut up." [2]

Because violence horrifies many of us, it does not follow that we do not want to see it, and it certainly does not follow that we ought not to see it, let alone that we should not be permitted to see it. Violence is often a political fact which helps a citizen reach a political conclusion.

As Hollywood has long known, violence does not horrify everyone. Quite the contrary. Robert Ardrey noted:

> We enjoy the violent. We hurry to an accident not to help; we run to a fire not to put it out; we crowd about a schoolyard fight not to stop it. For all the Negro's profound and inarguable grievances, there has not been a racial outbreak in America since the days

An unidentified television cameraman, doing his job, crouches beside police, doing theirs. Time and place: 1971, Winston-Salem, N.C., after police were fired upon when they went to a Black Panther headquarters to investigate a theft. (*UPI Photo*)

of Watts in which a degree of carnival atmosphere has not prevailed. I myself may have no great taste for Molotov Cocktails; it is because I am timid, not because I am good . . .

Action and destruction are fun. The concerned observer who will not grant it indulges in a hypocrisy which we cannot afford. He who regards a taste for violent action as a human perversion will not likely make any great contribution to the containment of our violent way.[3]

Another dilemma of the medium is that the television journalist cannot always see the violence committed by both sides. A camera crew traveling with American or allied soldiers can film the unpleasant acts of their soldiers. The enemy's violence goes unobserved. Camera crews filming riots are advised, warned or ordered by police to stay behind police lines, which the crews may be glad to do for their own personal safety. But so shielded, the violence they will witness and film will be mostly what police do to rioters. Even if police do nothing, most of the people filmed from the vantage of police lines will be policemen. And in a tense, angry riot, the likely lasting impression will be of tense, angry policemen.

As might be expected, some members of the general community react negatively to any television riot coverage, arguing that riots feed on television exposure. Television journalists have had to give serious thought to their policies on reporting riots, and particularly violence in the ghettos.

Here is another dilemma, stated succinctly by *TV Guide* reporter Neil Hickey: "Arabs, prison inmates, students—and scores of other identifiable pleaders—have absorbed with bewildering and unerring canniness the first lesson of the electronic age: calculated illegal behavior gets results. The formula, by now, is a proven one. It really works."

"Why Can't You Be Objective?"

Suppose a casual acquaintance told you that someone you loved and respected had done something horrible. Even if the casual acquaintance showed you some snippets of film of the deed or its aftermath, you are likely to doubt the story. If you have heard that this acquaintance is occasionally inaccurate, your doubts will grow. And if you believe this casual acquaintance is maliciously inspired and is probably influencing others with his story, who can blame you for becoming furious?

For many television viewers this set of responses occurs when a newscaster, the "casual acquaintance," reports unpleasant news about a person or cause the viewer admires. Reuven Frank put it this way: [4]

The important thing is that a large number of people who watch television for information saw information which disturbed them and which they resented. To one degree or another they refused to allow themselves to believe it. It bothered closely held values. Understandably and naturally, they clung to their values and rejected the information. The only possible explanation for what they saw in this frame of mind would have to be that what they saw was false, and then that it was arranged to be false, and then that it was arranged by a conspiracy to be false.

News director Robert Caulfield of WNAC-TV, Boston, said, "The whole question of balance troubles me greatly. . . . Viewers call me up and say, 'How dare you show film of those 20,000 uncouth demonstrators?' or 'How dare you put on so many liberal spokesmen?' And I say, 'Look, *you* sound like an articulate person. Why don't *you* come down here to the station and I'll put *you* on.' But they won't come. The silent majority is everywhere but on the telephone." [5]

The news director of another large station said the mailman regularly brings him piles of angry letters.[6]

> I keep hearing the same refrains: ". . . If you didn't cover demonstrations, there wouldn't be any . . . Why don't those kids get haircuts? Who cares what they think? . . . Your reporter was obviously biased; he asked such nasty questions . . . Why don't you put on some good news for a change?"
> We're not press agents for the established order of things.

The Des Moines speech by Vice President Agnew encouraged a sizeable segment of the American people to express the feeling that television news is presented in a biased way. A Gallup Poll taken soon after the speech reported that 42% felt that TV network news tends to favor one side, many (but not all) of the respondents saying it was the liberal side; 40% thought the network newscasts dealt fairly with all sides (18% had no opinion), and—among other findings—45% thought that newspapers tend to favor one side.[7] Those who supported Agnew's viewpoint generally thought the television news bias was leftward, liberal. Most television journalists who have written on this subject disagreed, but ABC news commentator Howard K. Smith, agreed, saying network news departments were almost exclusively staffed by liberals. "It evolved from the time when liberalism was a good thing, and most intellectuals became highly liberal. Most reporters are in an intellectual occupation."

Such a statement, levelled by a respected colleague, ought to concern television journalists. So, too, expressed opinion that some television journalists, especially on local stations, are conservatives. The concern is not that journalists should not hold personal political views, but that for some listeners, expression of these views gets in the way of the flow of information, breeding justifiable resentment and suspicion. Any citizen, including a journalist, may hold any political views. Indeed, the journalist who

*"So much for my version of the news. And now over to my
colleague for the same news but with a different set of biasses,
hangups, and axes to grind."*

Drawing by Donald Reilly; © 1970, *The New Yorker* Magazine, Inc.

failed to reach political conclusions would not be worth his weight in warm tapioca.

Smith's observation that most reporters are in an intellectual occupation should please reporters, not disturb them. After all, being intellectual, which the dictionary defines as having a notable mental capacity, being extremely rational, and pursuing things of interest to the intellect, is more desirable than being *unintellectual*.

Can a newsman work as a political neuter? Maybe not, but he must always try. To the degree he succeeds, he is an ethical professional. To the degree he fails, he is a propagandist. Reuven Frank put it this way: [8]

> To boil it all down, the essence of traditional American journalism at its best—and, in my opinion, at its most useful to our society —is an artificial innocence. As individuals, of course we have ideas of what we prefer. More important and less often discussed, we have ideas of the effect what we report will have. We think about impact. But we must pretend as well as we can that we have no such ideas

about impact on the one hand and the world we should individually like to see on the other. . .

David Brinkley is not an innocent. Vanocur is not an innocent. John Chancellor, who began as a demon Chicago police reporter, knows the facts of life. That is not what I meant.

"Innocence" may not be a very good word, but it is the best I could find for the newsman's necessary deliberate detachment from aiming his work or letting someone else aim it to changing society— for even the noblest motives. . .

The newsman's prime responsibility is to the news business itself, with its standards and traditions. Put that way, it might seem a simpleton's view of life. The alternative—the only alternative—is the newsman as a conscious instrumentality of social control. To me, that is a frightening and abhorrent idea. I hope it is to you. But in one form or another, it is often suggested. Those who suggest it are rarely aware of this implication of their suggestion. In my experience, it is always suggested for the highest unselfish motives by people who sincerely want a better world and want news to help them achieve it. News doesn't do it. News doesn't know how. News which knows how isn't news.

Strangely, complete uninvolvement by a knowledgable journalist almost defies common sense, for it would mean, as an extreme example, that a newscaster could not look unhappy if the stock market averages skidded, or smile if they recovered, because the stock market short sellers are delighted with a price collapse. And if perfect detachment were possible, it would be too dull and wooden for interest or enjoyment.

David Brinkley on the subject: [9]

A person presumably is expected to go on the air and be objective, which is to say that he is to have no likes, no dislikes, no feelings, no views, no values, no standards; to be a machine. Well, if I were objective, or if anyone was, he would have to be put away somewhere in an institution because he'd be some sort of vegetable. I'm not objective, make no pretense of being objective. There are a great many things I like and dislike, and it may be that at times some indication of this appears in my facial expression . . . or anyone else's. If it didn't, we'd be in a pretty sad, indeed pitiful, condition. Objectivity is impossible to the normal human being. Fairness, however, is attainable, and that's what we strive for—not objectivity, fairness.

Edward R. Murrow said, "It is not, I think, humanly possible for any reporter to be completely objective, for we are all to some degree prisoners of our education, travel, reading—the sum total of our experience." Kenneth Stewart, a newspaperman, stated, "If you mean by objectivity absence of convictions, willingness to let nature take its course, uncritical acceptance of things as they are (what Robert Frost calls the 'isness of is'), the hell with it. If you mean by objectivity a healthy respect for the ascertainable truth, a readiness to modify conclusions when new evidence comes in, a refusal to distort deliberately and for ulterior or concealed motives, a belief that the means shape the end, not that the end justifies the means, all well and good." [10]

In workaday terms, the ethical journalist should follow these guidelines in newscasts:

1. Film should be shot and edited, and copy should be edited and written solely because of his perception of its importance and interest to the viewer, never because it puts a political cause or a politician in a good or bad light.

2. No viewer should be able to guess a journalist's political party or candidate preference from the way he reports a news story. However, his attitude toward an individual news event may—and perhaps should—on occasion be made plain, depending upon the event. Common sense and common decency should guide him. Labelled commentary and documentaries (such as *The Selling of the Pentagon*) give the journalist latitude for political expression, but he must be accurate and he must always be fair. Documentaries are part of the long American tradition of investigative journalism, which seldom pleases the subjects.

3. The journalist's primary goal should be to report what exists, let the chips fall where they may. In a totalitarian society, the primary goal is different.

Howard K. Smith, who saw a liberal slant in reporting, does not advocate blandness. "I find an almost excessive lack of bias on television. We are afraid of a point of view. We stick to the old American belief that there is an objectivity. If a man says the world is round, we run out to find someone to say it is flat."

"WHY DON'T YOU PUT ON SOME GOOD NEWS FOR A CHANGE?"

Most news, or at least most *hard* news, is a report of change. Change disturbs the usual state of affairs which, considered broadly, is more pleasing than not. Where the usual state of things is displeasing, change might be for the better, which results in "good news." More often, especially when the change is unexpected, change from the ordinary is change for the worse. It is ordinary that buses and planes reach their terminals safely and that cats get out of whatever they get into. When a bus or plane crashes or a cat gets stranded in a tree, that's news. With this concept, journalism reflects human nature. Pa doesn't tell Ma that his teeth chewed their way easily through lunch. Pa does tell Ma that one back tooth aches. If he did digress on the efficiency of his teeth, Ma would tune him out. A working newsman who admitted that he could devote more space to good news than to crime said people wouldn't remember it. "I go home at night and my wife doesn't say, 'Gee, the neighbors got along swell today.' But if the wife threw her husband out the window, I hear about it."

Former NBC newscaster Chet Huntley said, "Journalists were never intended to be the cheer leaders of a society, the conductors of applause, the sycophants. Tragically, that is their assigned role in authoritarian societies, but not here."

A different attitude, expressed, interestingly enough, by a national civil rights leader, the Rev. Jesse Jackson, is that journalists often seem obsessed with the sensational—war protests, riots, burning ghettos, crime, immorality, drugs—all the nation's fractures and cancers, yet say little about quiet progress, small decencies, the things that go right. Essentially, Jackson asked for balance and perspective, two commodities not always to be found when the teletypes clack out bad news from a dozen datelines.

Television news, limited in time, focusing on what matters to and/or interests many viewers, must deal with information many viewers find troubling. For network and large city audiences, troubling information all but crowds out pleasant information. The more troubling the news is, the more unusual it is, the further it is from normal activity. For example, few stories in recent years have been so upsetting to Americans as the reports of the My Lai massacre. Seldom has news been so bad and unwelcome. A congressional committee investigating My Lai stated, "In fact it was so wrong and so foreign to the normal character and actions of our military forces as to immediately raise a question as to the legal sanity at the time of those men involved."

The choice of a totalitarian society would be to suppress such news "in the interest of the nation." The choice of a libertarian society, such as that of the United States, is to look at itself openly, warts and all. That we don't like this news, that it is not good news, must not matter in reporting the news. CBS president Frank Stanton stated, "The troubled pages of this century's history are writ dark with the death of liberty in those nations where the first fatal symptom of political decay was an effort to control the news media." [11]

Unfettered television news has had, is having, and will continue to have an effect on history. Consider television coverage of the war in Vietnam, the world's first televised war. The London *Economist* declared, "The United States is the first free country that has ever tried to fight a televised war under the rules of democracy—free reporting, opinion polls, the lot— and if the result has been the unsurprising discovery that people loathe war, that is something that all democracies will have to chew over in the future." To which, BBC-TV's Robin Day added, "One wonders whether in the future a democracy which has uncensored television in every home will ever be able to fight a war, however just. . . The brutal details of military action may be there on the television screen to shock and to horrify, sapping perhaps the will of the nation to resist the forces of evil or even safeguard its own freedom."

Washington Post television editor Lawrence Laurent said the Vietnam War was the worst reported war in history because television coverage was ridden with stereotypes. "The North Vietnamese soldier is invariably shown as captive, ragged, undernourished, small. His American captor looks well fed, well equipped and huge by comparison. This image —so contrary to the tradition that the hero does not fight with anyone smaller than himself—may be the reason why so many people, especially the young, oppose the war."

In response to a statement by affiliates that network newscasts should not give so much "publicity" to people who oppose government policies, NBC president Julian Goodman said NBC News does not "make, or advocate, or favor the news it presents. All of us should recognize that disturbing developments presented on television loom far larger in viewers' minds and memories than the developments viewers take for granted and approve." [12]

To say that people prefer good news to bad is to state the obvious. So, too, to say that people are distressed by bad news. But it is quite another matter to guess that people will choose good news programs to the usual run. From time to time, one hears of newspapers devoted solely to good news. Their circulations are reportedly minuscule. The author once worked for a newspaper which, each Christmas, printed an edition with only good news on page one. I observed that readers glanced quickly at the pap on the front page, then turned to page two for the news which mattered to them and really interested them. To prefer good news is not necessarily to prefer to read good news, to hear it on radio, or to watch it on TV.

However, television stations sometimes go far in the other direction. Their newscasts feature every minor traffic accident, every one-alarm fire, and every shooting they can film. "Fender benders" matter to few viewers and cannot interest many others. Then why are they shown? Perhaps they are shown because the news director lacks imagination. Five minutes of daily reflection would yield story ideas containing, potentially, more action film than two month's worth of crumpled bumpers, and many of these stories would fall in anybody's category of "good news."

News director Richard Buddine, WSLS-TV, Roanoke, Va., said, "If there is a million-dollar fire in the middle of town, all of the stations in the area will have film of it that night, and it will all look pretty much the same —unless somebody had processor trouble. And chances are most of the reporting will be pretty similar. The same thing is true if there's a plane crash at the local airport, the mayor resigns or a local bank is held up. The flashy, obvious stories are easy to cover. So the station which is determined to be outstanding in news coverage . . . must push above this common level and press for a higher standard of excellence."

Finally, on this subject, take note that television broadcasting gets it on the chin both for entertainment shows which are too bland and news shows which are too upsetting.

The medium isn't always the mesmer.

"WHAT CAN WE DO ABOUT WHAT YOU SHOW?"

Along with the three critical questions already cited comes a fourth. This question is raised less often, but it is more thoughtful and it is harder to answer except to admit that current television news practice leaves something to be desired. The question is: "How can we cope with your emphasis on our abnormalties?"

This question may be directed at a television news department by a university president who senses that many citizens have formed an impression of a university dominated by dirty, bearded, wlid-eyed hippies egged on by nutty or politically radical professors. Consider what San Francisco State College president S. I. Hayakawa told the 1969 RTNDA convention: [13]

> The first thing they asked me was do I expect any violence the following day? It's as if there is an abnormal interest in violence on the part of the networks and when there's violence there are hundreds of cameramen around and reporters and so on and when there is no violence, when normal operation of the colleges are going, there is nobody in sight except to come around and ask the question, when do you expect more violence.
>
> Now I understand this. In many ways television is a medium that requires action and motion in order to keep interest focused on the screen. On the other hand there are many other things that involve action and motion in a college or university, like pictures of education classes dealing with handicapped children, pictures of the dance programs, pictures of athletic programs, poetry readings, therapy sessions. All sorts of things involving human interaction could just as well be shown as the riots on a campus. . .

TV Guide published a series of articles by reporter Neil Hickey, which were combined in a booklet, *Television and the Troubled Campus.*[14] Here are some quotations:

TV Guide editor Merrill Panitt: "There is little doubt in the minds of many social observers that the widening breach of understanding between college students and the American public is traceable directly to television. Students themselves contend that television contributes to the generation gap by concentrating more on the violent acts that grow out of their 'cause' rather than on reporting the real issues. Society, on the other hand, sits glumly watching the riots and sit-ins, interpreting them as an attempt to destroy the very fiber of a well-ordered community. Caught in the middle are television news directors who lament both parties' failure to understand the limitations of the medium."

TV Guide reporter Neil Hickey: "Activist students almost universally dismiss television as unresponsive, obtuse, and largely irredeemable as an instrument for illuminating the root issues of student unrest. . . . the 'pig press' . . . (When 18-year olds vote) it will be even more crucial that what America *thinks* is going on in the universities coincides with what is *really* going on there. That can't be accomplished without the enlightened complicity of television's journalists. It is not yet certain that they are equal to the task."

TV newsman Ronald Mires, KPIX, San Francisco: "It's all complex and difficult. If we gave six sides to every story, people would say there were six sides we missed."

TV newsman Tom Dorsey, WBNS, Columbus, Ohio: "The truth is we don't know what the hell the truth is."

Student activist at Ohio State: "No station will devote sufficient time to unraveling all the issues, many of which are, admittedly, both complex and unpleasant. But the minute a bunch of students seize a building, the TV reporters come rushing to the campus, taking pictures and demanding to know why the building was seized. They should *know* why the building was seized. But they never do and probably never will."

KRON news director Vic Burton, San Francisco, saying he could use 30 men to cover the campus beat: "It doesn't take a top-notch reporter to cover violence, but it takes a good man to see the *real* news, and not just the police car being burned and the helicopters spraying tear gas. We need people to cover campus militancy before it erupts in violence. We don't spend as much time at Berkeley as we should. Did I say we could use 30 men? Hell, we could use a hundred."

Former Berkeley student body president Leigh Steinberg: "If TV news is nothing but reconstructed adventure stories—if television's main function is to entertain—then obviously TV will gravitate to what is exciting and what thrills its viewers."

Scranton Commission Report: "Again and again, the cameras focused on what was most bizarre, dramatic, active or violent. Few television or radio and newspaper reporters had the time or knowledge to explore the causes. . ."

Berkeley philosophy professor John Searle: "I watch television news not to find out what's happening, but what *other people think* is happening. Any time you're personally involved in a news event, as I have been at Berkeley, and then you later see it on television, you're often struck by the fact that somehow they just didn't get the story quite straight."

Sol M. Linowitz, chairman of the Urban Coalition, ex-chairman of the board, Xerox Corporation, former ambassador to the Organization of American States: "Worry that viewers channel-hop when the news becomes dull is an unspeakable response to a grave national problem."

On Television Coverage of Demonstrations and Riots

The problems of television coverage of riots extend beyond the techniques of filming them. The presence of a camera crew at the scene of an unruly demonstration may incite participants to acts of mischief or violence.

One of the Chicago Seven defendants, Abbie Hoffman, declared, "So what the hell are we doing, you ask? We are dynamiting brain cells. We are putting people through changes. . . . The media is the message. Use it! No fund raising, no full-page ads in *The New York Times,* no press releases. Just do your thing; the press eats it up. Media is free. *Make news."*

FCC Commissioner Nicholas Johnson wryly observed, "Demonstrations are happening, and the news media—like moths to a flame—run to cover them."

As ghettos in the summers of their discontent vent their frustrations and angers, television newsmen must cope with a paradox of objective reporting. If they do not report, they are not treating this major news objectively. Yet if television newsmen do report the riot or demonstration as its news value dictates, with cameras, they may affect what they report, and cannot maintain their desired role of uninvolved observer.

The camera in a demonstration catalyzes what it sees. At work is a kind of Heisenberg Principle of Uncertainty, in which by observing, we alter.

ABC News correspondent Don Farmer put it this way: [15]

> Television can report the action better than any medium, but with the same cameras that are required to report the action, we get ourselves involved in the story, whether we want to or not.
>
> When television newsmen are going to cover a demonstration, a march, or a rally on film, they obviously have to know about it ahead of time, whereas a newspaperman needs only enough time to get himself there before it is over. The television people must have more time because of the equipment and the extra manpower needed to do the same job the newspaperman does with a pencil and a telephone. When you call ahead of time and say, "When are you going to demonstrate?" some Negro leaders have taken this as an invitation to demonstrate. Maybe they hadn't planned to. The answer I received a couple of times on the phone to "When is your next demonstration?" was "When would you like it?" This is a problem. I think here is where things must change.

The same problem is related by William B. Monroe, Jr., in a couple of anecdotes: [20]

Television newsmen, local and national, are accustomed by now to the phone calls from civil rights groups with the details of when and where demonstrations are to be held. The civil rights group quickly became sensitive to the possibilities of television. In Alabama, a group of demonstrators was praying in the streets. They saw a TV newsman beside a camera pointing a microphone at them from across the street, trying to pick up the sound as well as the picture, and immediately started praying a little louder.

Frank McGee saw a civil rights demonstrator, a white woman, lying down on the floor of the Republican convention hall. McGee told the NBC control room about it, but he was told that they couldn't put him on the air for at least two or three minutes. McGee bent over the woman and asked, "How long are you going to lie here?" The woman said, "How long do you want me here?"

And a few years ago, someone called the WMAQ-TV newsroom in Chicago:

"We're going to stage a sit-in at the Main Loop post office."
"When is it going to start?" asked the newsman.
"As soon as you get here."

"The last time I was in New York," recalled British critic Malcolm Muggeridge, "I happened to catch a glimpse of Newzak at the production end. I was walking back to my hotel, and came upon a little group of people standing about in the road. It was, in fact, a demo. There were the usual bearded academics and lib-females carrying slogans, a little group of police with a van, and one or two reporters. Nothing seemed to be happening, and when I asked why, I was told that the cameras hadn't turned up. Shortly afterwards they arrived and set up; someone snapped a clapper-board and shouted "Action!" and the demo slogan began. The bearded academics and lib-females raised their slogans and shouted in unison; the police grabbed one or two of them and pitched them in their van. Then someone shouted, 'Cut!' and it was all over. Later in the evening I caught the demo on television in my hotel room. It looked fine." [17] *Muggeridge, who coined the word "Newzak" to compare television news with Muzak, tells a good story. The clapper-board and shouts of "Action" and "Cut" sound like a tall tale, unless someone in the TV crew was joking, but the rest is almost believable.*

The television newsman's rueful amusement at his predicament in a demonstration gives way to concern and sometimes fear in a riot. Nothing about a teenager wielding a brick is funny. The young rioter in the ghetto wants the world to know his feelings. He sees a television camera crew,

BROOM HILDA   R. Myers

and he thinks that through them he can reach beyond the ghetto to tell it the way it is. He knows from his own television watching that other young men in other city ghettos spread the word this way. And so he picks up a brick and shouts to attract the cameraman's attention.

Even if he does not see a cameraman, the rioter senses that he and his friends are making news, and that the more lawless they become, the more news they make.

As might be expected, some members of the general community react negatively to any television riot coverage, arguing that riots feed on television exposure. Television journalists have had to give serious thought to their policies on reporting ghetto violence.

It is unthinkable that television news abrogate its duty to report one of the most vital stories of our generation, rebellion by blacks in our cities. Yet television news must not encourage rebellion, with its attendant bloodshed, destruction, and polarization of black and white communities.

Here is a dilemma.

In several cities, television newsmen from competing stations have met to formulate guidelines for riot coverage. They were concerned not only with their responsibility to their community and to their professional standards of reporting the news without fear or favor, but also with the safety of the camera crews sent into the ghetto streets. Some cameramen, soundmen, reporters, and film couriers have been abused, injured, even hospitalized. Plainly marked television station cars have been singled out for burning. Expensive equipment has been smashed. Couriers' motorcycles are obvious targets.

Television news crews must face the hostility of rioters resenting any whites, and the hostility of those policemen who contend that television reporting, especially live reporting, worsens and lengthens a riot. Some police also feel that the television newsmen concentrate too much on police action in controlling the riot and arresting suspected troublemakers, leading to allegations of police brutality from the general community.

Among some guidelines generally accepted:

1. Riots are to be fully covered.
2. Militants without a substantial following are to be regarded as

publicity seekers, and are to be ignored. Newsmen subjectively determine what constitutes a substantial following.

3. Camera crews should stay out of neighborhoods where trouble seems to be brewing, but violence has not yet broken out.

4. Wherever possible, camera crews are to remain inconspicuous.

5. News personnel who go into riot zones must wear hard hats and, weather permitting, padded jackets.

6. News personnel are to say and do nothing to encourage further depredation. They must not linger, waiting for something to happen.

Other advice for camera crews: [18]

Don't be a hero. Run scared. Stay close to police or national guardsmen when you can.

Dark clothing is advisable. Avoid wearing a coat and tie.

Travel in pairs if possible. If it is safe to drive into the area do it with two men—one driving, one taking the pictures.

Be mobile. Keep your equipment to a minimum so that you can move fast if a mob starts after you. Strap an extra lens to your belt and stuff extra film in your pockets.

Don't carry firearms or Mace.

Use telephoto lenses whenever possible so you don't have to get too close to where the danger exists.

Tape windows of your car to avoid being cut by flying glass. Tape down the light switch on your car door so that when you open the door the light doesn't go on.

Never use flash. . . . you'll become a target from both sides.

Avoid getting involved in a dispute with anyone. Treat everyone with respect.

Keep in touch with your office.

A clever cameraman who works for Britain's VISNEWS emptied the works from a transistor radio whose case was just large enough to contain a flat Bolex silent camera with a two-turret lens. He has walked through riot areas with the "radio" perched on his shoulder against his ear and a bland smile on his face as he listened to the music of 16mm film clattering through the gate.

In a memorandum to assignment editors, reporters and camera crews, William Sheehan of ABC news wrote:

We cannot be too careful in our coverage this summer of riots, disturbances and incidents. Our purpose must be to keep the stories in perspective so that a scuffle doesn't become a riot in its reporting.

Please keep in mind these guidelines and see that the questions are answered in our coverage:

Describe the nature and extent of the problem with precision. We don't want to give the impression a whole city is aflame just because someone has started a bonfire.

We must know the reasons for the trouble insofar as they are discernible. This requires some follow-up reporting after the initial trouble. Talk to civil rights leaders, merchants and residents in the area who were not directly involved in the disturbance. If the issue that triggered the problem is not clear, let's say so.

The police are not the sole source in stories of this kind. Neither are those on the street leading the demonstration.

It may be stating the obvious, but I feel it's worth repeating: ABC News wants nothing to do with staged stories. If you miss an element, don't ask for a repeat. Be careful that the cameras are not the cause of a demonstration.

Of the entire black rebellion in the age of television, William B. Monroe, Jr., said this: [19]

Negroes are the architects, bricklayers, carpenters, and welders of this revolution. Television is their chosen instrument—not because television set out to integrate the nation or even to improve the South, but because when the Negroes got ready for their revolution, television was there. Television was coming of age as a journalistic medium. It was, unlike the newspapers, a national medium; it had the courage—in most cases, a courage drawn from the old tradition of the American press—not to shrink from the fierce and often ugly scenes growing out of the Negro struggle; and it conveyed the emotional values of a basically emotional contest with a richness and fidelity never before achieved in mass communications. When you *see* and *hear* a wildly angry man talking, whether he is a segregationist or an integrationist, you can understand the man's anger, you can feel it—the depth of it, the power of it, the suffering in it. But if you *read* a description of what the man said, you find that, by comparison, the words are dried-up little symbols through which only a fraction of the story comes.

FOR THE STUDENT

1. Why might a news director choose to cover routine accidents and fires? Defend or criticize these reasons.
2. Why might he send a film crew to where violence is brewing—for example, at the main gate of a struck factory?
3. How should a reporter cope with the matter of his own political views when the man he is interviewing expresses opposing views?
4. Can news be presented objectively? Fairly? Discuss.
5. Should newscasts have more "good news" than you usually see now?
6. Should a demonstration be covered if the news department feels it is being staged for television news cameras?

7. Arrange to read all letters sent by viewers to a newsroom over a one-month or six-month period. Write a paper about them.

8. Should a newscast be balanced? If so, how?

9. For several weeks, watch and analyze one news program's coverage of one controversial topic. Report your conclusions about the news department's objectivity.

10. Read Vice President Spiro Agnew's 1970 Des Moines speech criticizing network television news practices. List the points he makes. Which do you agree with? Which do you dispute? Which do you feel have some truth but are exaggerated?

2

THE DAY

AT SEVEN O'CLOCK each weekday morning, the dayside assignment editor at one of our large city television stations arrives at work. Let us consider him and his co-workers, for they are fairly typical of local television news staffs of comparable size everywhere. Even where news staffs are much smaller, most of the same tasks are performed, although on a reduced scale, by employees with combined job functions.

The dayside assignment editor of our typical news staff walks into the newsroom and goes straight to the bank of teletypes, even before he hangs up his coat. In a few seconds, he scans the last 30 minutes of copy transmitted by the AP, UPI and the local news wire (if his city has one). Seeing nothing that will require the immediate alerting of camera crews, he hangs up his coat, plugs in the coffee pot, and begins his day. For the rest of the day either he or the nightside assignment editor will either rip or glance at the "wires" (all the teletype wires) roughly every 15 minutes. As air time nears, the trips to the teletypes will be increased to every five minutes; this frequency will be maintained until the newscast is done. Throughout the day other staff members will look at the wires, out of professional and personal interest and the knowledge that when a major news story breaks, they will probably learn of it first by teletype.

THE BULLETIN

The dayside assignment editor is not the first man on duty at the station. At least one engineer begins work before the station goes on the air.

An early morning announcer reports in soon after. If the assignment editor sees a bulletin on the teletype which he feels should be broadcast as a bulletin (the ratio of broadcast bulletins to teletype bulletins may be one in a hundred), he will direct the engineer to cover whatever program is being broadcast by a bulletin slide * and he will give the announcer bulletin copy to read. A news editor has the authority to interrupt programming at any time with a bulletin. As a rule he will not interrupt a station break or a commercial with a bulletin which is not of overriding importance. Of course, when a bulletin is of major importance—the kind which once would have been called a "flash"—anything on the air is interrupted; in the event of war or the death of a president, regular programming does not resume after the news is announced; instead, the available fragments of news are repeated and amplified as new information appears until such time as the network takes over or the local staff can organize its reportage.

A bulletin may read as follows:

HERE IS A BULLETIN FROM THE KLMN NEWSROOM: AUTO WORKERS HAVE GONE ON STRIKE AT FORD FACTORIES ACROSS THE COUNTRY. 154 THOUSAND WORKERS AT 62 PLANTS ARE IMMEDIATELY AFFECTED. STAY TUNED TO KLMN FOR FURTHER DETAILS.

Brief introductory and tag lines sandwich the bulletin, in order to put the news announcement into the context of the programming situation. The facts are kept to a minimum, and the bulletin is very short, for it is meant only to declare that an event has taken place. Details of that event are reserved for the regular newscast or for a special news program.

Sometimes the significant fact of a bulletin is repeated. For example:

WE INTERRUPT THIS PROGRAM FOR A NEWS BULLETIN: RURITANIA HAS DECLARED WAR ON CARPATHIA. RURITANIAN BOMBERS STRUCK DEEP IN CARPATHIAN TERRITORY, HITTING AIRFIELDS AND RAILROAD DEPOTS. RURITANIAN TROOPS CROSSED THE FRONTIER AT THREE POINTS.
TO REPEAT: RURITANIA HAS GONE TO WAR AGAINST CARPATHIA.
KLMN WILL BULLETIN MORE DETAILS THROUGHOUT THE DAY.

News may be worth bulletin treatment, but not immediate program interruption. Some viewers were furious when a WABC-TV, New York, news editor interrupted a Bolshoi Ballet performance of "Swan Lake" to report the murder of Malcolm X. They felt that bulletin could have been delayed for a few minutes. Another program was interrupted to report that Richard Burton had just married Elizabeth Taylor. The seasoned news editor asks himself how important it is to viewers to learn this news at this moment, before he commands the television equivalent of "Stop the

* The Glossary at the end of this book gives brief explanations of technical terms.

presses!" He also asks himself if a bulletin reporting a tragedy should be inserted into a comedy program, when the bulletin will be followed by a return to comedy.

DAILY ASSIGNMENTS

If the dayside assignment editor has found nothing on the wire requiring his immediate attention, he begins to plan the day's camera schedule for three crews. From a box containing 31 consecutively numbered "future" folders, one for each day of the month (after a date has passed, that folder is used to accumulate assignments for the same date of the following month) he takes the folder for the present day. In the folder he finds six items:

1. A letter from a viewer discussing a neighborhood problem. Along the margin, the nightside assignment editor has penciled an address and a time, 10 a.m.

2. A handout from a local department store announcing ground-breaking ceremonies at noon for a new store.

3. A typewritten note from the news director, setting up an interview with the author of a best seller at 9 a.m.

4. A wire advisory of a noon news conference for an important out-of-state senator.

5. A wire feature story about plans for a local shopping center financed by a black group dedicated to self-help. Undated.

6. A newspaper clipping about an all-day conference on air pollution.

The three camera crews are assigned to begin at 8 a.m., 10 a.m. and 2 p.m. Based solely on this future folder, the assignment editor makes this tentative schedule:

	CREW 1	CREW 2	CREW 3
9 a.m.	author		
10 a.m.		neighborhood	
noon	senator	new store	
1 p.m.	lunch		
2 p.m.	air pollution	lunch	
3 p.m.			shopping center

Any schedule requires some assurance that persons to be interviewed will be ready when the crews arrive. In this schedule, meetings with the author and the neighborhood spokesmen had already been set up. The senator and the store dedication had established their own times. The air pollution conference could be done at any time, although it would be necessary to call ahead if some particular spokesman was wanted for an interview. Only the black shopping center story has to be arranged. However, today's wire file has not yet been read.

The assignment editor rips all the wires. His practiced eye runs down each item, searching for several kinds of stories:

   a. A story which should be covered today.

   b. A feature story, which can be filmed any time.

   c. A future news assignment.

   d. An out-of-town, national or international story with a local angle.

   e. A story which should be presented with still photos, maps or drawings.

   f. A backgrounder or some other story which should be called to some staff member's attention. The editor will send it along with the letters "FYI" (For Your Information) scribbled on top.

   g. Out-of-town stories for which film might have been shot—or yet might be shot—by another television station or a free lancer.

   h. Hard news: major news stories which can be reported as is. As the day wears on, almost every major story will have been updated several times.

   i. A cute "brite."

   j. Specialized items of interest to the sports editor and the weather reporter.

As the assignment editor scans the wires, the first news team arrives to start their day. A reporter, a cameraman and a soundman report to work. (On smaller stations, the cameraman doubles as soundman. On very small stations, the reporter does it all. But a network news team might consist of a producer, a reporter. a cameraman, a soundman and an electrician.) The editor tells the cameraman that he is tentatively scheduled to cover interviews with an author, a senator and air pollution officials. This informs the cameraman that he will probably mount his camera on a tripod all day, rather than on a shoulder pod, and that he will be lighting static indoor scenes. He and the soundman go off to assemble their gear and, if they haven't already done so, load film into magazines. They also know they have an hour to get to and set up for their first assignment. This time, the camera is not hooked to its shoulder pod, but the pod goes along in the car, just in case.

The reporter is given the note from the news director. Fortunately, he has made a practice of thumbing through the future folders, and knew that he would be assigned to interview the author. The reporter has already spent an hour in the public library leafing through the author's latest book, a critical review, and a reference work on the topic covered by the author. This interview promises to be an enlightening and intelligent one, with some wry humor and some sparks flying.

After the first crew leaves, the assignment editor completes his reading of the wire. He has added two more assignments to the six tentatively made:

7. A midnight high-speed car chase after a robbery suspect. Interviews with police and film of suspect.

8. A beautiful starlet in court to seek a divorce. 10 a.m.

The editor gets on the telephone—he will spend most of his day either on the phone or checking the wires. He calls Crew 1 on their car mobile phone to tell them to wrap up the author story quickly in order to get to court for the starlet. If he cannot reach the crew on the mobile phone, he will phone the author at his hotel to request that the crew call in when they arrive. If the story is an important news beat, he will not inform the crew by mobile phone, knowing that rival station crews might be using the same radio frequency. Instead he will tell the crew, via car phone, to get to the nearest phone booth and call him back by "land line." The editor, realizing the crew may be late to the courthouse, also calls a bailiff he has befriended at the courthouse to ask him to inform the starlet that a news crew is on its way, if she will only be patient. Starlets being starlets, she will almost certainly wait. The car chase story arrangements must also wait. It is a weak story to begin with, and by the 6 p.m. newscast, it will be 18 hours old. The assignment editor notes it as marginal, to be covered only if nothing else develops.

Later in the morning, something unexpected does turn up. A freelance cameraman brings in film he shot of the conclusion of the chase and the capture of the suspected robber. The film is sent to the lab. If a writer judges the quality to be good, the later interviews will definitely be scheduled.

The editor phones the neighborhood problem spokesmen to say the camera crew and reporter will be almost 30 minutes late. Please be patient. His phone call not only keeps the people there, it is good public relations.

At 10 a.m., the members of the second news team arrive: the cameraman and soundman assigned as Crew 2 and the reporter who will work with them. Although a cameraman and a soundman usually work together week after week, the assigning of reporters is more flexible. Some stories may not need reporters; for example, the filming of an art exhibit, a parade, or a circus performance. Camera crews are sometimes assigned to non-news tasks such as filming segments of a documentary. On the other hand, reporters may be sent where camera crews are not needed (e.g., to search records) or not allowed (e.g., at a trial). Also, camera crews necessarily move from story to story more slowly than reporters do. A reporter may be assigned to work with different camera crews during the day, either to cover more stories or because he has particular knowledge in a certain subject area. And if a reporter edits his own film (i.e., determines the cuts —a film editor does the physical editing) he may have to leave his crew in mid-afternoon. Sometimes the reporter travels in his own car; sometimes he travels with the crew, and takes taxis if he has to break away.

Crew 2 and the second reporter are quickly briefed about their assignments and sent on their way. Stories of neighborhood problems, such as a demand for a traffic light or objection to a zoning decision, usually require no advance study by a reporter. Sympathetic questioning by a skilled reporter plus intelligent camera work at the scene of the problem usually produce a good story. If both sides to the dispute can be brought in front of the camera, the story is even better, especially when a writer can later intercut the arguments to produce short and punchy statements by each party in turn. Very rarely, a camera is witness to a heated discussion by both sides present at the same time, perhaps brought together by the reporter. One or both parties may grow quite angry at the television newsmen off camera. On the other hand, the camera may record an absolutely fascinating argument, either with the reporter or, more properly, between the antagonists. If a film editor intercuts statements by opposing parties who did not actually confront one another, the newscaster must be careful to point out that a face-to-face debate did not take place, and that the film was edited this way so that points of view on the same subject could be presented together.

At 10:30 a.m., the lab man arrives at the station. He begins to heat the chemicals in the tanks of his color film processor (his tasks became more complex when the station "went to color" in news). The smaller black-and-white film processor remains on the premises, but it is rarely used now. All news film at his station is shot in color, including the film shot by "stringers," the free-lance cameramen (sometimes they are students) who earn extra cash each week by filming spot news stories, often at night when the station's regular camera crews are off duty. The midnight chase film was shot in color by a stringer. It will be the first film to go through "the soup" this morning. Also waiting for color developing are some documentary footage and some footage for a local commercial. But these will be delayed until the news film has been processed, or "souped."

Two other men begin their day at 10:30 a.m., a writer and a film editor. The film editor is ready to begin work almost immediately. Before the night newsroom film editor (who arrives at 3 p.m.) leaves each night, he clears the editing bench of the day's debris. The morning film editor's first task is to take apart the reels which comprise the previous night's late news. The station presents two news shows, at 6 p.m. and 11 p.m. The 6 p.m. reels are broken into individual story segments after the program ends. Some of the stories are re-edited for the 11 p.m. newscast. The 11 p.m. reels are broken the following morning. The film editor spends about 30 minutes breaking the two 400-foot reels into a dozen or so smaller reels. He labels each little plastic reel and types a file card. The cards are catalogued alphabetically by topic and/or person, and are cross-filed if necessary. All the reels are placed in a film can, which the editor dates and stores on a shelf.

Meanwhile, the first writer to arrive spends his first 30 minutes scanning the day's shooting schedule, the morning wire copy and the newspapers to which the newsroom subscribes. He keeps up with the news events on all levels from local to international for several reasons:

1. He may be called upon to look at film or tape concerned with this news event or a subsequent event related to it.

2. The news event may be mentioned by someone whose words he must edit.

3. He may find in the news event something worth following up. Here, his purpose duplicates that of the assignment editor. It is a useful redundancy. The more staff members who read news extensively, the more depth of coverage the newscasts are likely to have.

4. He may write a non-film story, an editorial or a humorous essay based on a news event.

5. He may refer, in passing, to a news event in his copy on another story.

At 11 a.m., the newsroom messenger arrives. Until the news department hired its own messenger, it had to make do with commercial messenger services or use whatever staff member had some free time. The messenger makes frequent trips to the airport to get or ship film. He intercepts camera crews, picking up their film in order to save them a trip to the lab. He brings them spare parts if any of them report equipment failure. When available, he carries film between the lab and the film editing room. He carries reels from the film editing room to the projection room, and brings them back after the newscast. All the while, he learns the workings of the television news operation and, when he has time, apprentices for the job which interests him most. The previous newsroom messenger is now the soundman on Crew 3. The present messenger is learning film editing.

About 11:30 a.m., the assignment editor receives three phone calls. Crew 1 calls in to say they have finished the starlet story and are now heading for the senator. Crew 2 calls in to say they have finished the neighborhood story and are heading for the groundbreaking ceremonies at the site of the new department store. The assignment editor decides to dispatch the messenger to the senator's news conference to meet Crew 1 and get the film of the author and the starlet, when he receives the third phone call. A fire dispatcher on the west side of town, who was befriended by one of the newscasters and now feels a degree of loyalty to the station's news department, telephones to report a fire out of control at a paper box factory located just down the street from a paint factory.

The editor immediately contacts each crew by car telephone. Their orders are to head directly to the fire, ignoring their next assignments. As the assignment editor speaks to them, he is looking at a large city map

THE NEWS FLOW

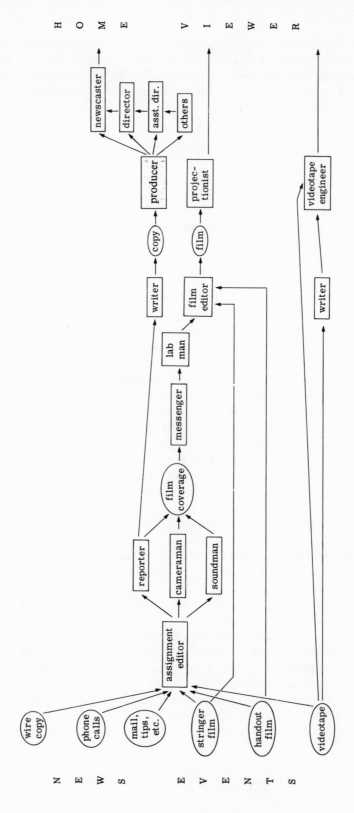

over his desk. He learns where each crew is, locates the place on the map and mentally traces two lines to the fire scene. Somewhere along each line he finds a major intersection to use as an intercept point for film pickups. The crew may remain at the scene of the fire for two hours. Between them, they have three film stories. He cannot afford to wait until the crews have finished the fire story to get those stories "into the house." Therefore, he tells each crew to drop the film they have already shot at an intersection he has selected, and to call him back to let him know at what gasoline filling station or what store they have deposited the film. He and the crews know from experience that filling station attendants and storekeepers are more than obliging in this regard. They tend to become keenly interested in what is going on. They get caught up in the excitement of the news. and they make sure to watch that night's newscast, pleased that they have played a part in making it possible.

The messenger is dispatched to one of the intersections. When he arrives he will telephone back to the office. By that time, the assignment editor should have been given a precise location by each crew. Because he does not wait to hear from a crew before he leaves, the messenger may advance by 30 minutes or even an hour (depending on how far those intersections lie from the station) the time that those three films are available for screening and editing.

The news conference for the senator is now lost to the station. As for the store dedication, there is still a chance that the store itself will have commissioned a commercial photographer to film the event, in which case a print of the film can be given to the station without charge. The editor pulls the original handout from his future file, notes the phone number of the public relations firm which mailed the handout, and telephones. He learns that film is being shot and, yes, it is color film. However, the commercial photo lab usually used to develop this agency's film could not have it ready before tomorrow. The lab is not geared for the exigencies of news. The assignment editor is tempted to give this story up also, since it is of marginal value at best. However, this experienced newsman discovered long ago that it pays to make an extra effort to get a film story. It is not up to him to determine by telephone the value of a piece of film not yet shot. A writer has that responsibility, after he sees the film. If the story is worth assigning at all, it is worth trying to get, so long as the getting does not become too expensive and it does not interfere with the getting of better stories. So the assignment editor gives it one last try. He tells the public relations agency man that the station's news lab will develop the film free of charge. A writer will screen it. If it is worth using, the film editor will cut it, then restore it after the newscast. Only a few frames will be lost in the splices, and the film will be essentially in its original condition. If it is not worth using, the agency will get it uncut. With virtually nothing to lose by this arrangement and a chance to get his client's film on a newscast, the agency man readily agrees.

Both duty crews are now occupied at the fire. The assignment editor telephones the cameraman and soundman of the third crew and asks them to come in as soon as they can. A call to the home of the third reporter gets no response, so the assignment editor calls Crew 2 by mobile phone and tells the reporter to take a taxi to the air pollution conference, line up a story and wait for Crew 3. The Crew 1 reporter will handle the entire fire story.

At noon, the assignment editor's news line-up looks like this:

In house:	robbery suspect (stringer)		
Completed:	author		
	starlet		
	neighborhood		
	CREW 1	CREW 2	CREW 3
noon	fire	fire	
1 p.m.			air pollution
2 p.m.	lunch	lunch	
3 p.m.			shopping center

THE NEWS DIRECTOR

The news director makes his own schedule and keeps it flexible. At 10 a.m. he arrived at the station for a management conference on the news budget. Unlike some television news departments run on a shoe-string and producing lackluster newscasts which do little but keep the Federal Communications Commission at a safe distance, his news department actually makes money for his station. The twice daily newscasts are interesting and informative. Their audiences represent a large slice of all viewers in the city, and the viewers tend to be faithful. Watching one or both newscasts is as much a part of their day as eating supper. Local advertisers request time within or adjacent to the newscasts, and some segments are sponsored. Station management, aware that it takes money to make money, plows much of the profit back into the news department in salaries, equipment and a budget to cover purchases of film, artwork, rental of helicopters and other costs to improve the newscasts.

At noon the news director goes into the newsroom. As he looks over the line-up of stories, the assignment editor describes the fire story. A phone call to the fire department dispatcher tells him the fire is still out of control and has spread to the building adjoining the paint factory. Everyone in a three-block radius is being evacuated, and engine companies throughout the city are converging on the area.

The story is assuming major proportions, and the news director elects to exploit its possibilities. He phones a helicopter service at the airport and hires a "chopper" and pilot to fly to an empty field a mile from the fire.

He is told to wait for a cameraman. At the same time, the assignment editor tries to reach either crew by car mobile phone. He gets no response, as he expected, because both crews are away from their cars, filming the fire. He instructs the mobile phone operator to turn on the red alert signals at each phone. When a crew member finally returns the call, the assignment editor orders a cameraman to meet the helicopter. Only a cameraman will go aloft, using his silent camera. Even if the helicopter were roomy enough for a soundman and a sound camera, the sound of the fire would be drowned by the noise of the "chopper." Besides, some cameramen prefer to lean out the open door of helicopters when shooting, eliminating the glass barrier between camera and subject. Leaning out of a helicopter while holding a heavy sound camera would be foolhardy.

THE WRITER

Now the early writer returns from the screening of the car chase film. He reports that the film is excellent, as far as it goes. He recommends sending a crew to the police station to seek statements from the suspect, a detective and, if possible, one of the officers who made the arrest. Learning that no crew is immediately available, the writer calls the detective handling the case to get the story and to learn when the arresting officers will begin their duty shift.

The writer then calls the art department of the television station. That department is separate from the news department. The artists print and draw cards for commercials, for the morning children's show, and for every other locally produced program. They make slides and "crawls," the rolls of paper which are drawn slowly past a television camera lens at the start of a program to show titles and at the end of a program to show credits (the crawl usually carries names into a frame at the bottom of the screen and out at the top). The station has ordered an electronic titling machine, but it has not arrived. The writer wants the art department to produce three line drawings showing the chase at various stages. He intends to tell the story "over" cards until it reaches the point where the film begins, instead of trying to cram both the beginning of the story and its conclusion behind the film of the conclusion of the chase. Hopefully, if a camera crew can be freed, he will round off the story with interviews.

With the cards ordered and the later film pending, the writer decides to delay writing the story. Instead, he and the film editor begin to screen the next three films to arrive from the lab: the author, the starlet and the neighborhood problem.

The author has sent along a copy of his latest book. The writer removes its jacket, which will be mounted on a card to be placed on a rack in front of a television camera. At the moment in the filmed interview when the book is first mentioned, the director will order a four-second dissolve from film to card, so that the viewers may see the jacket. The writer also calls the art department to order a "super" card of the author's name. (The electronic titling machine will eliminate the need for this artwork.) From the 200 feet of film shot of the interview, which rolls through a projector at the rate of 36 feet per minute, the writer chooses four silent segments totaling 12 seconds for a lead-in to the sound interview, and one minute 15 seconds of sound. His script will have copy to cover the opening 12 seconds, and will indicate to the director when the super card and the book jacket are to appear. He will give the times of the various segments and an end cue, so that the director will be able to cut on the closing word. It is his news department's policy to time the super and other internal cues from the start of SOF. Other news departments prefer to time their cue from the start of film, so that the super cue, below, would be at 30 seconds into film (adding 12 seconds of silent film to the 18 seconds of SOF before the super is taken).

author/6 p.m. /march 20/ runs 1:27

:12 SIL	William Johnson has written one of the most controversial books of the year, "A Spy in the Department of Commerce." Since its publication, he has been in constant battle with critics. He is here to visit relatives . . . and talked with Carl Miller.
1:15 POS COLOR	SOF
AT :18 SUPER: WILLIAM JOHNSON	
AT :30, DISSOLVE TO BOOK JACKET FOR 4 SECS.	
AT 1:00, AGAIN SUPER: WILLIAM JOHNSON	ENDS: " . . . expression will prevail."

The starlet proves to be quite dull. She was only willing to plug her next picture, and would say nothing about the divorce or anything else. However, the cameraman, using his sound camera to get natural sound of court corridors and her heels tapping on the marble floors, asked the starlet to walk into and out of the courtroom, toward him and away from him, and to pose chatting with her lawyer. From these scenes, the writer constructs a 30-second film story. He ignores the interview.

The neighborhood problem is a demand by residents that a school crossing guard be placed at what they consider a dangerous intersection. When requests to the city and the school district failed to get action, the residents turned to television and newspapers. The television reporter asked the group of neighbors who had assembled in their spokeman's living room to accompany him to the intersection. There, with the traffic in the background, he interviewed the spokesman at some length, then took short statements from as many of the other residents as he could coax to speak up.

Additionally, the cameraman filmed establishing shots of the neighborhood, the school and the crossing from several angles. To further illustrate the story, the writer asks the art department to draw a "pull-tab" map which shows the busy street, the intersection, the school on one side and the houses on the other. A black tab is built into the map, with the end of the tab jutting slightly outside the card. The card will be placed on a rack during the newscast and a television camera will focus on it. At a signal, a prop man (stagehand) will slowly pull the black tab out, exposing a white line beneath it, showing the path children take from home to school. On the television screen, it will look very effective, establishing the perspective clearly.

At 3 p.m., two more writers, a film editor and the nightside assignment editor report to work. The fire is under control, all the fire footage is "in the house," and crews and reporters have been given lunch breaks. Crew 3 is out on its assignments. Crew 2 is dispatched to the police station after the assignment editor phones ahead to set up the interviews. Crew 1 is given time to check equipment before going home for the day. Newsreel cameras and sound gear get rough handling, yet they are precision built. All the equipment needs attention and frequent maintenance. Otherwise, the cameraman and soundman risk equipment failure at crucial moments.

The night film editor and one of the two late writers are assigned to the fire story. The other writer goes to a television monitor for both the incoming "feed" from New York of the network news, and a special network videotape service of international, national and sports film stories for use on local newscasts. From some 15 available clips in the videotaped special service, the writer may choose four. He will edit them if necessary, but keeps his editing to a minimum, for videotape editing remains a slow process, although much improved with the advent of electronic editing capability built into videotape machines. Instead, he directs the videotape engineer to dub the clips he wants onto a separate reel in the order he requests, with cue marks in between. He will prepare a script for each videotape clip, so that the director will have timings and end cues. The writer will also strip the wirephoto machines, looking for stills to use in connection with the videotape, usually at the beginning or end of the tape. He will also look for stills which will stand by themselves as the only visual elements in a story. All stills will be sent to the art department with instructions for touching up and cropping. Then they will be photographed with positive transparency film, which is mounted as slides. Some of the slides will be shown full on screen, others will be used in rear projection Chromakey behind the anchorman. (On some stations, wirephotos are simply pasted, taped or stapled to cards for televising through a camera in the studio.) Thirty slides may be used in a 30-minute newscast.

The nightside assignment editor will take over duties from the dayside editor in the space of half an hour. The transfer of responsibility and information must be smooth and complete. If not, the nightside editor may not do what the dayside editor promised would be done: important phone calls will not be made; phone calls that are received will not be understood, (e.g., "Say, anybody know why Detective Joe Green was supposed to call us?"); and news stories will not be assigned as they should be.

BUILDING THE NEWSCAST

As the afternoon hours pass, a pile of individual story scripts grows on the news director's desk, for he serves also as the producer of the early evening newscast. At 4 p.m. he begins to build the newscast from wire copy, film scripts, videotape scripts and local material such as a weather report. The writer who looked at the videotape and monitored the network news also rewrites news stories from the wire copy. He chooses the major stories of the day, selects the latest information available and summarizes it briefly, writing in broadcast style. He will continue to watch the wires closely until both the local and network newscasts have been completed. The network newscast may be received from New York one to three hours before it is played back (depending on national time zones). If late news contradicts what has been taped already, or if a bulletin of overriding importance appears on the teletype, the writer will write a script to cover a portion of the taped network newscast with a slide, or with a local newscaster, live, to report it. Besides rewriting wire stories for the local newscast, the writer also chooses a half dozen wire copy stories which he doesn't bother to rewrite. He simply staples the copy to sheets of paper and writes the word "PAD" at the top of each sheet. If the newscaster runs out of copy before the end of the program, he will have these additional items to read.

The news director lists the elements of the evening newscast:

	SLUG	TIME
COPY	war	:30
	President	:30
	drug hearing	:30
	China	:30
	tax cut	:30
	court ruling	:30
	stocks	:15
	weather	:45
	elephant bright	:15
FILM	fire	5:00 (?)
	robbery chase	2:00
	author	1:30
	starlet	:30
	neighborhood	2:30
	shopping	1:30
	groundbreaking	:45
	air pollution	2:00

VIDEOTAPE	bombing	1:30
	floods	1:15
	Israeli army	1:00
	Arizona killer	1:30

The total time, as tentatively outlined, is 25 minutes 15 seconds. The 30-minute newscast, of course, does not permit airing 30 minutes of news. Its format includes an opening one-minute commercial, four one-minute commercials within the program, a 20-second opening, a 20-second closing and 20 seconds at the end for a "promo" (a promotional commercial for a later television program) and a station break, leaving 24 minutes for news.

However, five minutes each day is allotted to sports and weather news. A sports reporter and a sports writer have been working independently of the main news operation, assembling the items for their segment. They add two films to the reels being built by the film editors. One clip is of a night baseball game filmed the previous evening by Crew 3. The other clip is of an afternoon horse race at the local track, filmed by the track and supplied free. For the sports reporter, the race is legitimate news. For the race track, it is inexpensive advertising, and the managers are happy to rush the film to the station each day of the racing season.

Subtracting five minutes from 24 leaves the news director with 19 minutes of time available for 25:15 of film, tape and copy. The news director now has a chore he must cope with each day: what to cut. He always has more news available to him than he can use. If he did not have more, he would worry, for he would sense a weakness in the overall quality of the newscast material. He would also worry if too much had to be trimmed away, because that would mean a lot of effort and expense was going to waste. Ideally, he wants to trim the script to 18:45, with 15 seconds for leads into commercials. But first he assembles his individual scripts for each story into a newscast script within the framework of the format. Where an individual script is not yet available — for example, the fire script will not be complete for another hour — he simply writes the slug (e.g., "fire") on a sheet of paper and inserts it into his arrangement. In a few minutes, the script looks like this:

OPEN

FILM: fire

COMMERCIAL

war

VTR: bombing

China

VTR: floods

President

FILM: air pollution

drug hearing

COMMERCIAL

VTR: Israeli army

court ruling

FILM: shopping center

tax cut

FILM: author

COMMERCIAL

VTR: Arizona killer

FILM: robbery chase

FILM: starlet

SPORTS: 1. baseball

           2. racing

stocks

COMMERCIAL

FILM: groundbreaking

weather

FILM: neighborhood

elephant bright

CLOSE

    The news director now has his script. It is, however, 6:30 too long. Many of the times are approximate. Taking out a stopwatch and reading at the pace he knows the newscaster uses, the news director reads the rewritten wire stories, all of which are marked, arbitrarily, as segments of 30 seconds. As he reads, he edits out a phrase here and a sentence there, finishing with a saving of 45 seconds. He knows the five minutes allotted to the fire story is also approximate. He may be able to trim this story, but he does not want to cut anything out that would hurt a major local story, his lead story of the day, one which the news staff covered in depth. He goes to the screening room, where the writer and film editor are now piecing together on paper what they have just seen. The news director asks about the quality of the story and its length. The writer praises the film and asks the news director how "tight" the newscast is. When he is told, the writer asks for at least four minutes. The director asks him if he wants more. They settle on four and one-half.

A director (arm raised) stares intently at a monitor as he prepares to give the technical director (to his left) the command to dissolve from one chain to another. Meanwhile, the assistant director (pencil poised) clocks the length of the program segment.

The news director again looks at his script. He decides to cut the air pollution story to 45 seconds and to hold the author story for another day. He kills the Israeli army story after talking to the writer who looked at the videotape about the comparative merits of the four tapes. The news director makes one or two additional cuts, and the script is soon at the length he wants it.

THE DIRECTOR AND THE ASSISTANT DIRECTOR

It is now 4:30 p.m. The newscaster, the director and the assistant director, or A.D., arrive. Each page of the script has been typed in quintuplicate. The assistant director sorts the pages into five separate scripts, slipping in "slug" sheets where pages are still missing. The top copy goes to the newscaster. The second copy to the director, who circles a word five seconds ahead of each film and videotape. When the newscaster reads that word, the director will order "Roll film" or "Roll tape," knowing that each film clip and each tape story will be physically halted in their machines precisely five seconds of rolling time ahead of the first frame of film or the first videotape picture that is wanted. The director also calculates which of three television studio cameras he will focus on the newscaster each time he appears, which camera on the sports reporter (and, if the newscast used stills mounted on cards, which camera on each card on the two easels in the studio; additionally, he decides which cards go on which easels).

The newsroom set in the studio is fixed. It does not change from day to day. It is never "struck" unless it is redesigned. The set is pre-lit; that is, once the director has arranged the lights, no changes are made in lighting so long as there are no complaints and no changes are made in the set; the single exception is the occasional need to light a prop used to illustrate a story.

The third copy of the script goes to the assistant director. During rehearsal he will time each story and keep a running time as well, marking these times on the pages of his copy. The fourth copy will go to the audio engineer. Although the audio engineer gets instructions from the director, his copy of the script enables him to cut away from film and tape exactly at the final word of the end cue, so that the studio sound comes crisp and clear, with no unwanted words going over the air or 'upcuts" (the loss of words because the sound was brought in a second or two late). The final copy goes to a TelePrompter typist, who reproduces the script in large letters on a roll which will fit into a device above a television camera lens. As the newscaster reads, someone will electrically roll this script to keep pace. To the viewer at home, the newscaster seems to be looking right at him, telling him the news. Actually, he is reading. Sometimes, he uses the script in his hand just as a prop. Other times, he reads each in turn. That final copy may end up in the producer's hands, and later in the files.

As a rule, except on some smaller stations, neither the director nor the assistant director are newsmen. They consider a newscast a "show" which is handled much like any locally produced show, except that they get the script very late, feed it live and occasionally accommodate changes while the program is on the air. Otherwise, to them it is another show using two or three cameras, one or two film chains, videotape, slides, etc. It uses a set which must be lit, and it begins and ends at specified times, with breaks for commercials. Their concern is not with content, but with format. An hour earlier their concern was with Jumbo the Clown and 20 squealing children in the audience. An hour later, they will be concerned with commercials and station breaks during the run of a movie or of network programming. At the network level, directors assigned to news usually do nothing else.

THE PRODUCER

At some television stations, a member of the news staff, perhaps a writer or assignment editor, doubles as director, assistant director or as producer. A producer is responsible for the content and production of a newscast. In many cases, the news director serves as the producer. In some news operations, there is no producer as such; several staff members share the work and the responsibility for the content of the newscast.

THE NEWSCASTER

The newscaster, or anchorman, has the most desirable job in the television news department. He is paid more than others, sometimes disproportionately more. To station management, he (and on large stations anyone who appears on camera, including field reporters) is the "talent." To everyone, in and out of the station operation, the newscaster alone is identified with the news program. On the network level, the viewer says he tunes into the "Cronkite news" or the "Brinkley news" or the "Smith-Reasoner news" and, on the local level, to the "Joe Doaks news" or the "Joe Doaks show" or "Joe Doaks and the news." The newscaster is the representative of the station and the news department in addressing Kiwanis luncheons, and the like. However, accompanying the occasional glamour and star system treatment is a measure of insecurity. If audience ratings fall, the newscaster is likely to be blamed and may be replaced. Chances are he will seek employment in another city unless he chooses some other occupation. He also feels the competition not only of newscasters elsewhere, but of reporters and other news staffers who aspire to his position.

On some stations the newscaster is an announcer who was appointed newscaster by virtue of his stage presence, his authoritative voice, his delivery skill or his looks. If he does not immerse himself in the day-to-day news operation, but merely contents himself with picking up a finished script, other news staffers scornfully label him a "reader."

Today, many newscasters go considerably beyond such detachment from news and the building of the newscast. The newscaster is often also a reporter; on small stations he is likely to be *the* reporter. Even further, the combination newscaster-news director is common, with the job of producer thrown in. The newscaster then has responsibility for the content of the newscast. Or, to put it another way, the news director not only produces the newscast, but delivers it.

READING THE SCRIPT

While the director and the assistant director mark their copies of the script for cue words and camera cuts, the newscaster reads his copy for content. He is particularly concerned with factors which may be detrimental to delivery. If he comes across a name or a word which he is not sure he will pronounce properly, he checks it with a writer or looks the word up in a dictionary or a gazetteer. The newscaster also watches for words he feels a writer chose in error.

The newscaster takes his script to a quiet corner and reads it aloud to himself, getting a feel of words, phrases, meaning and a rhythm pattern. He pencils slash marks at places he will pause for breath and he underlines words he will emphasize. Here and there he edits words and phrases, eliminating those he considers unnecessary to the meaning and changing others to permit a smoother reading. He may break a series of sibilants or words ending in "th or "ths" ("The death of a sixth youth in that bus accident. . . ."), or he may remove the word "today," probably the most overused and unnecessary (in most stories) word in television newscasts.

After he has read the script and is satisfied with it, the newscaster either goes to the make-up department or puts some on himself. Make-up for a newscaster is usually limited to "pancake," to avoid appearing washed out under the hot studio lights, although sometimes features are highlighted or subdued, depending upon the skill with which the make-up is applied. As a rule, newscasters grin and bear this "show biz" aspect of presenting the news.

CONTROL ROOM AND STUDIO

At 5 p.m., one hour before the 30-minute newscast begins, everyone connected with the air production of the program (as distinct from news assembly) gathers in the studio and the adjoining control room. More dis-

A studio control room may confront a director with wall-to-wall monitors. At a remote location at Cape Kennedy, a director (at left) for ABC News not only sees what is available through several live cameras, videotape and projector channels, but also what his own network and its competitors are airing at the moment.

tant rooms, such as master control, quality control, projection and video-tape are already staffed. The reels which the film editor has built of the individual stories, based on an order list from the news director, are taken to the projection room and mounted on sound projectors.

In the control room are the director, the assistant director and the technical director, who is seated before a panel of buttons and levers called a switcher. On the wall in front of the three men is a bank of television monitors showing what each studio camera sees, what each projector sends, what the videotape room sends, what the control room is sending out and what the television station is beaming. During the rehearsal and the newscast several monitors show the same picture. For example, when the newscaster begins the program, his face will appear on a camera monitor, the studio monitor and the "air" monitor. During rehearsal, a film will appear on one film-chain monitor and the studio monitor, while one camera monitor shows the newscaster waiting, another is focused on a still photo, the tape monitor and the second film-chain monitor are blank and the "air" monitor has Jumbo the Clown or an old movie.

In a room adjoining the control room (or "control booth") is the audio control booth, with a plate glass wall, enabling the audio engineer to see the director and the monitors while shutting out all unwanted sound. His room is equipped with turntables, tape recorders, audio switching controls and volume "pots."

In another room is a booth announcer. He introduces the newscast and the newscaster, gives station breaks, reads "promos" for the later programs, reads some commercial copy and some public service spots, and introduces the next program. The only equipment in his soundproof room is a micro-

---

SIMPLIFIED JOB CHART *

NEWS DIRECTOR—Oversees entire news operation and administration, often including documentaries and editorials.

NEWS PRODUCER—Responsible for a single newscast each day.

NEWSCASTER (or ANCHORMAN)—Reads news on air, introduces film reports and reporters in studio.

REPORTER—Reports news stories on film, voice over film, or in studio.

WRITER—Writes copy, makes film editing decisions.

FILM EDITOR—Cuts film, also makes film editing decisions.

ASSIGNMENT EDITOR—Assigns reporters and cameramen to news stories.

DIRECTOR—Has charge of actual presentation of newscast, including studio cameras, film and videotape projection.

---

* Different news operations combine these functions in different ways. This chart, meant only as a guide, does not describe every television news roster.

phone and a television monitor, except for his headset, consisting of earphones and a tiny microphone, which can be shoved aside. Everyone in the control room has a similar headset, and so do the stage manager and each cameraman in the studio. The projectionist and the videotape engineer have either headsets or a two-way speaker system to complete the informational hookup under the control of the director. Sometimes, especially in live coverage of major news, the anchorman will wear an earpiece, called an IFB (Interrupted FeedBack), through which the producer gives him instructions and advises him of upcoming films and switches.

In the studio proper are the television cameramen (not to be confused with the film cameramen who go into the field to record news stories), a "boom mike" man responsible for all the studio microphones, a prop man responsible for cards and furniture (he will pull the tabs on the "pull-tab" maps), the man who operates the TelePrompter, an electrician responsible for lighting (he doubles as a cable man, whose responsibility it is that the camera cables trailing along the floor don't snag, which would cause the camera to jerk), a stage manager who is both a sub-director and the man who cues the newscaster, and, of course, the newscaster plus others who will appear in the newscast, such as the sports reporter, a news reporter, a feature reporter, the weatherman or a guest.

REHEARSAL

The rehearsal brings together for the first time all the elements of the newscast. The headlines or the "tease" film or statement which may precede the newscast give the audio engineer a chance to adjust his "pots" to get the sound levels he wants. He also balances the announcer's mike level during the "open." More importantly, for the first time, the written copy for each story is read against the edited film and videotape. The newscaster paces himself and may edit some more words so that copy matches film. If something on film escaped the watchful eyes of the film editor and the writer, a dozen other pairs of eyes will catch it at rehearsal. If the film editor has transposed two film stories in a hurried assembling of the projection reel, it will be caught here. Like theatrical rehearsals, a rehearsal of a newscast starts and stops, as the director orders changes. The TelePrompter man runs through his script roll. *Many local newscasts are unrehearsed and look it.*

While each segment is practiced, the assistant director times the segment with his stopwatch, and notes that time on his copy of the script. When the rehearsal is finished he adds up the segment times, and informs the director, producer and newscaster of the total. It may be necessary to cut some copy, or even to excise a film or tape story, which usually means rolling quickly through the film or tape during the program when the reel has reached the point where the particular story begins. Only if the script allows no time for a roll-thru, will the film be physically cut.

A studio control room is a busy, crowded place during air time. The man beside the microphone is the technical director. The switcher, the panel of buttons and levers on the table in front of him, lets him cut in any camera chain, videotape chain or projection chain. He acts at the command of the director, who is guided by the rows of monitors.

On the other hand, if the newscast runs short of its allotted time, the newscaster will "fill" with "pad" copy, (either until the program ends, or a pre-set "backtime" segment is reached, enabling the newscaster to conclude strongly, rather than sloppily with pad copy).

While the rehearsal continues, the technical director glances frequently at the clock. Everything stops when he reports, "Two minutes to air." Now the projectionist and the videotape engineer rewind the reels back to the first cue positions. The television cameramen swing their heavy cameras into opening position, "get on" the suitable lenses, and focus. The TelePrompter is rolled back to the newscaster's opening words. The director, the assistant director and the audio engineer stack the pages of their scripts, and leaf through them to make sure all pages are in numerical order. The newscaster does the same with his copy. He straightens himself in his chair, picks up a pencil or whatever other prop he uses, and assumes an expression of intelligent seriousness.

"One minute to air."

"Thirty seconds."

The stage manager gives a final flip to the trailing cord of his headset and calls out, "Fifteen seconds. Quiet on the set. . . . Ten. . . . Five. . . ."

With his eyes fixed on the sweep-second hand of the clock mounted on the wall in front of him, the director addresses, in turn, the technical director, or T.D., beside him and the stage manager listening by headset: "Four . . . three . . . two . . . one . . . Up on one (telling the T. D. to fade in from black to camera number one) . . . Cue him."

The stage manager, standing beside the camera designated as number one, jabs a forefinger toward the newscaster.

And the newscast begins.

FOR THE STUDENT

1. Watch a local newscast for one week. List the things you like about it. How can it be improved?
2. If you were a news director, would you rehearse each newscast? All of it or just film and tape portions?
3. What does the newscaster mark on his script? The director? The assistant director?
4. Watch a newscast to see if you can detect the reading of pad copy and the start of the backtime segment.
5. Read an evening newspaper before watching a network newscast. List the stories you think the newscast might cover. Then monitor and compare. Why the differences?
6. Compare one network newscast plus one local newscast with the evening newspaper. What front page stories were left out of the newscasts? Did the newscasts cover any stories the newspaper missed? Compare differences in emphasis.
7. In this newscast, do you think any stories were created for or by television journalists?
8. Monitor one local newscast to guess, for each story, whether a public relations man or a press officer was involved. If not, guess what the source of the story was. Compare your impressions with those of other students.
9. Cull the local newspapers for two "anytime" feature stories and two dated assignments for a television newsroom future book.
10. Spend a day in a newsroom. Keep a log of newsroom activities.

3

PUTTING IT TOGETHER

WITH FEW EXCEPTIONS, everything in a daily newscast — every film clip, every videotape, every still photo, every map and every scrap of news — is prepared and assembled on the day it is aired, all done within the space of a few hours. In a few minutes it is over. The careful work is shelved or scrapped. Tomorrow it must be done again with fresh news, and the tomorrow after that with still other news.

Television newscasts are presented so often and, as a rule, so smoothly that all those who have participated in the television news operation forget what they may have concluded the first time they saw a newscast from the vantage of a studio control room: an informative television news program is an achievement.

The gathering of news and the preparation of a newscast follow familiar paths, despite the diversity of the news itself, so that what may seem to a newsroom visitor near deadline as chaos is actually an orderly haste, an organized system going at top speed.

SOURCES OF NEWS

In theory, television news departments and newspaper editorial departments have identical sources of news available to them. In practice, it does not quite work out this way. One reason for the difference is that the two media differ in the kind and degree of news they use; for example, newspapers have no use for motion picture film sources, while television newscasts have no use for the Dow Jones wire.

From time to time another difference becomes manifest. Television has a greater appeal to office holders and office seekers. Robert Kennedy admitted that he would rather appear for 30 seconds on a network evening news program than be written up in every newspaper in the world. Former President Lyndon Johnson's press secretary, Bill Moyers, said his boss felt that "television offers him the most direct, straightforward and personal way to communicate with the people. It is not someone else's attitude or interpretation of what the President said. It's the purest form of communication, and I think the most desirable." It may be a hard fact for newspapermen to swallow, but it is a fact nevertheless that many politicians and public relations men make themselves more available and put themselves to greater trouble for a television newsman than for a newspaperman, with the exception of reporters for a few of the nation's major newspapers, "the quality press." Yet this is an important exception, because as someone once remarked, sometimes political figures prefer to reach "people who count instead of people who are counted." Certainly, television news also reaches "people who count," but it is most influential as a mass medium, and television journalists should never forget that.

Let us examine the sources of news available to a television news department. What follows is a fairly complete list of sources, fully available only to networks and large city stations. Yet even small stations have most of these sources open to them. The small stations differ in degree, rather than in kind. They have fewer people, fewer facilities, fewer news sources, and fewer man-hours to gather the news.

Wire Services

The Associated Press and United Press International offer their subscribers a variety of wire services:

1) "A" wires, emphasizing international and national news.

2) "B" wires, emphasizing feature stories, reports in depth and regional news.

3) Sports wires.

4) Broadcast, or radio, wires, in which news is rewritten in broadcast style, condensed, and arranged into five-minute and 15-minute summaries for "rip-and-read" newscasts. Except for the occasional feature or major news story, a broadcast wire treats news quite superficially. The broadcast wire has a "regional split" once an hour, a period when the news is fed not from the main "trunk" feed but from a regional bureau of the wire service. Most states have a regional office in their largest city. Here, at random, are a few of the AP broadcast wire splits from the Minneapolis regional office:

> 6:25 a.m. — Minnesota road information; in depth dateline pieces; regional news.

10:25 a.m. — Minnesota pre-noon news summary; weather forecasts as available.

1:25 p.m. — Minneapolis grain closing; Minneapolis final grain bulletin; Chicago live beef futures; Chicago hog futures; closing South St. Paul livestock; Northwest afternoon sports roundup.

6:25 p.m. — regional temperatures; five-day forecasts, evening Northwest sports capsule.

8:25 p.m. — Minnesota evening news summary.

11:30 p.m. — midnight highlights, late sports.

Note: Garbled wire copy can sometimes be unscrambled using this key:

A B C D E F G H I J K L M N O P Q R S T U V W X Y Z
- ? : $ 3 ! & 2 8 ' ( ) . , 9 0 1 4 ' 5 7 ; 2 / 6 "

So: &99$, 32' becomes: GOOD NEWS

5) Still photo machines, such as AP's "Photofax" and UPI's "Unifax," which reel off still pictures and maps, already captioned. The machines work by feeding chemically treated paper between a straight blade (which should be changed daily) in front of the paper and a helical wire mounted on a drum (which should be wiped clean daily) behind the paper. Excited by a photo-electric cell in the sending mechanism, the straight blade deposits a layer of iron on the paper proportional to the strength of the current, creating a shading from light gray to black on the paper. The current

flows between the blade and the helical wire as the drum revolves, scanning across the paper. The paper, of course, is slowly and continually fed upward past the blade to offer a new surface to the scanning line with every turn of the drum.

The AP serves some 3,100 television and radio stations in the United States alone. UPI reaches 2,100 television and radio stations. There are in the United States approximately 680 commercial television stations (508 on VHF), including a handful of satellites which lack their own news departments. There are also 182 non-commercial television stations (77 on VHF). For radio: approximately 4,270 AM stations, 2,475 FM stations. (Approximations are preferable in a book, because new channel licenses raise the totals.)

Taking advantage of new technology, AP and UPI have computerized their news flow. Both also offer a 24-hour newswire designed for display on a CATV channel. AP also produces news documentaries for television and for the educational and video cassette markets.

Reuters, the British news agency, has expanded its worldwide coverage to include correspondents in a few American cities. *The New York Times* and *The Los Angeles Times-Washington Post* offer news analyses not available on AP and UPI, but excellent as they are for newspaper readers, these wire services have little appeal to television news directors, who prefer to spend budget money in other ways.

Some large cities have a separate city news service, which deals only with local and area events. A city news service provides not only news, but tips, and usually both a news calendar of upcoming events and a court calendar indicating some of the more interesting cases on tomorrow's docket.

The weather wire is provided by the National Weather Service at no charge to subscribers except for machine rental and drop charges. Television stations, radio stations and newspapers in large cities have benefitted from this arrangement for some years. In the early 1970's the service was extended to media outlets in smaller communities through what is called the NOAA (for National Oceanic and Atmospheric Administration) weather wire. The feed is identical to the major city weather wire feed. In some communities the long distance line charges are paid for by the subscriber; in other communities, by the National Weather Service. Weather news is routine almost all the time, but no other news can match it for its broad and continuing appeal to the public. Newscasts which just give weather reports casually are overlooking a very popular ongoing news event. Weather news ought to be imaginatively and fully treated. (Some examples can be found in the section, *Illustrating Weather News,* chapter 14.)

Other Media

Metropolitan newspapers contain rich veins of news leads for television stories. The leads may be found in local news coverage, feature stories, items in local columns and nationally syndicated columns.

Suburban and small town newspapers should be regularly scanned for local stories which have potential for development into television newsfilm stories.

Other television stations ought to be monitored for several reasons: to learn what the competition is doing, to learn what the competition is missing and to learn what the competition has that your station is missing. While a station should never present stories that will have viewers muttering, "Heck, we saw that yesterday on the other channel," it must still be alert to developing news.

Radio newscasts can be monitored at home before the newsman starts for work, and on the car radio whenever he is driving. Radio news can alert him to breaking stories, and send him and other newsmen of the station scurrying to grab cameras and head for the scene of a major story.

Magazines provide occasional leads to local stories. More often, their treatment of a national event or their reporting of national attitudes can lead a local television station to an interesting feature, perhaps by interviewing local residents on the same topics.

Network television newscasts may be mined for ideas. One network news feature showing how easy it is for a burglar to open most door locks led a local station some months later to cover the same subject with a different approach. A locksmith went from door to door in an apartment house corridor. Using the simplest of tools, he flung open each door in turn. It will be instructive to note that, in addition to the useful warning this news feature gave to householders, it angered many viewers who phoned the station to complain that the film was so explicit that it was a lesson, especially for the young, in how to burglarize.

Sources for Visuals

Because television is primarily a visual medium and because it is virtually the only medium which is able to show action (the only other medium is the now extinct movie theater newsreel), the sources of news must include the sources of newsfilm and videotape. Many news programs are built each day around film and videotape. The variety of sources supplying these commodities, film and tape, depends upon the news department's budget.

1. The news department's own camera crew(s) will shoot most of the local film stories used, and often will cover stories within the television station's reception area. The farther away the stories are from the television station, the more important they must be to merit coverage, not only because of the added expense of sending a cameraman or camera crew and perhaps a reporter to a distant locale, but also because the time required for travel cuts down the number of stories which can be shot in one day, and because the lengthy absence of a camera crew may leave the station unprotected in the event of a major breaking story close to home.

2. Stringers are free-lance cameramen (Note: newspaper stringers are reporters) who are paid per story used. In large cities, stringers may

only be permitted to sell breaking news stories. Some stations have union contracts with their own cameramen which forbid the station to assign a story to a stringer or to buy film of a scheduled event, like a parade, from him. In smaller towns, where such union contract provisions do not exist, the stringer may provide everything up to full coverage for small stations which lack their own camera crews. The stringer uses his own camera equipment, rents equipment or borrows it from the station. Some local stations even equip regular stringers.

3. A regional network of stringers or of television stations which interchange film clips will effectively extend the reach of any television news department that takes the trouble to set up such a network and keep it functioning smoothly and fairly. If done strictly on an exchange basis, the cost of a regional film network can be very small compared to the coverage—and protection—gained. Even where film stories are bought, a stringer system can be relatively cheap, costing only the agreed fee if the clip is bought on speculation (or if the story was assigned by the station to the stringer), plus the film replacement whether the clip is purchased or not (certainly an inexpensive way to maintain goodwill), plus the cost of shipment (usually by Air Express or by an airline's own freight service).

4. Special network videotape feeds of news clips reach subscribing stations daily: CBS Late Afternoon News, ABC Daily Electronic Feed, and NBC Network Program Service.

5. A newsfilm shipping service, also by subscription, is a supplemental source.

6. Videotape is taken from network newscasts for use on late local newscasts. It is a common practice of local stations affiliated with a major network to pepper their late night news reports with videotape lifted from the early evening network newscast. For example, battle film which appeared in the dinner hour CBS Network newscast will reappear in the 10 p.m. or 11 p.m. newscast of many local CBS affiliates.

Stations in the Pacific and Mountain time zones sometimes delay network newscasts until 6 p.m. or 7 p.m. local time, which may mean that a videotape of the evening newscast will be on a shelf for three hours before people in Los Angeles or Seattle see it. A news editor must monitor that incoming feed in case breaking news requires that it be updated. Not only must he know what each news item consists of and where in the feed it is located, so that a videotape engineer will be able to fast-forward to the right spot, but the editor must also know what news items near the top of the newscast can be blocked out if a totally new event requires reporting. Updating a network feed consists of writing copy which will exactly cover an existing news segment, allowing a smooth transition into and out of the network videotape. The local update copy can be read by a newscaster on camera or by an announcer over a bulletin slide.

7. The news department's own film library can often supply just the right footage to illustrate a story. A good library is well worth maintaining.

8. Handouts are either locally or nationally produced by companies with something to sell or a name to keep before the public. When handouts are well done and based on genuine news, they can be a useful addition to the sources of newsfilm. The fact that they are non-exclusive (everyone getting the same film) is a minor drawback. The fact that they are free should not be a drawback either.

Public relations men have discovered that many television news producers welcome intelligently crafted handout film, which is a mixed blessing for the newsroom. An article by William McAllister in *The Wall Street Journal* questioned a relationship which may seem to public relations men and some broadcast newsmen to be symbiotic: [1]

Alaskan caribou prance playfully across the TV screen. The scene is the chill Arctic tundra, where conservationists would have you believe that such animals would be threatened by the proposed Trans-Alaska Pipeline.

Not these caribou, however. They seem unperturbed by a long, wooden mockup of the pipeline. Indeed, most of these calm caribou simply scamper over it on special ramps or scurry under elevated sections. The local newscaster assures viewers that such environmental safeguards would be integral parts of the controversial project.

The conservationists' fears undoubtedly seem unfounded to TV viewers in Baltimore, Chicago, Boise and numerous other cities who recently saw the caribou feature on their nightly newscasts. In fact, it would appear the pipeline interests couldn't have put together more effective newsfilm if they had made it themselves.

That's because the pipeline interests *did* make it themselves.

Facing nagging governmental delays and constant harangues from environmentalists, Alyeska Pipeline Service Co., the pipeline consortium, turned to what it says is one of the most effective, yet one of the least known weapons in the public-relations arsenal. It's the television news release. The pipeline concern, like a growing number of other companies, has discovered that the nation's TV stations are often willing and sometimes eager to air company-made films during their news shows. The reason for the stations' attitude is simple: They have time on their hands—and on their screens—especially since some have recently expanded their local newscasts. All a company has to do is supply a short film and an accompanying script to a station.

Thus, it's becoming increasingly difficult for the TV viewer to know where the news ends and the puffery begins in local shows. Of course, PR men have been trying to get free plugs for their clients since the early days of broadcasting—or, indeed, of print, for that matter. But the advent of the so-called film handout has given public relations men a sophisticated tool that its advocates say is all but indistinguishable from news that a station's own staff has gathered. . . .

Some newscasters are troubled by the situation. "Ninety-nine times out of 100, I'll throw the film into the trash can without even looking at it," says Dick Williams, news director of WTNH-TV in New Haven, Conn. "It's almost a matter of ethics."

It may be more than ethics. In 1952 the Federal Communications Commission required stations to identify the sources of films and other materials they receive from outside sources for use in political programs "or any program involving the discussion of public controversial issues." The FCC once refused to rule specifically on whether that applied to a piece of film supplied by an aerospace concern for a news program. Nonetheless, many broadcasters hold that it does.

Westinghouse Broadcasting Co. requires its stations to superimpose on the screen a slide identifying the source of such film, says Ron Myers, news director of KPIX, the Westinghouse station in San Francisco. "The viewer has a right to know who paid for the film," he says. . . .

Because the film clip and the script are usually closely coordinated, it is difficult for editors at local stations to make extensive revisions to the film, the producers contend. Even so, the onrush of numerous companies putting out TV releases plus the growth of local news staffs has forced some producers to rely on more subtle, less blatantly commercial news films. "In the old days you could get away with anything," recalls Jerry Wyler of New York City's Vavin Inc. "The standing gag was you could send out blank film to 100 stations and get at least five to use it."

(See chapter 6, *Radio News,* for audio sources.)

The Community

1. Notices of scheduled events, either mailed or telephoned, help an assignment editor plan his day's shooting.

2. Public relations representatives, either making the original contact to the television newsroom or receiving a call from the newsroom, ease the work of setting up stories involving their clients.

3. Politicians are sometimes their own best "PR men." They or their secretaries will call television stations "just to let you know" what they will be doing or where they will be speaking later that day. Politicians are almost always cooperative (unless they are being indicted for something). When election time rolls around again, they will have to pay cash for the television exposure.

4. A disgruntled or concerned expert will sometimes call in to draw the news department's attention to something of public concern.

5. An angry citizen will do the same. .

6. A neighborhood representative (e.g., for a group of mothers protesting the lack of a traffic light near an elementary school) will do the same.

7. Colorful characters will do the same. Every town has them. They may be hermits or cat collectors, and they may be delightful interview subjects when they are in trouble with the law or come to public attention in some other way. But a word of warning: the colorful character on Tuesday's newscast may become Wednesday's nuisance when he tries to talk the news department into another appearance, and Thursday's pest, and Friday's pain. . . .

8. A traffic dispatcher will alert camera crews and reporters to fires, accidents and crimes reported over the special police and fire department radio bands. Dispatchers are hired by many stations in lieu of a full-time assignment editor. The student preparing for a career in broadcast journalism should consider applying for a part-time job as a traffic dispatcher at a station near the university.

PROCESSING THE NEWS

To a visitor, a television newsroom around air time on a busy day is a place of shouting and confusion. People seem to be running into each other in wild dashes. Wire machines clack. Half a dozen employees yell at once. Newsmen are familiar with the stranger's wondering comment, "How do you get anything done in this madhouse?"

In fact, a great deal does get done, and in a very short time. These daily feats appear even more remarkable when we consider the penalties of making errors of one sort or another: dead air, the wrong film coming up, splices that break in the projector, the embarrassment resulting from bad judgment and bad taste, and even libel suits.

Errors seldom occur in competently managed and staffed news departments because newsmen and television studio personnel know their jobs thoroughly and care about doing them well. In creating and processing the written and graphic materials which comprise a newscast, experienced personnel have learned what it is possible to accomplish within any given span of time.

Processing written and graphic materials can be broken into a series of steps (Note: not every news operation takes all the following steps):

Film

Shooting. A good local newscast depends upon good film stories, especially those breaking news stories covered by sound camera. The better newscasts are built around the film available each day. Of course, important news without visuals should take precedence over film of minor news value, but the producer structures most segments between commer-

A station's master control engineer performs the electronic equivalent of a railroad switching master's job. He sends programs to the transmission tower from any of the station's studios, the projection room or the videotape room. At the same time, he receives programs from the network for later transmission, or he transfers incoming programs directly out.

cials around a core of a film or a videotape, or two or three shorter films. Separate network videotape stories may be tightly edited and dubbed into a single "world and national news" segment which the local anchorman "voices over."

Transporting. As each deadline approaches, the problems of getting film to the lab loom large. Even early in the day, assignment editors scan maps to keep camera crews moving from story to story without constant trips to the lab to drop off film. Means must be devised to bring the film in.

Developing. Many television stations own their own developing tanks. Others rely on commercial agencies in town. The popularity of color news film has meant the expense of bigger, more complex laboratory systems, for color film cannot be developed in black-and-white film tanks. The newsroom should alert the lab when film is due to arrive, to make sure the chemicals have been heated to the proper temperatures and that someone else's film is not in the way.

Screening. A writer or the reporter on the story and a film editor may view the film together. The writer holds a stopwatch or follows a timer wired to the projector in order to locate the scenes he wants. It takes months and perhaps years of film screening experience before a writer gives accurate times and accurate cues, and makes firm, confident editing decisions immediately after screening a film for the first time. The film editor jots down the cues and times of the wanted scenes, suggesting changes. Creating a good writer-film editor relationship is perhaps more important than establishing any other working team relationship in the entire news operation.

Editing. The film editor cuts and assembles a film clip from the developed reel. He must constantly watch for frames which should be removed and for scenes which should not be spliced together. As deadline nears, he often finds himself rushing to finish a clip in time, but never rushing so much that he does not tug lightly at each splice to be sure it will hold.

Scripting and integrating with other visuals. While the editor builds the film clip, the writer builds the film story, which is based on all the copy available, phone calls if needed to garner added facts, and other visual elements, such as maps, photographs, super cards and other films.

Projecting. Finally the finished clip headed by numbered leader goes to the projection room, perhaps as part of a reel containing several clips in the sequence determined for the newscast. The story may actually be on two reels mounted on two projectors, if it is to be double chained (see Chapter 13, FILM EDITING). At the command "Roll it" from the director in a studio booth—the command coming over a loudspeaker or through a headset—the projectionist flips the switch that starts the projector, sending the film through the film chain and out over the air.

Videotape

Recording. Film or live programming transmitted from one television station to another, or from a network to a station, is either broadcast immediately or it is recorded on videotape for broadcast later.

Playing. The network newscasts are replayed just as they were recorded unless in the intervening hours either: a) a major news event has occurred; b) a story reported in the newscast has been significantly altered by subsequent events.

Editing. Evening newscasts on tape and network interview programs, such as "Meet the Press," are often raided for short segments to be used in local late newscasts. Segments are sometimes also extracted from library tapes. A writer "screens" reels of tape just as he screens freshly developed film, using a stopwatch or a built-in counter.

Dubbing. The desired segment will either be marked on the original tape at a spot exactly five seconds before it is to begin, in order to allow the machine to achieve full speed and the picture to stabilize, or else the desired segment will be dubbed from the original tape to a smaller tape, where a five-second cue is also applied. When it is dubbed, it "loses a generation." A second generation tape lacks some of the quality of the original, but the loss should not be noticeable to the untrained eye.

Scripting. Writing to videotape is just like writing to film. In each case, the writer must cover the five-second cue with an "intro" lasting at least five seconds. When the director gets the script, he will circle the word which comes five seconds before the tape is to begin. If there is no on-camera intro, the director puts his roll cue five seconds from the end of the preceding item.

Feeding. When the newscaster reads that circled word, the director will order the videotape engineer to "Roll tape" or the projectionist to "Roll film." Ampex videotape machines equipped with fully automatic "Amtec" capability and RCA videotape machines equipped with "Pix-lock" allow dissolves into and out of tape. Other machines allow only cuts.

Audio Tape

Recording. Like film, unlike most videotape, audio tape may be recorded anywhere without elaborate preparation. In fact, it is the most flexible recording medium of all. It is lightweight, unobtrusive, independent of light and power sources (when battery operated) and unrestricted by time needed for developing or even transporting, for audio tape can be sent to a studio from any telephone. Tape interviews by telephone are also common, so that a reporter can get interviews which time considerations would not otherwise permit.

Playing. Broadcasting an audio tape is little more complicated than playing the tape on a home tape recorder. If the tape holds a complete program, the audio engineer will keep it on a reel. If it is a short interview segment, he is more likely to transfer the sound to an audio cartridge.

Editing. Depending on the union and personnel situation, physical editing is either done by the audio engineer following the instructions of the writer, or by the writer himself. Splicing tape is not a difficult task. An inexpensive audio splicer and some practice will turn out professional quality audio tape.

Scripting. Audio tape is used in television, but only in connection with visual elements. Sometimes the newscaster on camera holds a telephone or headset to his ear, as if he is joining the audience in listening to a live report. An alternative to this bit of staging is to play the tape behind a visual, such as silent film (fresh or stock footage), silent videotape, or a series of cards. The film for a live camera might show a tape recorder with the tape rolling. The film or videotape often has sound already on it, but this sound is suppressed in favor of the audio tape. The writer determines which elements will be used in conjunction with which other elements, and outlines what he wants in a story script.

Feeding. The audio engineer shares space in the studio control room with the director and the technical director, sometimes in a closed cubicle of his own, while the projectionist and the videotape engineer are off in other rooms (other studio control personnel, such as the video shader, may also be in the control room). The audio engineer gets a copy of the script to guide him, but he still awaits the director's command to "Roll audio tape."

Graphics

Cropping. Photographs arrive at a newsroom in all sizes and height-width relationships. But a television receiver shows pictures in a relationship of three units height to four units width. To fit square photographs or tall and narrow photographs—both of which are sometimes transmitted by AP Photofax and UPI Unifax—into television's 3 x 4 aspect ratio, it is necessary to crop them, trimming top and/or bottom, or to extend them by drawing additional background on either side.

Outlining. Sometimes background must be removed. For instance, when two dignitaries meet, lesser officials are likely to be present. An air brush, a dark pen or a pair of scissors can remove these unidentified and unwanted figures from the photograph. It is also necessary sometimes to use a pen to outline a figure in order to bring it into sharper relief. Such jobs fall to a newsman in a small station. Large television stations have graphic arts departments.

Drawing maps, graphs and cartoons. A higher degree of drawing skill is required here. However, a newsman using a little care can draw a serviceable map or graph. When a map is needed, nothing else will do so well, and television newsrooms need maps often. A good world atlas and some state, county and city maps are a worthwhile investment for any television art department.

Stills on cards. The simplest and quickest way to prepare a photograph for air use is to brush some glue on the back and fasten it to a card, preferably of a dark gray hue, so that it will be less noticeable if the camera picks up part of it. Stapling a picture to a card is even quicker, but the result is not uniformly satisfactory. When a personal picture is borrowed from a private citizen, however, masking tape or paper clips should be used to protect it.

Slides. The disadvantage of cards is that they tie up a television camera. When a script calls for a sequence of cards, two cameras are needed. On the other hand, slides require only a slide projector which can share a chain with a film projector. A Polaroid camera mounted on a stand and using positive transparency film is sufficient to make quite good slides in minutes. Any newsroom staff member can learn to make such slides.

Super Cards. White lettering on black cards identifies persons, places and dates, appearing over film, videotape, persons in the studio or in live remote situations. The super card or super slide is simply a slide or card whose image is electronically superimposed over the image of a film, tape, etc.; that is, the card and the film are blended in transmission. The black disappears. Super cards can be made of block type run on a proof press with white ink, small white cardboard letters pasted on a black background, white plastic letters on a cafeteria menu sign, or some similar device. Electronic titling machines do the job better, but they cost more. (See Chapter 14, STILLS.)

Copy

Selecting and Sorting. Newsrooms receive far move copy than they can ever use. The bigger the newsroom, the more teletypes and the more copy. One or more staffers may have no other job than controlling this flood of information. From it, the day's file of significant and film-related news must be pulled, some likely features must go into a future folder, and fresh leads must be attached to stories already slected for use. Additionally someone must open and at least glance at the news releases arriving in the mail, for some of these are also useful.

Script Information. All information pertaining to stories to be included in the newscast must go to the writers assigned to those stories. The information may be in wire copy, handout (mailed news release) copy, the cameraman's dope sheet, the reporter's notes, facts garnered by telephone or captions on photos.

Writing. The writer combines all pertinent factual information with his own scribbled notes about visual elements which will form part of the story. His resulting story script is essentially a unit which can be placed anywhere in the overall newscast script. He also rewrites wire copy into short news items for the newscaster to deliver on camera, tightening and simplifying the stories, phrasing them in broadcast style, emphasizing local angles and altering them to include new information.

Late News. Television, like radio, offers immediacy of information. This sometimes means that carefully constructed newsfilm stories must be redone or discarded at the last minute. The newsroom also has a responsibility to the public every moment the station is on the air. General programming must sometimes be interrupted for bulletins. A mark of a television station's quality is the willingness of station management to put bulletins and live news switches on the air, and the ability of a newsroom to cope with major news breaks quickly, smoothly and informatively. This responsibility includes covering ("updating") delayed network newscasts with later news.

Script Assembly

Arrangement. Some newscasts begin with international and national news, move on to state news, then to local news, then to sports, stocks and

Nothing in the video cameraman's manual tells him how to keep cool. But his imagination is likely to be as varied as his field assignments. While waiting for a countdown at Cape Kennedy, a cameraman uses a beach umbrella to keep the Florida sun off his camera, his zoom lens and himself.

the weather. Others restrict themselves to local news, sports and weather. Some stations lead off with local news, unless a world news story is of un- usual importance, and end with a feature. In every newscast there is a segmented organization according to some pattern, or format. Within each segment, stories are usually arranged in order of news value and according to visual elements (e.g., so that all film is not in a block).

Commercials. Whether a newscast is unsponsored or partly spon- sored, it is often the preferred place for commercials known as "spots"— commercials from companies which buy time rather than programs. Many newscasts are profitable endeavors, a highly desirable state of affairs when some of the profit is plowed back into the news operation to improve quality of coverage. Care should always be taken to spread the commer- cials evenly across the time span of the newscast. Leads into commercials are a matter of policy: some newscasters mention the company's name and may even plug the product ("I'll be back after this message about de- licious, bite-sized Yunks"); others strictly separate news and advertising ("More news in a moment"). Some newscasters lead into commercials with a tease ("Another ax murder on a lonely farm. That story . . . after this message"). Although the practice is not applauded, some newscasters are required to read their own commercials, with the result that news and product promotion are mixed up and the newscaster is regarded by some viewers as a huckster, whereas a commercial announcer saying the same things would be held in greater esteem. (This matter is further discussed in *A Word from Our Sponsor,* Chapter 19.) As many newscasts across the country have proven, the best showcase for a commercial is a com- petently produced news program. Grateful viewers will make a point of buying the products advertised. Separation of news and commercials re- quires an extra measure of care in script assembly. There should be no juxtaposition of product and unfavorable news about the product. For ex- ample, auto accident stories should not immediately precede or follow automobile commercials; airlines have a standing order that airline com- mercials are to be cancelled on any day an airliner crashes.

Timing and Back-timing. The newscast's assistant director times in- dividual stories and segments. This makes it easy to tell if a program is running late and permits a quick decision about what items may have to be dropped. During the minute a commercial is on, a director is busy checking timing, consulting with others and reaching decisions about the balance of the program. Newscasts are often "back-timed," that is, timed to a closing segment whose time is known, so that the end of the news- cast will be clean and strong. The raggedness of reading short pad items is much less obvious when a script is back-timed, because these items are in the middle of the program, just before the back-timed segment.

Pad Copy. If a program runs less time than expected or if film breaks in the projector (or similar minor catastrophe), the newscaster fills the gap with pad stories. These are short news items which have no news connection to other news items in the program. They are delivered on camera without visuals. In most cases, pad is simply wire copy edited with a pencil and stapled to 8½" x 11" sheets.

Protection Copy. Every so often, even in the most carefully managed news programs, something goes wrong mechanically or electronically. Telephone line troubles interrupt a live switch to a remote truck or another city. A videotape machine quits. A projector bulb goes out. On local stations there is usually no provision for such calamities, and the newscaster apologizes as gracefully as he can, although he may feel he has been left "with egg on his face." Networks provide anchormen with "protection copy," summaries of what was said or shown in the remote feed. Reporters phone these summaries to New York.

ASSEMBLING THE NEWSCAST

As newspaper readers we can scan headlines. If a headline interests us, we read the lead. If that interests us, we read the second paragraph. And so on, breaking off as soon as the story ceases to matter. As radio news listeners and as television news viewers, we lack this option. If a story does not interest us, we have two choices; we wait it out or we reach for the dial.

The newspaperman need not care if a story lacks wide appeal. The broadcast newsman must care. If a long, dull story in the middle of a newscast sends 10 per cent of his viewers station hopping, the effort and expense in producing the rest of that newscast is lost on those 10 per cent. They won't be back that day. Some may never come back. The broadcaster knows that his audience can get rid of him with a slight twist of the wrist. It's that easy.

Therefore, stories are chosen, written and organized into a newscast with as broad interest as possible within the framework of news value and good taste. Stories of limited concern are either omitted or are left until the end of the newscast.

For example, sports news is awaited by many men and a few women. They want very much to hear the scores, and will leave any newscaster who ignores these daily doings. But other listeners could not care less. They would leave a newscaster who wasted their time with scores when they want to hear about today's solution to yesterday's global crisis. The newscaster lifts himself from the horns of this dilemma in a way familiar to us all. The sports report follows the news. Those who wish, may stay. Another subject of only partial interest is the stock market's activity. The newscaster solves this problem by giving a very short report after the bulk of other news has been delivered. Sometimes he describes the market's activity in one sentence, the behavior of the Dow Jones Industrials in the next, and he is done. Still a third subject getting cautious treatment is the weather forecast. While everyone is affected by the weather, not everyone is willing to spend 30 seconds of his time learning that the stationary high front over the city is likely to remain for another day, and that tomorrow's high will be 86 after an overnight low of 52, while today's high was 85 and this morning's low was also 52, except near the airport where it was 51. Weather reporting can be much more imaginative, but many stations seem unaware of this.

If any of these normally routine stories becomes extraordinary—if its news value increases sharply—the story moves into the general news section. A world's series score, a sudden drop in the stock market, a blizzard—all these stories have wider appeal and move toward the front of the newscast.

This might lead us to the conclusion that the top story of the day is read first, followed by the second most important story, and on down to the least interesting story, which ends the newscast. However, this is not the usual arrangement, although short radio newscasts often follow this pattern.

The most frequent arrangement of stories—or line-up—in a television newscast begins with the top story of the day, whether local, national or international. This might be followed by world news, with stories being melded into one another, tied with a verbal bridge, or at least put in proximity because of similarities of subject or region. Within this world news section, there might be such subsections as world and national news, or hard news followed by feature stories. The world news section is likely to be followed by a local news section. Here, the same connections and separations prevail. Stories that can be linked are linked. Features follow hard news. Political news may be separated from murders and accidents. Finally, a filmed feature story or on-camera "brite" may wrap up the report.

The time available for a newscast is not simply an open area to be filled with news. Commercials must be spaced within the newscast and this, too, affects the arrangement of stories. Some newscasters go into commercials and come out of them on camera. Therefore, a story that ends with a piece of film will not be slotted before a commercial spot, unless the newscaster is willing to appear just long enough to say, "I'll be back with a report on an air crash, right after this word from . . . . . ." And it better not be a word from an airlines company.

Another consideration in arranging stories is the avoidance of the monotony of having too many on-camera stories following each other, or too much film, without the appearance of the newscaster.

A Typical Arrangement

Here is the arrangement of local stories and graphics used on a typical day by KABC-TV, Los Angeles. (See *Glossary* for abbreviations.)

STORY	VIDEO	AUDIO
1. Catholics end Friday meat ban	still: man catching fish	story and intro to videotape recording
	vtr: interview with fisherman	vtr
2. legal fight over sunken ship	o/c	
3. TV strike threat	o/c	
4. commercial		
5. youth seeks draft deferral	still: draft board	story and intro to vtr
	vtr: youth and ill wife	vtr
6. incoming and departing governors meet	o/c	
7. exclusive interview with political figure	silent film: 10 secs	intro
	sound-on-film (identifying supercard after 30 secs)	sof
8. City Council buys rollcall machine	o/c	
9. French TV show to unwrap mummy	o/c	
10. humorous intro to sports reporter	o/c	
11. Dodgers may trade Maury Wills	o/c still: Walter O'Malley	
	sof: Wills (identifying super-card)	sound under sports reporter continuing story.
12. odds on Army-Notre Dame game	o/c	
13. auto racing	vtr dissolves to 2 stills, each sandwiched by vtr	sports reporter ad libbing event
14. boxing	o/c	
	sof of boxer (identifying supercard)	sound under sports reporter

STORY	VIDEO	AUDIO
15. horse race	o/c	lead into film of race
16. story tease	o/c	
17. commercial		
18. football feature	o/c	lead into feature
	silent film	music
19. commercial		
20. feature about Job Corps	feature reporter o/c	
	sof	sound under reporter
	o/c	
21. commercial		
22. Job Corps feature continues	o/c	
	sof	sof
	o/c	
23. commercial		
24. mistreated dog	silent film	story and lead into sof
	sof (interviewee identified by supercard)	
	sil	
	sof	
	(another supercard)	
	sil	
25. commercial		
26. mistreated dog story continues	sil	newscaster
	sof	sof
	(another super)	
	sil	newscaster
	sof	
	(another super)	
	sil	newscaster
	card	newscaster
27. commercial		

STORY	VIDEO	AUDIO
28. join network for 15 minutes of national and international news		
29. county official arraigned	still	newscaster
	sof	sound under newscaster
	sof	and intro sound on film sof
	repeat opening still	newscaster
30. lead into commercial	o/c	
31. commercial		
32. Sunset Strip without rioting teenagers	silent	feature intro and lead into sound
	sof (supercard)	sof
	sil	newscaster
	sof (supercard)	
33. lead into commercial	o/c	
34. commercial		
35. car crash kills jet ace	o/c	
36. helicopter crash	silent film	newscaster
37. lead into commercial	o/c	
38. commercial	sof	sof
39. actress arraigned	still	intro story and sound film
	silent film	
	sof (supercard)	sof
40. weather	map	newscaster
41. good nite	o/c	

Several elements were taken into consideration in the organization of this script. The first is the network news report embedded in the middle of a news hour. National and international news, unless of major importance, was left to the network. On what was regarded as a slow news day, the only major story reported was a reaction by a commercial fisherman to the ending of the Catholic Church's ban on eating meat on Friday. A second consideration, not evident from reading the story outline, is that this newscast, which begins at 5 p.m., increases its audience as it goes along, picking up viewers returning home from work. Therefore, the most interesting stories are saved for the last quarter hour, after the network news. A third consideration, again not immediately evident, is that the guidelines for a newscast in a metropolitan area may be partly based on audience analysis. With seven channels to choose from in this instance, urban television news viewers tend to sort themselves out according to such demographic factors as occupation, age, education and race. Young city-bred university professors and retired midwestern farmers may live side by side, but their tastes differ in many ways, including preferred news programs. Television station executives know this.

The script outline for this particular newscast gives only an indirect indication of the interest value of each story and of the graphic elements. In television news, what is on film very often determines whether a story will be used, and this is always weighed in determining the time allotted to the story.

Yet another consideration is what has been uncharitably called the amount of "jiggle" on the screen. A newscaster on-camera for long stretches can be tedious. What television news does best is to present action, showing the viewer what happened, visiting the place it happened, watching and hearing the people involved giving their sides of the story. Certainly, a newscaster can sum up the bare facts of any story in less time than it takes to use film, and at much less cost, but if he does it too much he will lose his audience. Here a balance must be struck. Editorial judgment comes into play. Film for the sake of "jiggle" is as wrong as eliminating film to squeeze in as much hard news as possible. The test—within the bounds of good taste—should always be: what will our viewers get out of this? What will they remember when the program ends? The answers to these questions form the framework for practical news judgment.

FORMAT

Following the old radio news pattern, television newscasts began as segmented presentations: for example, 10 minutes of world and national news, followed by 10 minutes of local news, followed by 5 minutes of sports, followed by 5 minutes of weather—all of this less commercials, with the individual segments sponsored when sponsors could be found. So the local news was brought to you by the First National Bank and the weather news was brought to you by Smiling Sylvester, the used car dealer.

Over the years television newscasts have broken out of this rigid format to the more flexible "magazine" format. The news of the day is considered in its entirety, and any news item, at least in theory, can go anywhere. On World Series days, sports may lead off. Another day the lead story will be local. If local news justifies 15 minutes, it gets it. If it

justifies only 3 minutes, it gets that. In actual practice, the magazine format as often as not ends up looking a lot like the segmented format. The
weatherman comes on 18 minutes into the newscast, give or take 2 minutes. The sports editor comes on 24 minutes in, give or take a bit. Perhaps the key difference is that under the magazine format the pattern
can vary, if the news justifies variation.

Another kind of format change has come in the studio arrangement.
The Scene Tonight, initiated by WCCO-TV, Minneapolis, has been widely
copied. The anchorman, the weatherman, the sports editor, and sometimes
a commentator or a field reporter are all on the set. The anchorman, besides reading the national and local news, calls on each of the others, and
sometimes exchanges light banter in the process.

Eyewitness News, as presented by WABC-TV, New York, takes the
banter considerably further. The concept of *Eyewitness News* is that the
viewer prefers to invite friendly, outgoing people into his home, people
who obviously like each other, and can take some of the sting out of the
usual catalogue of daily troubles which form so much of our news. Viewer
surveys have indicated a strong positive response to this format, although
it is not without its critics, among them other broadcast newsmen who
feel that *Eyewitness News* takes too light-hearted an approach to serious
matters.

Said Travis Lynn, executive news director of WFAA, Dallas, "On a
bad night the format can be embarrassing. The dangers in this thing are
really twofold. One is trying to be funny when you're not. The other is
using inside jokes. If you can't think of anything natural to say, then you
ought to say nothing." On the other hand, Los Angeles newscaster Tom
Snyder argued, "I have never subscribed to the theory that the product
we're delivering has been graven in stone by the Lord God."

This format may include the mini-documentary, the filmed, episodic
treatment of a story over a period of days. Unlike the standard 30-minute
or 60-minute documentaries, the segments are tightly edited, fast-paced,
and rather simple, dealing with a single facet of a topic at a time, and
giving the viewer who may have missed earlier episodes some fill-in and
perspective.

Eyewitness News, as its name implies, brings field reporters into the
studio each evening to report their stories, aided by film shot earlier in
the day. "Every other news operation has reporters, cameramen, editors,
producers, writers and anchormen," said one news director. "By the time
that an anchorman reads a story, it has gone through the hands of about
eight people. We send a reporter out and he does everything: reports it,
edits it, and delivers it on the air. You get a purer report."

While some television journalists describe the *Eyewitness News* format
in less printable terms, Marshall McLuhan calls it "friendly teamness." He
adds: "Since the user is always the content of any medium or service, the

news is much shaped by the public . . . The TV public is a part of the action . . . The 'friendly teamness' broadcaster *shares* the news with his audience instead of merely passing it on as an impersonal package."

FOR THE STUDENT

1. From today's newspaper pick out some stories which a newscast could report using library film.
2. What stories in today's newspaper could be helped by maps and other graphics?
3. Monitor a newscast for one week to determine its format. Is it a magazine format? A segmented format? Something in between? What is the studio setting?
4. Interview a local news director to learn what pool arrangements, if any, exist among the stations in your city, and how the system works. Write a short paper about what you learned.
5. Interview the news director of a local station with network affiliation, or the news director of an O & O, to learn how a network news operation gets a local film story. In a short paper, describe the logistics of both an air express shipment and a wide-band feed.
6. Interview all the assignment editors in your city and write a description of all the stringer operations.
7. Write a list of guidelines for stringers.
8. Arrange the stories on the front page of today's newspaper into a newscast. Compare your organization with what other students put together.
9. Go through a copy of *Time* or *Newsweek* for stories which can be given a local angle.
10. If, as a news director, you could afford only one news wire, which would you choose? Which, if you could afford two?

4

REPORTING

AT A NEWS CONFERENCE for a United States senator one day in one of the nation's large cities, local newspaper and wire service reporters were casually asking their questions, which the senator answered perfunctorily. Suddenly the door opened and, making a fair amount of noise, six men strode in. They were a reporter, a cameraman and a soundman from each of two local television stations. With sound cameras mounted on the cameramen's shoulder braces, with film in the cameras, with portable lights and with amplifiers and microphones already hooked up, these two television news teams needed only a minute or so to get ready to shoot, not much more time than a pencil-and-paper reporter takes to settle himself and prepare to jot down replies.

The atmosphere in the room became electric. The senator sat up, obviously more attentive. He completely ignored the newspaper reporters present. The television reporters were no-nonsense men. The newspaper reporters dropped back as the hot lights went on and the television reporters moved into position. Each television reporter crisply fired three or four questions at the senator, who responded just as crisply. In five minutes it was over. The lights went out and the television news teams departed, hurrying to the next story. The senator slumped back in his chair. The air of casualness resettled through the room. For the remainder of the news conference the senator behaved as if he could not care less whether the other reporters stayed or went, or even what they wrote. For him the most significant portion of the news conference had already occurred in a five-minute blaze of hot lights, because the film would carry his face and his voice to more voters than he would reach in a dozen speeches in that city, to voters he could reach in no other way, even by visiting supermarkets and standing outside factories when shifts changed.

For the reporters, the attitudes and events which had just transpired were by no means unusual, and were remarkable only in their degree of acceptance by all participants. Quite possibly, each television news reporter was not a whit more competent than his newspaper colleagues and, just as possibly, was less versed in the topics under discussion. He and his questions were favored solely because they were the means by which the senator could appear on television.

If from this event, which one can find repeated dozens of times daily across the nation, a lesson can be drawn, it is that the television news reporter should train himself to take advantage of the opportunities the television medium gives him.

A NEW RHETORIC

The mechanics of the television process and the persons involved in the process represent what we might term a new variable in the equation of persuasion. The other variables have been analyzed for two thousand years, dating back to the *Rhetoric* of Aristotle, which counseled the speaker in the ways to win over his audience, whom Aristotle referred to as "judges." Rhetoric is one of the oldest of the behavioral sciences. It is the study of the means of persuasion, a study avidly pursued across the centuries by ambitious men aware of the power which comes with winning the minds and hearts of other men.

In our own era, the television medium does more than project the *voices* of ambitious men. Much more. Every nuance of tone, gesture and facial expression is projected into the parlors and even the bedrooms of those whose minds and hearts the politician seeks to conquer. He reaches his audience when they are relaxed and secure, perhaps more receptive than in any other situation—except being in a great crowd hearing martial airs, and seeing flags and uniforms.

Understandably, the politician wants television coverage. He holds news conferences wherever he thinks a camera crew can be coaxed from its station. He allows ample time for the film to "make" the newscast. He sets aside space for tripods at his public addresses, and alerts the television stations. He makes himself available for interviews, and more available for television interviews. If he can afford it, he hires an advance man and a public relations man skilled in the requirements of television news. Should anyone question the expense, the politician can recall that it was the television medium's presentation of four debates in 1960 that is frequently credited with electing John F. Kennedy as President of the United States.

Richard M. Nixon learned the hard lesson well. His successful 1968 campaign was in media more than in motorcades. The media push was described by Joe McGinniss' *The Selling of the President 1968,* which is less remarkable for its exposés than for its examination of a means of political campaigning which will intrude upon us more and more. In politics as in pro football, winning isn't the main thing. It's the only thing.

"I know we're being used," David Brinkley admitted. "I simply decide how to handle the story on the basis of who is using us, and how, and why."

Professor Walter DeVries of the University of Michigan and V. Lance Tarrance, former Republican National Committee research director, in their book, *The Ticket Splitter,* claim that independent voters are more influenced by television news, documentaries, news specials and newspapers than by paid political spots on TV. (A survey taken by DeVries is cited in the Preface.)

For all these reasons, and others, the television newscast has come between the speaker and his audience. Without television, the speaker reaches 500 people or 5,000 people. With television, he may reach 50,000 people in a medium-size city or 500,000 people in a metropolis. If the speech is reported on a television network, the politician's good, earnest face and his stern or honeyed words may enter 50 million homes. Even those who hear him in person, if they see cameras present, are anxious to hear him again on television, perhaps curious to learn what the television newsmen regarded as important. Certainly what they will hear repeated in the newscast will remain with them longer than anything else they heard in person. Every television cameraman, soundman, and reporter is accustomed to having members of the audience come up to him to ask, "What station will this be on?" and "When will it be on?"

Curiously, after a generation, television seems to codify reality. Two brief examples may serve. When Robert Kennedy's body was flown from Los Angeles to New York, reporters waiting at the airport were standing just a few feet away when the coffin passed, yet they had their backs to it, choosing instead to watch the event on a portable television monitor nearby.

It has been observed that in television studios, people often prefer to watch the performers on monitors. Billy Graham claims he gets more converts among closed-circuit TV viewers than among audiences who watch him in person.

The role of mass communications in rhetoric today should be studied not only by journalists and students of mass communications, but by students of rhetoric and students of political science, and most carefully by political aspirants. Today we have a rhetoric of television. We might even call it a rhetoric of television news.

As a sign of the times, consider the lead paragraph of *Time's* 1967 Man of the Year cover story about Lyndon Johnson: [1]

Even if the television tube and a ubiquitous Texan had yet to be conceived, the President of the U.S. in the latter third of the 20th century would almost certainly be the world's most exhaustively scrutinized, analyzed and criticized figure. As it is, the power of his office and the Jovian electronic eye insure that the Chief Executive's visage and voice are available for instant dissection from Baghdad to Bangkok, from factory cafeteria to family living room. Depending on the man and the moment, he may come across as heavy or hero, leader or pleader, preacher or teacher. Whatever his role, in the age of instant communication he inevitably seems so close that the viewer can almost reach out, pluck his sleeve and complain: "Say, Mr. President, what about prices, Napalm? The Draft?"

GUIDELINES

Some guidelines for a television news reporter's preparation and conduct can be laid down:

A television reporter should have at least a conversational knowledge of the specialized field of every man he interviews.

He should know enough about each specialized field to ask sensible questions.

He should know enough to recognize what is new and interesting and important.

He should not embarrass his station, the man he interviews or himself by asking stupid questions. He may lean on friends who are experts in various fields for the kind of incisive questions that really get to the heart of the story. The best reporter has friends whose knowledge spans much of the field of general information. A fast phone call often is all that is necessary to prepare the reporter for the technical or complicated story.

He should not waste time with sophomoric questions. If he must ask an elementary question, he should be aware that it is elementary, and he should ask it unobtrusively, off camera, before the interview begins formally. However—and this qualification is significant—if his elementary question is likely to produce an interesting answer, he should go ahead and ask it. For instance, it would be amateurish to ask a visiting NASA official on camera, "How many manned flights have there been so far?" But try one like, "Why should my tax dollar go toward sending more men to the moon?" and he may get the best story on tonight's news show. (Or, the reporter may be brushed off with the same reply the NASA spokesman gave to the last ten reporters who asked that question.) Note, too, that the second question is open-ended. Unlike the first, it cannot be answered with a word. The reporter asks for opinion, not facts he himself could easily get by doing his homework. And by asking for opinion rather than facts, he flatters the man he questions. (It should be added that this

It takes just a little imagination to hold an interview in some place other than an office. Here, the late Bill Lawrence interviews George Romney in a garden setting, creating a relaxed and pleasant, but thoughtful mood. Often, the topic will suggest the setting, such as a freeway background for an interview with a highway commissioner, or a lab setting for an interview with a scientist.

is not the sort of question ever asked during a space shot, nor is likely to be asked by a veteran science news reporter.)

He should be aware of the interview situation. He should not start an interview with the sort of tough question asked toward the end of "Issues and Answers." A friendly opening question or comment, maybe stated before the camera rolls, breaks the ice.

A somewhat green television reporter, accompanied by a cameraman and a soundman, once arrived late for the opening of a candidate's store-front headquarters. The small store was packed with well-wishers. Other camera crews had arrived early and had set their gear up on a platform facing a stand reserved for the candidate, due to arrive momentarily. With no time to shove through the crowd and no space to set the camera up, the cameraman suggested setting up on the sidewalk outside, collaring the candidate before he went into the store, and getting a quick statement. Agreed. The crew set up, the candidate arrived, was collared, persuaded, and festooned with a lavalier mike. As the cameraman adjusted his focus, the reporter politely told the candidate the question he intended to ask in order to get that quick statement. The candidate was taken aback, for it was a very tough question indeed, the sort a reporter should build up to. The candidate did not know if the camera was rolling (it wasn't), but decided to take no chances. He not only did not want to answer the question, he did not want the question itself used. So he proceeded to destroy the reporter. With one hand he tried to tug the mike off, meanwhile covering it, which muffled the sound. With the other he pointed at the reporter and barked, "I answered that question two weeks ago on your network. Don't you watch your network's newscasts? It was reported in the papers. Don't you read the papers? How come a station sends a reporter out who doesn't watch his network's newscasts or read the newspapers?" Etc. Etc.

The cameraman, observing what was going on, stepped away from his camera, waved his arms over his head and told the candidate the camera had not been turned on yet. (Which was really a shame.) He walked up and put a friendly arm on the candidate's shoulder, smoothed the ruffled feathers and asked for a fast 40 seconds on what the candidate thought of having such a nice turnout of nice supporters on such a nice sunny day. The candidate curtly nodded agreement, threw a last dirty look at the reporter, who stood there stunned, and—at the cameraman's signal—flashed a warm smile and launched into a "I'm delighted so many of my. . . ." statement. Then off to the storefront. (*The reporter eventually came to appreciate the lessons that day taught, and offers them to you in this book. The candidate went on to become president of the United States.*)

THE INTERVIEWEE'S KNOWLEDGE

The reporter should keep his questions within the field of the interviewee's competence (unless he intentionally seeks a humorous counterpoint, such as asking a British M.P—perhaps near the end of the interview—what he thinks of modern London fashions). It makes no more sense to ask an astronomer about the latest military policy than to ask a flyer about the climate of Mars.

For that matter, it is unlikely that the flyer is an authority on military policy. He knows something about air attack, military morale around him, air strategy and the outward condition of the local populace. The reporter should talk to the flyer about what the flyer knows. The story will be more informative, more exciting, and less likely to be misleading. To be sure, Captain Hiram Jones may be perfectly willing—indeed, anxious—to spend five minutes of the television station's film giving his views about foreign policy. But the reporter is better advised to save the policy question for the ambassador, the senator or the professor who has spent years of his life studying the complexities of political events in the war-torn region.

Ralph Paskman of CBS News opposes what he calls "indiscriminate interviewing of the so-called man in the street." He asks, "What purpose is served, what information is gained by asking somebody's mother 'Should Red China be admitted to the United Nations?' You are not providing news or information when you ask somebody to be an expert on something they cannot possibly be qualified to discuss. Man-in-the-street assignments are really not valid unless you are asking people questions they are qualified to answer." [2]

Radio news director Gary Franklin disagrees in part. "MOS's won't add to the viewers' basic knowledge of events. But they're interesting. People like to know what others think. It's like a newspaper's Vox Populi."

When astronaut Virgil Grissom, later killed in preparing for Apollo I, made his 15-minute sub-orbital flight in 1961 in the Mercury spacecraft Liberty Bell 7, the entire nation thrilled to the news. Los Angeles television station KABC-TV sent a camera crew out to do a man-on-the-street interview asking two questions: 1. What do you think of the space flight? 2. Who is Virgil Grissom?

Everyone who was interviewed glowed with pride in answering question 1. Some spoke knowingly about its effect on the Cold War. But two-thirds of them did not know who Virgil Grissom was. Someone thought he was a barber.

Fools speak knowingly on any subject. And sometimes their opinions get pride of place in the press and on the air. One reason is that ignorant opinion usually comes across as less stuffy than informed opinion, a generalization supported by considerable observation. But the danger of disseminating misinformation should weigh heavily on a newsman's conscience. Non-expert expertise gets far too much play, at the expense of the thoughtful views of authorities in a field. And in an MOS on a political question, a few views taken at random are an insufficient sampling of public opinion, even with the best of editorial motives and the greatest editorial discretion. Majority opinion exerts considerable influence in swaying belief. Quoting three or four individuals with similar views gives those views an aura of universality.

For instance, *Newsweek* once bannered a non-expert survey as its lead story: "War Over Berlin: The Brutal Question." [3] The question, "Should the U.S. risk a nuclear war to defend Berlin?" was asked of "mother of an Air Force man," "Marine veteran at Harvard," "assistant pastor," "father of four," etc. *Newsweek* used a nice folksy approach, but at a critical moment in our foreign policy, they saw no need to pose this question to a diplomat, a general, a political scientist, or anyone else who was likely to have given more than five minutes of consideration to the matter in his life. Understandably, the folksy replies fell mostly into the "yes" or "no" category, without anyone replying with such an obvious question as: "Do you mean defend Berlin against invasion, or against blockade, or

The reporter translates the complexity of events into terms we can understand. ABC News science editor Jules Bergman uses a model of the lunar module to explain what the astronauts are doing.

the tactical move of East German police replacing Soviet soldiers at Checkpoint Charlie?" If such a question was asked, *Newsweek* ignored it.

In the hands of a biased and unscrupulous newsman, an MOS can harm a political candidate. In a political sidewalk interview film once made for showing in local theaters, everyone supporting one candidate was pleasantly ordinary. Supporters of his opponent looked odd or were sloppy or stuttered.

THE REPORTER'S KNOWLEDGE

An intelligent reporter who covers a story over his head need not be at a disadvantage. The vast majority of his audience will not know any more about the subject matter. And once the reporter understands the salient points, he may be in a better position than the expert to explain them simply to the audience.

Obviously, a reporter cannot be an expert on everything. Ideally, he will have a broad liberal arts education, a comfortable command of the English language, a friendly manner, a clear voice and an up-to-date awareness of what's going on in the world and in his backyard.

The television reporter should be able, in the course of a morning, to shift mental gears from quizzing a detective about a homicide to a news conference with the visiting Secretary of Agriculture to an interview with a local civil rights leader to a chat with a minister's wife just home from the Congo.

Yet, even this is not enough. The reporter must be a translator. A pencil-and-paper reporter translates the expert's information and opinions into a story the reader of his newspaper or magazine understands. The television reporter leads the expert to do this himself, and to do it with brevity and a measure of excitement, if possible.

Brevity is a factor that must always be in the back of a reporter's mind when his camera is rolling. Words that fall to the cutting room floor represent dollars in the news department's budget. However, many a veteran television newsman will argue that, once out on a story, the cheapest thing a crew has is film. That is to say, it is false economy to be stingy with film when the station has invested half a dozen expensive man-hours in the story. This argument obviously cannot be settled in the abstract, without reference to particular cases. Experience will dictate the best course to follow in each case. Here, it is enough to note that brevity is the soul of television reporting, but it must be tempered by common sense.

Brevity can also be the soul of witless reporting, and chances are it will not be the reporter's fault. Prepared to explain, lucidly, what happened in the state legislature today, he is told by the producer of the evening newscast that he must limit himself to a 25-second wraparound, maybe 15 seconds intro to an SOF statement and a 10-second tag. Who can blame him for muttering, "That's fine, but when do I get to report the news?"

A television reporter, especially in a standupper, in which he speaks directly to the camera, should communicate the importance and the excitement of what he is reporting. Sam Zelman of CBS News remarked, "The biggest weakness of the beginner, it seems to me, is a lack of urgency in his delivery. News is urgent and exciting. But so many of us are somewhat matter-of-fact and casual about news. This attitude is not designed to attract attention either on the air or across a dinner table. To impart urgency, you needn't talk louder or faster. But you certainly must somehow communicate your own excitement and interest in the material. If you do, you'll look bright-eyed and alert on the air — and that's considered rather attractive." [4]

DIGGING FOR FACTS

The value of a story sometimes is exposed only when the reporter probes for it. In many interviews, the man facing the camera tries to limit the matters he willingly discusses. When a reporter inquires about matters beyond those limits, the interviewee will fend off the questions. A skillful politician can turn a question so deftly that most reporters will not be aware that he is not answering it. A reporter is well advised to listen carefully to answers. Too many reporters pay little attention to answers, devoting their attention instead to the framing of the next question.

The give and take of questions and answers can produce statements which the interviewee would not include in a speech. For example, when

Barry Goldwater announced formation of the Free Society Association, a CBS reporter questioned him as follows: [5]

REPORTER: Will there be any stronger ties between the Free Society Association, Senator, and the John Birch Society? Will they work together and have any common goals?

GOLDWATER: Well I would say that all organization goals are common in this country. We're interested in the country. If a member of the Birch Society wanted to come into this organization there's no stopping him. We welcome members — everybody but Communists.

REPORTER: You say everybody but Communists. Would that include the Ku Klux Klan?

GOLDWATER: Oh you know what I mean, for God's sake. We don't want members of the Ku Klux Klan and I don't think members of the Ku Klux Klan would join a thing like this.

A few days later, a television news reporter evoked laughter by close and clever questioning of his subject, Democratic National Chairman John Bailey, who had just announced a fund-raising jingle contest:

BAILEY: There's two parts to this contest: One is for sustaining members who secure the largest number of sustaining members in his state. Then there is a second part, an essay of twenty-five words or less on why I am a Democrat. (LAUGHTER)

REPORTER: Why does it take so many words?

BAILEY: (LAUGHTER)

REPORTER: Suppose you don't know twenty-five words?

BAILEY: Well, we assume that — as I said, twenty-five words or less. (LAUGHTER)

REPORTER: Why are *you* a Democrat in twenty-five words or less? (LAUGHTER)

BAILEY: I guess I was born one. (LAUGHTER)

Digging for a story frequently means work away from the camera. Studying an issue is important. Books, old newspaper clippings, public records and telephone calls to knowledgable persons are source material. A rule to remember is that where there is an issue, there are individuals in opposition to each other. Get the arguments of each side, and face the other side with those arguments, preferably on camera.

TOUGHNESS, SYMPATHY, AWARENESS, GALL

A television reporter's qualities should include toughness. He needs a thick hide if he intends to cover more than supermarket openings. A politician who feels a reporter is prying into what the politician prefers hidden may not be above trying to silence the reporter in the presence of others with a scathing personal crack about the reporter's ignorance or amateurishness. If the reporter lapses into blushing muteness — or if he snaps back angrily — the politician wins. If the reporter keeps his head and has confidence in his line of questioning, he may dig out a story in the public interest.

A reporter should leaven his toughness with sympathy. At times he will need both. Every reporter on general assignment sooner or later faces a story he prefers not to cover. It is not easy to shove a microphone near a father whose child has just drowned. No final answer can be given to the question, "Then why do it?" The question and the answer fall into the realm of news department policy, and can be debated endlessly. For most reporters, the only answer is, "It's part of my job." This is not a crass, callous answer without ethics. Covering one child's death may save another child's life through a safety precaution that would otherwise have been neglected. Not every distraught father, suddenly seeing a microphone, will turn away or get mad. Many a parent has poured out a heart full of grief, communicating to the television audience more emotion and understanding than will ever come from a soap opera. But be careful. A reporter for one Cleveland television station interviewed a 10-year-old boy who survived a Lake Erie boating tragedy in which his companion, another boy, drowned. The reporter asked the youngster if he was sorry they had gone out on the lake that day. (And if that wasn't bad enough, the question was used on the air.)

NBC News executive producer Reuven Frank, in a memorandum to his staff, said, "The best interviews are of people reacting — not people expounding. Joy, sorrow, shock, fear — these are the stuff of news. No important story is without them . . . And no qualified reporter can afford revulsion at random contact with other humans."

It was stated, above, that the reporter must be a translator. He must interpret or have the interviewee interpret specialized information for the public. First, the reporter must understand the topic himself. This point cannot be stressed often enough. A reporter who brings no background of knowledge to the interview is as blameworthy as the cameraman who forgets his film. Where the subject is highly technical, the reporter who feels ill-prepared should at the least get some information from the interviewee or a public relations associate (if one comes along) before the cameras roll.

With an awareness of the subject, the reporter must then guide the interview so that it relates to what will be understood by the viewers at home — by the rich man, poor man, beggar man, thief, etc. Suppose the visiting Secretary of Agriculture is in town to give two speeches on new proposals for wheat parity pending before Congress. Wheat parity doesn't mean a thing to the worker who just came home from an eight-hour shift at the Ford plant. An explanation of parity would bore him. So the reporter asks the Secretary of Agriculture. "How much more will I pay for a loaf of bread if this goes through?" "Nothing," comes the reply "if the bread companies will absorb it. Otherwise, about a penny." Now the reporter has his story in the film can. This, the factory worker will understand. And if he turns his head toward the kitchen and yells, "Hey, Mabel, did you hear that about the bread?" the reporter has done his work well. He has helped an expert to communicate a complex matter across the air waves so that people at home understand and care. And that is what this business of television news is all about.

The reporter could have phrased his question differently. Instead of asking, "How much more will I pay?" he could have asked. "What would be the average cost increase for the quantity of wheat needed for a single loaf of bread?" But then he would not be translating fully. He would not be speaking the viewer's language. The factory worker might not have caught it. Instead of calling to his wife, he might have reached for the television program guide to see what movie the station was showing after this dull newscast.

A reporter's preparation for a story varies with both the reporter and the story. To learn a day ahead that you will interview the Pakistani ambassador is far different than being told to rush out to cover a fire. Given a day's notice on the Pakistani ambassador, one reporter will spend an hour at home that night leafing through recent issues of *The New York Times* for the background and latest facets of the dispute with India. Another will ask the assignment editor to suggest a couple of questions. Another will go to the interview cold, except for some half-remembered headlines in yesterday's tabloid. One reporter will write his questions down on paper and will read them to the ambassador. Another will also write his questions down, then will throw his paper away just before he gets to the door, or will keep the paper pocketed to refer to in an emergency. The reporter who "sort of remembers" headlines probably won't bother writing anything down, or even thinking of questions in advance. He depends instead on his toothpaste smile to charm the ambassador.

As for a decision on whether to read questions from paper or to avoid this crutch, there can be no final answer. What is best is what is most suitable and most comfortable. The only certain rule is that preparation is better than no preparation.

Two anecdotes illustrate the point.[6] Before he became Attorney General, Robert Kennedy flew to Seattle to look into the affairs of the Teamsters Union, then under Dave Beck. A radio reporter sent to the airport to interview Kennedy could think of no better opening question than, "Mr. Kennedy, are you an attorney?"

A few weeks later, Beck returned from Washington, where he appeared before the Senate Crime Investigating Subcommittee. Another radio reporter with another microphone greeted the president of the Teamsters

Union with this, "Mr. Beck, I don't know what is going on. I haven't been paying any attention to the news. But what is the situation?"

Some other questions to make us wince, and then maybe make us wiser:

In New Orleans, a TV reporter asked the head of a teacher's union if teachers should unionize.

In Chicago, a sports reporter asked someone, "Is good physical condition important to success in sports?"

In Santa Monica, shortly after President Kennedy was shot, a TV reporter asked a friend of Pat Lawford, the President's sister, "Does this shock you?"

Besides toughness and sympathy and background information, a reporter should carry a dram of gall. There will be times he will either bluff his way into a story, or he won't get the story. Other times, he will have to elbow his way in, or again, no story. These times are not as frequent as the movies would indicate, but they exist. When gall is required, a reporter may choose to sit outside on his ethics and watch another reporter barge in, microphone in hand, cameraman close behind, grinding away. Or the reporter can do his own barging in. This, too, is part of "the game."

When Lyndon Johnson was Vice President, he rode to an auditorium in one of our major cities to address 5,000 persons waiting inside. Television reporters knew they would see him for about 30 seconds as he emerged from his car, shook a couple of hands, crossed the width of the sidewalk and vanished inside the auditorium. Every reporter but one instructed his cameraman to establish himself near the Vice President's path to catch the general noise and hubbub of those 30 seconds. That one reporter figured this was a moment for boldness which must be nothing less than effrontery.

When Mr. Johnson stepped out of the car and began to shake hands, he shook one hand which refused to let go, and reinforced its grip by using the other hand at the heel of the Vice Presidential elbow.

With the cameraman, supporting the sound camera on a shoulder pod, close behind him and recording all that was happening, the reporter held on while Mr. Johnson's Secret Service men tried to separate the two men unobtrusively. It took Mr. Johnson just a few seconds to realize that this reporter was not going to release his grip without a scene. He grimly nodded to the Secret Service men to step back. He would answer the reporter's question. Now the reporter let go of hand and elbow and asked one incisive question on some pending legislation. Johnson replied fully, then moved away briskly and entered the auditorium where those 5,000 persons were waiting.

The reporter's behavior is open to criticism. It might be said that he acted less like a responsible and ethical professional than like one of the "papparazzi," the notorious free lance photographers of Rome, who go to

CBS cameraman Lauren Pierce (on the left) went to Meridian, Mississippi, where nightclub bouncer Alton Roberts (right) was one of 17 men who pleaded innocent to charges of plotting the deaths of three civil rights workers. Outside the Federal Court Building Roberts grabbed at Pierce's camera. Pierce struck back with a handle he was holding. Roberts dodged and knocked Pierce down. Pierce needed six stitches over his eye. (*UPI Photos*)

any lengths for an exclusive. It might also be argued that the reporter's maneuver worked, leaving the other reporters chagrined, with little on film but a record of a competing reporter talking to the Vice President.

"Don't let him off the hook"

Ralph Paskman of CBS News pointed out that all interviews are not necesarily interesting: "All too frequently interviewing somebody in the news is used as the easy way out. We are not covering a story if we get somebody to say on camera what has already been published in the press and broadcast on radio. Unless the interview carries the story further, provides new information or sheds new light on a development, there's little reason to use it. Of course, one cannot always know whether a film interview will carry the story one step further, so we often have to try it, and see what happens. But just because it has been shot doesn't mean it must be used . . . Too frequently, we are content, because of the various pressures on us, to settle for what is really token coverage of an important story instead of doing the kind of job television can do. The city, state or federal government passes legislation or undertakes some project. So we interview the man who sponsored the bill or heads the project. In doing so we are being dull. We are guilty of not taking advantage of the very special capability of this medium." [7]

How does a television newsman offset a strong opinion just expressed by an interviewee? Jim Overbay, KMBC-TV, Kansas City, Mo., said, "If a newsman takes the Joe Pyne approach, he's stepped beyond the realm of a newsman. But an interviewer who can be the devil's advocate and still not join the battle himself—that's the ideal. It's a thin line, and one must be careful not to cross."

If the reporter, having asked a pertinent question, thinks the answer is shallow or evasive, he should not hesitate to bore in. Almost invariably the real news, especially in a tense situation where the interviewee wants to stay tight-lipped, comes on the pressing follow-up questions which make it perfectly clear that the reporter will settle for nothing less than a direct answer or a flat refusal to answer.

In the case of a pertinent question, a refusal to answer sometimes is as revealing as a direct reply. As Ed Arnow, a veteran television reporter, put it. "When the fish has important information, don't let him off the hook."

Individuality

Any reporter, and especially a television reporter, needs to project his own individuality. When Edward R. Murrow reported for CBS, lesser newsmen tried to imitate his deep voice. When David Brinkley came along a few years later, other reporters copied his pacing. This is wrong. The best newscasters, commentators and reporters ought to serve as guides to a re-

The reporter is part of a team. Members of the team work in harmony while trying to overcome any problems which will detract from the professional quality of the final product. During this interview, set up in front of a helicopter, a big problem was noise, both from wind and aircraft engines. The wind screen (the gray cover) on the microphone diminishes the wind noise. The reporter places the microphone close to the officer's mouth to overcome the noise of the engines. The soundman hugs his earpiece to his head to be sure he hears nothing but what is being recorded on film.

porter who is developing his own manner, but the reporter who apes them only appears foolish. CBS correspondent Morley Safer was asked to comment on the "maverick" label pinned on him. He replied: "I don't think I'm much of a maverick. We live in such a rotten society of tags. We live in a society where anyone who veers that much is considered a maverick or daring. I don't think I'm a maverick. What it is, I think, is that television is such a maverick medium. The formalizing technique hasn't happened yet. Nothing has really changed in newspapers since Gutenberg. Every paper has a style guide. The day that TV has a style guide, that's the day I want to get out of TV." [8]

TECHNICAL TRAINING

A thoroughly professional knowledge of the technical requirements of television news demands still more broad background not only of the reporter, but of every television journalist who prides himself as being a member of a profession and compares his professional status with that of, say, optometrists or architects. For it is a certainty that truly professional men consider that a knowledge of the equipment they use is an integral part of their profession.

An award-winning cameraman and laboratory consultant, Morris Bleckman, put it — somewhat optimistically — this way, "There was a time in television news when, if you could tell the difference in a picture between a man and woman, it was good film. But no more. The schools graduate journalists who know gamma, pH, color, temperature, and spectral response. These men have made the lab aware that the old order is gone. The cry now is quality-control-delivery and that's the reason there is no more newsfilm. There *is* film developed in highly sophisticated machines that, in one batch, contain a film used for teaching, a film to sell a product and — heading the list — a film to be used on television news." [9]

In truth, Bleckman states an ideal, yet this ideal of education and technical knowledge is not beyond the television newsman's grasp. For, as we saw in Chapter 2, television journalism depends upon many skills meshing smoothly. Any member of the news operation who fails to understand or refuses to concern himself with his colleagues' tasks risks the loss of his own efforts.

THREE CASE STUDIES

Three television news reporters who covered City Hall in the same Midwestern city were accompanied for one week each by Dan Drew, who was doing a research study at Indiana University.[10] These are some of his observations:

> Reporter A pictured the journalist's main function as informing audience members about "important things" that take place in the community. He described these as "things that affect the welfare, livelihood, and comfort of members of the community." The newsman thought his audience consisted of white, middle-class homeowners who were deeply "interested in the welfare of the community." Since the reporter was middle-aged and deeply entrenched in the community, his audience appeared to be a reflection of himself. . . .
>
> The reporter seemed to pay little attention to what he thought were the policies of his news organization. He said that his editors were interested in "anything that catches the eye or ear" and complained that much of what went on the air was not news . . .
>
> Reporter A chose most of the nine stories that he covered during the week of observation. He particularly liked stories that showed the city, its police force, or its officials in a favorable light. Of the stories he covered, six were scheduled events, one resulted from a

friend's tip, one was the result of reporter initiative, and one was a story that he saw first in the local newspaper.

City officials were used almost exclusively as sources of information. In fact, the newspaper and criminal court records were the only written sources he checked on a regular basis. Reporter A's typical story consisted of a sound-on-film interview with a city official.

The television newsman was on extremely good terms with his sources. He was friendly, cooperative and positive in his interactions with them. The reporter and officials often discussed personal matters, and he sometimes offered advice or suggestions for dealing with either personal or civic problems.

One of the most noticeable aspects of Reporter A's behavior was his reluctance to broach subjects that he thought sources would not want to discuss. He usually began such conversations by going off the record. When they told him not to use certain information, he carefully obeyed. As a result of this he sometimes got information that the other reporters did not have, but would not use it. The newsman seemed to view events through the same frame of reference that city officials used. He explained that both he and the officials were interested in the "welfare of the city."

The television journalist interacted with radio and newspaper reporters several times each day. They traded bits of information about stories and discussed what they were going to cover later in the day. Reporter A summed his relationship with the other reporters saying, "I give a little and get a little." . . .

Reporter B said that he felt strong pressure from his superiors to produce as many visually interesting stories as possible each day. This appeared to be the major factor that governed his daily activity. The reporter's search for news was rather random. He started at the top floor of city hall each morning and wandered from office to office asking secretaries: "Any news today?" . . .

In his interactions with sources, Reporter B was careful to be friendly and cooperative. He was afraid that if he offended them, they would not cooperate, and he would not be able to meet his daily quota of stories. After one particularly frustrating day, he told the observer, "I'm tired of kissing ass to get stories." He was shy about asking questions that he thought the source would not want to answer and went off the record before making such inquiries. At one point, a city official said that someone had offered to make it worth his while to vote the "right way" on a municipal land transaction. The reporter ignored the statement. Afterwards, the observer asked if the official had been talking about a bribe. The reporter said that probably was the case. He did not mention it again . . .

Of the three reporters studied, Reporter C was least concerned about newsroom policy . . . Reporter C appeared to be more satisfied with his job that the other subjects . . .

Reporter C made most of the decisions about what he would cover each day. Of the 11 stories he followed during the week of observation, seven were scheduled events, two developed from conversations with sources, one grew from a tip, and one was picked up after the newspaper printed it. The main information source was the interview with city officials, but he checked more written records than the others. Reporter C looked at such documents as zoning filings and city procurement forms.

In his interactions with sources, Reporter C was less cooperative and more tenacious than the other newsmen. In return, sources were more cooperative with him than they were with the others. Perhaps they either respected him or feared him more. The television newsman did not go off the record when dealing with sensitive issues, but he did try to separate himself from the questions. He would be extremely friendly with the source, then suddenly turn serious and say, "Officially I'm here to . . ." Sometimes he prefaced his questions with phrases such as, "Some would say . . ."

About all three television journalists, Drew concluded:

It was quite obvious that the newsmen had little time for digging. Each had to cover the same territory that was handled by two or three reporters for the local newspaper. Also, each interview with a government official involved meeting a photographer, setting up equipment, filming, and editing the finished product.

A lack of knowledge about such specialized topics as law and budgets also limited the reporter's effectiveness. The source sometimes took on the role of educator in order to explain basic facts to the reporter about legal or economic matters. Under these circumstances, it seems highly unlikely that the journalist can do much probing.

COVERING A NEWS CONFERENCE

In 1967, Barry Goldwater held an early morning news conference in his Phoenix, Arizona, hilltop home to talk about South Vietnam. Lyndon Johnson had crushed Goldwater decisively at the polls two years before largely because of Goldwater's outspoken militarism. But Johnson followed up his election victory by adopting some of the very military policies which Goldwater had advocated. Clearly, what Goldwater would say at the news conference was of interest, not only because of the man himself but because of the nagging possibility that his present attitude presaged future military policy.

That was the background to the news conference, which was attended by NBC and ABC teams flown in from Los Angeles (a team being camera-man, soundman and either one or two men serving in the functions of pro-ducer and reporter), three local television teams, and reporters from AP, UPI and Phoenix newspapers. Goldwater made a short statement describ-ing the trip, then opened himself to questions.

The television cameraman, or the producer or reporter who advises the cameraman when to start and stop, must pace a news conference. He knows film runs through his camera at the rate of 36 feet per minute, and that his camera has a 400-foot magazine. Even where the cost of raw film stock is not a problem (as it is on most local stations) the cameraman should not simply turn his camera on and let it run out because:

1. Precious minutes are wasted developing, screening and removing unwanted film.

2. The film might run out at the wrong time during the shooting. Of course, there is less chance of getting caught short if the camera carries 1200-foot magazines, but these are seldom used for daily news work except by networks.

3. The cameraman would have to carry many extra magazines. They are heavy. Loading them with film and hooking them into the camera sys-tem are troublesome processes.

4. The cost of raw film stock should never be completely ignored.

5. At a news conference it usually is neither prudent nor practical to keep the camera rolling. It is rarely necessary to use up a 400-foot maga-zine. Half that amount should be ample. This means selective filming. The re-porter who misses a good question and realizes it while the answer is being given should not waste film by instructing the cameraman to record the remainder of the answer. Instead, he should wait until the interviewee has finished and then, with camera rolling, he should ask for a clarification or extension of the reply. Likely as not, the reply will be much the same, some-what paraphrased and often tighter, the interviewee now having had a chance to consider his words.

The cameramen, reporters and producers at the Goldwater news conference made dozens of individual decisions about when to turn their cameras off and when to turn them back on. Everyone was "rolling" when Goldwater entered the room and sat down. Some shot silent. Some shot sound. These scenes might be needed to introduce the story, with a news-caster's voice over the film. Everyone was rolling when Goldwater made his opening statement. As it turned out, the statement was not important, but it might have been. No one could afford to miss it. All cameras con-tinued to roll for the first two or three questions and answers. Once again, some important pronouncement might have been forthcoming. After the third question, the cameraman and producers became selective. The cameramen's fingers could be seen hovering near the on-off switches. The cameras would usually roll as a question was being asked by any reporter.

The reporter usually doubles as the producer of news coverage. He decides what approach will be taken to make a news story out of the situation confronting him. Such decisions may not be required during a breaking news story, but they must be made in covering a feature story. Above, the reporter (left) looks on as a cameraman shoots silent film of children drawing posters.

Sometimes the cameramen do not pick up the reporters' questions, especially if the reporters are not from their stations, but they listen to each question, and pick up the answers to those questions which they feel may elicit a valuable response Sometimes, a reporter signals his cameraman that he is about to ask a question, giving the cameraman the few seconds notice necessary to flip his switch on and get the camera up to speed. The signal may be a wave of the reporter's hand held discreetly behind his chair. This signal is not always possible at a large news conference, where the reporter may be some distance from his camera, or crammed close to other reporters, so that a hand behind a chair cannot be seen in the confusion. An equally discreet wave of a pencil behind his neck may serve the reporter. But in the turmoil of a crowd of reporters and cameramen collaring some news figure in a hallway or at an airport, the reporter and cameraman must forget about signals. They are busy enough just keeping their

balance, getting some picture and some sound, and squeezing in one or two
questions. Here more than anywhere the cameraman must have his wits
about him and, if the impromptu news conference lasts more than three or
four minutes, begin to pay attention to what is said, so he can stop using
up film if he feels that something being said has little news value. Once
again, experience counts, for it brings, or should bring, judgment.

After the opening statement, reporters fired questions at Senator
Goldwater. (Although he was not a senator at this time, it is customary
politeness to address a politician or military officer by the highest title he
was ever accorded unless, like "General" Eisenhower, he prefers another).

The first question, sensibly, was a broad question: "Senator, how do
you feel the war is going in South Vietnam?" Mr. Goldwater's response
included, among other opinions, the belief that the United States was winning the war.

The reporters then began to narrow the range of the questions. They
probed for the headline-making statement. Possibly their subject had such a
statement in mind all along, and was waiting for the suitably phrased question. This is not uncommon in interviews, a kind of courtship dance in
which the interviewer and his subject feint, parry and maneuver around the
topic circle, gradually coming closer together until the climactic moment of
thrust and response. *(If this seems to be an overdramatic description, per-*
haps it is because the author has attended and edited too many news con-
ferences called by politicians).

Following the broad opening question, the reporters then asked, in
sequence: How do you think the United States should proceed in Vietnam?
(Mr. Goldwater called for more bombing of border targets). Do you favor
saturation bombing? (A qualified yes.) Do you favor an invasion of North
Vietnam? (Not at present, but it may be necessary to go into Laos now and
Cambodia soon because North Vietnamese troops are hiding there.)

Here, to several of the experienced newsmen, was the story they had
come for: the suggestion by the recent presidential candidate that we invade
two neutral nations neighboring on South Vietnam. The questions went off
in another direction for a while, for not all reporters present caught the
import of the statement or felt it significant. While the topic veered, the network cameramen used the time to advantage. They turned off their cameras
and loaded fresh magazines. When they were ready, the reporters bore in
again: Senator, would you clarify your statement about going into Laos and
Cambodia? (He did.) Are you advocating that we invade Laos? ("I'm not
advocating anything. I'm saying it may be necessary. . . .").

Soon it was done. The news conference had been short — about half
an hour, not counting a pause to adjust the lighting to compensate for the
rising desert sun creeping above a window curtain and, at the same time
down Mr. Goldwater's forehead. The interviewee exchanged a friendly
word with reporters, permitted himself to be cornered for a few minutes
longer by pencil-and-paper reporters, then left to catch a plane, while the

television crews wrapped up and the reporters and producers hurried to get their film to the lab, and their audio tapes to radio studios.

The major story broadcast and published that day on the Goldwater news conference was the talk of invading Laos and Cambodia. Interestingly, the first story printed by the Associated Press had a different lead: Mr. Goldwater's feeling that the United States was winning. The comments on Laos and Cambodia were buried several paragraphs down. But a short time later — possibly when the story came under the scrutiny of a veteran editor — a new lead was filed, and Laos was on top.

Editing Problems

A television news reporter should know the technical requirements of his medium.

A windy airport creates an audio problem. So does a "boomy" room, with hard walls, no windows or rug, and little furniture. So does a school cafeteria at lunch time. A freeway at night creates a lighting problem. So does a cathedral.

The reporter who doesn't know or doesn't care about these built-in problems is likely to be reminded by the cameraman and soundman, but not by the film editor, who doesn't go along on the assignment. His complaints may be heard too late to help the story.

Lack of cutaways

More good film has been thrown away for want of a two-second cutaway than for any other reason. If the Secretary of Agriculture made two usable statements in the course of an interview, but had his eyeglasses off for the second statement, the editor who lacks a cutaway must use: (a) roll thru film — not seen on the air — while the newscaster bridges on camera (some newscasters don't like this because the rapid switching sometimes works badly); (b) a roll thru or Academy leader (numbered, 10 seconds long, for roll-thrus lasting more than 10 seconds) for a cut to a card in the studio during the show; (c) a jump cut, cutting directly from one statement to the other, leaving the audience wondering what happened to the glasses; or, (d) just one of those two statements by the Secretary of Agriculture.

Unfortunately, especially when time for editing is at a minimum, (d) may be the choice, and a good piece of film goes into the trash barrel. Many a harried film editor has spent half an hour searching through his cutting room for just two seconds of usable cutaway film. The thoughtful editor will lay aside a stock of indoor and outdoor cutaway shots, but he won't be prepared for every eventuality. And when he's on deadline, he won't have time to look. This might be considered a cameraman's concern rather than a reporter's concern, except that a reporter has charge of the crew. Sometimes, a film editor who asks a cameraman why he didn't shoot cutaways on a certain story is told that the reporter was in a hurry to get the next assignment, and did not want to spare the time.

It should be noted that natural SOF (sound-on-film) cutaways are better than silent cutaways on an SOF story. Silent cutaways cause a drop-out in the audio level. But getting SOF cutaways requires added time and trouble by the cameraman, because a sound camera is unwieldy. It is easier to leave the sound camera on the tripod and wander around with the smaller silent camera to shoot cutaways.

Cigarettes and pipes are even worse than eyeglasses, because eyeglasses usually stay on. If possible, the interviewee should not smoke while the camera rolls.

Up-cuts

A reporter who forgets to allow three or four seconds between the start of the camera and his opening question will find his first words lost. The camera needs those seconds to get up to full speed. The loss of words is called an up-cut. The reporter is also likely to get into trouble by beginning his second question before the interviewee finishes his first answer. He jeopardizes both question and previous answer, if the editor finds it necessary to cut at that point. The reporter who wants to have the interviewee terminate a drawn-out answer should learn to give some meaningful, silent gesture with hand or eye that signals the start of speech (i.e., that indicates a desire on the part of the reporter to say something). This is not as difficult as it may sound.

To avoid an up-cut in the reporter's question— when the reporter begins to ask the question before the camera is up to speed — the pre-question is used: "Governor, a question about the university. . . ." In the three or four seconds it takes to say this, when stated leisurely, the cameraman can flip the "on" switch and the camera can accelerate to full speed.

Reverse angle questions

The filmed interview should show the reporter asking questions, a technique which gives the interview perspective, gives the reporter visibility, and gives the film editor cutaways.

For the interview itself the best camera position is behind the reporters' shoulder. The interviewee is seen head-on; the reporter is not seen at all.

Commonly, when the interview ends, the reporter sits still and the cameraman moves his camera close to where the interviewee sat. The reporter then repeats his questions. The interviewee need not be present. If he is not, the reporter might be asking the questions of the floor lamp a foot to the right of the camera, because the camera does not pick up what he is looking at. To be sure he asks the same questions, the reporter can carry a small tape recorder. Without this he either consults his notes or jogs his memory. Later, the film editor will intercut questions and answers.

The reporter should allow three seconds of silence before and after each question.

Interviewees who are present when this occurs sometimes get confused and start to answer the questions all over again.

If the interviewee remains and is willing to be a silent prop, the cameraman should set up behind the interviewee for the reverse angle questions. Now the reverse angle catches the reporter full face and the interviewee one-quarter face.

The reporter has another reverse angle option besides asking questions. He makes a pre-question statement, such as, "That brings up another point" or "Well, let me ask you this. . ." The film editor bloops this cutaway statement in front of the question actually asked during the interview.

Let us say that the editor wants to splice two statements made by Mayor Jones. The first, at the start of the interview, concerns the new airport site. The second, at the end of the interview, is a response to the reporter's questions, "Will you be looking for new taxes?" With a pre-question statement in hand, the editor can put it together like this:

VIDEO	AUDIO
MS, MAYOR	(statement about airport site)
MS, REPORTER	"Well, let me ask you this . . ."
MS, MAYOR	(REPORTER'S VOICE): "Will you be looking for new taxes?"
	(mayor replies)

Lack of Alternatives

In the field, the reporter may get a clear, sudden vision about how the story should be cut. The story will be "edited in the camera." Well and good unless, foolishly, no other film is shot. For example, the reporter may start with a stand-up intro outside the victim's house. Then he'll invite the camera to come inside for a tour of the room where police found signs of struggle, then to the room where the body was found, then to the room where the knife lay, all bloodied. Unfortunately, the reporter's brainstorm may not look so grand two hours later in the screening room. Often as not, the resultant film story is too long. A reporter in the field can never know how the flow of the day's news affects the time which can be devoted to his story. If he has constructed an elaborate film story whose parts are so interwoven that none will stand alone, then the whole story may be junked, or it may be butchered beyond recognition in a desperate effort on the editor's part to salvage something from three hours of work by a reporter, cameraman and soundman. (These three worthies, after viewing the wreckage on the tube, will mutter furiously about the clods who call themselves film editors.)

The solution: give the film editor as much flexibility as possible.

Lack of time

The reporter will also be asking for butchery of his film if he doesn't allow enough time to have the film brought to the station, developed, screened, edited, scripted and put into sequence with other films for the projectionist. All the reporter's care and preparation is wasted if he doesn't give his co-workers back at the station enough time to do their work well, too. The difference between a story being used or not being used, or between a story being well cut or being hastily chopped up, frequently has a direct correlation with the story being tightly conceived and edited in the field, with the addition of shots necessary to give the film editor flexibility.

ADD A DASH OF HUMILITY

Finally, the reporter should retain a sense of humility, of proportion, of his role in the news situation. He is a medium through which news is

The reporter not only serves as an interviewer, but sometimes also assists in capturing on film the natural elements of a scene or event. Above, ABC newsman Peter Jennings stands off camera holding a microphone (also off camera) in front of an officer briefing his men.

clarified and imparted. Nothing more. Bill Beutel, newscaster for WABC-TV, New York, stated:

"I think there's a very great danger on the part of television reporters to become drugged by their own power, so drugged that they find themselves developing a mystique — a mystique about television reporting that even they believe. This eventually ends with attempting not only to report but to control what goes on in a precinct station or a city hall. When we near the point where all of us carry that mystique around in our breast pockets — I think the time then comes for re-evaluation." [11]

The reporter should remember that he is, after all, just one link in the chain that begins at the scene of an accident or a news conference and ends in a viewer's living room. Reporters and all other on-air personnel have been pinned with the designation "talent," a relic from early broadcasting days. No connection exists between "talent" and talent. Some "talent" are talented, just as some non-"talent" personnel are.

The reporter is the representative of the public at a newsworthy event. He is their ears, their eyes and sometimes their conscience. His primary responsibility is to the public. His questions are asked on their behalf. If he ever represents a conflicting interest, he betrays his proper role. There are degrees of betrayal, from the favor to a public relations man of a free plug to an attempt to shape attitudes toward a candidate for public office because of the reporter's personal views, to doing a thing because "there's something in it for me." A television newsman cannot excuse himself because his ethical lapse is small. A little betrayal of the public trust is, to quote an old joke, like being "just a little bit pregnant." The betrayals are sure to grow bigger.

The reporter's job is demanding, but rewarding. It is the most varied and exciting job in the television news department. Except for the jobs of news director and newscaster, it is the most desirable job on most stations, and one to which a student can aspire soon after graduation, especially at smaller stations.

THE ANCHOR SPOT

Kids aspire to be television anchormen the way they once wanted to be railroad engineers. The glamour of the railroad engineer went with the steam locomotive, and Walter Cronkite has predicted a day when the newscaster will follow: [12]

There is a canard abroad in our business that television news always will be limited by the simple fact that many, if not the majority, of news stories cannot be illustrated.

Horsefeathers! as the saying goes.

We can't illustrate many stories only because we don't know how. *I* don't know how, or I'd be doing it. But there will be some bright young men coming along who will figure out how, you can count on it. . . .

When all this happens there are going to be some radical changes in news programs. If we can illustrate *all* stories, there is no further need of a news broadcaster to read half the items to the public. Disembodied voices can narrate the film, reporters on the scene will be seen when the situation demands, and there will be no need for a news master of ceremonies in the studio.

For the foreseeable future, the anchorman — a name interchangeable with newscaster — will be with us, the most visible member of what Vice President Spiro Agnew called "a small group of men, numbering perhaps no more than a dozen. . ." He is the physical embodiment of all those mysterious figures who have something or other to do with television news, even if people are not sure what it is they do. People certainly know what he does because they can see him do it once or twice every evening, which makes it all the more important that he do it right.

For an anchorman, "doing it right" includes: 1) speaking clearly; 2) imparting the sense of the news; 3) convincing viewers that he knows what he is talking about; 4) keeping the newscast moving smoothly; 5) maintaining contact with his audience.

Speaking Clearly

To present information clearly, the anchorman must speak in an understandable manner, enunciating so he does not slur word endings. He should not try to pitch his voice low to give it "authority." If he does not naturally sound like Edward R. Murrow, so what? Elmer Davis sounded authoritative with a high voice.

He should "woodshed" his copy; that is, he should rehearse it, either aloud or sub-vocally, so that he won't stumble on the air. He may discover unfamiliar words or names. He may also come across tortuous sentence structures.

Because we have been breathing all our lives, it does not automatically follow that we have been breathing correctly for voice projection. Nor does it follow that we place our vowels correctly. Some lessons from a competent voice coach could be the best investment a future newscaster makes today. Repeat: a *competent* voice coach.

Sense of News

To impart the sense of the news, the anchorman should, above all, keep up with the news even if he is only a reader who picks up a script others have prepared. His rate of delivery should reflect the mood of his copy. So should his inflection. He should know when to pause. When he "woodsheds," he may place oblique lines, called virgules, between words to indicate pauses, one for a brief pause, two for a longer pause. He may underline words he intends to emphasize.

In sum, the newscaster reads his copy aloud before air time not for pronunciation alone, but for content. An intelligent newscaster makes hack writing sound intelligent. A news reader who could care less makes intelligent writing sound glib, and just plain awful. On the air his attitude, reflected in his voice and expression, will indicate his understanding of the news. One of the leading local newscasters in the United States reportedly began his career by trying to smile his way through every news item, aware that he had a charming smile and pearly, evenly spaced teeth. Luckily for him, the people he worked with got through to him fast.

Psychologist Israel W. Charny thinks newscasters and reporters should go considerably further than a grim expression and a serious voice to present somber views.[13] He feels that objective reporting of violence says in effect, "Well, folks, it's happened before, it's still happening, and there's nothing we can do about it." He said newscasters should develop "a more human language" to get across their feeling of sadness over loss of human life, anger over the wastefulness of violence, and a feeling of hope that man can live peacefully. A story would not begin, "Three persons died today when. . . ." but instead, "A sad accident today claimed the lives of . . ." The author knows of no newscasters who report news this way. Among the objections to this kind of reporting would be its abrogation of objectivity and its maudlin tone. Also, few accidents are *not* sad and tragedies are *always* terrible. Nevertheless, Charny's approach has supporters.

Knows His Subject

To convince viewers he knows what he is talking about, the anchorman must, of course, keep abreast of current events. He must also know how to pronounce the words and names he uses, including foreign words. As a rule, a foreign term or name should be pronounced accurately, but with an American accent; that is, the stresses should be on the right syllables and the pronunciation of the vowels should resemble the pronunciation a native speaker would give them, but the newscaster should not try to imitate a Frenchman or a Russian or a Spaniard when he refers to their cities or native dishes. A newscaster or reporter who is rattling along in midwestern American, then suddenly purses his lips to form an umlaut, sounds as though he is trying to impress someone with his worldliness. He sounds phony. Best bet: a slightly Americanized version of the original. (See *Guide to Pronunciation,* below)

Smooth Flow

The studio stage manager uses these signals:
Two minutes to go: two fingers.
One minute to go: index finger .
30 seconds to go: one index finger crossing another, making a plus sign.

15 seconds to go: a fist.

5 seconds and count down: a wide open hand, with the fingers dropping as the seconds tick away.

Cut: a finger cutting across the throat.

Slow down: palms drawn apart slowly.

Speed up: an index finger making a fast turning motion.

Watch me for cue: finger pointing to eye.

You're on: index finger jabbing toward newscaster.

To keep things running smoothly, the anchorman must hit his cues and must be depended upon for the director's cue timing; that is, if the director sets up a film roll cue on a word five seconds before the copy ends, the newscaster must be depended upon to read those last five seconds of copy *in five seconds*. If he cuts it short, the director has little choice but to stay on the now silent newscaster or go to black. If the director takes the film chain, viewers will see academy leader numbers. On the other hand, if the newscaster runs over the five seconds, the director has the unpalatable choice of cutting him off or, more likely, upcutting the film.

A smooth newscast requires mental agility when fluffs occur—and they occur in the best rehearsed newscasts. The newscaster fluffs a word, or the wrong film comes up, or the the remote switch does not come in, or the audio fails, or a splice breaks. The newscaster must decide on the spot whether to apologize or whether to ignore it, and if he apologizes, what to say. Usually, a short apology with the briefest explanation and no embarrassment is the best way to handle an error. At times a sense of humor helps.

"I'm sorry. We seem to have lost our sound. We'll try to rerun that film later."

"My apology. We have line trouble between here and Chicago. But we heard most of that report."

"That is 'she sells sea shells'."

(To sports editor) "John, how come we never catch those words on the editing bench? You'll have the only sports report in town with an X rating."

Rapport

Maintaining contact with his audience is more than just staring at the lens or the TelePrompTer when the red light is on. Certainly a maximum amount of eye contact and a minimum amount of nose-in-script helps. (When reading a direct quotation, the reporter should be looking at his script.) Beyond this, the anchorman must realize he is talking to one person somewhere on the other side of that lens. Like the writer, the anchorman should imagine an audience he can visualize, one, two or three people at most who are letting him into their living room so he can tell them what's been going on today that will interest them and may be important to them. The best newscasters have an instinct about this. They go *through* that lens. They talk to *you*.

They also share with you an interest in films and switches. Notice how often an anchorman will introduce a film or a switch, then will settle back and turn his head slightly to look at a camera monitor located beside his desk or recessed into it. After the film ends the camera may catch him still staring at the monitor. An instant passes, then he looks up and continues with the newscast. All quite natural. The newscaster and you at home have shared the experience of viewing that film.

Guide to Pronunciation

The pronunciation of unfamiliar names and places should not be guessed at. Nothing is more likely to irritate a viewer or make him think the newscaster is a rube as much as the mispronunciation of the viewer's home town or the city in Italy where the viewer's grandfather was born. Admittedly, a mispronounciation is not the worst of offenses. It's just one of the most glaring.

A guide to the correct pronunciation, in brackets, should follow the unfamiliar name: Robert Cholmondelay (CHUM-lee). The stressed syllable is capitalized.

If you are not sure of the pronunciation, use the telephone. Call the source. If you are calling a wire service, better give the local man an hour to check with the regional or national office.

UPI uses these phonetic conventions:

- A -

AY for long A (as in mate)
A for short A (as in cat)
AI for nasal A (as in air)
AH for soft A (as in father)
AW for broad A (as in talk)

- E -

EE for long E (as in meat)
EH for short E (as in get)
UH for hollow E, or schwa (as in the)
AY for French long E with acute accent (as in Pathé)
IH for middle E (as in pretty)
EW for EW dipthong (as in few)

- I -

IGH for long I (as in time)

EE for French long I (as in machine)
IH for short I (as in pity)

- O -

OH for long O (as in note or though)
AH for short O (as in hot)
AW for broad O (as in fought)
OO for long double O (as in fool or through)
OW for OW dipthong (as in how)

- U -

EW for long U (as in mule)
OO for long U (as in rule)
U for middle U (as in put)
UH for short U (as in shut)

CONSONANTS

K for hard C (as in cat)
S for soft C (as in cease)
SH for soft CH (as in machine)
CH for hard CH or TCH (as in catch)
Z for hard S (as in disease)
S for soft S (as in sun)
G for hard G (as in gang)
J for soft G (as in general)
ZH for soft J (as in French version of Joliet)

Where the pronunciation runs counter to the spelling, use the word "like":

Roger Blough (like NOW)

Among books listing the pronunciation of names or words are the *NBC Handbook of Pronunciation, A Pronouncing Dictionary of American English* by Kenyon and Knott, the *English Pronouncing Dictionary,* and Noory's *Dictionary of Pronunciation.*

OMBUDSMAN

Like many newspapers, a few television stations run an ombudsman service, which may be called "Direct Line," "Action Line" or "Action News." These regular features are so popular that viewers will wait out news segments they find dull just to listen to someone's problem and to learn how the news department solved it. In at least one newscast, which runs 45 minutes, the ombudsman service starts at the half hour, presumably keeping viewers from switching channels to catch the start of another program.

The service is quite simple. The "Action Line" reporter invites letters from viewers who have a problem "we can help solve," which translates to problems involving some level of government or a private business firm. The letters pour in from the woman who is wakened by garbage trucks at 6 a.m., the man who can't get a replacement part to fix a broken lawn mower, the youth who sent three job applications to a distant company and got no response, and so forth.

The news department should establish a policy of answering every letter, knowing that this alone may require someone's full time attention. One or two letters of particular interest become part of the newscast. After a problem is solved, the letter is read on the air. The steps taken by the news department and the eventual outcome follow.

Baltimore's WJZ-TV has a program called "Solution." It presents a problem, such as welfare, alcoholism, housing, or prisons. Viewers are asked to write in with solutions. The mail is screened. Writers of the best letters are invited to present their solutions on film or in the studios.

Washington's WTTG-TV created the Consumer Help Center, with telephones manned by students at the George Washington University School of Law. People with problems call in. The law students direct them to a source which may help. Individual cases and overall statistics provide raw material for the news staff to produce consumer features.

Chicago's WMAQ-TV has published questionnaires in Chicago newspapers, asking readers for their opinions on several issues. A videotape unit went to four Chicago locations to tape responses.

An "Action Line" program is first cousin to investigative journalism. In the former, reporting can be triggered by a viewer's problem; in the latter, by a news event. In both, the reporter may seek to expose a condition he considers harmful to consumers or to the general public.

When a string of Ohio River barges struck a pleasure boat, killing seven aboard, Cincinnati's WCPO-TV conducted an experiment on film to argue that legally minimum barge lighting was inadequate. The film was aired and a Coast Guard board of inquiry requested a copy.

Documentaries and news specials are sometimes devoted to consumer issues. To cite just one example, a single issue of CBS' "60 Minutes" featured two consumer topics, an examination of the $30 billion-annual auto repair industry, and the dangers and illusions in plastic surgery.

As part of a report on welfare fund mismanagement, a reporter at KTTV, Los Angeles, gave social workers a false name, a false social security number and a false story at two local welfare offices. In return she got $138.90. KTTV aired its "swindle" and invited county welfare officials to reclaim their money. At first the welfare director demanded that the reporter be jailed. The embarrassed director later changed his mind and congratulated the news department for its investigation.

FOR THE STUDENT

1. Assume the Secretary of State will hold a news conference in town tomorrow morning. Prepare some questions, based on current news.
2. Assume you have secured an interview with the Secretary of the Treasury for tomorrow morning. Prepare some questions.
3. Assume you have an interview an hour from now with the new Miss America. Prepare some questions.
4. Discuss the author's contention that there is "a rhetoric of television news"—that is, an art of persuading people through the use of television news.
5. Using either a sound camera or an audio tape recorder, do an MOS on what people think about television news. Sample questions: How often do you watch? Do you think it could be more interesting (or useful to you)? How? Are the newsmen you watch fair and unbiased? (If not, specifically what's wrong?)
6. Interview a public official or a professor who has been interviewed by a television reporter. What did he think of the interview? Where could it have been improved? Was the reporter well enough informed about the general topic?
7. Draw up some guidelines for a reporter at a news conference.
8. Interview another student, on tape, about his job last summer, his hobby, or some other subject in which he has first-hand experience (not just opinions). Prepare some questions in advance and, if possible, bone up on the subject before the interview, after learning what the topic will be.
9. Tag along with a television reporter for one day. Report to class.
10. Evaluate each local newscaster on the five factors cited as "doing it right."

5

TELEVISION NEWS
AS NEWS

Is TELEVISION NEWS fundamentally different from newspaper news? If we strip format and technique away, are they not just the same? Certainly any lively discussion of the merits of television news raises comparisons with the printed medium.

The answers are not simple. Fundamental differences *do* exist because of the fundamental differences between Man as Reader and Man as Listener. Yet the similarities are just as fundamental, because Reader and Listener are frequently the same person, whose interests, desire to comprehend and standards of taste are indivisible in terms of differences in media.

It's Still a Small Town

A veteran Los Angeles newscaster has managed for years to give viewers the comfortable feeling that they live in a small town, sort of. The neighborhood squabble over whether to replace a stop sign with a street light at one corner does not seem to be "worth" two or three visits by reporters and camera crews plus ten minutes of air time in that megalopolis with its million street corners, but the crews from his news department are dispatched nevertheless. Pull-tabs maps help the newscaster explain how the neighborhood kids must now walk three blocks out of their way if they want to cross at a traffic light.

This story *ought* to have no importance to 99% of the viewers, but curiously it *does* matter. Ignored by the viewer is the fact that the corner is located in Long Beach, while the viewer lives in Van Nuys or Malibu or Whittier. All that matters is those kids, whom we see on film dodging through traffic. The newscaster has localized this story by treating an urban sprawl of eight million people as if it were North Platte, Nebraska.

A more familiar way to localize a story is to feature a local angle in a national story:

> *"Three St. Louis area residents were on the airliner which crashed. . . ."*
> *"Like the rest of the nation, Missourians this morning found. . . ."*
> *"The President announced he'll make an airport stop in St. Louis as part of his 15-state. . . ."*

In our electronic age, the time of what McLuhan calls "the global village," such a provincial approach seems anachronistic, out of date. Mobile and upwardly mobile viewers who lack a strong community feeling won't be turned on by localizing. But for the majority of viewers, the newspaper city editor's hoary admonition that names make news and his testy demands for local angles have a meaning even in the global village.

A WEWS-TV (Cleveland) crew raced to Miami while an airliner from Cleveland was being hijacked via Miami to Cuba. The crew got there minutes ahead of the airliner and got film and videotape interviews with passengers from Cleveland. The interviews were fed by wide-band phone line back to WEWS for the evening newscasts.

TELEVISION NEWS VS. NEWSPAPER NEWS

Television news writing is not newspaper writing read aloud. Television news differs from newspaper news in content, arrangement, style and delivery. The receiver of the information is different also, although in many cases, the television news viewer is also a daily newspaper reader. He is different because the medium of television requires different degrees of attention and participation than does the medium of print. Print is a medium in which the reader must be actively involved to get the message. The reader must concentrate. He must focus his attention on the printed word, and he must let his imagination, his mind's eye, fill in the picture the text describes.

Quite opposite demands are made by the television medium. The viewer sits passively. He doesn't come to the news, as he would by turning the pages of the evening paper. The news comes to him. It follows him around the room if he gets up from his chair. It follows him into the kitchen when he goes for a snack, until he is out of earshot. While he watches the tube, his sense of sight is captured, so his imagination is not called forth. However, television news does not demand the viewer's full attention. His mind may wander. The newspaper reader is not likely to be doing much else while he is reading that occupies his attention, but when he watches the news on television, he may also be carrying on a conversation, building a model airplane, or even glancing through a magazine, depending upon his degree of interest at any moment.

What this means is that the television news writer has a more elusive target at which to aim his information than does the newspaper writer. The television news writer who offers the audience nothing but newspaper news read aloud will not keep his audience tuned in for very long.

A 15-minute television newscast gives the audience approximately the same number of stories as does a newspaper front page and a local news page, each at a depth of one to three paragraphs. For a 30-minute newscast, add page 3 of the newspaper, and a few more paragraphs of depth from the front page. That's all.

It has been repeated often that television news will never replace newspapers. Television news, and radio news as well, cannot provide the number of facts a newspaper provides. Actually, television newsmen should not try. The viewer would not absorb that much detail, and would soon grow bored.

Let us consider what a newspaper tells its readers. A story about a day's fighting in a distant war goes into considerable factual detail. We learn the identity of the battalion and the number of jungle miles it pierced that day and how far it is from some city we use as a reference point and how many enemy soldiers it encountered, how many it killed as against its own losses. We learn who the officer is who gives us this information, and what he has to say about the battle and the battle which is likely to follow. The story gives us similar information about the activities of a regiment a certain number of miles (we are told how many) away (we are told which direction). The same story also tells us about the day's bombing, which means learning how many bombers left from where to what targets to drop how many tons of explosives how far from what referent points, and to what degree of success according to what Air Force source. The same story may also tell us of the day's political activities in that distant country, the internal maneuverings, the attempts to control or the attempts to get out from under. We learn the names and titles and assignments of the visiting political officials and where they are going and who is meeting them and how long they intend to remain, and what they say about what they have seen so far.

Detail after detail, fact after fact. Furthermore, this is just one story, or at least it is wrapped up under one dateline. Ten other stories on the front page carry just as many names, places, quotations and numbers. If there is any characteristic which makes newspaper writing unique, it may well be its use of numbers. Here are some examples taken from the front page of one edition of *The Minneapolis Star:* [1]

Gov. Wendell Anderson today urged the Minnesota Legislature

to extend the powers of the Metropolitan Council, make it an elected agency in 1974 and enact other Twin Cities-area legislation. In an unusual action, Anderson sent a 3½-page letter to the 201 legislators. He wrote that he is "concerned that this session of the Legislature take positive steps to carry forward" policy decisions made in the 1967 and 1969 legislative sessions.

SAIGON, South Vietnam — Forty-five Americans were killed in action last week, pushing the death toll for U.S. servicement above the 45,000 mark in the Indochina War. The U.S. command said that since Jan. 1, 1961, 45,019 Americans have been killed in action. It is the third-highest number of U.S. dead in any war. The week's toll was a drop from 56 dead the week before. However, American wounded rose from 195 to 518 last week due to some rocket and mortar attacks on U.S. bases.

SAIGON, South Vietnam — U.S. Navy planes tangled with enemy missiles over North Vietnam for the second time in six days and attacked antiaircraft batteries 85 and 115 miles northwest of the demilitarized zone, the U.S. command announced today.

Several Grow Township residents who live in $35,000 to $45,-000 homes are fighting to stop construction on a development of $19,900 houses because, they say, the buliding permits for the development were issued illegally and the houses don't meet the building code.

To try to duplicate this detail in a broadcast not only would be hopeless. It would be foolish. It would be wrong. Television news is not a good vehicle for carrying great volumes of little facts. As a test, read the above stories to a friend. Read one or all. Wait five seconds, then ask the friend to repeat what he heard.

The News vs. What Really Happened

Plato's allegory of the man in the cave, in Book VII of *The Republic,* pointed to the difference between what we think exists and what really exists. We also have Herbert Spencer's tragedy of the murder of a Beautiful Theory by a Gang of Brutal Facts. Walter Lippmann discusses the difference between reality and "the pictures in our heads" in *Public Opinion,* which should be must reading for every journalist. Lippmann cites opposing French and German military communiques in February, 1916, about the "battle of Fort Douaumont.[2] The Germans announced they had taken the fort by assault. The French Staff knew nothing of such a battle, but they felt impelled to say something because the German communique was being flashed around the world. So the French issued the following communique, which was translated and published in *The New York Times,* Sunday, Feb. 27, 1916:

LONDON, Feb. 26—A furious struggle has been in progress around Fort de Douaumont which is an advance element of the old defensive organization of Verdun fortresses. The position captured this morning by the enemy after several fruitless assaults which cost him extremely heavy losses, was reached again and gone beyond by our troops, which all the attempts of the enemy have not been able to push back.

According to Lippmann, what actually happened was that the position somehow had been forgotten in a confusion of orders during a shifting of front line troops. Some German soldiers saw the door open, crawled inside, and captured the few French soldiers they found. There had been no battle and no losses. Nor had the French troops advanced beyond it.

We may be sure the French Staff would not have printed the truth even if they knew it: the position was taken because of the stupidity of a French officer in issuing orders. And probably a news correspondent, had he known this truth, would not have cabled it, because he depended on the French headquarters for information, and he would have offended them by telling the truth. Or, military authorities might have censored the cable.

Lippmann also reprints the following dispatch: [3]

WASHINGTON, Dec. 23—A statement charging Japanese military authorities with deeds more "frightful and barbarous" than anything ever alleged to have occurred in Belgium during the war was issued here to-day by the Korean Commission, based, the Commission said, on authentic reports received by it from Manchuria.

Of this dispatch Lippmann comments, "Here eyewitnesses, their accuracy unknown, report to the makers of 'authentic reports'; they in turn transmit these to a commission five thousand miles away. It prepares a statement, probably much too long for publication, from which a correspondent culls an item of print three and a half inches long. The meaning has to be telescoped in such a way as to permit the reader to judge how much weight to give to the news."

As factors standing between reality and report, Lippman includes censorship, the desire for privacy, limited public interest in current affairs, the superficiality of news reports, and the restrictive stereotype patterns into which most of us fit the news we read and hear.

UNWRAPPING THE TRUTH

A story selected at random from the Associated Press radio wire reads as follows:

THE SOVIET AND YUGOSLAV FOREIGN MINISTERS HAVE ANNOUNCED THAT THEIR NATIONS' POSITIONS ON MOST INTERNATIONAL PROBLEMS COINCIDE. THE

STATEMENT WAS ISSUED AFTER A WEEK-LONG VISIT TO
MOSCOW BY YUGOSLAV FOREIGN MINISTER KOCA POP-
OVIC (POP-O-VICH'). THE ANNOUNCEMENT INDICATED
RELATIONS BETWEEN THE 2 NATIONS ARE THE WARM-
EST IN A LONG TIME.

A listener, in the year 1961, might fairly conclude that Yugoslavia
is after all, a Communist country. Its break with Russia does not really
amount to much, certainly not enough to keep the Yugoslavs from presenting a united Communist front against the West. If the listener should
hear later that his congressman intended to vote for something that would
improve relations between the United States and Yugoslavia, he might be
more inclined to write a wrathful letter to Washington.

Actually, the story is meaningless. Discovering why is a little like
playing detective:

1. The story says not a word about the purpose of Popovic's visit to
the Soviet foreign minister (Andrei Gromyko) or the subject of their conversation. Two sophisticated, skillful, busy diplomats do not meet to decide
that their government agree on "most international problems."

2. The story contains only one fact taken *from* the official statement
issued jointly by the foreign ministers: "positions on most international
problems coincide." The rest of the story contains facts *about* the visit
and an inference.

3. That one fact is a pleasantry. Joint statements always mention
areas of agreement. Two foreign ministers would hardly emerge from a
meeting to say that positions on a *few* international issues *do not* coincide.
Yet this statement is a corollary of the other.

4. No support is given for the inference that relations were the warm-
est in a long time. With heightening tension over Berlin, Gromyko might
have preferred Popovic's agreement to a joint statement about solving that
crisis.

5. Gromyko and Popovic would certainly agree on one matter: what
they talked about was none of our business. Not only are diplomats close-
mouthed, but Communist government officials do not feel that the public
must be kept informed via privately owned newspapers and broadcasting
stations in the West.

6. The one fact, "positions on most international problems coincide,"
is given from an obviously longer official statement. Such statements are
carefully worded. Taking one phrase out of its context might be a gross
simplification.

7. Even that sole phrase might bear little relation to the original joint
statement after going through the hands of one translator and several
editors.

8. It would be difficult to reach a higher level of abstraction than the

three words, "most international problems." These are "words cut loose from their meanings." [4]

9. The words "announced" and "announcement" connote something new being disclosed. People "announce" an engagement or the arrival of a baby. But there is nothing new in the phrase quoted by the A.P. The two governments' foreign policies have not suddenly veered so that their positions on most international issues now coincide, where they did not hitherto. If either government had shifted its views on just one issue, and had revealed this, the story would have been far different. No, it was not an announcement. It was just a statement, as we understand the term.

To sum up, the A.P. story actually says nothing except that the Yugoslav foreign minister spent a week in Moscow, during which he met with the Soviet foreign minister, and that Popovic's name is pronounced pop-o-VICH'—which Yugoslav-speaking radio and television listeners might conceivably dispute.

The likes of this news item can be found day after day on the news wires, leaving vague, yet perhaps indelible impressions of states of affairs which do not exist. This particular item may have reinforced a stereotype about Yugoslavia: that it is strongly pro-Russian and anti-American, whereas Yugoslavia has actually pursued neutralism avidly and has provided the inspiration for other Eastern European nations to try to break the embrace of the Russian bear.

James Bormann, a veteran Minneapolis radio newsman wrote: "Every radio and television newsman, striving for professional status in a relatively new field, has a stake in the preservation of the kind of broadcasting that demands the whole story. If we were to surrender to the philosophy of broadcasting that news is something to be glossed over quickly—something to be "capsulized" like bad medicine and then washed down with a torrent of discordant platter music—then our days as newsmen are numbered. And so are the days for public reliance on broadcasting for aggressive coverage and informative newscasts. . . . You can't kid the public into thinking it is well-informed when the news diet offered contains only a kernel of news, heavily coated with showmanship." [5]

WRITING AND EDITING DECISIONS

Unlike the professional ballplayer, an editor grows nimbler as he grows older, and his worth increases, provided he takes pride in his work. If he does not, he becomes a hack. The difference between the hack and the competent journalist is imagination. Or, to put it another way, the difference is a willingness on the part of the competent journalist to *think* as he makes the dozens of decisions every newsman routinely faces each working day. The hack tends to react automatically. He bases his decisions, pragmatically, on the easiest way to do something. The competent television writer should be able to defend with logic every scene he chooses, every word he uses.

The British statesman Edmund Burke stated, "If it is not necessary to change, it is necessary not to change." The television newsman, wondering what film sequences to select and what copy to write, might paraphrase Burke's credo: "If it is not necessary to include, it is necessary not to include." Or, less fancifully: if you don't need it, drop it. Each day provides far more news than any newscast has time to present. And if each day doesn't also provide far more film or at least opportunities for film than there is time for, the assignment editor should be replaced.

The decisions a film writer is called upon to make usually involve winnowing the material available to him. What scenes and facts should he include? The element of information (a scene or a fact) ought to meet either of two tests: it is important to the story? or, is it interesting? If the element of information meets neither the standard of interest nor the standard of importance—the standards being those of the writer or editor —the element should be dropped. The day's file of news will contain other important and/or interesting elements to include in the newscast.

The factors of news choice are the factors of attention: what will or ought to make someone pay attention. The most important news to you is news which vitally concerns you: "Mr. Smith, I'm happy to tell you the tumor is benign." "Charles, I've decided to leave you." "Stick 'em up, buddy."

Consider the written news item on the slip of paper passed to the bank teller: "I have a bomb in this paper bag. Give me all your folding money. P.S. Don't make any sudden moves." That news contains these attention-getters:

1. Personal involvement
2. Danger
3. Excitement
4. Economic effect
5. Immediacy (time)
6. Nearness (place)
7. Human interest
8. Novelty

All these elements make an event news. Add two other elements:

9. Magnitude of the event
10. Fame of the person involved

and you have the factors which determine news choice.

Every television news story should have one or more of these factors, but more factors do not necessarily mean more important news. A single factor may lift the news event above every other news event. For example:

"The Pope died today."

A memorable occasion, such as a Pope's visit to the United States, brings out video cameramen (atop panel truck) and film cameramen. While their products duplicate each other to some extent, they are really non-competitive, for the immediacy of video transmission and the flexibility of film are unique and not comparable, at least at present.

The fame of the person involved places this story at the top of virtually everyone's list of news stories on any day, yet other factors of news choice in this story are minimal or non-existent.

One of the reporting tasks for any news medium is finding "a local angle" in a story with a distant dateline. Usually the local angle will be the name of a local person or the local concerns of a national event; for example, the likely effect on a local shoe factory of a bill to lower tariffs on Italian shoes. Occasionally, a writer produces a local angle where none exists, and in the process makes the distant event more understandable and more personal to his audience. Don Buehler, news director of KSTP radio, St. Paul, delineated an anti-war demonstration in Washington this way for Twin City listeners: [6]

> To visualize Washington today . . . picture 35W southbound on a Friday afternoon . . . picture a burning car, or cars . . . across 35W northbound, cutting off the downtown Minneapolis exits and I-94 eastbound. Picture an overturned truck on Highway 55 and 7th Street . . . picture a crowd of 500 youths thumping on automobile

hoods at Highway 12 and Cedar Lake Road . . . mentally conceive
the 8th Avenue, Broadway, Hennepin and 10th Avenue bridges
blocked.

Or note I-94 near St. John's hospital in St. Paul . . . Snelling
closed at County Road C . . . Shephard Road at a standstill . . . Lex-
ington choked with demonstrators led by a pediatrician.

You have a mental picture of Washington . . . gleaming on the
banks of the Potomac, in view of the world. If you're familiar with
Washington . . . M Street . . . through Georgetown . . . clogged. The
14th Street Bridge . . . that's where Cal Thomas is stationed.

What is news is relative to what else is news. "Man bites dog" is
the top story on a lazy July Fourth, when government offices are closed.
"Man bites dog" does not get into the newscast on the day war breaks
out. In short, there are slow news days and busy ones. The writer must
adjust his judgment to the total flow of news. For instance, on a slow
news day, he cuts a film clip running two and a half minutes of a quarrel
between two city councilmen over rezoning a residential block to allow
construction of a supermarket. The story contains these elements:

VIDEO	AUDIO
1. The street in question, various scenes. 20 secs. silent.	1. Newscaster sets the scene. Where we are, what the quarrel is about.
2. City hall, Councilman Smith's office door, Councilman Smith. 12 secs. silent.	2. Newscaster introduces Smith, who is pushing hard for the rezoning.
3. Smith, sound-on-film. 40 secs.	3. Smith tells why.
4. Councilman Brown's door, Brown. 8 secs.	4. Newscaster introduces Brown, who is speaking for the folks who live around the corner, and like the neighborhood as is.
5. Brown, sound-on-film. 35 secs.	5. Brown tells why not.
6. The neighborhood, 5 secs. silent.	6. Newscaster says most neighbors agree with Brown.
7. Tightly edited (3 to 8 secs. each) comments by a half-dozen neighbors. Neighbors are filmed outdoors. (This is sometimes known as an "MOS", or Man-on-Street, a variation on random interviews of passers-by on a downtown street to some question of the day.) 30 secs. sound-on-film.	7. Four oppose the change, one favors it, one is uncertain.

Half an hour after the clip is edited, an explosion on the other side
of town tears open a dry cleaning plant, killing two and injuring seven.
Today is no longer a slow news day. The news director automatically re-
evaluates the news stories in his line-up, including the quarrel between

Smith and Brown. If the quarrel had not erupted on the Council floor that day, the entire story, all two and a half minutes, might have been set aside as a news feature usable tomorrow or the next day. But the quarrel did occur, and this is today's news. The clip will have to be re-cut to about one minute. Out goes the MOS of the neighbors and the 5-second intro. That shortens the clip to 1:55, with :55 yet to be chopped out. He listens to Smith and Brown on the film editor's sound reader, and cuts each man to 20 seconds. This leaves 20 seconds of film to be removed. Out go the silent leads to each man. The writer retypes the opening 20 seconds of copy to include the news of the quarrel and to "intro" Smith and Brown. Super cards identifying the men will do the rest. The clip is now one minute long. A minute and a half has been saved for use in the explosion story.

In a radio or television newscast, all stories must fit the inexorable limitations of time. The writer assigned to the story of the governor's arrival or the seizure of a heroin cache will ask, "How much time have I got?" He doesn't want to know how much time he has to write his script but rather to know in advance how much air time will be allowed for the story, so that he can frame his editing decisions within that span of time. The news producer may say, "Keep it under a minute thirty," or he may say, "Take a look at it and see what it's worth." In either case, after screening the processed film, the writer may call the news director to say, "This stuff is pretty bad. I'd either keep it to 20 seconds or drop it completely," or he might say, "We've got some great footage here. Can you let me have two minutes?"

What has happened in this interchange between writer and producer is that the producer was considering the importance of the story based on the day's news-file, and the writer was considering its interest, based on the scenes he has just viewed. Similar conversations occur many times each day in newsrooms across the nation.

Some actual examples of decisions considered should be helpful. Unlike the fictional news item above, about a quarrel over zoning, what follows is a filmed news story which appeared in one of the American Broadcasting Company network newscasts. It was edited in Los Angeles, headquarters of the Western Division of ABC News, and fed to the network over telephone lines that were leased at a cost of approximately $2,300. The film editor, who advised in the choice of scenes, was in California with the writer. The producer was in New York, and conferred with the writer by telephone.

SCRIPTING AND EDITING A FOOTBALL GAME

On Sunday, Jan. 15, 1967, the first Superbowl game was played in Los Angeles, the first match between the champions of the National Football League and the champions of the American Football League.

The Green Bay Packers, representing the NFL, defeated the Kansas City Chiefs of the AFL 35 to 10. ABC news sent a "sound crew"—sound cameraman and soundman—plus a silent cameraman to the game. The sound crew shot every play, taking no chance that they might miss a touchdown run. Between plays they stopped the camera. Because of time pressures—in this case, the hour reserved for feeding the network—it was decided that the film of the first half would go immediately by motorcycle messenger to the lab for developing. The messenger returned to the Coliseum to wait for the end of the second half. This enabled the writer and film editor to screen and assemble about half of the film clip before the second half was available for screening. As it happened, three-fourths of what was aired occurred in the first half, because the most interesting and important plays took place then. The writer and editor enjoyed the luxury of an extra hour-and-a-half of working time which would have been denied them had they been forced to wait for all the film at once. The producer, weighing the value of this news story against the other news of the day and the time limitations of the newscast, asked the writer to keep the story under 1:30.

The reel of the first half of the game, fresh from the lab, was mounted on a projector in a small screening room. As the first frame of picture appeared, the writer clicked his stopwatch. From this point on, he would identify a scene that interested him by the watch; for example, the pass that set up the third Green Bay touchdown began 27:14 and ended 27:42, measuring from the head of the reel.

Before the reel of the second half arrived, the writer and editor roughcut a clip of the first half. It consisted of these shots:

SCENE	TIME
1. kickoff	:15
2. first Packer TD	:18
3. cutaway of scoreboard	:02
4. long twisting run by Chief back (visually exciting scene)	:22
5. long Chief pass that set up TD	:07
6. Chief TD	:10
7. scoreboard	:02
8. second Packer TD	:14
9. scoreboard	:02
10. Chief, field goal (dull, extreme long shot)	:07
11. scoreboard	:04
Total:	1:43

Plainly, the rough cut was far too fat. It was already 13 seconds over the limit, and the second half was not in yet. With its three Packer touchdowns and its scene of an injured Chief back being carried off the field, the film of the second half could not be ignored. The writer called the producer to ask for an additional 30 seconds. The film was interesting and, after all, when the original 1:30 allotment was made, no one knew the score would be so large; that is, so many touchdowns would have to be accounted for. The producer looked over his line-up and agreed to 15 added seconds. That still meant some scenes would have to go. But which scenes? The kickoff was the only scene in the rough cut showing the entire stadium. The writer felt it was necessary to show the stadium and/or the spectators because he wanted to begin the script with a mention of the sultry weather the spectators enjoyed while most of the nation was in the grip of January cold. The three touchdown scenes and the field goal scene were important because they showed how the points were scored. The long run was the most interesting play of the game, and had the crowd roaring. The long pass was needed to show how the Chiefs went from midfield to scoring position. The shots of the scoreboard were needed as cutaways. (The writer and the film editor later chided the sound cameraman for not shooting sound cutaways of the crowd. Silent cutaways were available, but the writer ignored these because they would have caused sudden drops in the sound level.)

What should be cut? The writer and the editor talked it over. Seven seconds could be saved by cutting out the field goal, but this was the last time the Chiefs scored. The writer, who had the final decision, wanted to remove it, but the editor persuaded him to leave it in. The editor wanted to eliminate the long run, but the writer refused. The editor also wanted to eliminate the kickoff. Here the writer yielded, substituting in its place a four-second silent camera shot of spectators wearing makeshift eyeshades to ward off the bright sun. The long pass was also cut, and two other scenes were tightened. The clip now ran 1:18. That left :27 seconds for what was probably to come in the second reel: three touchdowns, three cutaways, and an injured player.

The second reel arrived and was screened. The writer and the editor again talked over the editing decisions. One touchdown and the injury would not be used. What was added to the clip was an intercepted pass and two of the three Packer touchdowns made in the second half of the game.

The final clip ran 1:43. It was scripted as follows:

FANS: WITH SHIRTSLEEVES AND EYESHADES :04	Blue skies and a hot sun in January over the Los Angeles Coliseum.
FIRST PACKER TD :18	77-degrees, shirtsleeve weather, as the Green Bay Packers began to roll over the Kansas City Chiefs. . . in professional football's first world championship game. Bart Starr to Max McGee.
SCOREBOARD :02	After the conversion, the Packers led 7 to nothing.
LONG RUN :22	In the second period, the Chiefs. . .rated as the underdog. . . fought back. Mike Garrett had the crowd on its feet with a twisting run into Packer territory.

CHIEFS TD :10	Two passes by Len Dawson brought the touchdown. First to Otis Taylor on the 7. . . then to fullback Curtis McClinton.
SCOREBOARD :02	The conversion tied the score at 7 all.
SECOND PACKER TD :09	Green Bay went back into the lead with a 14 yard sweep by fullback Jim Taylor.
CHIEFS FIELD GOAL :07	With less than a minute left in the first half, Kansas City kicked a field goal. . . its last points of the game.
SCOREBOARD :04	The score at half-time: Green Bay 14, Kansas City 10.
INTERCEPTION :10	The second half was all Green Bay, as defensive half Willie Wood intercepted a Kansas pass, and ran it 50 yards to the 5.
THIRD PACKER TD :05	Elijah Pitts . . . took it over for the Packers third T. D.
FIFTH PACKER TD :10	But the star of the game was a star . . . Bart Starr, the Packers quarterback, hitting McGee for another touchdown. Starr . . . voted player of the game . . . . which the Packers won 35 to 10.

EDITING A SPEECH

The television news writer fulfills a unique function when he screens film of a speech. Willy-nilly, he is a censor.

The cameraman, reporter, or producer at the scene are also censors. But unless they are severely limited in the quantity of film they may shoot, their censorial functions are limited to "cutting out the dull stuff" and to pacing the speech so that the speaker does not say something important during the minute or more the cameraman needs to change film magazines. If the camera crew receives an advanced text of the speech, they can pace themselves with greater certitude. Otherwise, the cameraman is likely to hold back his last 50 feet of film (about a minute and a half) as a protection, to cover an important statement, while he waits for the speaker to embark on what the cameraman feels is a dull or non-essential part of the speech. Television-wise speakers try to provide advance texts. For even when the cameraman has plenty of film in the camera and an ear cocked for an important statement, the speaker may have launched into his major topic before the cameraman can flip on the camera switch and the film can accelerate to normal recording speed.

The news writer has many matters to consider as he waits, with stop-watch in hand or his eye on the film timer, for the film to begin:

Time

The amount of time allotted for this film story may be allocated in

Changing a film magazine in the middle of a breaking news story requires not only manual dexterity but also enough judgment to estimate when to take the camera out of action without risking the loss of an important statement or action.

advance by the newscast producer ("Keep it under 1:15"), or it may be the result of haggling, such as:

> WRITER: "Can we let the senator's speech run two and a half minutes?"
> PRODUCER: "Impossible. Wrap it up in 45 seconds."
> WRITER: "I can't do that. Even if I just use the part where he calls the governor a fool, it will be 1:15. Add a 15-second silent intro, you have a minute and a half, and that's without his talking about the highway scandal."
> PRODUCER: "Suppose you just use the highway scandal."
> WRITER: "It's not as strong, and we'll only save 15 seconds."
> PRODUCER: "I'll give you a minute 10, tops."
> WRITER: "Make it 1:20."
> PRODUCER: "O.K. 1:20, but it better be worth it."

If the producer were assembling a 15-minute newscast, which permits about 11 minutes of actual time for news, a minute and 20 seconds represents a significant slice of the show. Yet it is not untypical of the time usually given to a speech on television. The 1:20 must include the silent film, or on-camera introduction to the speaker, leaving perhaps 1:05 of a speech that may have gone on for an hour.

Appeal

Most speeches excerpted and presented on a newscast are political. Few politicians, or non-politicians speaking on political matters, sustain

general interest very long. A television news audience is far different from
a politician's live audience. The live audience has voluntarily surrendered
its time and attention to hear the speaker. The television audience is not
present to hear the speaker, but to hear the news. News writers tend to assume, quite sensibly, that the audience has a low threshold of boredom
which few speakers can overcome by charisma.

Significance vs. interest.

Frequently the writer finds himself torn between using a significant
statement and an interesting one of not much significance. In the above
example, the senator's comments on the state's highways quite possibly were
of greater importance to the citizenry than his waspish criticism of the governor. Yet the writer, who could choose only one, chose the latter. It was
more interesting, more likely to hold the attention of the viewers, in his
opinion. Another writer, equally capable, might have reached the contrary
decision. No doctrinaire rules may be laid down about this. Each writer
must choose for himself, again and again. He must base his choices upon
his news department's policy and his own predilections. Hopefully, as his
experience grows and he himself matures, his choices will be wise, popular
and defensible.

Writer's objectivity

It may be generalized that most experienced news writers are objective
about most stories. They can cut a speech or a news conference without
bing affected by their own political opinions. The few newsmen who have
an ax to grind do not deserve their jobs, for they are propagandists, not
journalists. Yet many a decent, objective news writer occasionally finds
himself absolutely furious at the mouthings of the man on the screen in
front of him. He is sorely tempted to make the speaker look bad. Perhaps
the speaker is a Nazi or a Communist, a John Bircher or a New Leftist and
the news writer is infuriated, because of his own political bias. If this is the
case, the writer ought to turn the editing over to another writer, or ask
another newsman to screen the film with him and share in the decision making. To make such a request is a mark of personal strength.

Film problems

The writer can never ignore the physical realities of film. An otherwise usable statement by a speaker may have to be omitted for technical
reasons. The cameraman may have turned the camera on an instant too
late, so that the camera hasn't reached full speed when the speaker begins
and the opening words are up-cut. The camera may run out of film before
the statement is completed. The speaker may not have paused for a breath
before beginning that usable statement, thus innocently creating the problem of "lip flap" (see FILM EDITING) for the editor who tries to separate

the usable statement from what has gone before. And most unforgivable, the cameraman may not have shot a satisfactory cutaway, forcing the writer to choose one segment of a speech instead of two because he cannot use both without a jump cut. Cameraman should make it standard practice to get several brief shots of the audience at every speech they cover, and the audience should be caught listening attentively, not fiddling with their napkins or key chains while waiting for the speaker to begin. If the cameraman wants to shoot his cutaways before the speech begins, so that they are done and out of the way, he might try asking several members of the audience to look off in one direction. Even if he asks them to stare at a wall, in a medium shot it will appear in a cutaway as if they are listening to the speaker.

Self-contained statements

Television-wise politicians use the enthymeme, the aphorism, the pungent phrase, the statement which can be taken alone out of context. They learn to pause between statements, knowing that the medium of film transforms the dimension of time into the dimension of length, and that a few inches of 16-millimeter film length ought to bracket a statement for easy removal from the rest of the speech. What these astute politicians do is not obvious even to the initiated, for the argument wrapped up in a couple of phrases the short and crisp remark, and the pause are all familiar rhetorical devices. On the other hand, editors shrug their shoulders when the speaker. on film, declares, "I have seven proposals. One . . . Two . . . Three . . . etc." The editor is not totally without recourse in this situation, but the effective remedy may involve the complexities of "double chaining" (see FILM EDITING) and the editor may feel that the speaker's point number three is not worth the trouble. The editor may decide to choose a less significant part of the speech because it is easier to edit, or because it will look better on the air. This rejection of the better statement also occurs when the speaker entwines it with another statement, perhaps by a reference buried within the statement, such as "My opponent will be rejected by the voters next Tuesday because he is guilty on all these counts, and the voters know it." The wise speaker also avoids involved explanations, pyramided arguments and sentences which begin with conjunctions or transitional words and phrases such as "however," "therefore," "as a result," "because of that," and so on.

STOCK MARKET REPORTS

Some listeners watch the news mainly for the stock market report. For them, the movement of the Dow Jones Industrial Average is a gut issue. If the Dow drops, their stomachs churn, because the value of their 100 shares of A.T.&T, their 17 shares of I.B.M. and their 40 shares of

American Zinc may have eroded the equivalent of a week's pay. If the Dow soars, so do their spirits. An extra week's pay! The morning newspaper will give them the grim or delightful specifics, but they can't wait, so they watch the evening newscast for a clue.

Most newscasts limit themselves to a minimal report. Anchorman and/or still will report the amount of rise or fall in the Dow Jones Industrials. Sometimes other indices appear: the closing Industrials average, the Dow Jones Rails, the Dow Jones Utilities, *The New York Times* Index, the rise or fall of the American Stock Exchange. Except for arrows on the stills of RP's, the report consists totally of numbers. Like baseball scores, the stock market numbers intensely interest some viewers, are of passing curiosity to others, and bore or irritate the rest.

But economic news can be considerably more than this. Prices, especially food prices, wages, taxes, and mortgage rates affect us all. Some large stations and all the networks assign men to cover the economic "beat." The quality of their reports depends on clarity: how clearly can the reporter explain to each listener what a 0.3% rise in the cost of living index actually means to us all? Visuals help, provided each still contains only a little, easy-to-absorb information. For example, a photograph of a lamb chop with the words: UP 15c IN JUNE tells it like it is to everyone. Graphs are not quite as effective, but better than just a newscaster or a reporter on camera. Rule: *For economic news, get away from the "talking heads."*

KOMO-TV, Seattle, filmed a daily report on stock market activities at a local brokerage office. News director Jack Eddy said: [7]

> We feel the secret is to avoid, like the plague, a recitation of quotations. If that's what people want, they can get them from the financial page of the newspapers. Secondly, most people don't care. What they are interested in, is how will "what happens on Wall Street" affect them, and we approach it from that angle.
>
> We also look for the news peg. When the President eases the freeze of Federal construction, who will it affect? The construction industry and the money lenders. How did specific stocks respond to such news, particularly those with local ties?
>
> You can almost always find a news hook. We also look for the human interest angle. For example, we came up with a chart showing the relationship between hemlines and the market. It's great for the slow day.
>
> Also the unusual. Ever hear of stock called McIntyre Porcupine? Or do you know why gold stocks seem to go up when the rest of the market declines? Or what in the heck is ex-dividend?
>
> The other element for television is making it visual. Instead of doing a straight talking head interview, we are able to utilize some of the electronic equipment in the Merrill Lynch office, to

punch up and read market figures, the hi's and lows, the trading on a particular stock, any number of things that give the report a little pizazz.

In the morning on our 8:00 AM TV news program, it's a little different. The newscaster is connected by telephone patch to Keith Patrick at Merrill Lynch; and with some general film of the board room, we get a report on the market at that moment, in an informal, conversational manner.

A UHF station in Los Angeles, KWHY-TV, simply transmits the New York Stock Exchange ticker from the time it opens until it closes. Small brokerage houses which cannot afford their own tickers tune in. So do investors, many of them retired and elderly, who can sit at home and watch their fortunes grow or diminish.

News for Youngsters

World and national news bewilder many adults. When the economy dominates the headlines, television reporters do more explaining and clarifying than straight reporting for their adult listeners. But who tries to communicate with kids?

KCET-TV, Los Angeles, for one. The public television station created a prime-time, half-hour weekly newscast called "Newseekers." Some 30 to 40 teenagers, under the direction of two junior high school teachers, reported, wrote, produced and presented news and commentary, using the junior high school's closed-circuit television equipment.

It is not necessary to employ a 13-year-old anchorman in order to get through to youngsters on a newscast aimed at youngsters. However, it *is* necessary to write clearly enough so that children can understand what the newscaster is saying, to illustrate the news with maps and other graphics so that a youngster can differentiate between the Middle East and the Middle West, and to relate a news event to a youngster's frame of reference. In short, it is necessary to do for children what the newsman ought to do for adults, only more so.

FOR THE STUDENT

1. How does the television audience differ from the newspaper audience?
2. Quietly observe people at various places watching television newscasts. What can you say about their behavior and degree of attention?
3. Rewrite a newspaper's local story leads for television.
4. Between the reality of a guerrilla battle in some distant jungle against government troops and the television news report in the United States of that battle, what possibilities exist for distortion?
5. Separate fact from inference in three stories on the front page of today's newspaper.

6. What makes a news story interesting? What makes it significant?

7. Find a particular "interesting" news story you would choose in preference to a particular "significant" news story. Justify this preference for television news. Then find a "significant" news story you would prefer to either. Again, justify your choice for a television news audience.

8. If a political candidate hired you as his broadcast news consultant, what would you advise him to do?

9. Suggest some ways to improve a local television newscast on a slow news day such as July 4.

10. Look again at the report of how the first Superbowl game was edited. Given the same film and the same time limit, recut it and write a new script.

6

RADIO NEWS

A ROBBER HELD UP A loan company in a Texas city. The manager pressed the silent burglar alarm. A police dispatcher sent a patrol car. A radio newsman, hearing the dispatcher on his newsroom police monitor, looked up the address in a cross-listed telephone directory and dialed the phone number on his beeper line. At the loan company the phone rang insistently. The robber told the manager to pick it up.

Hello, the manager said.

The reporter said he heard the loan office was being robbed.

The manager allowed how that was now happening.

Now?

Yes.

The reporter paused for a moment's thought. Could he speak to the robber?

He wants you, the manager said.

Another pause, longer.

Hello, the robber said.

The reporter and the robber chatted for a bit, but the conversation was interrupted by the police arriving at the front door. The robber was arrested.

And the radio reporter had it all on tape.

FIRST MORAL: It pays to have a cross-listed telephone directory.

SECOND MORAL: Don't underestimate radio news or resourceful radio newsmen. Television has not walked off with all the marbles, and never will.

The event just described is not unique. Reporter Don Harris of Chicago's WGN News interviewed a bank robber, also in the course of the robbery. Their taped conversation was interrupted by the arrival of police.

ADVANTAGES AND DRAWBACKS

Radio news beats the competitive media in these ways:

1. For bulletin news, it is fast and adaptable compared with the lumbering giant, television, which puts the bulletin on, then ignores the story until the next scheduled newscast unless the story is bad enough to shock the nation. Newspapers are out of the running.

2. When you want the latest news, you can find it on the radio, somewhere on the dial, within 30 minutes in most of the country. You may just hear headlines, but if the story you want is big enough, the headlines will include it. A survey by Opinion Research Corporation reported that 52% of all Americans 18 years and older used radio as their main source of news in the morning.

3. For live coverage of a breaking story, as for bulletins, radio again is the lithe, fast runner up against the lumbering giant, television. Unless the story warrants a television mobile unit or a helicopter with video transmission gear, radio news will beat it with on-the-scene information now. Again, newspapers are out of the running. A word of caution belongs here. Do not intercept and rebroadcast police or other official broadcasts. It is illegal and it may endanger lives. For example, the Federal Aviation Agency criticized several radio broadcasters for transmitting radio conversations between pilots and FBI agents during a hijacking.

4. For economic reasons, radio stations can present a variety of specialized newscasts on a regular basis, which television will not match (a television station *could,* but no station *does*): regular newscasts, sports news, business news, extended weather reports, farm news, science news, political commentary, news for women, feature news. The list goes on. Television is not in the running, but newspapers definitely are. So are magazines.

5. People can learn the news while absorbed in other activities: driving, working, housecleaning, sunbathing, even trying half-heartedly to wake up.

6. For some people, including Richard M. Nixon, radio provides a better means than television for getting through to people with complex information. When pictures are either unwanted or unavailable, radio may be the best medium of all for convincing. CBS News reporter Dan Rather said, "Richard Nixon believes in radio. He thinks that in complicated matters you can get through on radio better than you can get on television because you don't have the visual element to sort of muck things up."

7. During blizzards, floods and other emergencies, radio keeps peo-

ple in touch with what's happening. For some, a lifeline. Of prime importance: school closings, street and highway closings. Television often does not compete, especially in the mornings. Newspapers cannot.

8. Certain small segments of our society can get news in no other way. Among them: people who live in remote areas, prisoners, the blind. Automobile commuters fall into this category twice a day.

So much for advantages. The biggest disadvantage of radio news exists for both the public and the practitioner. Most radio news is sketchy and inadequate. The listener who really wants *news* is merely exasperated unless he can find a station committed to news.

The radio journalist may eventually leave the field in despair, battered by too much rip-'n-read, too many five-minute newscasts written in 15 minutes, too many demands for a fast one-line-in, one-line-out of a taped insert in a newscast which goes on in 30 seconds, too little time to check a source or make a phone call, no time at all to consider or weigh or think. It is haste, not speed, and the product reflects this in local newscasts across the land. Intelligently crafted newscasts, invariably beamed from intelligently—and profitably—run stations, are oases in a national radio wasteland. Discussion of radio news quality usually terminates in a quarrel over radio broadcasting economics—that is, to permit a journalist to spend more time preparing a newscast means either presenting fewer and/or shorter newscasts, which no responsible journalist wants, or increasing the radio news staff, which costs money.

The difference between a shoddy rip-'n-read news operation and a modestly adequate news operation is relatively small. "Modestly adequate" might mean an extra man, hired at a respectable salary, and a budget which will cover a few more stringers, some long distance calls, and an out-of-town trip now and then. To satisfy FCC requirements, news is the main "front" which enables stations to renew their licenses. All stations should put up a good front. Some stations do, because their owners care. All station owners should care.

An angry radio news director told colleagues, "The reason the lousy stations exist is management. Hear their cry 'we would like to have a better news operation, but you know news is a costly proposition . . . all stations lose money on news.' Bunk. Our noon news blocks on AM or FM nearly pay the bill for our entire news operation during the year. . . . Those ("lousy") operations detract from my news, and your news, and still put us in the class of second-rate journalists. We are going to remain in that category until management get their heads together and begin making accusations against each other about sloppy, incompetent newsrooms."

The popular conversation-pit newscast, with the anchorman, editorialist, weatherman and sportscaster exchanging banter, has not been matched by radio newscasts. KSFO, San Francisco, found warm listener reaction, to a variation on the pattern. The newscaster and the disc jockey on duty talked about the news in what was described as "a free-hand, unrehearsed, give-and-take session." The newscaster reported what was happening, the disc jockey asked questions which sprang to his mind, and the listener found himself "drawn into the discussion because the questions being asked by the DJ are the same ones generally that the listener is asking himself."

EXAMPLES OF RADIO NEWS OPERATIONS

A 1967 survey by RTNDA, the Radio Television News Directors Association, of more than 800 television and radio stations in the United States and Canada showed these averages:

Radio newsroom employees: 1.08 full time, 1.01 part time.

TV-radio combination newsroom employees: 3.7 full time, 0.9 part time.

Daily radio newscasts that were longer than 5 minutes: average of 3.

Nearly 100% of the radio newsrooms had beeper telephones, with 9.8 beepers or outside reports weekly.

95% of the radio newsrooms had tape recorders.

60%-70% had mobile units of some type.

63% of the radio stations editorialized, 13% of these on a regular basis, with 48.5% of the radio newsrooms writing at least some of the editorials aired on their stations. (For TV the comparable figures were: 60%, 13%, 62%.)

28% of the radio stations (50% of the television stations) used stringers, but many radio news directors were displeased with what they had.

75% of the news directors, radio and television, reported to management; 25% reported to the program director.

UPI took a survey of radio stations to determine news practices and operating philosophies. Here are three reports from, respectively, a small town, a small city, and a medium-size city.

STATION #1

Operating Conditions

Market, 6,000; power, 1000W; on air, daytimer; owned locally; independent.

Philosophy

Wants to be more than a jukebox, so it has strong local news department with authority to break in with any important news. Features bloc programming, country-pop music (stays away from R-and-R image).

News Operation

Tools: Newswire, two-way mobile, working arrangement with with other stations on regional breaks, mutual cooperation with a newspaper.

Staff: News director responsible to manager, one staffer.

General: Uses wire service copy every half hour. 15 minutes at 8:30 a.m. and noon. Local newscasts at 7:05 a.m. and 5:05 p.m. Ten are under five minutes, 8 are tens and 2 are fifteens. News mixed according to significance. Writes two local newscasts and "unashamedly rip-and-read other times. We use nearly all UPI features and in-depthers in our bloc programming i.e. farm, women's, commentary, sports, record information. Also religious section."

Success Key

"We feature news and information and brag about it and sell it."

News Revenue

News big factor in a "very profitable" P-and-L statement. 18 of 20 newscasts sponsored, and it gets a 30% premium for two local newscasts. Merchants buy time because "they know people listen to us." News sold both spot and package. Listeners say they stay tuned all day because of the variety, the information and the fun provided. One hardware store has been with station steady for 17 years, one drug store for 12 years and three auto dealers 8-10 years.

Editorializing

Five days per week, written by general manager. "We've been praised and we've taken our lumps. Above all we've gained stature in the process."

Looking Ahead

Feels there is more and more listener demand for actualities. Now gathers some locally and gets some from Washington headquarters of two major political parties.

STATION #2

Operating Conditions

Market, 200,000; power, 1000W; on air, daytimer; owned, group; independent; TV-affiliated.

Philosophy

"Attention to detail will bring success." Uses two full-time news-men to produce and broadcast the news. No jockeys. "Newsmen never turn a record or touch a mike switch. They do what they're paid to do. News." Up-tempo music, but no rock 'n' roll, mixed with news.

News Operation

Tools: Newswire, audio service, helicopter, mobile phone, beeper.

Staff: News director responsible to manager, 1½ newsmen, two stringers, arranging working agreement with other stations.

General: 12 newscasts in 12-hours. A fifteen on each hour, ex-cept thirties at 7 a.m. and noon and a sixty at 5 p.m. Saturdays and Sundays show tens every hour (but plans to make them fifteens). Non-news personnel NOT permitted to make newscasts. Four times as much news carried today as one year ago. Sports car-ried 45 past the hour.

Success Key

"We are only five months old in terms of a change in format but have no reservations in saying that news is the only way to go."

News Revenue

"Still struggling to shake the good-minimum news format but can say that news has been our 'saving grace.' We have hired news-men, produced good news and sold our station on the basis of news concept. Sales have doubled. Listener comments are great and an-ticipate 50% of our net will come from news in the near future. Six of 12 newscasts sponsored and sold on spot and package basis. We're building community acceptance and long-range solidity this way. And it's paying off. An air-conditioning company moved up its season 45 days on the strength of newscast promotion. A nursery sponsor got one complete landscaping job on basis of a newscast. We can and will corner the market by staying ahead of our competition in news."

Sales Aids-Promotion

Salesmen carry A.R.B. information, brochures, audition tapes, news oriented success stories. Advertise in newspapers and on TV.

Looking Ahead

Gearing for more local in-depth coverage. Plans brief but comprehensive local news documentaries. Anticipates expanding its fifteens to twenties per hour.

STATION #3

Operating Conditions

Market, 495,000; power, 5000W; on air, 24 hours; owned, locally; independent.

Philosophy

Hires only high calibre newsmen, gives them an efficient news center, serves listeners 24 hours per day with whatever is happening.

News Operation

Tools: Newswire, audio service, regional news network covering seven states, 6 mobile units, 1 airplane, 2 leased helicopters, 3 tiny-talkie units, 5 portable tape recorders, working agreements with stations.

Staff: News director with vice-president's title and responsible only to management, 7 staffers (each working part of day in news center, rest in field and each with a mobile), 10 stringers.

General: Features hard news, editorials, airborne traffic advisories, weather and road conditions, school and industrial closures, features, in depth on big stories. 20 scheduled newscasts: 19 fives at 55 plus 1 fifteen at 7 a.m., plus 7 headline summaries, all locally produced. Has live sports, beepers, mobile, regional network feeds, audio, special reports from news center. "We interrupt for important news." Volume up 15% in last 12 months by adding four regular news reports; volume up 50% in last five years. Non-news personnel never allowed to air newscasts. Newscasts a mixture of all news according to significance.

Success Key

"Only way an independent can be a real force in a community is through an extremely news-oriented approach. News as it happens from where it is happening. Be vital."

Radio news writers rewrite wire copy for a newscast. There is no "rip 'n read" here. In the shaping of a radio newscast, the information transmitted by the press associations will be examined, combined, sifted, simplified, and sometimes written to conform to a particular newscaster's style.

News Revenue

"News, without question, is the reason for our #1 rating." All 20 newscasts sponsored, two with same sponsor for seven years. Sold as spots. Charges 10% premium for all time during AAA drive time periods to defray cost of airborne coverage. 50% of net comes from news; up 25% in five years.

Editorializing

Daily, written by news director, general manager and commentator, approved by news director. Has helped commercially and is "credited with election of a mayor."

Sales Aids-Promotion

Salesmen have tapes and brochures. Tours of news center.

Costs

Examples abound. A three-man news staff in an Iowa town of 8,000 *turns out* 23 newscast daily and *turns over* $78,000 a year to the station above newsroom operating costs.

Cost of setting up a small radio news operation will include equipment bought once (presumably), weekly salaries, weekly costs for tele-type wires and audio services, and supplies which must be reordered. Naturally, these costs vary. A large radio station in Philadelphia will pay more than a small station in Wet Hat for the same AP "A" wire. It will also pay more for an acceptable journalist for the obvious reason that it can afford to demand a higher degree of skill.

Initial purchases of equipment include standard size typewriters, portable tape recorders, a special telephone installation, a roving police monitor, and perhaps a file cabinet in addition to other office furnishings.

Travel, stringers and tipsters should also be budgeted. A radio news stringer is a part-time correspondent, usually in another community within the station's transmission range. Stringers are paid by the word or by the story. Sometimes their voices are used, sometimes just their information. Stringers may be small town reporters, housewives or students who have the spare time and the flexible schedule needed to cover stories at odd hours, either at their own direction or on assignment from the newsroom (in the latter case they should be paid whether or not the story goes on the air).

Tipsters are found where news is found. The court bailiff, the police sergeant, the fire dispatcher, the probate clerk, the parole officer, the air traffic controller, the highway patrolman may all call from time to time with leads which develop into hard news or feature stories. For the tip, the station pays a flat $3 or $5. Word of tipster payments spreads and the news department which establishes a policy of paying for tips soon finds itself getting news tip telephone calls from people who were never solic-ited. The station will eventually have a substantial network of informants. Many of the tips prove worthless, but lots of wheat lies amid the chaff.

A variation of the tipster network is to advertise that the station will pay $25 or $50 for the tip leading to the best story of the week. Not only is the sum paid but, with his consent, the tipster's name is announced.

Audio news services—reports from correspondents, interviews and some actualities—are sold by the UPI Audio Network, Radio News International, and Metromedia Radio News. ABC, CBS, NBC, Mutual (supplemented by Reuters), and Westinghouse supply affiliates with a steady flow of on-the-spot news coverage. ABC Community Newsfeed focuses on stories of interest to minority groups. AP offers a weekly mail service of audio commentary and features. New York's Ecu-Media News Service offers 3½-minute religious features. Group-owned stations, includ-ing Capital Cities, Triangle, Westinghouse, and Storer, supply their own stations with reports and actualities. During a major news crisis, a news service may provide an open-line, live report running for hours. On-the-spot reports flow in reverse, too, as radio newsmen sell reports to net-works, usually for fees of $10 to $50 per cut.

The closed circuit news service feeds can go over ordinary telephone lines, or over better grade, wider band, special broadcast lines.

The UPI Audio Network feeds about 75 spots a day through a permanently open telephone line to a subscriber's tape recorder which is actuated by sound to turn itself on and off. The UPI broadcast wire periodically transmits an "Audio Roundup" describing the spots UPI has fed, so that a news editor can quickly locate those spots he wants to use in a newscast.

Branches of government, politicians, and some private business firms mail audio tape handouts. Some of these spots are quite good and can be edited to make them both better and less commercial.

A number of special radio networks exist in the United States independent of outside business interests. Several stations band together to exchange voice reports, actualities, or live programming. The stations may belong to the same owner, they may be in the same state or region, or they may have a community of interests and be commercially run, like the Black Audio Network, or non-commercial, like a network of college radio stations. For a little extra trouble and expense, the radio station belonging to a regional network extends its reach quite a bit.

Radio newsmen feeding a spot to a network sometimes forget to stop. Radio news consultant Jerry Graham: "There is a tendency to have actualities just for the sake of actualities and to let them run too long. Tight editing is needed. Secondly, reporters in the field have to refine their techniques. They should get to the heart of the story in the first few seconds of their reports, so that the stations that cannot carry a full segment won't lose the important element of a story that may be at the tail end and be cut out."

Voice inserts (called "beepers" even when there is no beep) should be short. Sometimes 30 seconds is too long. Usually it is ample. Not many beepers should be allowed to run as long as 60 seconds.

Get live or taped beepers from: eyewitnesses to a breaking news event, including those involved, like the bank teller who was just held up and the runner who just won the race and hasn't quite caught his breath; the people who will be affected by a decision, like the homeowner whose taxes are about to rise or the president of the company that won the contract; the important citizen who says surprising things and the important citizen who is miffed at what that other important citizen just said, even if he hadn't heard about it until you called him.

NEWSCAST SCHEDULE

The radio news audience ebbs and flows. It is greatest at three periods of the day: morning, noon and late afternoon.

Morning (6 a.m.—9:30 a.m.): Clock radios wake people with the news. Mothers want to know how to dress children for school. Commuters want to know what freeways are jammed. Car radios keep them company all the way to work. Everyone wants to know what's been happening.

Noon: Radio news accompanies lunch for the housewife, the construction worker, the farmer.

Late afternoon (4:30 p.m.—6:30 p.m.): Commuters again want to know about the traffic. Investors wonder what the Dow did. Everyone wants to know what the day has brought.

Some listeners like to tune in at bedtime. Has the world survived another day? What will tomorrow's weather be? Who won the Detroit game?

Both inside and outside these peak listening periods a pattern of headlines, brief weather reports, 5-minute summaries, and 15-minute newscasts can give form to the daily news schedule. For example, headlines and weather on the half-hour and 5-minute summaries on the hour. Or, 15-minute newscasts on the hour, headlines at the half-hour and 45 minutes past the hour. Or, 5-minute summaries at quarter-past, half-past, and five-to. And so on. Because the audience increases during three periods of the day, the amount of news offered should increase also. That is the time for the daily business digest, the science report, the "news behind the news," news for women, the sports report.

Not all these newscasts are produced locally. Many radio stations affiliate with CBS, NBC, Mutual, or one of the four ABC networks. All networks provide newscasts on regular schedules. Affiliate stations sometimes attach local newscasts back-to-back to the network newscasts. Sometimes they present completely separate locally produced newscasts which include national and international news. There is no "best way" to set up a radio news schedule. Some stations want to duck the competition. Some want to meet the competition head-on. If any rule exists it is this: *Don't change the schedule without a good reason.* Listeners establish radio news habits. A newscast is a constant in the lives of many people, as dependable as the rising of the sun.

ALL-NEWS RADIO

"News," said Dick Wald of NBC News, "is like salted nuts. The more you inform, the more people want you to inform."

Today, about a dozen radio stations in major cities have gone to an all-news or news-and-information format. But "salted nuts" for the listener has not always brought peaches and cream to the station owner. Several stations tried all-news and dropped it. Those who survived are glad they held on for the year or more it took to break old listening habits and build the sizeable audience which exists in every major city for all-news radio. Unlike radio music audiences, all-news audiences pop in and out.

Said one newsman: "Only a moron would listen to us for very long at a stretch." Switchover to all-news format is usually accompanied by billboard, bus and/or newspaper advertising. WTOP, Washington, gave political leaders transistor radios locked to WTOP.

Station managers considering all-news fret over the cost. Staff may double, if it was thin to begin with. Other overhead costs rise. On the other hand, revenue should also rise considerably. Some stations are making more than they ever did spinning platters. Beyond money, the station manager finds himself with influence and prestige in the community beyond anything he had experienced as just a businessman whose business was running a radio station. WAVA, Washington, general manager John Burgreen observed, "This sort of operation gives you the feeling you're really doing something in broadcasting."

All-news format varies with the hour of the day. During morning and evening commuting hours, the pace picks up: shorter stories, more rapid reading rates, more headlines, more frequent time and temperature checks, more sports reports, fewer features. Between 10 a.m. and 3 p.m., most listeners are housewives. News tends to get softer: longer stories, more features, slower pacing. Here is a WBBM, Chicago, noon to 1 p.m. format:

> Network news
> Local news
> Weather
> Stock market report
> Editorial
> Local feature
> Headlines
> News summary
> *Direct Line* (an ombudsman service)
> Book reviews
> Hollywood report

Says John Callaway of CBS Radio, "We view news as reporting on the reality of what's happening. War is a reality, sure—but so is a book, so is a play, so is a restaurant. When you give immediacy to them, you're in soft news—and this is a significant part of our approach to housewives' time."

Another example: WTOP reports weather news every seven minutes, time checks every three minutes, headline summaries every fifteen minutes, and twice an hour runs two-minute special reports which may be sports, news analyses, commentaries, or special interviews. A daily off-beat local feature is run three times a day.

A charge levelled at all-news radio is that most of it is shallow [1]: "The news is often billed as 'stories in the making.' They emerge from nowhere; they live briefly and blend indistinguishably into new emergencies.

One-sentence headlines, flecky details, weather, traffic, sports, stocks, compressed catastrophes, affairs of state, revolutions and coups, stabbings, shoot-outs, local fires, fender-benders, the jingle and the sell of endlessly procreating commercials—they drone, they clip (fast, fast, no introspection, no navel) without emphasis, change of pace, or emotional tone in a sort of instant omnipresence, never *to* or *from,* only *at,* the re-creation of a mythical pattern of nowness. . . .

"No one can stay in the all-news world for more than ten minutes at a time. For the lineal mind, instant omnipresence is dreaded nothingness. . ."

One day a brave television broadcaster will try all-news television. Signs of it are increasing. One major commercial station, KNBC-TV, the NBC O & O in Los Angeles, extended its evening news package to two and one-half hours. Several CATV channels show nothing but the AP- or UPI "A" wire. With the coming proliferation of CATV channels and the FCC requirement that CATV originate programming, the likelihood of all-news television in this decade increases.

MOBILE UNITS

Vehicles with two-way radios give a radio newscast what the disc jockeys call the "now sound":

". . . The men at the levee have been working 16 hours without relief. There with them now is WWW reporter Jerry Jones."

And in comes Jerry Jones, with an on-the-spot, right-this-minute report of the sandbag loading, plus the playback of a tape he got five minutes ago at a place to which he could walk while carrying a portable tape recorder, but could not reach by car.

The mobile radio unit may be as simple as a journalist's private car containing a two-way radio, or it can be as elaborate as the radio news car designed for KSTP, St. Paul. The KSTP newsman can transmit sound from either a portable or AC-power tape recorder, or several microphones through a five-channel mixer. He can feed either to the station or directly on the air, using a transmitter mounted on the car. In addition, the car has eight-channel police receivers, one low band sending frequency, two high band sending frequencies, a typewriter, a desk, and foul weather gear. It can transmit live broadcasts of news conferences, interviews, breaking news, MOS reports. Wireless mikes can be fed to the car and "tripped" to relay back to the station on another frequency, so that reporters can work without cords. An inverter provides the necessary AC power. The car is a rolling radio station.

Mobile units run on more than wheels. Some stations use helicopters, not only for those daily traffic reports, but for getting to distant places fast, especially when roads are blocked. Hovering over parades, helicop-

154   TELEVISION NEWS

ters advertise their radio stations as they deliver running commentaries heard on portables carried by the good folks below. Mobile unit power boats cover fun or disaster. And at least one radio station uses an amphibian car. The newest kind of mobile unit is the snowmobile. Canadian station CMHL, Hamilton, Ontario, sends its snowmobile out during snowstorms when even police cars get stuck. Radio listeners learn which roads are still open, which are hopelessly clogged. Sometimes people, seeing the snowmobile go by, turn their radios on in a hurry to discover where it is going and what is happening.

The FCC grants remote pickup licenses to licensed broadcasters for two-way radios. The "base station" at the broadcasting station gets an identification of three letters followed by three numbers: ABC-123. Each "mobile station" gets two letters and four numbers: AB-1234. The car's transmitter-receiver usually goes in the trunk, with the mike and controls under the dashboard, and if the car does not already have one, an alternator in place of a generator, in order to keep the battery up to strength.

Sometimes a mobile phone substitutes for a two-way radio. The conversation goes through a telephone operator. The audio quality will probably be inferior to that of a good two-way radio hookup and it may not be possible to patch in a tape recorder for playback, at least without extensive modification. Most radio units can be modified for playback from portable tape recorders.

A video camera crew draws on the batteries of their automobile to supply the power to run their camera and microwave transmitter, which beams the signal back to the station. The automobile is equipped with an inverter, which converts 12-volt DC battery power to 120-volt AC current. Crew members do not have to hunt for an electrical outlet to plug into at every story location.

Besides communications equipment, a mobile unit should carry emergency equipment: a tow line, battery cables, lanterns, flares, etc. In winter when the reporter goes where the blizzard is, he will find foul weather gear useful. More than one journalist has been rewarded with an interview after pulling a driver out of trouble.

TAPE RECORDING

Most radio stations have at least one telephone linked to a tape recorder, so that a telephone conversation initiated at either end can be taped. These phones may have a beeper, which emits a short beep every fifteen seconds to let both parties know their words are being recorded. The newsman at the station should be able to switch off the beep, which degrades audio quality and distracts the listener when the tape is played over the air. Anyone being interviewed must be informed at the start that his words will be aired live or will be recorded. The beep tone is not required if the interviewee is warned that the conversation is being taped, and the warning itself is on the tape. Nor is a beep needed if a reporter or stringer calls in, because he knows that his words may be broadcast. And stations may inter-connect for a live station-to-station feed without the beeper. Finally, there is a system for sale which puts a beep in the ear of the interviewee, but the beep does not register on the tape.

Radio newsmen will not be sorry to see the beeper go to a museum. It has been a (BEEP) nuisance.

With good, inexpensive, reel-to-reel and cassette tape recorders now on the market, all radio newsrooms should have at least one portable tape recorder. A cassette will do if it can be patched into a studio tape recorder. A reel-to-reel tape recorder permits the newsman to edit the original tape. Several types of audio tape splicers can be bought. Simplest is the splicing bar, used with a single-edge razor blade. Sliding a forefinger along the groove holds the tape in place. Each end of the tape is cut at the angled cross groove (to avoid a "pop"), the excess tape falls away, and a bit of splicing tape bonds the two ends firmly. Steel and plastic splicing bars are available for just a few dollars.

A popping sound or any other unwanted noise can be eliminated by splicing or by replaying that segment of tape with the record button down, the volume pot down, and the feed and takeup reels guided by hand past the record head. A little practice is advisable before trying it on a cut meant for a newscast. A third way to eliminate unwanted sound is to put a magnet on the tape. Again, practice first.

Steps are saved—to say nothing of valuable seconds—if a tape recorder in the newsroom can be patched directly over the air. Regular newscasts need not come from the newsroom, but bulletins should.

(For using audio tape in television newscasts, see section on *Audio Tape* in Chapter 3.)

Mark W. Hall, author of *Broadcast Journalism,*[2] has some advice to the reporter doing a beeper interview, including:

1. Identify yourself, your station, and the purpose of your call.
2. Tell the person you are calling that you are recording the interview. If he objects, turn off the tape recorder.
3. If he still objects, explain that you are trying to get a balanced report.
4. If he still objects, ask him why.
5. During an interview, ask open-ended questions, like why.
6. Don't murmur "I see" while he is talking. Keep quiet. Editing will be easier.
7. Don't ask permission to use a comment. Don't agree to let him preview the edited tape.

REMOTE TAPE REPORTS

The radio news reporter away from his station faces a dilemma if he has an interview or MOS on tape which he is anxious to get on the air quickly. If he is near his car, equipped with a high quality radio transmitting unit capable of taking a tape recorder patch, and he is within transmitting distance of his station, his problem is solved. But what if he is not?

One solution would be to dial his station on a nearby phone, and play the tape, with the tape recorder speaker next to the telephone mouthpiece. Quality: awful.

A common practice among radio newsmen is to establish a hardwire connection using a telephone. This is done by running two wires from the tape recorder speaker, fastening alligator clips at their ends. The reporter unscrews the mouthpiece of whatever telephone he happens to be near and attaches the alligator clips to the two protruding metal tips. Sometimes microphones with alligator clips are used the same way for live transmission. Telephone companies frown on this practice, as they do on the attachment of any foreign equipment to their equipment without their own interface gear. The practice flaunts the provisions of their telephone tariff rate structure, which is approved by a state regulatory agency, but—as far as the author has been able to determine—attaching a tape recorder to a telephone is not illegal, provided, of course, the instrument is not damaged. To the best of the author's knowledge, it is not a *crime* and there are no legal penalties. The telephone company may be within its rights to cut the user's service, however. So be warned.

In recent years AT&T has lost decisions on the use of the Hushaphone, a rubber mouthpiece attachment designed to concentrate the sound of the voice, and the Carterphone, which hooks two-way radios into the telephone network. But—again as far as the author can determine—no court ruling has come down on hard wiring tape recorders to telephones.

The Telo/Talk Earphone connects a tape recorder to a telephone for either sending or receiving sound of a fairly high quality. Because the device attaches to the outside of the telephone instrument, no question arises about the journalist's right to use it.

A perfectly legal and inexpensive device, the Telo/Talk Earphone, works by induction to transmit or receive audio tape sound over telephone lines. A "donut" with a rubber sleeve fits on the mouthpiece or earpiece of the telephone. A wire with a jackplug at the end runs from the "donut." The plug goes into the microphone input jack for recording, into the speaker output jack for transmitting. Among its advantages as a recording device, it enables newsmen to get remote tape reports while at home.

A simple telephone tap, even less expensive, consists of a suction cup wired to a jackplug which goes into the microphone input jack. The suction cup attaches to the outside of the telephone, usually on the telephone base near the transformer or on the receiver behind the earpiece.

FOR THE STUDENT

1. Assume you are news director of a radio station with one mobile unit and one news wire. A budget increase now permits you to add either another mobile unit or another wire. Which would you choose? Defend your choice.
2. Why should a radio station develop a strong news department if it could get as much income at lower expense and with fewer headaches by spinning platters and keeping news to a minimum? Build an argument for news.
3. Suggest ways to promote a radio news operation to the public and to advertisers.

4. How does getting radio news actualities on the air differ from getting television news actualities on the air?

5. Format an hour-long block from 10 a.m. to 11 a.m. for an all-news station. Format the 6 p.m. to 7 p.m. block.

6. If the station programming were not all-news but instead provided blocked-out three-hour morning and late-afternoon news periods, how would you change these formats (see question 5)?

7. Accompany a radio news reporter in the field for an entire day. Write a paper describing what he did.

8. Spend a day in a radio newsroom. Write a paper, including what surprised you.

9. Scan today's newspaper for out-of-town stories which could be updated with local beepers.

10. Monitor a radio network newscast for the purpose of extracting remotes for a later, locally produced newscast. For each cut, note the running time (the time it starts and ends, taken from the top of the newscast), the item time (start-time subtracted from end-time), intro cue (the newscaster's lead-in to the cut) and the outcue (the last words of the cut). If possible, use a stop watch. As you will discover, monitoring accurately takes practice.

7

WRITING

CONSIDER THE VIEWER. Or for radio news, the listener. Ask yourself, what does he look like? The answer should not be, "That's a stupid question. Viewers look like everyone." Indeed they do, but the writer who imagines an audience of everyone is actually imagining nothing. He writes with no one in mind, which is a mistake.

The news writer, the reporter and the newscaster should regard the audience as a single person, not a great faceless mass. One person. For the radio journalist, that one listener may be a commuter driving his car along a freeway, listening at 60 miles an hour as he changes lanes in his effort to get to work or get home three minutes earlier than usual. For the television journalist, that one viewer may be a housewife trying to catch the news while supper is cooking and she's ironing and the kids are yelling. Or the one viewer is her husband, home from his eight-hour shift, tired and irritated, wondering when the newscaster will finally shut up. That driver, or that housewife, or that factory worker is the audience. There is no convention of political scientists listening intently to catch every nuance of the information presented. If you, in delivering, reporting or writing the news confuse that tired workingman or bore him, he can turn you off—CLICK!—just like that. From that moment, all your clever imagery, all your projected sincerity, all your carefully edited film, presented at considerable expense, and all the rest of your news department's hard work is wasted, so far as that viewer is concerned. He may not come back tomorrow. He may never tune in again.

You can, if you wish, pander to him in an effort to enthrall him (if you don't like the image of a tired workingman as your audience, choose someone else, but choose some *one*). Play up the sex stories, the crime stories and the light features, especially the film with what used to be called cheesecake, while you provide a minimum of important news. Some news directors do this, especially during rating periods when the station buys space in the newspapers and along the sides of buses to advertise a "courageous" examination of marijuana in the nearest university sorority houses, or some such. It is the author's opinion that this kind of journalism equates with the diet pill business in medicine and the promotion of whip-lash injuries in legal practice.

Or, you can give your tired workingman the important news of the day in a manner which *will* interest him, which will have him call out, "Say, Maud, did you hear that?" Although he may still be waiting for the ball scores, he is watching the news to learn what has happened today. He pays taxes, he has children in school, his family breathes the air and drinks the water, he doesn't want prices to go up, he doesn't want to lose his job and he doesn't want to go to war. Above all, he is nobody's fool. If you can present the news to him clearly, so that he can understand it, and interest-ingly, so that he pays attention to it, he will stay tuned and you will be acquitting yourself professionally.

EVOLUTION OF BROADCAST NEWS STYLE

In the course of two centuries of American journalism, a unique style of newspaper writing evolved. Its most distinctive feature is the "in-verted pyramid." The most important facts are told first, followed by lesser facts in descending order of importance. The first sentence usually has the "five W's": Who, What, When, Where, Why; and sometimes How is thrown in for good measure. The headline first tells the story in micro-cosm. The 5-W lead retells it more clearly and with a little detail. The next three paragraphs or so may provide a further retelling, with still further detail. The remainder of the story may retell it all again, this time in chronological form with additional detail.

This writing style has been developed to a high degree by — and tends to be peculiar to — American newspapermen. It is not the style of Fleet Street, whose sub-editors prefer a less stilted style, narrative rather than structured. Nor is it universally liked, or used, by all American newspaper-men.

The inverted pyramid style has one big advantage over a chronological or narrative style of writing. It enables a busy newspaper copy or make-up editor to trim a story, either in copy or type, from the bottom as he assem-bles a page. And so, because stories are written to be trimmed from the bottom if necessary, important elements of each story are retained, despite drastic chopping.

When radio news emerged in the twenties and thirties, it was written by men trained in the newspaper tradition. Radio news was fed through newspaper wire services or stylistic copies of newspaper wires. Gradually, however, it became apparent that radio news must not be just spoken newspaper copy. A listener cannot skim radio news items looking for a story in which he is interested. In radio (and television), trimming from the bottom would mean throwing out entire stories.

Another difference between newspapers and radio news is that, in radio, a narrative treatment immediately after the lead sounds more natural than the retelling of a story in an ever-expanding lead. Further, some words and word pairs which look perfectly good in print feel awkward on the tongue ("youths," for example). A newscaster plowing through a long sentence must catch his breath in the middle, a physiological fact the newspaper writer need not consider. The radio news listener's continuity of thought is threatened by lengthy noun clauses between subject and verb, or between transitive verb and direct object. (For instance, "Senator Brown, who visited Judge Jones yesterday after a talk with Congressman Smith, cancelled all other appointments.")

Over the years, radio news writers altered newspaper style to suit their own medium. The changes were ad hoc: if an innovation sounded good, it stayed, and was used again another time. No overall style was imposed in radio news writing. Although radio news drew men like Edward R. Murrow, who was trained in public speaking, the fountainhead of radio news writing has been journalism, not rhetoric.

Television news grew out of radio news, just as radio news grew out of newspaper journalism. Like Topsy — and like radio news — it just grew. It, too, evolved on an ad hoc basis to suit a new medium. Although there are many similarities, the style of radio news writing is not completely the style of television news writing. When film is shown, words must relate to pictures. Audio and video elements work in concert to tell the story. Silence is sometimes part of the television script. A good radio story is often trimmed or rejected for television because it lacks graphics. A good television film story is often rejected by a radio news editor because it is weak.

The television news or documentary writer who fails to balance audio and video elements, or who thinks the sound will take care of itself, is practically begging to be misunderstood. Experiments by university researchers indicate that words compete poorly with pictures if the words separately clamor for the viewers' attention. As an example, it is foolish policy to grab any piece of war locale film which happens to be in the library in order to illustrate the latest wire copy from that locale. If the film shows a village with a medium shot of a chicken scampering across a dusty road, the copy can report anything from a political upheaval to a major battle, and a lot of viewers may remember nothing but that chicken. (See section on *Research,* Chapter 19.)

An effective bit of humor can occasionally be derived from sharply contrasting what the television audience sees with what it hears. For example, a feature story about a flying grandmother began with film of a private plane taxiing toward the camera while the newscaster said something like, "Everyone knows that when a grandmother reaches her sixties, she likes nothing better than to stay at home with her rocking chair, her knitting and her pussy cat." (SOUND UP FULL FOR ENGINE ROAR). "David Brinkley's Journal" showed scenes of automobile graveyards, highways jammed with billboards, and streets jammed with pawn shops, with no audio but a recording of "America the Beautiful." It was effective, powerful rather than humorous, with the kind of impact Simon and Garfunkel delivered with their "Seven O'Clock News," as they sang "Silent Night" against a radio newscast of tragedies. Two separate SOF elements can also be contrasted by tight intercutting. When Oklahoma ended statewide prohibition, an Oklahoma City television news cameraman shot film of "dry" ladies outside a liquor store stubbornly singing "Onward Christian Soldiers." He also shot close-up film of the liquor store cash register ringing up sales. A film editor intercut the two scenes, with each phrase of the song followed by the counterpoint ringing of the cash register.

BROADCAST COPY

Here are some rules:

1. Type copy. Don't write in longhand. If changes involve more than two or three words, type them in. If only two or three words, print them. If the page looks messy, retype it.

2. Double space or triple space.

3. Put only one story on a page.

4. Slug each story with one or two words in the upper left corner, followed by your last name and the date: FIRE-JONES-7/3. If your newsroom has a different slug-line style, follow it.

5. If your story continues onto a second page, print MORE in big letters and/or draw an arrow pointing down. On the top of the second page, type FIRST ADD, then the slug word: FIRST ADD FIRE.

6. Put script page numbers in the upper right corner when the script is assembled.

7. Never break a sentence on a page. Try not to break a paragraph on a page.

8. Never break a word on a line.

9. Don't change a word gingerly, like this: tomorrow; or like this: tomorrow. Change it boldly: TOMORROW.

10. Be sure your typewriter ribbon is black enough and your typewriter keys are clean.

11. Leave margins: 2 to 3 inches on top, 1 to 2 inches at bottom, ½ inch at left and right.

12. Radio copy goes the full width of the page. Television copy is split down the middle, with an inch of white space between video and audio. If the station's practice is to put video material on the left and audio matter on the right, keep it that way.

13. Figure on 4 seconds to a full line of copy, 2 seconds to a half-line, as a rough guide.

14. Words to be read aloud should be typed upper and lower case. ALL OTHER WORDS, BOTH VIDEO AND AUDIO INFORMATION, SHOULD BE TYPED IN CAPS.

15. Use a series of dots . . . to indicate a pause. Use pairs of dashes — two dashes on each side — to set off a phrase. Use parentheses (now and again) for "throwaway" phrases. In broadcast copy, punctuation has no function other than clarity.

16. All elements of a number should be written so that they can be read from left to right, and symbols should be spelled out. $4,687.14 should be written: Four thousand six hundred 87 dollars and .14 cents. Also acceptable: 4 thousand 687 dollars and 14 cents. Better yet, round off the number: 47 hundred dollars *or* nearly 47 hundred dollars. 14.3% should be written: 14 — point — 3 percent. June 16 should be written: June 16th *or* June sixteenth. 1972 can be left as is. The decade can be written as: the 1960's, *or* the nineteen sixties. Fractions are written out: two-thirds, one-half *or* half (NOT: a half) *A* million sounds like: *eight* million. Set off telephone numbers with hyphens: Central 6-5-4-3-1. The number 1 looks like the letter l, so write *one* and *eleven* unless they are part of a larger number.

17. Underline words to be emphasized. "Not" should usually be underlined or spelled in caps.

18. Use phonetic spelling for unfamiliar names. Capitalize the stressed syllable: He drove from Cairo (KAY-ro), Illinois, to Paris (PAY-ris), Kentucky. (See section on *The Anchor Spot,* Chapter 4.)

19. Spell correctly, even though only one or two other staff members will see your copy. Misspelled words can cause confusion and can lead to mispronunciation. Keep a dictionary and a gazeteer or atlas. Besides, why let your co-workers think you are stupid?

20. Read your copy aloud. Whisper if you like. You'll catch awkward phrasing or a succession of silly sounding or sissy sounding sibilants. Veteran broadcast journalists subvocalize as they write.

21. Don't abbreviate, except for Mr., Mrs., Dr. and St., as in St. Paul. Use initials if you want them read aloud: the F.B.I. *or* the F-B-I. Where the initials are not all that familiar, precede or follow them with

the full name: the S.D.S.—Students for a Democratic Society. Where the initials form an acronym, don't use periods or dashes: NATO.

Sine Qua Non

Never write anything you don't fully understand.

"That's what the wire copy said" is the feeblest excuse around.

If *you* don't understand it, don't expect anyone else to understand it.

Attribution

Attribute a statement to its source when the statement is controversial ("All the Democrats do is spend and tax, spend and tax."), when the source is needed to establish credibility ("Smoking a pack of cigarettes a day definitely shortens the average life span by four years."), and when the source is an integral part of the story ("The governor will not run for re-election.").

Don't attribute without a reason.

If the source is trustworthy and obvious, don't attribute. For example:

POOR: The vice president in charge of production at Mammoth Studios, Harvey R. Lurch, says shooting begins next week on "Son of Anchorman."

BETTER: Shooting begins next week on the Mammoth Studios picture, "Son of Anchorman."

Don't use vague or pointless attribution, such as "unimpeachable sources" or "highly placed informants," unless you are a diplomatic correspondent.

Limit attribution: Police said, *not* Assistant Police Chief Melvin Grover said (unless there is a reason for using Grover's name).

Start the sentence with the attribution.

Contractions

Use contractions, but don't feel that broadcast style requires contractions. Broadcast style requires only a natural, conversational manner of writing and speaking. If you are more comfortable with "should not" you should not feel obligated to write "shouldn't." But eschew "ain't."

Quotes

Quotation marks by themselves may not sufficiently separate a direct quote from other copy, but they should be used, along with an introductory phrase. With a lengthy quote add a concluding phrase:

The mayor said — and I quote — "Let's work together."

The mayor called it "a misguided, overblown project."

Quoting the mayor: "We have no other choice."

The mayor's exact words were: "Not while I still draw breath."

The mayor said — to use his words — "Councilman Jones is dead wrong."

The mayor praised what he called, "The company's concern for the health of our community."

Break up a long quote by inserting a phrase like: And still quoting the mayor . . . *or* The mayor went on to say . . . *or* The mayor continued. . .

For a longer quote: . . . must meet this challenge." The words of the mayor. *Or sometimes:* End of quotation.

Do not write: . . . must meet this challenge." Endquote (*or* unquote). It sounds stilted. The quotation marks alert the newscaster to provide a pause or inflection.

When you quote someone saying "I," be sure the copy is written so that no one thinks the newscaster is referring to himself.

Names and Titles

Omit first names of well-known people addressed by title. Make it: President Nixon, *not* President Richard M. Nixon; Britain's Prime Minister Heath, *not* Prime Minister Edward M. Heath of Great Britain.

If the name is not a household word, don't lead with it. Use his title first, or the reason he is newsworthy:

Secretary of State William Rogers (or *the* Secretary of State, William Rogers):

One of the girls convicted in the Charles Manson trial . . . Susan Atkins. . .

Or, you can use the title or reference in one sentence and the name in the next: One of the girls convicted in the Charles Manson trial briefly left prison today. Susan Atkins walked . . . *etc.*

Said

"Said" and "says" are perfectly good words, no matter how many times you use them. "Points out" is tricky. So is "claims."

"Told" is better than "said in a speech to. . ."

So is "promised," where it fits.

Slang

Whether you use a slang word depends on whether it gets in the way of communication. Some slang is O.K. Other slang words get some folks uptight.

A couple of words about dialects: don't ever . . .

Gobbledygook

Nobody grows old these days. Instead, people become senior citizens. Kids are no longer lazy in school; they're underachievers. Military prisoners are not tortured; they undergo deep interrogation (unless they're our soldiers, in which case they are tortured). The poor have vanished from our slums, replaced by the culturally disadvantaged. For that matter, the slums have vanished, replaced by the inner city.

Wherever something unpleasant exists, it seems, we can make it disappear by giving it a nice ringing phrase. Bureaucrats create many of these euphemisms, but journalists proliferate them, which is a particular shame because journalists should know better.

Accuracy and clarity remain the touchstones. If a delicate phrasing more accurately and clearly identifies a condition, the delicate phrasing should be used, but if the old Anglo-Saxon word (like old or lazy or poor) does the job better, the old word should be used. Ignore the delicate phrase. Learn to suspect new terms which government officials, military briefing officers and professors drop at news conferences.

Other confusion

Avoid "the former" and "the latter." They are confusing.

Beware of "it." Be sure its referent will be understood by listeners. If in doubt, repeat the original word or phrase or identification.

Again, don't lead with an unfamiliar name. *Instead of:* Herman Hicks was fined 15 dollars by a municipal court judge, *make it*: A municipal court judge fined Herman Hicks 15 dollars.

If you lead with a familiar name, precede it with a title or an identification: The football hero of the nineteen forties . . . Tom Harmon . . .

The usual broadcasting practice is to give the identification first, the name second, no matter where in the story they appear.

Today

Most stories reported *today* happened *today*, especially if they are reported on an evening newcast. Unless there is something special about the event occurring today, such as a reference to an event yesterday or tomorrow, avoid the temptation. Leave *today* out.

If time is important, if you want to show how fresh the news story is, or if leaving the "when" out bothers you, try *this morning, this afternoon, this evening*, or *tonight*.

CLEAR WRITING

The most important consideration of a broadcast news style is clarity. Radio and television news share this need. Unlike the newspaper reader, the radio listener or television viewer cannot go back over a sentence to fathom its meaning. Either he understands it the first time through, or he loses it forever. Any listener who stops to think, "What was that he just said?", loses not only that bit of news, but also the news that is being told while he is puzzling over the last bit.

Clear writing is not a matter of luck. Nor does it automatically develop in a newsman. Clarity of writing style has been studied for two generations as a behavioral science called "readability." Its best known advocate is Rudolf Flesch. In its early days, readability was the province of educators who searched for formulas to measure children's schoolbooks. Later, Robert Gunning and a few others applied their skills to dispel the fog in business writing, periodical publications and news wire copy. Today, readability researchers use computers and follow investigative lines similar to those of linguists seeking machine translation of language. Among the products of labored research, which at one time included hand counts of the letters in thousands of words, have been formulas which objectively test for clarity.

Without a formula, there are only two ways to determine whether a news story is understandable to a broadcast audience. One way is to test the audience. Several research studies have done just that, reading news items to groups of volunteers, then questioning them. This method may provide guidelines to the researcher, but it obviously cannot be used by the news writer to provide guidelines for the story he has just written. Therefore, he turns to the second way to decide whether his copy is clear. He evaluates it based on his experience. Or his editor does. Either way, the judgment is subjective. Sometimes, this judgment is very good. Sometimes it is not.

In deriving formulas, readability researchers have used such yardsticks as lists of difficult words, average sentence length, number of prepositional phrases, average letters-per-word, use of "personal" words and sentences, complexity of sentences, ratio of clauses, percentage of abstract words, number of pronouns, and much, much more.

For the news writer faced with the practical task of checking his copy, most formulas are too complex to be of value. He needs a guide to clear writing he can remember easily and apply easily. He needs a guide he can also mentally put aside. Such a guide will become integrated into his total writing experience, called up involuntarily when a sentence sounds or looks cumbersome.

THE EASY LISTENING FORMULA

With the need for a simple, practical formula in mind, the author, aided by an IBM 1401 computer, did his doctoral dissertation on the subject of clear writing in television news. From an analysis of 36 network and local scripts, plus stories from six major U.S. newspapers, a total of 152,890 words, a writing formula emerged. It is called ELF, for Easy Listening Formula, but it is also useful to test newspaper copy and any other prose written primarily to communicate information.

The Easy Listening Formula is simply this: *In any sentence, count each syllable above one per word*. Take a second look at any sentence

By permission of Johnny Hart and Publishers—Hall Syndicate, Inc., 1971.

scoring above 20. It may be perfectly clear, but chances are it can be improved by trimming adjectives or adverbs, extracting clauses or dividing into two sentences.

A one-syllable word is not counted: hat, check, girl.

A two-syllable word counts one: bowler, grabbing, hostess.

A three-syllable word counts two: radio, distributes, beautiful, misery.

A four-syllable word counts three: democracy, implausible, conscientious.

And so forth.

It is no accident that, as the words used above as examples are replaced by longer words, we climb the abstraction ladder. We also climb ladders we might call "difficulty" and "infrequency." Put plainly, long words are usually harder to understand than short words—not always, but usually. As Winston Churchill put it, "Short words are best, and old words, when short, are best of all.' One-syllable words are often either familiar verbs, pronouns, function words (the "glue" words which hold content words together), or concrete nouns. Polysyllabic words (like the word "polysyllabic" itself) are often abstract nouns or seldom-used verbs or adjectives. Obviously, there are exceptions to these statements, but language as a whole hews closely enough to the "long-hard, short-easy" pattern to make the *length* of a word a rough guide to its difficulty. One obvious reason for the pattern is our natural tendency to shorten words we use often. Gasoline becomes gas. Telephone becomes phone. Television shrinks to TV.

The Easy Listening Fomula is based on the concept that a sentence is a package for information, and the corollary concept that the information in long words is usually more difficult to absorb. The ELF permits considerable variety in writing. It does not require short, static sentences to produce a pleasingly low score. Here is a sentence with an ELF score of zero: "This is the cow that kicked the dog that chased the cat that killed the rat that ate the malt that lay in the house that Jack built." It is also a clear sentence. Children have delighted in it for ages. Notice that it contains not one abstract noun.

What sends the Easy Listening Formula soaring is a long sentence full of long words. Consider this monstrosity from a book about science. The book was written not for scientists, but for average readers:

> The fatal legacy of science, as it is unfortunately interpreted in contemporary anthropomorphic culture, is the too frequent insistence that the symbols do themselves constitute a logically autonomous and self-sufficient system, and that in the syntactical structure of that system resides the logical reality that has formerly been supposed to subsist in the extra-linguistic entities symbolized by the system.

What does the author mean? Is he saying it's too bad that we depend more on scientific symbols than upon their meanings? If so, why doesn't he say so? This kind of writing—and the above passage is not an isolated example—is dreadful enough when it is set down for readers. A sentence like this aimed at listeners should be drawn and quartered.

To sum up, long words often communicate abstract ideas: capitalism, totalitarianism, communication, psychotherapy. In writing news, we cannot always escape long words. However, when we must get an abstraction across the air waves, we should do so as simply as possible. The abstract information should be sent in "small packages"—that is, short sentences.

Writing is a way to transmit information, attitudes and emotions from one brain to other brains. We may regard television as a medium for information, attitudes and emotions, using writing-read-aloud and pictures. We employ television as our medium because it carries farther than sticking our heads out the window and shouting. What is important is the communication of information, attitudes and emotions—not television, not the means of communicating. Writing, radio, television and shouting are means to communicate, and nothing more. Let us disagree with Marshall McLuhan as concerns news, and say that the medium is not the message. The message is the message. However, if we fail to communicate the message—which is the content of each day's newscast— if we do not get our information across to the viewers clearly so that they understand the news, then we are wasting paper, ink, breath. vocal chords, a great deal of money and everyone's time, including our own.

TIGHT WRITING

Deadwood

Journalism has been called a process of elimination.

If a word isn't needed, omit it. If a sentence adds nothing to the communication of information, omit it. Padding is just a hindrance to thinking. Don't try to write everything there is to say about a person or an event or an idea. You can't do it. And if you could, who would want to hear it?

Despite its masthead, *The New York Times* does not give us "All the news that's fit to print." *The Atlanta Journal* does not "Cover Dixie like the dew." And the radio newscaster does not give us "a complete summary" of the news, whatever that means. "Complete summary" is a contradiction. If it's complete it's not a summary. If it's a summary, it's not complete.

What should you tell in a news story? Tell what is important or interesting, based on your judgment, which derives from your training, skill and experience. Then stop. Do not use a piece of information just because you happen to have it. A news story is not a dumping place for data. Waste baskets were built for that purpose.

Summary or "Throwaway" Leads

A short sentence or a sentence fragment at the start of a broadcast news item acts like a headline. It tells the listener what to expect. It is also a one-sentence lead-in to a silent film story, a billboard at the start of a newscast, or a tease preceding a commercial:

> *A wet finish to the State Fair . . .*
> *Another day in the auto strike . . .*
> *Three accidents are in the news . . .*
> *Today's storm was one for the record books . . .*
> *And school opens tomorrow . . . maybe . . .*

Beware of the forced transition phrase. Because one story follows another does not mean the stories must be connected. Even when a connection exists, the news writer should not feel obliged to write a bridge (or "a coupling pin"). Spare us from cute leads like:

> *A war of a different sort happened here at home when the mayor and the city council tangled over the location of the new airport.*

Don't use question leads. They are acceptable for newspaper feature stories. On the air they sound like introductions to commercials.

"Hey, Fred, listen to this . . ."

Not only is a 5-W lead unnecessary in broadcast copy, it is most undesirable, for it throws a great deal of information at the listener all at once. Equally undesirable is any large and formal assemblage of facts. Veteran broadcast newsmen, professors and textbooks exhort the student and the young journalist to write in a conversational style, but worry as the young writer will, a conversational lead still eludes him.

You might try this mental trick. (It may not work for you, but it's worth a try.) Vocally precede a lead with the phrase, "Hey, Fred, listen to this. . . ." Then read your lead. If the words in your lead sound cumbersome and stiff, rewrite them. You may find that "Hey, Fred (or "Mom" or "Uncle Charlie," if you prefer), listen to this. . . ." is a useful phrase which keeps you from writing awkward leads full of little facts which hardly anyone could care about or remember.

If you preface a story with such a phrase, say it aloud, then read your copy aloud. In any case, read your copy aloud.

On the left is copy which was read on a television newscast over silent film of a school ceremony held outdoors. On the right is a version rewritten in a conversational style and considerably shortened. Read each version aloud, preceding each reading with "Hey, Fred, listen to this. . . ."

Original	*Rewrite*
New facilities at Breck School were dedicated this afternoon in the name of the Reverend Canon F. Douglas Henderson. Canon Henderson is recognized for seventeen years of leadership as rector and headmaster of the school. The new additions to existing facilities included a science hall, library, girls' gym, and hockey arena. Breck is a co-educational college prep school with an enrollment of about 500. The school has often been cited for new innovations in traditional educational methods.	Breck School has a new science hall, a new library, a new girls' gym, and a new hockey arena. And today, they dedicated them. Breck is a co-educational college prep school, with 500 students.

Note that the rewritten version says "they" without revealing who "they" are. In context, especially with film showing who "they are, "they" needs no more elaboration than "it" does when we observe that "it's raining." The original version, fiilled with details viewers will not absorb, reads as if it were written by a publicity man.

COLORFUL WRITING

Clear writing will produce a competent news writer, considering style alone. But by itself, it will not produce a quotable writer. Few things in life give a worker more satisfaction than the praise of his fellows for his workmanship. The journalist is no exception. There is deep satisfaction in having a phrase cited by a co-worker. "Hey, did you hear Charlie's tag on that lost horse story?" Or having the studio crew break into laughter when the newscaster reads a line. Or having them suddenly grow attentive, suddenly grave. (For example, one newscaster was so moved by copy reporting the death of a beloved actress that he was unable to finish reading it. He sat there, on camera, biting his lip until the director went to black.)

The sources of color are many. They should be used sparingly, and they should be built upon the framework of clear writing.

Pungent verbs

These are usually active, not passive, verbs which *describe* what occurred rather than merely *reporting* it.

POOR: A temperature inversion brought eye-burning smog and then heavy fog into the Los Angeles basin Friday, shutting airports and making driving hazardous.

BETTER: Another temperature inversion in Los Angeles. Drivers whose eyes smarted from the smog later had to peer through a gray gloom as heavy fog rolled in. The airports turned away incoming planes.

Narrative treatment

Sometimes David Brinkley succeeds in telling us what happened because he tells what happened first, what happened next, and what happened after that. The wonder of it is that writers don't copy his writing style the way reporters and newscasters copy his delivery. The narrative writing style is as old as "Once upon a time. . . ." which got buried somewhere in the folds of the 5-W lead.

On the left is a silent film story used on the air by one station (with the names changed). On the right, a narrative rewrite.

Original	*Rewrite*
LIVE	**LIVE**
A Lincoln High School student has failed in a bid to get back into school.	Howard Green wants to get back to Lincoln High School. So far, he can't.
FILM	**FILM**
At a meeting this afternoon the County Board of Education rejected an appeal by the parents of Howard Green, who was expelled for allegedly violating school regulations regarding the use of dangerous drugs. Although the youth admitted taking barbiturates, an attorney hired by his parents claims medical tests indicated he had not consumed drugs. The attorney says the parents, Mr. and Mrs. John Green, indicate they will go to court if necessary to get their son reinstated.	The school expelled him for taking barbiturates. Howard admitted it. But his parents hired a lawyer. And this afternoon the County Board of Education heard the lawyer say that Howard did not take drugs . . . and there are medical tests to prove it. The Board thought it over . . . agreed with the school . . . and rejected the appeal. Howard can't return because he broke the rule about taking drugs. But his parents, Mr. and Mrs. John Green, say they aren't quitting. They're ready to go to court to get Howard back into Lincoln High.

Instead of the usual summary lead, the story is told from beginning to end. In the following example—John J. Goldman's byline story on page 1 of the *Los Angeles Times* of January 14, 1967—note also the use of periodic sentences:

NEW YORK, Jan. 13. Patrolmen O'Connor and Keating knew they didn't have much time. Before dawn Friday, minutes before a normally quiet neighborhood in Queens was transformed into an inferno, O'Connor and Keating heard a fantastic, roaring sound rising from under the street.

The policemen radioed for help; then ran, pounding on doors, ringing doorbells, shouting:

"Don't bother to grab anything. Just get out."

And out into darkness, heavy with the odor of gas, raced mothers in bathrobes with babies in their arms and fathers in pajamas, dragging other children behind them.

By now there were other policemen and firemen with bullhorns warning:

"This is an emergency. Everybody out."

Out poured more than 300 residents, some in slippers, women with overcoats thrown over their nightgowns, all running for their lives.

Periodic sentences

Here the normal clause pattern is inverted. The dependent clauses precede the independent clause. The sentence builds, sometimes until the last word. Used often, this construction creates a stilted style which may intrude and irritate. Used cautiously, it can create emotional impact.

Consider one sentence in the example cited above: "And out into darkness, heavy with the odor of gas, raced mothers in bathrobes with babies in their arms and fathers in pajamas, dragging other children behind them."

Several figures of language are used here: the absence of the article "the" before "darkness," the identification of the darkness as "heavy," the hyperbole "raced" instead of "ran" (another effective and perhaps more accurate word might be "stumbled') and the balance of "mothers in bathrobes . . . fathers in pajamas."

Compare the reporter's periodic construction with a standard construction of the same sentence: "Mothers in bathrobes with babies in their arms and fathers in pajamas, dragging other children behind them, raced out into darkness heavy with the odor of gas." Plainly, this sentence lacks the tension of the original.

Metaphor and simile

Metaphors embed themselves in a language. Yesterday's metaphor becomes today's household word and, by a metamorphosis, the only word which will do, the only word which expresses exactly what we want to express. Because words are symbols, because words stand for things, actions, qualities and relationships, we can almost regard language itself as a body of former metaphors. By definition, a metaphor is a word or phrase which substitutes for another word or phrase. A comparison is implied rather than stated, as in a simile, which sets out the comparison with "like" or "as."

Of all stylistic devices, metaphors and similes are probably the best known and most abused:

> Tiger Jones flew out of his corner of the ring like a bulldozer, with that right arm cocked for a haymaker.

It takes imagination to find a fresh metaphor or simile, one which brings the listener an involvement in a mood. That mood might be as somber as a state funeral, as light as a humorous Harry Reasoner commentary, as tense as a battleground on the day before battle, or as pathetic as a battleground on the day after. The metaphors and similes either add to the mood or, by not adding to it, automatically detract from it. In sum, metaphors and similes are too important to be written thoughtlessly. It isn't necessary to use metaphors. It is necessary to avoid stale metaphors, meaningless metaphors. If you want a slogan to hang above your desk in place of THINK, you might consider:

EXPUNGE

CLICHES

> POOR: "Speculation was rampant in local and Eastern financial circles today as to the possibility of a merger between Douglas Aircraft Co. and giant North American Aviation, Inc., of El Segundo."
>
> BETTER: Some financiers here and in the East are saying that Douglas Aircraft Co. may merge with North Aviation, of El Segundo.

The rule for using metaphors and similes should be: Use a figure of speech only if you can justfy using it.

An extended metaphor, or analogy, may sometimes etch a picture the writer wishes to create. For example, a *Newsweek* journalist in a cover story on Harlem Congressman Adam Clayton Powell, extended a metaphor based on a quotation: " 'I am an irritant,' Powell once declared quite accurately, and as such he rubbed great welts of resentment."

Or, consider this example from a KNXT, Los Angeles, newscast: "The Los Angeles County Funeral Directors Association uttered a piercing cry of pain today, claiming it was cut to the quick by Dr. Kildare's scalpel . . . It claims the show portrayed funeral directors as people who try to capitalize on grief . . ."

However, the mixing of metaphors, like the mixing of many colors, produces only a muddy picture. The careless mixing of metaphors is easily found in news writing:

POOR: "A deluge of late selling on the New York stock exchange tumbled prices to their lowest level of the year. The market suffered a similar low blow early this morning and just managed to recover before the second wave of selling hit."

BETTER: A wave of late selling on the New York stock exchange tumbled prices to their lowest level of the year. The market had just managed to recover from an early morning selling wave when the second wave came.

Repetition

Note that the revised version uses "wave" three times. Repetition is a useful writing device, particularly in writing meant for the ear. The idea contained in a word is reinforced by repeating the word. But repeating should be done consciously and with purpose. Repeating a word because you cannot think of another, because it jumped to mind, or because you will not bother to take the time to look in a dictionary or a thesaurus for a better word marks you as careless.

Some sportswriters, among others, go too far in the opposite direction. Nouns and verbs are never repeated. Instead of writing the word "ball" more than once, they will write *sphere, spheroid, pill, apple, melon,* and so forth. Instead of *beat* or *defeated,* we get *downed, dumped. crushed, creamed, slaughtered, smashed, walloped, wiped, flattened, floored, smashed,* and *sneaked past,* all by the score of 3 to 2.

Simplicity

Mark Twain, who was paid by the word, said, "I never write 'metropolis' for seven cents when I can get the same price for 'city'."

The UPI radio manual advises us to:

    send, not transmit or dispatch
    call, not summon
    buy, not purchase
    leave, not depart or evacuate
    act, not take action
    try, not attempt
    arrest, not take into custody
    show, not display or exhibit
    get, not obtain
    need, not require
    see, not witness
    help, not aid or assist
    break, not fracture
    build, not erect or construct
    meet, not confer, convene, or hold a conference.

And don't hold your breath until you hear some kid holler, "Oh, I just sustained a contusion" or "I've suffered an abrasion" or "I've received a laceration." Bruises, scrapes and cuts are *in* these days.

The abstraction ladder

In *Language in Thought and Action*,[1] S.I. Hayakawa uses a cow named Bessie to explain how we abstract words. Near the bottom of the abstraction ladder is the one and only Bessie, the name we give to that particular creature grazing over there, whom we can see and touch and describe from her big brown eyes to the way she switches her tail. If we climb one rung of the abstraction ladder we come to the word "cow." We still have a picture although we have lost some of the characteristics of the cow we call Bessie. Climbing higher, we come to "livestock." That's somewhat blurry. Harder to picture. More characteristics gone. Higher still, we find "farm assets." Next, "asset." Finally, at the top of the abstraction ladder, "wealth." If we try to visualize that, we are forced back down the abstraction ladder, perhaps to a pile of coins.

Sometimes we have to talk about "farm assets" in reporting news, but when we do we should be aware that we are way up on the abstraction ladder. What we are discussing is hard to comprehend, to give form, to put edges around. When we can manage it, we'd do better to write about Bessie.

As examples of how this is done, here are the leads on two front page stories of one issue of *The Wall Street Journal*:

> During the final two nights of last October and the first two of November, four 30-man guerrilla teams led by North Korean Lieutenant Chong Dong-choon slipped ashore on South Korea's rugged and bleak eastern coast. They quickly faded into the mountains.

This story concerned North Korean subversion of South Korea. Do we want to read on? You bet we do.

Here's the second lead:

> DETROIT. Just before dusk on a recent snowy afternoon, a car on the crowded Edsel Ford Expressway near here skidded on a patch of ice. It came to a halt broadside across three lanes of fast-moving traffic. A trailing car plowed into it, followed by another and another.

Again, a narrative treatment and concrete words low on the abstraction ladder carry us into the story. The story begins with just that: *a story*. This story dealt with multiple car collisions and their insurance problems.

If *The Wall Street Journal* chooses to talk to its highly literate readers in short, clear sentences and in terms they can visualize, and if the *Journal* can do so with complex economic and political matters, a broadcast newsman might conclude there is not much information that he cannot offer up just as simply and clearly.

Newspaper reporter Fred Othman advised young reporters: [2]

> Tell about the taste of things and, especially, smells. People like to hear about smells. Both good and bad. Take the man smoking a Turkish cigarette; it smells like burnt chicken feathers. Say so.
>
> Don't write about ideas, or even things, but about the people who have the ideas, or who build (or break) the things. Let the ideas and the things be described, but by all means make them incidental. Get as many personal references into the story as possible.
>
> Conflict between two men is better than conflict between two armies. If the battlers are doing it with words, quote them accurately. Really accurately. If they mangle the language or split infinitives, let them do so in your story; makes 'em sound like humans. Entirely too many people, when quoted, sound like English professors.

A word of caution here, and a plea for charity. True, many people speak in ungrammatical, broken sentences. Probably so do you. If you would like to see your own words quoted so that you sound "human," even if you sound foolish or uneducated, then let the bad grammar of others show. Otherwise, be considerate of the man you quote. Do not read his words so that he sounds ignorant. If you must change a word to make a statement grammatical, then change the word, so long as you don't alter the meaning.

Informality

A primary difference between broadcast writing and writing for print is the conversational style of the former. Within the limits imposed by the need for brevity and clarity in imparting information, the rule for writing for the ear is *write as you talk*. For example:

> "The unsettled conditions in Algeria may well mean a postponement of the 50-nation Afro-Asian summit conference, scheduled to open one week from today in Algiers. And the *up-in-the-air situation* is causing problems for Red Chinese *boss* Chou En Lai, who stopped in Cairo . . then planned to *head to* Algiers for the meeting. Chou is *killing time* until a decision is made on the conference. *He's even* visiting museums . . . and *he'll* probably visit the Pyramids and the Sphynx, too." (ABC News)

In the above example, also observe the frequent use of the conjunction "and"; conjunctions are more common in normal conversation than in formal writing.

Incomplete sentences and truncated words also mark the conversational style. ". . . Much cheaper than a 'copter, too—but six thousand dollars, as compared with 30 thousand." (KNXT News).

Sparkle

We have already observed that a sharp contrast between audio and video elements of a story may create an effective bit of humor. There are other ways to make the viewer smile, to brighten his hour. Learning them is worthwhile, because the day's news report is so often an unrelieved catalog of death and taxes. No one reports about the bus which safely negotiated the hairpin turn.

Obviously, not every story ought to be brightened with a felicitous phrase. If the news is grim, let it remain grim. Where it is not, a touch of sparkle here and there helps. However, too many light touches are worse than none at all, because then the writing intrudes on the story rather than enhances it, and the news report sounds corny, sophomoric.

Here are some sources of sparkle: 1. famous quotes, including poetry, and proverbs; 2. commercial slogans ("I'd rather fight than switch" has been incorporated into dozens of stories); 3. twists on popular movie and song titles; 4. allusions to unrelated but well known news events, historical events, or persons; 5. irony; 6. understatement (less often used than hyperbole, but often more effective); 7. the pun.

Numbers

A City Council meeting might produce this story:

> The City Council last night tentatively approved a Department of Parks and Recreation budget request of $6,500,000 for the coming fiscal year, an increase of $1,250,000 above the current budget.

What meaning does this story have for the milkman, the machinist, the stenographer, or you? Maybe a vague unease, because somebody wants to spend more on something, and taxes will go up for sure. Had the newscaster reading this item said "sixteen million" or even "sixty million" some viewers, perhaps many viewers, would have sat quietly waiting for some news of interest to them. After all, $6,500,000 doesn't have much physical reality. In dollar bills, could you lift it? In quarters, would it fill your living room to the ceiling? How much of that money affects *me*?

Suppose, instead, the City Council meeting produced this story:

> This year, the cost of running the city's parks is, on the average, two dollars and 63 cents for every man, woman and child living here. Next year, it may go to three and a quarter, up 62 cents. The

Department of Parks and Recreation is asking for the increase . . .
and last night the City Council tentatively agreed to it.

Now the milkman, the stenographer, and you have information in a
dosage you can gulp down. Are you getting your $2.63 worth? Are the
parks well tended and is it such a big deal to spend another 62¢ to keep
them from looking scruffy?

Maybe you can personalize even more by naming an average family.
If the federal government announces an income tax hike, and you work
on a station in, say, Louisville, it is cheap and easy to localize the story
by saying, "Kentuckians will pay more when. . . ." There's a better way,
but it takes a little trouble:

"Arthur Simpson, his wife and their two children live in east Louisville on Simpson's weekly take home pay of one hundred 24 dollars and
47 cents. Starting January first, they'll have to manage on one hundred 18
dollars and eleven cents. What happens to the other six dollars and 36
cents? Uncle Sam is taking a bigger bite out of Simpson's paycheck . . .
and mine. . . . and yours. . . ."

It is easy to get enchanted with numbers. Numbers are obvious, and
come easily to hand. "Three men were injured. . ." "A budget of 6 million 500 thousand dollars." . . . etc. But life is more than numbers. Instead
of learning that the City Council approved a record budget of $6,500,000,
the viewer might prefer to learn that the City Health Bureau will have a
little more money to do its job next year, but not enough to add a dormi-
tory to the School of Nursing, while the Department of Sanitation will get
considerably less than it asked for, and will have to do without new garbage trucks.

Obviously, this kind of writing forces the journalist to pay more
attention to the budget statement, make a couple of phone calls and consider what is meaningful to people. A sum like $6,500,000 isn't meaning-
ful to many people. If you heard it on the radio, you'd forget it immediately. You wouldn't care if the budget was $6,500,000 or $7,500,000,
and yet the difference is enough to make you a millionaire. Now you're
interested! Somebody is now talking about making you rich!

The point is, do not use numbers just because you have them at
hand. If the City Council passes a six and one-half million dollar budget,
you must mention that sum in a story about the new budget. But you do
not have to lead with it, and you do not have to limit yourself to it.

The rule here is: *a number which means little to you will mean little
to most listeners.*

The same rule applies to "Three men were injured. . ." This is such
a standard lead that an editor may jump down your throat if you fail to
use it. But it would be more interesting to say that a dump truck filled
with sand took a corner too sharply and tipped over. The three men inside

were taken to the hospital. All three were cut and bruised, and one of them, John Rogers, may have a skull fracture. You cannot get away from numbers, but play down the flood of numeric facts which come your way. Approximate numbers where you can and make them meaningful where you can.

Personalization

The repetition of personal pronouns gives a personal, even an intimate feeling to a piece of copy. Here is a passage from William Manchester's controversial book, *The Death of a President,* New York: (Harper & Row, 1967):

> He was also nervous. He was afraid that later she would regret having gone. He wanted her to enjoy this trip so she would make others. And he was determined that his wife should look her best in Texas. For the first time in their marriage, he asked her what she intended to wear. Dallas especially interested him. "There are going to be all these rich Republican women at that lunch, wearing mink coats and diamond bracelets," he said. "Be simple—show these Texans what good taste really is." So she tramped in and out of his room, holding dresses in front of her.
>
> "If it's so important that I look all right in Dallas," she asked him, "Why do I have to be blown around in a motorcade first?" He explained: Exposure, like patronage, was a source of political strength. You had to be seen. You had to move through crowds. And you had to move slowly.

In broadcast news writing, a degree of personalization is achieved by tying the viewer, the newscaster and the community together by using such pronouns as "we," "us" and "our." For example, it is better to write "The City Council voted to raise *our taxes"* than to write "The City Council voted to raise taxes" or "The City Council voted to raise your taxes." Also: "We are due for some rain tonight"; "The income tax form will not confuse us this year as much as it did last year"; and so forth.

However, newsroom policy decisions guide the use of "our" in the sentence, "Our bombers again hit hard at enemy positions." Some news directors prefer the strictly neutral, "U.S. bombers . . ." or "American bombers. . . ." Other news directors consider the use of "our" in this context to be acceptable.

Prose rhythm

The rhetorical devices which create rhythm must be used sparingly and with discretion in delivering news. Balance, meter, rhyme, alliteration, onomatopoeia are the stuff of poetry. Yet they have been an integral part of great speeches since Demosthenes. The cadence strikes the ear and moves the hearer. In news writing, prose rhythm enhances the story which tugs the heartstrings. Even straight reporting deserves variation in sentence length. And what should be said of writing about the funeral of Winston Spencer Churchill and the burial of John Fitzgerald Kennedy?

Theodore C. Sorenson wrote many speeches for Kennedy, and is probably the author of some of the ringing phrases we recall from the speeches of the late President. In the prologue to his biography, *Kennedy* (New York: Harper & Row, 1965). Sorenson used stylistic devices familiar to those who recall Kennedy's speeches. Here, Sorenson is a reporter and commentator, yet note the employment of contrast and balance, alliteration and metrical flow—in short, style. He uses style to talk about style, to make the point that John Kennedy's style underscored the substance of his message, but that there was more to Kennedy than style. Without calling attention to what he is doing, Sorenson underscores the substance of his own message:

> Most regrettable, in my view, are those memorials and tributes which speak more of his style than of his substance. The Kennedy style *was* special—the grace, the wit, the elegance, the youthful looks will rightly be remembered. But what mattered most to him, and what in my opinion will matter most to history, was the substance— the strength of his ideas and ideals, his courage and judgment. These were the pith and purpose of his Presidency, of which style was but an overtone. I would be the last to diminish the value of his speeches. But their significance lay not in the splendor of their rhetoric but in the principles and policies they conveyed.
>
> During his days at the White House he became weary of hearing the cynics say that his personality was more popular than his program. In his view the two were mutually reinforcing and inseparable. Now the same people—unwilling or unable to perceive the changes he wrought—are writing that his legacy was more one of manner than of meaning.
>
> For still others the tragedy of his death has obscured the reality of his achievements. In emphasizing the youthful promise left unfulfilled, they overlook the promises he kept. His death, to be sure— symbolic though senseless—should never be forgotten. But I think it more important that John Kennedy be remembered not for how he died but for how he lived.

THIS MAN IS NOT SMILING

The headline you've just read is information-less. It tells you nothing you haven't already learned from looking at the picture.

If someone tells you your own name, he again transmits no information: you already know it. He doesn't resolve any uncertainty for you.

This idea—that whatever resolves uncertainty is information—was used by Dr. Claude E. Shannon during his years at Bell Telephone Laboratories to define and measure information for the first time in a way that was usable to scientists. Starting from such basic concepts, Shannon built a theory which has many applications to problems in communication and in other fields. In 1948, he published his classic paper, "A Mathematical Theory of Communication."

Before this there was no universal way of measuring the complexities of messages or the capabilities of circuits to transmit them. Shannon gave us a mathematical way of making such measurements in terms of simple yes-or-no choices—conveniently represented by binary digits, which Dr. John W. Tukey of Bell Labs and Princeton University named "bits."

As a result, we now have a benchmark. We know how much information a business machine, for example, can theoretically produce. We have a means for comparing this with the information of a telephone call or a television program. We have tools to help us design for high quality and high efficiency at the lowest possible cost.

Shannon's quantitative measurement of information is not only invaluable to the Bell System but to scientists and engineers the world over. It is exciting much interest among psychologists and workers in other fields in which information handling is so vital.

AT&T 🔔 **Bell System**
American Telephone & Telegraph
and Associated Companies

Emphasis

An advertisement for the American Telephone and Telegraph Company's Bell Telephone Laboratories several years ago showed a dour man and a headline which read, THIS MAN IS NOT SMILING. The copy claimed that this headline was informationless. "It tells you nothing you haven't already learned from looking at the picture," alleged the ad writer, who went on, "If someone tells you your own name, he again transmits no information: you already know it. He doesn't resolve any uncertainty for you. This idea—that whatever resolves uncertainty is information—was used by Dr. Claude E. Shannon during his years at the Bell Telephone Laboratories to define and measure information for the first time in a way that was usable to scientists."

Shannon's mathematical equations serve as the basis for communication theory. Communications engineers must be forever in his debt. However, the ad writer was quite wrong when he said the headline, quoted above, contained no information. The reason: the ad writer is unable to tell whether the reader has already learned, by looking at the picture, that the man is not smiling. To be sure, if someone asked the reader whether the man was smiling or not, the reader would reply in the negative, possibly accompanied by some choice words about the mentality of the questioner. But the headline called attention to the fact. Without the headline, the fact might have been overlooked.

Let us apply this to television news. Let us identify the man as John Jones, a local banker just arrested for embezzlement. We have either this still or some film of Jones with the same expression on his face. The copy might read:

VIDEO	AUDIO
CU: JONES. 15 SECS.	Jones was obviously unhappy as our camera caught him at this troubled moment in his life. His eyes were slightly bloodshot. His lips were pursed. A worried frown creased his brow. His face seemed to reflect a mixture of anger and despair.

Normally, of course, we do not write such copy. But if we did, can it be said that we offer no information? What we have provided is emphasis. We have taken a small bit of information and, by hammering at it, have driven it home to the television viewers. At least, hopefully we have done so. But chances are if we were to ask the viewers, five minutes later, how Jones appeared, a few might answer, "He looked fine."

Among the dictionary definitions of information are "the telling of something" and "knowledge acquired." For some people, information will not be acquired by being told only once, in passing, along with the thousand other bits of information they will receive in the course of a newscast. They may have to be told again and again, perhaps in different ways. The television journalist can count himself successful if viewers retain just the core of the information he tries to transmit by word and picture. Very few will recall the details.

FOR THE STUDENT

1. Draw up a minimum list of news publications a writer or reporter should read regularly. Defend your choices.

2. Describe a viewer or listener that you, as a broadcast journalist, may be writing for.
3. Write a news story with contrasting audio and video.
4. Newspaper and television news writing styles differ. Why should they?
5. Write a story in inverted pyramid style. Rewrite it in narrative style.
6. Write three news stories observing all the Do's and Don't's in this chapter.
7. Get ELF scores for each sentence of each story. What was your highest single count? What were the story averages?
8. Rewrite the story with the lowest ELF average in order to raise that average markedly. Show each version to a member of your family or a non-college acquaintance. Which version is clearer? Which version does he prefer? Why?
9. Choose an abstract word from one of your leads and build an abstraction ladder. If possible, build it in both directions from your word.
10. Monitor each newscast in your reception area for writing style. Write a short paper comparing them.

8

THE FILM STORY

PEOPLE WATCH TELEVISION news, in large measure, because it brings events in action into their homes. We see and hear naval guns booming, a fighter plane swooping down, a soldier on patrol stepping carefully. We watch a demonstration, a parade. We follow police searching for a lost child or groping through the wreckage of an airliner. We hear and observe the highlights of a speech, a football game.

We do not watch television only to get the latest news. Radio does a better job. We do not prefer television because we want to get all the news: local, national and international. The newspaper does a better job. We do not prefer television for depth of coverage or penetrating analysis. A news magazine usually does it better.

We, as television viewers, benefit from our newscasts because they take us to the scenes of action and show us what is happening and what has recently happened. What we see on the television screen during a newscast can move us more deeply than what we merely hear or read. "A picture is worth a thousand words" applies to a newscast.

An example of the impression that a film story can make occurred with the showing of film from Vietnam of a brief engagement between some attacking G.I.'s and three Viet Cong who chose to dig in and fight, rather than melt away in the swampland. The story, sent by war correspondent Don North, was shown on the ABC network at 11 p.m. on a Saturday night. Because those, in San Francisco and New York, responsible for its cutting and presentation knew that what was on film was strong stuff, the editing was done very carefully and with several long dis-

185

Camera crews have risked their lives many times to get combat footage. Several cameramen have died in battle. Television camera crews burden themselves down with more gear than the soldiers they accompany. And the soldiers may be half their age.

tance phone consultations. Viewers' reactions were immediate and vocal, split about 50-50 between those who thought it should not have been presented and those who felt the film brought home the ugliness of the war as it should be brought home. More viewers phoned about this film than about any film ever presented on an ABC weekend newscast until then. One viewer, a Northridge, California, housewife, was able to recall scene and word in the two minute 15 second film clip almost exactly, and did so in a moving letter:

      I am writing because of something I saw on the ABC Saturday night news.

      It was a film report from Vietnam showing fighting between American and North Vietnamese soldiers. Later the film showed American soldiers dragging a wounded North Vietnamese soldier out of his fox-hole. The Vietnamese was wounded so very badly and his face was twisted in pain. As they dragged him out of the hole, an

American soldier said, "What's the matter, V.C.? Did I hurt you?" He said this in a whiny, sarcastic voice and he reminded me of a school-yard bully whose victim has finally broken down and cried.

A medic did try to save the soldier's life, but he died. Then he was pulled by the feet, his face dragging in the dirt, and thrown into a hole to be buried.

I couldn't believe what I saw and heard and I couldn't believe that every person watching the newscast wasn't as horrified as I was.

What I want to say is this: There doesn't seem to be any hope for this world when man cannot have sympathy for another man's pain and a man's dead body is treated with disrespect. How can God ever forgive us?

I feel that I must say these things to someone.

Thank you for reading this.

This story from a battle zone in Vietnam used words and pictures to create an indelible impression. Obviously, not every story can do the same. Yet the creation of the indelible impression remains the goal. A film story can inform by reaching the emotions rather than the intellect, by touching rather than telling.

An Absence of Detail

From an understanding of this quality of newsfilm, we can draw an important rule for the editing and writing of a film story: *Do not cram a film story full of details.* Unless a viewer has an exceptionally keen mind and pays full attention to the screen, he is certain to have difficulty absorbing a film story containing dozens of minor bits of information in the copy and a succession of varied and "busy" scenes on film. Certainly, most viewers are not likely to be either moved or informed much by such treatment.

One Los Angeles news director regularly reports the funerals of celebrities without any voice-over whatever. The report of an actor's funeral may begin with a still of the actor, a face familiar to everyone. The still is followed by a dissolve into film of the funeral, including close-ups of celebrities who attended. Finally, a dissolve to a card on which is printed the actor's name and underneath, the years of his birth and death. Then a slow fade to black. And from start to finish, music, not lugubrious, but gentle and light. Nothing more. Simplicity.

An example of a story crammed with facts is reprinted below, in the left-hand column, from the City News Service of Los Angeles.[1] Admittedly, the story was not written to be read on the air, but it will serve as an example. The AP version, on the right, is a far better treatment of the same news. (A few hours later, CNS rewrote its original story, improving it considerably.):

3/11/67

LOS ANGELES (CNS) — THE FAST THINKING OF A GREYHOUND BUS DRIVER IS CREDITED WITH PREVENTING A MAJOR TRAGEDY WHEN AN 800-FOOT "RIVER OF GASOLINE" IGNITED FOLLOWING A TRAFFIC ACCIDENT ON THE SANTA ANA FREEWAY.

LOS ANGELES, MARCH 11 (AP) — TWENTY-FIVE PASSENGERS ON A GREYHOUND BUS RAN THROUGH BURNING GASOLINE TO SAFETY LAST NIGHT AS A 15-FOOT WALL OF FLAME RACED TOWARD THEM.

ACCORDING TO BATT. CHIEF CLYDE BRAGDON OF THE COUNTY FIRE DEPT., THE BLAZE ERUPTED FOLLOWING A SERIES OF CRASHES ON THE INBOUND LANES OF THE FREEWAY EAST OF THE WASHINGTON BOULEVARD ON-RAMP SHORTLY AFTER 11 O'CLOCK LAST NIGHT.

POLICE SAID NOBODY WAS INJURED. WITNESSES GAVE THIS ACCOUNT:

THE MASSIVE SCENE OF DESTRUCTION BEGAN WHEN A CAR REPORTEDLY WENT OUT OF CONTROL ON THE RAIN-SLICK FREEWAY, CAUSING SEVERAL OTHER VEHICLES TO SLAM ON THEIR BRAKES TO AVOID THE ERRANT AUTO.

A TANKER TRUCK SLOWED IN HEAVY TRAFFIC ON THE SANTA ANA FREEWAY AND WAS STRUCK BY ANOTHER TRUCK, WRECKING THE TANKER AND SPILLING 1,825 GALLONS OF GASOLINE.

SEVERAL VEHICLES ASSERTEDLY SKIDDED TO A STOP ON THE SLIPPERY FREEWAY, POINTING IN ALL DIRECTIONS. BUT NO DAMAGE OR INJURIES WERE REPORTED.

AN UNIDENTIFIED MOTORIST STOPPED AND SET OUT FLARES TO WARN ONCOMING VEHICLES. A FLARE IGNITED THE GASOLINE. THERE WAS AN EXPLOSION AND FLAMES ROSE AS HIGH AS 20 FEET ALONG 200 YARDS OF THE FREEWAY.

AT THIS POINT, A GASOLINE TRUCK AND TRAILER ENTERED THE FREEWAY FROM WASHINGTON BOULEVARD AND IMMEDIATELY BEGAN TO SLOW DOWN TO AVOID THE TANGLE OF STOPPED VEHICLES.

AS THE GASOLINE RIG BRAKED TO A HALT, A HUGE SOUTHERN PACIFIC RAILROAD SEMI-TRUCK AND TRAILER, REPORTEDLY TRAVELING ABOUT 45 MILES PER HOUR, WAS TO JAM ON ITS BRAKES AFTER SUDDENLY COMING UPON THE SCENE.

AS THE GASOLINE RIG BRAKED TO A HALT, A HUGE SOUTHERN PACIFIC RAILROAD SEMI-TRUCK AND TRAILER, REPORTEDLY TRAVELING ABOUT 45 MILES PER HOUR, WAS TO JAM ON ITS BRAKES AFTER SUDDENLY COMING UPON THE SCENE.

AS IT SLID TO A STOP, THE SEMI-TRUCK CLIPPED THE END OF THE GASOLINE TRAILER, CAUSING AN 1825-GALLON OF FUEL (SIC) TO SPILL ONTO THE FREEWAY. THE SEMI-TRUCK THEN JACKKNIFED INTO A FREEWAY GUARDRAIL.

THE GASOLINE BEGAN FLOWING DOWN THE FREEWAY TO A DRAIN ABOUT 800 FEET AWAY AS OTHER VEHICLES, INCLUDING A GREYHOUND BUS WITH 25 PASSENGERS ABOARD, PULLED TO A STOP.

THE BUS DRIVER, WHO HAS NOT YET BEEN IDENTIFIED, IMMEDIATELY SPOTTED THE DANGER FROM THE ESCAPING GASOLINE AND EVACUATED HIS PASSENGERS. A FEW MOMENTS LATER, A MOTORIST AT THE EAST END OF THE TANGLE PURPORTEDLY PUT OUT FLARES AS A WARNING TO ONCOMING DRIVERS.

ONE OF THE FLARES WAS APPARENTLY TOO CLOSE TO THE DRAIN WHERE THE GASOLINE WAS ESCAPING AND THE FUEL IGNITED, SENDING A RIVER OF FIRE BACK TOWARD THE TANKER AND THE NOW-EMPTY BUS.

SEVEN UNITS OF COUNTY FIREMEN HAS (SIC) RESPONDED AND IMMEDIATELY PUT WATER ON THE FLAMES, PREVENTAN EXPLOSION OF THE REMAINING GASOLINE IN THE TANK TRUCK AND ITS TRAILER.

THE BUS, HOWEVER, WAS COMPLETELY DESTROYED BY THE BLAZE, AS WAS THE FIRST TRAILER OF THE SOUTHERN PACIFIC RIG.

OTHER VEHICLES STOPPED AT THE SCENE, INCLUDING THE CARS INVOLVED IN THE INITIAL MISHAP, WERE HURRIEDLY DRIVEN AWAY AND WERE NOT DAMAGED.

A SIGALERT WAS PUT OUT FOR BOTH SIDES OF THE SANTA ANA FREEWAY, AS THE FIRE AND THICK SMOKE PREVENTED TRAVEL ON THE OUTBOUND LANES.

MEANWHILE, A SERIES OF MINOR ACCIDENTS OCCURRED BEHIND THE FLAMING SCENE AS OTHER CARS WERE FORCED TO COME TO A FAST HALT.

THE DRIVER OF THE LOS ANGELES BUS, WILMER TURNER, BRAKED TO A STOP TO AVOID HITTING THE CRASHED TRUCKS. HE REPORTED:

"I SAW GAS SPURTING OUT OF THE TANKER. I GOT OUT OF THE BUS AND WALKED TO THE REAR AND SAW FLAMES. I RAN TO THE FRONT AND YELLED, 'HEY, ALL YOU CATS, GET OFF.' I NEVER SAW A BUS CLEAR SO QUICK."

THE PASSENGERS -- MOST OF THEM MARINES ON LIBERTY FROM CAMP PENDLETON 60 MILES TO THE SOUTH AND THEREFORE SCHOOLED IN SNAPPING TO AN ORDER -- RACED THROUGH THE FLAMES.

BEFORE FIREMEN EXTINGUISHED THE BLAZE, THE BUS HAD BEEN BURNED OUT, THE TANKER HAD BEEN DAMAGED AND THE OTHER TRUCK'S TRAILER DESTROYED. FIREMEN SAID IT WAS A MIRACLE THAT 2,700 GALLONS OF GASOLINE IN THE FRONT TANK DID NOT EXPLODE.

A WITNESS SAID ONE MAN'S CLOTHING CAUGHT FIRE AS HE RAN TO SAFETY, BUT HE APPARENTLY ROLLED ON THE FLAMES TO EXTINGUISH THEM.

4:40 AM

BATT. CHIEF BRAGDON ISSUED A PRELIMINARY DAMAGE ESTIMATE OF $31,000, INCLUDING ABOUT 150 FEET OF WOODEN CENTER DIVIDER RAIL WHICH WAS DESTROYED BY THE FLAMES.

HE ADDED THAT IT SEEMED ALMOST INCREDIBLE THAT NO DEATHS OR INJURIES OCCURED IN EITHER THE FIRE OR THE CRASHES.

FIREMEN REMAINED AT THE SCENE UNTIL THE
REMAINING GASOLINE FROM THE RUPTURED TRAILER
WAS TRANSFERRED TO ANOTHER TRUCK.

THE FREEWAY WAS CLOSED FOR ABOUT TWO
HOURS UNTIL THE FIRE COULD BE EXTINGUISHED AND
ALL THE WRECKAGE REMOVED.

                          3:59 AM

Facts can be jammed into film also. A picture by itself consists of facts. A close-up of a face tells us several things about the person: sex, age bracket, race, possibly his emotional state, possibly the state of his health. A medium shot gives us a clue to his financial condition and possibly even his place in society (is he a factory worker? a business leader? a student? a "long hair"?). A picture of two boys is "busier" than a picture of one boy. A picture showing two boys carrying placards we can read is "busier" yet. And so on. A shot held for three seconds followed by a different shot for four seconds demands more of viewers than one shot held for seven seconds. Two shots of different scenes demand more of viewers than two shots of the same scene, perhaps a long shot and a medium shot. More information is contained in two shots or two different scenes than in a single shot or a single scene, just as more information is captured in a "busy" shot than in a simple one. And so the rule, *Do not cram a film story full of details,* applies both to copy and to pictures.

As an example of "busyness," Patrick Trese of NBC News said, "We have absorbed from radio the tremendous fear of dead-air. I know one radio station where two men are on the air at the same time. If one pauses for a moment the other leaps in and starts talking. Sometimes they're talking over each other. There is absolutely no dead-air on *that* station. There is also no sanity. More important, for the audience, there is often no clear idea of what they are trying to convey. What happens orally can happen visually, too. If you talk about something that has no relation to the film, the audience will get no clear view of the picture. You will have talked the film to death." [2]

Leaving an Impression

What television news delivers best is impression. A minute of film showing bombers destroying a bridge and a flyer emerging from an air-sea rescue helicopter, when combined with a few facts about yesterday's raids and losses, will leave the viewer with more than he would retain if the newscaster read a long Associated Press dispatch. Viewers would not absorb the myriad details of the dispatch. The newscaster will not have communicated much to them. The many minor facts would bounce off minds dulled by other minor facts of no immediate relevance to their lives. In short, the words would be wasted.

In the following television news story by NBC's Trese,[3] observe how details are used to create an impression, instead of being just a collection of facts:

MORGANFIELD, KY., JOB CORPS

Camp Breckinridge, which is remembered with something less than fondness by thousand of Americans who found a home here in the Army, has been disintegrating in the hills of Western Kentucky since it was closed at the end of the Korean War.

OPEN ON SHOTS OF OLD CAMP
TO TRESE ON CAMERA

A few miles down Highway 60 is the town of Morganfield; population: 3700

This June, the War on Poverty brought the Job Corps to Camp Breckinridge and a few problems to Morganfield, Kentucky.

SOF: NEWSPAPER PUBLISHER.

Eventually, there will be two-thousand school dropouts at the Job Corps camp; but not many will visit Morganfield. "The boys spend their free time in nearby Evansville, Indiana--across the Ohio River--

GENERAL SHOTS OF MORGANFIELD

(There is not much action in Morganfield, Ky.)
If there was to be any sort of racial trouble it would have developed between the community and the Job Corps staff members—some of whom are Negro college graduates: not at all like the 400 Negroes whose families have lived in this paternalistic town for generations.

Morganfield is one of those small, bland American towns that exists because of the farms that surround it.

Hogs and cattle and corn have been bringing good prices lately; there has not been a crop failure for years; and so Morganfield has been enjoying a quiet, commonplace prosperity.

SOF: NEWTON MILLER

Every morning at nine o'clock, the unassuming, prudent men who maintain the status quo gather at Bee's Restaurant. Here, they debate--and solve--most local problems of government and commerce . . . over a cup of coffee or a bottle of Doctor Pepper's.

The Job Corps did not rely entirely on the persuasive powers of its community relations director. It spent money.

Local contractors were employed to help renovate the camp's old buildings. More than one hundred local people were hired to handle clerical chores and to work with the trainees.

The permanent staff soon numbered more than 400 adults--both white and Negro--and some of the payroll could be expected to reach the shops and restaurants of Morganfield.

The prudent men who lead Morganfield heard the
message quite clearly.

SOF: VARIOUS PEOPLE.

Last month, Morganfield, Kentucky, had its first civil
rights rally. It is noteworthy that it was directed not
against discrimination in the town but against alleged
discrimination in the Job Corps' hiring policy.

SOF: RALLY.

Since the rally, the Job Corps had its own internal
troubles--including a mess-hall brawl that resulted in
ten injuries and several expulsions.
But none of this damaged the relationship established
between the Joh Corps and the town.

The Job Corps is gradually changing the way of life in   CLOSER
Morganfield, Kentucky. There has been grumbling; tradi-   TRESE ON CAMERA
tional prejudices remain. But there has been no serious,
organized opposition. The leaders of Morganfield have
managed to lead their community through a difficult period
of transition, without incident.
Ten years ago, this would have been a different story.

Patrick Trese, NBC News, reporting.

To sum up, the experienced television writer uses just a few key
facts. He aims to give viewers an understanding of what has happened.
Call it a feeling or an impression. He leaves them with something they
can absorb. If he gave them a lot of names and numbers, they would recall nothing.

Yet another aspect of content must be observed. Except for major
news, most of the longer television news items are visual. Given a choice
between a 30-second report about a budget item being approved and a
30-second film about a fatal accident, most television stations show the
accident footage. Remember, television news is not newspaper news read
aloud. Of course, news judgment should always be the deciding factor. If
the television news editor decides the budget item has wide significance, it
ought to be aired, film or no film.

Visual impact is also weighed within a story. For example, given the
choice of a 30-second on-camera report of the judge's charge to the jury
or a 30-second film of the pretty defendant walking into the courtroom,
the walk wins every time in television. The newspaper will not mention
the walk, but instead will report the judge's charge to the jury. There is
good reason for the television editor's decision. If the newscaster reports
the judge's words, chances are that Mr. and Mrs. Viewer will sit there
unmoved, unless Mrs. Viewer starts rummaging around for her knitting
and Mr. Viewer heads for a beer in the refrigerator. But if the film of the
good looking defendant appears, you can bet Mr. Viewer will not be
thinking about a beer, and Mrs. Viewer is apt to comment that that

woman has guilt written all over her face, and besides is getting hippy. Both will be glued to the set.

People are like that. And who can say with certainty that the charge to the jury is more important than the defendant's wiggle? On a scale of importance, if a scale could be drawn in the first place, the entire trial would doubtless rank too low for consideration.

TYING COPY TO PICTURES

The copy and the film will either reinforce each other by carrying related information, or they will compete with each other for the viewer's attention. When this happens, the picture usually wins out. The viewer will recall what he saw, not what he heard. In most cases, this means he will have lost the central fact and the important details of the story. From this, we can draw our second rule of writing and editing a film story: *Relate words and pictures.*

The relationship should be indirect. An experienced writer does not say, "We are now looking at . . ." or "This picture shows . . ." Instead, he reinforces the picture by directing the viewer's attention to whatever is significant in the picture in terms of the story. For example: "On the hillside, a charred and battered helmet was one of the few indications that a battle had been fought here." Or, "The unexpected sunshine drew people to the city's parks."

Television copy must do more than relate to the pictures. Copy must tell the story. Words fill in the factual details pictures omit. But the writer can relate his copy to his pictures while he tells the story. For example, the copy which goes with a seven-second shot of a burned-out store front might read: "The fire then spread northward to the Acme Hardware store. It gutted the store. The estimated loss: 50 thousand dollars."

In rare instances, the writer may want to call attention to something on film before the audience sees it. If the event is startling and happens very quickly or happens in one corner of the picture, the writer may decide to alert the audience in advance to make sure they do not miss the event and will understand what they are about to see. For example: "As the police searched the alley, the suspect suddenly ran from behind a garage and disappeared over a fence. Watch the garage in the upper right hand corner . . . (PAUSE). Officers ran after him. They caught him crouching against the side of a house two blocks away."

The writer must be careful in using this approach, for the story can easily appeared staged. Advance warning can also make the newscaster seem calloused to the violence which may be about to occur. In a film story from Vietnam a television cameraman included a shot of a soldier being wounded by a mortar shell. The cameraman happened to be pointing his camera at a soldier some ten yards distant when the shell exploded. The reporter on the scene later did a "double chain" narration which contained a sentence alerting the audience to watch the soldier being wounded. An editor wisely struck out this part of the narration, replacing it with a "slug"—a piece of blank leader. The result was more effective and in much better taste—a pregnant pause in the narration, which in itself focused the viewer's attention to the scene. The mortar blast surprised the audience as much as it did the cameraman who happened to shoot it.

The following example from a KABC-TV News, Los Angeles, broadcast shows how film, still pictures and even pasted-up record album jackets can be combined to create a television news story, with the copy not only flowing smoothly, but matching each picture element and introducing each piece of film. Notice, too, that this news story, running approximately three minutes, uses three clips of sound film, both positive and negative, two silent lead-ins and one silent tag, plus seven cards.

CARD:JONES PIC	The death of Spike Jones, the maker of madcap music and zany sound effects, was due primarily to emphysema . . . a respiratory affliction. He died, at home, shortly after midnight following a long siege of respiratory trouble.
CARD:GROUP	Spike Jones and the City Slickers were famous during the 40's and 50's with recordings of "Cocktails for Two" which featured breaking glass and hiccups . . . and "My Old Flame" . . . backgrounded with sirens.
:06 SIL LEAD IN (GARNER)	The men he worked with have remained his friends. Mousie Garner was a member of the band. . and the butt of many of Spike's jokes.
:20 SOF	SOF
SUPER: GARNER	ENDS: ". . . great fellow."
:06 SIL ROLL THRU (BARTY)	Billy Barty joined Spike Jones in the early 50's. He was stunned by news of the bandleader's death.
:52 SOF	SOF
SUPER:BARTY	
	ENDS: ". . .really."
	MORE
:13 SIL (THOMAS)	As the news traveled, Spike's old friends began arriving at his Bel-Air home . . . . among them, Danny Thomas . . . . Thomas muttered, "What can one say?" He was greeted at the door by Jones' youngest daughter, 6 year-old Gina Marie.

ACADEMY LEADER TO
NEXT PART

CARD: ALBUM #1

CARD: ALBUM #2

:22 SOF POS: ("FIREMAN"
             CLIP)

AT CUE PUNCH. SLOW
DISSOLVE TO CARD:
PIC AND DATES.

Jones, who called himself "the dandruff in long-haired music" punctuated his arrangements with hiccups, burps, dog barks, cannons, kitchen utensils, and cow bells . . . and his public loved it. Later, in his career, he brought his special kind of madness to the movies . . . There was "Stop, Look and Laugh". One of his greater ilm successes was "Fireman, Save My Child."

SOF IS ALL MUSIC

Spike Jones, whose real name was Lindley Armstrong Jones, leaves behind . . his wife, singer Helen Grayco, and four children.

Here is another script used on the air, by KNXT, Los Angeles. This time, observe how a reporter, Paul Udell, on camera in the studio is assisted in telling the story by a meshing of sound and silent film with a slide and "supers."

TOTAL FILM 3:21
SIL NEG :35
STUDIO AUDIO UDELL
DISSOLVE AT :05 TO
SLIDE OF SLAIN POLICE-
MAN

BACK TO FILM AFTER
FIVE SECONDS.

This is where an Alhambra policeman lost his life today. Sergeant George Davis, thirty-five, married, the father of two small boys.

His blood was spilled fatally here outside this Alhambra Savings and Loan Company in the six-hundred block of East Main Street. This morning, two armed men walked inside, forced employees to help them gather up about ten-thousand dollars. Upstairs, a bank official heard the noise, and summoned police, while the vault was being robbed.

Officer George Davis was first on the scene, and the robbers decided on a hostage.

SOF 1:22 MAG NEG
SUPER: DAVIS

SOUND UP . . . "There was a wee bit of"
SOUND OUT . . . "And then I was shoved right down beside em."

SIL NEG :04

Meanwhile, another Alhambra officer had arrived on the scene.

SOF :53 MAG NEG
SUPER: HOSTAGE

SOUND UP . . . "Well, as I arrived."
SOUND OUT . . . "And by that time the suspects had driven east on Hidalgo Street."

SIL NEG :24
STUDIO AUDIO UDELL

This is the getaway car, found a few blocks away at Grand and Granada, where the suspects crashed into a tree. Found critically wounded inside was a man identified as Edgar Ball Weaver of Los Angeles, on parole from Chino where he served a robbery term.

Police and FBI agents began a house-to-house search which continues for the other suspect who, they believe fled on foot.

DISSOLVE TO STILL OF
   SUSPECT AT END OF
   FILM

He is identified as Jesse James Gilbert, alias James Mansfield and Henry Gatum. . an escapee from Folsom Prison where he was serving a burglary term. Police identify him as the man who fired the bullet which killed officer George Davis.

TELL IT THE WAY IT HAPPENED

Our third rule of writing and editing a film is: *Carry the viewer into the story.* (See also *Narrative treatment* in Chapter 7, WRITING.)

The family sitting at home in front of the television set tunes into a newscast because they want to learn—and see—what has happened in their community and in the world beyond. They are not tuning into "I Love a Mystery." While artistry belongs in newscasts, artfulness does not. The cunning news item which begins with a big close-up and does not settle down for 30 seconds may be the delight of the writer, but it will bewilder the viewer, who should never have to say after a story, "Now what was that all about?"

Unlike the inverted pyramid structure of newspaper stories, the television news story should be chronological, usually but not always after an opening summary of the main facts, and somewhat conversational. Consider a normal telephone conversation in which an item of news is related:

"Hello, Maud. This is Agnes. Jim just came home and told me the bank was robbed. It was two of them, with stockings over their heads and they got 18 thousand dollars. That's right. I said 18 thousand dollars. It happened just before the bank closed. Jim says these two guys pushed their way into the door just as the guard was about to lock it. They waved guns around and made everyone lie on the floor. Jim says one of them pointed his gun at everyone while the other one went around to the tellers' windows and began shoveling money into a shopping bag, coins and all—and endorsed checks. Jim was scared to death and he said a couple of the girls were crying until the fellow holding the gun went over to them and told them to shut up. They didn't try to get into the vault. I guess they were afraid somebody might have rung the silent alarm. Jim says the whole thing didn't take two minutes. The two guys ran out and jumped in a car and took off. I think the police threw up roadblocks. Anyhow, they got away, so far. Thank God nobody was hurt."

The structure of Agnes' narrative is essentially the structure of a television news story. The lead is contained in the first two sentences, for the essential facts are that the bank was robbed of $18,000 by two gunmen wearing stocking masks. The rest is chronological narrative. Had anyone been injured, you can bet that Agnes would have mentioned it in the beginning, "Jim just came home and told me the bank was robbed and old Mr. Peabody was hit so hard over the head that he's in the hospital."

A newspaper reporter might write the following story about the robbery:

> Two stocking-masked bandits held up the First National Bank, 212 Oak St., at 3 p.m. yesterday, escaping with an estimated $18,000.
>
> Police and state highway patrolmen set up roadblocks on all roads leading from the city, but as of last night the gunmen had eluded the police net.
>
> The loot was in bills, coins and negotiable checks scooped into a shopping bag from the cash drawers of the bank's six tellers' windows.
>
> No attempt was made by the bandits to enter the vault, which was closed but not yet under the time-locking device that prevented its being opened until morning. Police theorized that the bandits ignored the vault, containing an additional $56,000 because of fear that a teller might have set off a silent alarm, bringing officers before the pair had time to get away.
>
> The hold-up began at 3 p.m., as guard Sam Peabody, 62, 3412 Lincoln Ave., was locking the front doors. Two men, wearing nylon stockings over their heads to distort their features, shoved their way through the door . . . (Etc.)

The newspaper story is chock-a-block with facts. Until we are well into the story, we find no chronological organization. Quite the contrary. Some of the latest news is at the beginning. This is good newspaper and wire service practice, for a fresh lead can be written without having to change the entire story and perhaps reset an entire galley of type.

However, it is not a good broadcast news story. The way Agnes tells it is more interesting and more like broadcast news in structure. The television viewer finds himself in the role, here, of Maud, who must listen to the story from beginning to end rather than in the role of the newspaper reader, who can skip to another news item at any point in this story.

In summary, the television news story should be chronological after the lead, interesting, clear, devoid of unrelated details (like the age and address of the guard) and somewhat conversational (not chatty, of course).

The film which accompanies the story should be cut to match the copy, but should also make some sense by itself. Opening on a tight shot of a teller's empty drawer is cute and artful but it is not clear, unless the copy says something like: "Two hours ago this drawer held three thousand dollars in bills, coins, and negotiable checks. There are five other drawers like it." (CUT TO MONTAGE OF EMPTY DRAWERS). But even with this explanation, the viewer remains puzzled. Some viewers may never catch up.

Here is a standard treatment, which tells the story without fuss or fancy dressing:

VIDEO	AUDIO
LS: BANK EXTERIOR	Two bandits --wearing nylon stockings over their faces -- held up the First National Bank, and got away with about 18 thousand dollars.
MS: BANK FRONT DOORS	They forced their way past a guard who was locking the doors at the 3 o'clock closing hour.
LS: BANK INTERIOR	The masked bandits ordered customers and employees to lie face down on the floor.
MS: TELLERS WINDOWS	Then, while one bandit held a gun on everyone, the other cleaned out the tellers cages.
CU: EMPTY DRAWER	He went from drawer to drawer with a shopping bag, filling it with bills, coins and negotiable checks.
MS: TWO WOMEN TELLERS	At one point, his partner walked over to two young women tellers who were lying on the floor weeping, and ordered them to keep quiet. He did not touch them.
MS: VAULT DOOR	The bandits wasted no time on the locked vault, which holds 56 thousand dollars.
MS: POLICE, BANK PERSONNEL	They may have been afraid a teller had rung the silent alarm to summon police.
LS: REAR VIEW, BANK INTERIOR, FRONT DOORS IN BACKGROUND	It took the pair about two minutes to gather up the esti- mated 18 thousand dollars, and run out of the bank to a waiting car.
MS :POLICE IN BANK	Police have thrown up highway roadblocks.
MS: MARY ANN BEASLEY SOUND-ON-FILM INTER- VIEW WITH MISS BEASLEY	Mary Ann Beasley was on of the tellers who was ordered to stop crying.

Which version does this television story most closely approximate, the one given by Agnes or the one written by the newspaper reporter?

Notice that the choice of film shots carries us steadily into the story, starting with an establishing exterior shot. No scene is out of place or likely to confuse the viewer. Notice, too, that each shot matches the copy accompanying it, and that the story is told as it happened, following the summary lead. The story as a whole may be compared to a ladder. The two sides, video and audio, run parallel to each other and are joined at every rung—every scene.

MAKING CONNECTIONS

Our fourth general rule for telling a film story is: *Cut the film to establish relationships.*

The famous Russian film maker Serge Eisenstein taught that the joining of two pieces of film results in three ideas: the ideas in each piece of film and the idea in their relationship. An example of how this can operate is offered by Marty Smith, of Capital Film Laboratories, Washington:

> "Visualize a film of a train coming into a station, requiring about 30 seconds to chug in and stop. It has little intrinsic meaning and is too long. So I must cut it somehow. This I do by cutting in three shots from stock footage of a girl watching the train come in. By doing so, I actually shorten the film and change it by introducing a relationship. The secret of the power of motion pictures is this human need to relate things. Before, you had a train and a girl. They meant only themselves. Cut together, the two are related and a third meaning arises. In reality, they were not together at all. But relating them in the eye of the viewer gives them a brand new meaning unto themselves." [4]

Most news films seem to need cutaways. And most cutaways seem to be hackneyed: a camera rolling, a bank of cameras, a reporter's poised pencil, or a soundman's "pot." These are familiar cutaways for interviews and news conferences. We have seen them a thousand times already, and are likely to see them a thousand more. More imaginative cutaways are available. The subject of the interview has ideas to express. He is talking to people. Why not show people? Perhaps a cluster of them are standing to one side, listening. Perhaps the cameraman can get back far enough with a wide angle lens to relate the subject to the entire room, or at least to the reporter.

There have even been instances when an editorial decision was made to throw away the film story, at least in its conception, in favor of a short, humorous feature consisting of cutaways. Robert Brennan of CBS News once produced a "What's Going on Here?" story out of film submitted of a man in a "Buck Rogers" rocket suit entertaining a crowd. The film showed very little of the take-off, but lots of the crowd. By cutting it to emphasize reactions rather than the event itself, Brennan presented an imaginative little newscast item.

A similar result was obtained by Los Angeles station KNXT using a still picture mounted on a card, enabling a studio camera to pan across it, and a slide:

STILL: NIXON FACES (pan across from left to right on individual faces only— don't take cake)	Nixon, now a New York lawyer, spent part of the day going through a series of facial calisthenics. To the uninitiated, the grimaces and puckerings might have been confusing, not to say mystifying, but there was an explanation.
SLIDE: NIXON & CAKE OFF SLIDE	It was his 51st birthday, and he was merely doing what everyone does on his birthday, blowing out the candles on the cake.

With the rare exception of a scene which is intrinsically shocking, news film should not be spliced to jar the viewer, or to puzzle him. It may be demanding too much to say that film should tell some semblance of a story even without sound, but this is an ideal which ought to be kept in mind. For example, without words, we make some sense out of the following order of silent scenes:

1. Long shot of an accident scene.
2. Medium shot of one damaged car.
3. Medium shot of another damaged car.
4. An injured man lies on the ground.
5. An ambulance arrives.
6. The injured man, again.
7. Ambulance attendants walk; camera pans, discovers man.
8. Spectators look.
9. Man is put into ambulance.
10. Medium long shot of policeman directing traffic around accident.
11. Medium shot of ambulance pulling away.

Now suppose we eliminate the opening long shot. We do not establish the scene. The result is a slight bewilderment. We see two damaged cars. Are we in a junkyard? We see a man lying on the ground. What is he doing there? A little later we will figure it all out, but we may still be unsatisfied because we have not seen the relationship between the other pieces of film which the opening shot gives us.

Understanding the need for relating scenes is basic to the cameraman, the reporter, the writer and the film editor, permitting the viewer to see news film that was put together to produce clarity instead of confusion.

The opening long shot and the closing shot should run at least five seconds each. Seven seconds might be better. On the air, if the director up-cuts the start of a film story with a three-second opening scene, or jumps out early from a three second closing scene, the viewer only sees one or two seconds of the scene, and that is inadequate at the opening and jarring at the close. Both events happen often enough for the film editor to take the simple precaution of adding two or three extra seconds to both the first and last scenes. Besides, at the start, many viewers will need those extra seconds to absorb the establishing scene. As for the last shot, Hollywood tradition has accustomed us to the long fadeout.

FOR THE STUDENT

1. How could film of an accident scene detract from a viewer's understanding of what happened?
2. Without telling him why, have a friend watch a newscast while you monitor, noting which stories had film or other visuals. After it is over, ask him to recall as many of the stories as he can in as much

detail as he can manage. Is there a correlation between visuals and those news items which left an impression?

3. As an exercise, script a film story without copy, except perhaps for a title or super cards. Assume you have any silent or sound film you want. For example, script the funeral of a famous man, a world series game, or a campaign stop by a candidate for President.

4. Repeat the exercise, writing no more than three sentences. Let the film carry the story.

5. Again assuming you have any film scenes you want, script a film story using a front page story in today's newspaper.

6. Script a humorous film story based on cutaways. Use music, if you wish.

7. Script a story based on stills and graphics, assuming you can use any photo or drawing you wish. Story suggestions: a rise in the cost of living, the first day of summer, the anniversary of the death of President John Kennedy.

8. Monitor each local newscast you can receive. Record your impression of the way that voice-over copy and film are tied together.

9. Rewrite an inverted pyramid newspaper story in chronological style. Include the film shots which ideally would accompany the text.

10. Edit some old television news scripts to eliminate pointless detail and verbosity.

9

THE LEAD-IN

ALMOST ALL THE meaningful sound in a sound-on-film (shortened to the initials SOF in scripts) clip is talk. For convenience it will be assumed here that the "intro" to an SOF clip is an introduction to someone saying something.

The "intro," or "lead-in," may be:
1. A newscaster on camera.
2. A newscaster on camera with an RP (rear projection) still or freeze frame.
3. A still (card or slide) photo, map, cartoon, title card or prop.
4. Silent film.
5. Sound film with the volume lowered in the control room, so that the sound serves as a background to the newscaster's voice.
6. A "standupper" by the reporter who covered the story.

While each of these methods has its place, some are more desirable than others. A newscaster is more interesting to watch when he has an RP behind him. "Sound under" film is preferable to silent film. And film is usually preferable to a still photo. Nevertheless, a mix of all these methods is probably best of all, based on the adage that variety lends enchantment. But with the exigencies of time, available materials and a limited budget, a television journalist must temper what he would like to do with an awareness of what he can do. Let us consider each method in turn.

ON CAMERA

Going directly from a newscaster to a piece of sound film is weak, but sometimes unavoidable. This method is usually limited to small stations with a paucity of resources. Yet a news director anywhere has little option but to accept the abrupt cut to sound film if the sound film arrived late from the lab or on video tape (technically no longer film, but it will be so regarded in this context), if it contained no usable silent film, and no stills are available for RP's.

Rule: *The newscaster should introduce the story as if no film were to follow.* Unless he has some special reason for referring to the film (e.g., "We were fortunate to get . . ." or "The prime minister of Communist China made his first appearance before cameras in . . ."), the newscaster's lead-in to sound should ostensibly ignore the SOF which is to follow. He should not say, "This is what the mayor said about new taxes" or "Here is the mayor," and he should especially avoid unfinished sentences, such as, "The mayor declared . . ." The reason is simple: film does not always appear when you want it to appear. Even the best run newscasts occasionally suffer the embarrassment of a three-second pause between the newscaster's last word and the mayor's first word. Three seconds is a long time to leave a newscaster "with egg on his face." Yet without film to cut to, the director has no choice but to stay with the newscaster or, what is worse, go to black. Three seconds delay makes a newscast seem amateurish if the newscaster has introduced film with something like, "The mayor declared. . . ."

It is far better simply to let the film appear after the newscaster has prepared us with background information in the same way he would report any story. For example, "Mayor Tolliver said that the city may be forced to impose a hotel-motel bed tax. The prospect of a higher city budget led to the mayor's statement. It drew immediate opposition from the Chamber of Commerce. The mayor spoke at this morning's City Council meeting." The viewer is now prepared to hear the mayor, and even a Chamber of Commerce official whose statement is "butt-ended" to the mayor's statement, provided the official is identified by a super. The mayor should also be identified by a super. Should the film be delayed, the newscaster will not look foolish. Even if the film breaks in the projector—which also happens sometimes—the newscaster sometimes can go on to the next story, or fill with pad copy, without the need to apologize.

Here are some examples of lead-in copy used on the air. In each case the last sentence of copy was immediately followed by someone talking, someone who in most instances was identified in the final intro sentence. Some of this copy was read over silent film, some over sound-under film and some by a newscaster on camera, with or without an RP behind him.

In June, one of the most savage battles of the Vietnamese war was fought at Dong Xoai 60 miles north of Saigon. Nearly a thousand soldiers and civilians died, and much of the village was destroyed. Garrick Utley, who reported on the battle, has revisited Dong Xoai.

Indianapolis winner Sam Hanks--offical starter of today's 3-hour cross country navigational race in Los Angeles. 45 blind teenagers from the Braile Institute guided drivers after interpreting course instructions from the Braille System for the blind, One of the navigators . . . . Jerry Arakawa . . . .

Just in from Oakland: a filmed interview by reporter Roger Grimsby with Secret Service Chief Tom Hanson. His agents just cracked the biggest counterfeit ring ever uncovered in the West. They grabbed bags containing two million dollars in bogus bills of excellent quality.

Tomorrow at noon, the 35 foot yawl Viking will sail from Redondo Beach harbor bound for Hawaii. This afternoon we spoke with the pleasure craft's owner, John Brockman, about the trip.

. . . At a ceremony in the East Room today President Johnson called the three tax measures the mark of vigorous new philosophy in fiscal affairs. And he gave that philosophy credit for keeping an unprecedented peacetime expansion going. But he warned the full impact of the tax reduction won't be felt unless business passes it along and unless prices and wages remain stable.

. . . . The White House festival is unprecedented and has been well received by the artistic community. Former Ambassador George Kennan addres'sed a group at luncheon.

Gorgeous beauty contestants from Los Angeles gathered at the International Hotel this afternoon to compete for the title of Miss South Los Angeles. . . part of a run-off for the title, Miss California. Our cameras were on hand as the judges announced their decision.

. . . . The Secretary was speaking at the State Department, as he predicted mounting casualties for America's combat troops in Vietnam.

(AFTER ESTABLISHING SILENT FILM)
This little 3 year old girl is able to walk again after successful heart surgery at Loma Linda University Hospital. She was given a going away party today by hospital officials and members of the Heart Fund Volunteers. Little Afahan Zafar and her father are from Pakistan and came to this country in a final effort to save her life. The story has a happy ending.

The copy which leads into an SOF statement should not give away what will be said. To use the earlier example, if the mayor, on film, will say, "It is my reluctant conclusion that a hotel-motel bed tax is the only way to avoid adding to the heavy tax load of the already overburdened home owner," then the lead-in should not steal the mayor's thunder. It should not baldly state that "Mayor Tolliver said that the city may be forced to impose a hotel-motel bed tax." Rather, the copy should "set up" the statement. For example. "At the City Council meeting this morning, Mayor Tolliver proposed a new tax . . . one which immediately drew an angry reply from the Chamber of Commerce and from hotel owners. The mayor's proposal: a tax on travelers, visitors and people who come to the city for conventions." The mayor now appears on film to use the term "hotel-motel bed tax."

REAR PROJECTION

Not all television news studios are equipped with rear projection facilities. Even fewer use Chromakey, a color-keyed rear projection system which accomodates not only stills, but shows films, videotape and live transmission in color on the screen behind the newscaster, who must be careful not to wear a blue shirt or suit, for it will appear to have vanished.

All rear projection screens project still slides, which can be made with a polaroid camera mounted on a rack, using positive transparency film. The film can be produced quickly in the newsroom, snapped into plastic slide frames, and later stored for re-use. (See Chapter 14, STILLS.)

The studio director must establish his cameras so that the newscaster is close to the RP, yet does not obscure any significant element of it with his head. If the director has a free camera, he should set it up for a dissolve from a wide shot of the newscaster and the RP to a tight shot of the RP alone. The person in the newsroom who makes the slides ought to know the relationship of newscaster to RP screen. If the newscaster sits to the

Rear projection techniques combined with telephone and microphone hookups allow the newscaster to speak with the person on the screen behind him. Above, ABC commentator Howard K. Smith waits for the chance to engage in direct conversation with outgoing Alabama Governor George Wallace and incoming Alabama Governor Lurleen Wallace on election night, 1966.

left of the screen, the slide maker should reverse any profile pictures which face right, away from the newscaster. If the newscaster's head blocks most of the lower left quadrant, the slide maker must be sure no RP map contains an important element in that corner. The same care must be taken in the Chromakey process, which permits any electronic image to appear behind the newscaster. Of course, no picture containing words may be reversed, because the words would appear backwards.

No slide should be "busy." If the story concerns the death of a literary figure, and the only picture available shows him in the company of four other people, it may be advisable to cut him out of the picture and photograph him against a light gray background. A map "moved" (transmitted) on the wirephoto facsimile machine usually needs to be redrawn to remove most of the detail.

If the SOF to follow is a statement by, say, the British prime minister, the slide maker should not use an old library still of the prime minister as his lead-in. The prime minister probably looks older on film, has removed his spectacles and his overcoat, and is wearing a different tie. The old still, in short, looks like an old still. Much better: draw a map of the area the prime minister is discussing, such as Rhodesia or Britain itself, or use a photo, if the prime minister is discussing a person.

Again, the copy should neither refer directly to the film which follows nor should the newscaster repeat the thoughts or words on film. The newscaster must make reference to the RP and he should do so in the first sentence, but the reference should be oblique, never anything like, "This is the French foreign minister" or "We are looking at a map showing . . ." unless some special reason exists for calling attention to the RP. That might occur if, for instance, the map were a newly discovered treasure map, or the photograph showed a million dollars worth of Spanish doubloons. Even then, direct reference is not absolutely necessary.

As an example, let us suppose this is the day that Britain was accepted into the Common Market, and that a statement announcing this news was received by television stations either on film or videotape. A news director might order a map showing Britain and the Common Market nations, all in border outline. The names of the countries would be on the maps, but nothing else. No other countries would be shown. The copy could read: 'Britain today joined the Common Market. After ten years of dickering to enter the economic union of six nations across the English Channel, Britain was accepted. Prime Minister Edward Heath informed Parliament, then told his nation via the BBC."

This story can be written a dozen different ways. The foregoing version is just one of them. The newscaster immediately talks about what we see on the map. He then prepares us for the prime minister by naming him and his subject matter, but we are not told we are about to hear the prime minister nor—presumably—does the newscaster use the words of the prime

For a commentary during the Democratic National Convention, Howard K. Smith sits in front of a sketch of the Democratic donkey, with the important convention issues set out plainly. The essence of the backdrop is humor and simplicity.

minister. However, since the prime minister's announcement is of such importance, the newscaster may sensibly waive the rule about not announcing what the man on film will announce, as long as the newscaster's copy does not repeat the same phrases. *Writing is an art, not an exact science, and its rules may be broken if reasons for breaking the rules outweigh the reasons for keeping them.*

STILL PHOTOS, MAPS, CARTOONS AND PROPS

Rules which apply to RP's also apply to pictures and drawings which fill the television screen. A news program which lacks RP projection facilities may show still pictures and drawings either by making slides from the originals or by pasting the original photos and drawings to cards. The cards are placed on a stand, and a studio camera transmits them through the electronic system. If two studio cameras are available, as they would be in a three-camera program, electronic dissolves can create useful and pleasing montages.

The cheapest, simplest and quickest way to put a picture on the air is to slap some paste on its back, stick it to a card and place it in front of a studio camera.

Creating a montage is neither simple nor quick, nor is it especially cheap. As noted above, it can be done in a studio using two cameras. However, two cameras are not always available, and the opportunity for sloppiness is ever present. If time permits, a better method utilizes a motion picture camera, preferably a reflex camera. The camera is fixed in position. The stills are mounted on a rack which moves forward, backward and, if possible, up, down, left and right. The camera must be set for single framing; that is, adjusted so that it can expose only one frame at a time. It must also be possible to back up the film to permit double exposures. With these tools, a cameraman can create beautiful montages which could only be matched with expensive animation equipment. Practice and experimentation are needed to discover the distance a still should be racked between frames, how much a lens should be stopped down for fades and dissolves, and so forth. But the results are worth the effort, and a news department is stronger for having the capability to construct montages away from the studio.

SILENT INTRO

Perhaps the commonest way to introduce sound-on-film is with silent film. The cameraman's usual procedure in covering a static scene story such as a news conference or an interview begins with setting his sound camera on a tripod and arranging his lights. He must do this before any fixed-time event begins, or he will lose the opening statements while he fumbles with his gear. With his sound camera thus immobilized, the cameraman relies on his much lighter, much handier silent camera to give him the variety of scenes and angles he wants for establishing and cutaway shots. Unless he is under instructions to "edit in the camera," the cameraman tries to shoot enough different scenes to cover any approach the writer and the editor might later take to the story.

Over a period of weeks, an imaginative writer or editor will have assembled almost as many different kinds of silent intros as there are different kinds of stories.

1. The opening scene is often, but not always, an establishing shot: that is, a long shot or medium long shot which encompasses as much of the scene as is practicable. This may be followed by a medium shot of the speaker's table or lectern, followed by a cutaway of spectators, the reporter, one or more sound cameras, or any of a dozen other shots. Or, instead of a long shot, the opening scene may be the medium shot, followed by a close up of the speaker, followed by a cutaway. Or, the opening scene may be a close up of the speaker, followed by a medium shot or a long shot, in which case a cutaway probably will not be required.

2. Another way to avoid a cutaway, which at best is a necessary artifice, is to use the sound camera footage immediately preceding the first SOF used, with or without an establishing shot. In other words, the editor does not begin the first piece of SOF with the speaker's first words, but backs the film up to include four to six seconds of the speaker before he

utters those words. Unless the audio track contains only normal background noise for these four to six seconds, the editor must "bloop" the sound track, i.e., wipe it with a magnet to erase the sound. This film should not be used if the speaker was talking, because his lips would be moving. The film is eminently usable if a reporter was asking a question which the writer chooses not to use. The question is blooped, and the speaker's face in close up or medium close up appears as part of the silent intro. A cutaway is not needed. The intro could even be this shot alone, backed up 10 to 15 seconds.

3. In place of a static opening scene, the first silent film to appear on the air may be the speaker walking into the room. Even better, the cameraman can catch the entrance with his sound camera. The hubbub accompanying the entrance and the words of greeting to friends and newsmen make an excellent opening, especially if the speaker is famous.

4. If the event occurs in an auditorium or a banquet hall, the opening shot may be of the audience. It may also be of an exterior, say a building or a campus. It may be a sign on a door or at an entrance gate. Any exterior opening should carry us smoothly, shot by shot, to the speaker. For example, a brass plaque at the entrance to a multi-building factory might be followed by the exterior of the building where our speaker is located, followed by him in a medium long shot—presumably in a room whose equipment is important to the story—followed by a cutaway of the most important piece of equipment, followed by SOF.

5. The opening silent film might be a pan of a room full of interesting objects, or several shots of individual objects, followed by SOF of the speaker surrounded by the objects. A trade fair, a boat show, or an art exhibit may be treated with such an opening.

6. The silent—or SOF—intro might be of a plane arriving at an airport, or a car pulling to the curb.

Rule: *Whatever silent film is used, the writer should be able to defend his choices.* If he begins with an establishing medium long shot, he ought to be able to explain why, although it is unlikely that anyone will ask him to do so. It is a sloppy writer whose instructions to a film editor are "Give me 15 seconds of silent at the head." Any scene which appears on a television newscast—and there may be dozens in each newscast—is there because someone chose that particular shot in preference to everything else available to him. If the selection is careless and arbitrary, the newscast will reflect it.

Just as each scene should be used because there is a reason for using it, the length of each scene should be justified, and usually right down to the last second. The writer ought to make a rational, conscious decision that a shot should last four seconds rather than three. Indeed, a thoughtful writer and a careful film editor will occasionally dispute the addition of one-half second, and in an overlap cut the editor may count frames. (See

Chapter 13, FILM EDITING.) All this, of course, assumes that enough time is available to polish a film story. Where time permits, pride of craft should emerge in each film story. When the writer and film editor race the clock—as all writers and film editors must do sometimes—they will instinctively do things right if they are accustomed to thoughtful editing.

Among the reasons for letting a shot run, say, eight seconds instead of five seconds or ten seconds, are these:

1. An audio track which matches the film runs eight seconds.

2. The audio track on the film is needed for just eight seconds.

3. A quote or other copy which for some reason should not be altered runs exactly eight seconds.

4. It takes eight seconds for a pan (a horizontal turning of a stationary camera) to establish, move, and stop. An editor should not cut into or out of a moving pan.

5. Certain actions at either end of the shot must be included, e.g., a man walking into and out of frame.

6. Certain actions at either end of the shot must be omitted, e.g., nasty gestures at the camera by a prisoner, leaving a maximum of 8 seconds of permissible footage of the prisoner.

7. A scene is "worth" eight seconds, or the cutting rhythm calls for a shot here about 8 seconds long. These two considerations are highly subjective, but they are often soundly based on years of motion picture cutting experience which develops a feeling for shot value and rhythm.

8. Approximately eight seconds may be needed to permit a smooth dissolve or fade out of a shot which would otherwise be cut for five seconds.

9. A scene may be so "busy" (for example, a lot of words on a sign) that a shorter length will not give the viewer full comprehension.

The total length of a silent or SOF intro to an SOF story usually runs between eight seconds and 20 seconds, with 12 to 15 seconds being common. Little can be said in less than eight seconds which will suitably prepare the viewer for the sound-on-film statement. Anything more than 20 seconds would seem to be pointless or dull, unless the intro film sustains the interest of a silent or sound-under film story.

Rules which govern on-camera, RP, and still introductions to SOF also govern silent intros:

1. Copy should match picture.

2. A person seen in medium shot or close up must be identified the first time he appears. The viewer should never wonder who he is looking at.

3. As already mentioned, copy should never begin with phrases like "This is . . . ," "We are looking at . . ." or "Here we see. . . ."

Such words may prove embarrassing for the newscaster if the film is up-cut or rolls late. The viewer then will not be looking at what the newscaster tells him he is looking at.

4. The last words of copy before SOF should not refer to the SOF by phrases like "The mayor added . . ." or "Watch this scene," or "He had this to say. . . ." As noted in the last chapter, an exception to this rule occurs when something significant on film is likely to escape the viewer's attention because it happens very quickly or is very small or faint. Even then, the writer can usually refer to the object or action indirectly. For example, if the camera catches the third woman from the left in the back of the room suddenly fainting, the copy need not say, "Watch a woman in the back of the room," although this is a permissible digression from the objective reporting of the story. The copy can read, "As the lawyers wrangled, a woman standing in the back of the room fainted from the heat and excitement." The viewer's attention will be drawn there when the film appears just as surely as he would with a "watch her" admonition.

5. The intro copy, in sum, should be a story in microcosm, one that could stand—although weakly—without film.

6. Copy preceding sound-on-film should "set up" the SOF, but it should neither repeat the words that are coming, nor should it give away their import or surprise, unless a single fact of the story is so overshadowing that nothing else matters. Rather, the writer should indicate the overall tenor of the copy.

POOR SOF INTRO	BETTER SOF INTRO
Mayor Smith said Councilman Brown was misguided.	Mayor Smith criticized Councilman Brown.
Mayor Smith announced that all playgrounds would be closed.	The mayor had news that is sure to distress the city's children . . . and their parents.
The mayor surprised newsmen today by declaring, "I will not run for re-election."	The mayor surprised newsmen today by announcing that he will soon retire from public affairs.

The copy, above, which is labelled "poor" is poor only if it is immediately followed by the mayor on film saying, "Councilman Brown is misguided" or "I'm sorry to announce that all playgrounds must be closed" or "Gentlemen, I have decided I will not run for re-election."

The copy is adequate if the mayor does not repeat on film what the newscaster uses in his introductory copy. Indeed, the copy may be exactly what is called for if the mayor does not make the announcement on the film, but proceeds from that point with an explanation of the announcement; for example, "I say this about Councilman Brown because of his extraordinary opposition to the city beautification program," or, in the case of the playgrounds, "We are acting on advice of the City Health Officer because of two cases of meningitis reported in the county," or, in the case of the re-election, "I have served as mayor and as councilman for 26 years, and now it is time for a rest." With such opening statements on film, the direct or indirect quote becomes a needed part of the informational "set up."

7. The intro copy replaces a reporter's question when that question, as recorded on film, is inaudible, too long, connected to a prior answer ("In that regard, how can you . . ."), or asked by the reporter of a competing station, when newsroom policy requires the elimination of competitors' voices. Under any of these conditions, the intro must ask the question, because the film begins with the person answering it. For example: "On another subject, the governor formally announced that he's not a candidate for the Democratic nomination for vice president. Then he was asked if he would turn it down." (IN CUE) "I don't see how anyone could turn it down."

Roll-Thru

When two different men make statements which will be used in a film story, the statements are conveniently joined by means of a roll-thru. This is a length of film not meant to be seen on the air, used while a projector continues rolling at full speed to reach another film segment. When one man makes statements at two different times, e.g., a defendant chatting with reporters just before and just after he is sentenced by the judge, a roll-thru joins the statements.

The roll-thru, perhaps five or six seconds in length, may be leader film, with the newscaster on camera. More commonly, the roll-thru will be silent film, with the newscaster voicing over it.

The roll-thru is usually a bridge between two SOF statements. A film story may have several of them (referred to as "roll-thrus" not "rolls-thru"). SOF statements by different speakers also can be butt-ended: that is, spliced directly without a roll-thru, with supercards to identify the speakers.

The silent film and the copy used in a roll-thru must bridge either time or identity change. For example, between the defendant's two statements, before and after sentencing, the camera may focus on the courtroom door.

VIDEO	AUDIO
:32 POS MAG	SOF
	END CUE: " . . . really innocent."
:05 ROLL-THRU	Jones entered the court to hear his sentence. He was quieter when he returned.
:29 POS MAG	SOF
	END CUE: " . . . serve my time."

As another example, let us assume we have a statement by Mayor Smith saying Councilman Brown is misguided, and a reply by Councilman Brown that Mayor Smith has forgotten his promises to the voters. A five-second roll-thru might consist of three seconds of Councilman Brown's name on his office door, plus a two-second medium long shot of the councilman's office, with Brown seated at his desk.

VIDEO	AUDIO
1:04 POS MAG	SOF
	END CUE: " . . . him astray."
:05 ROLL-THRU	But Councilman William Brown was more concerned with budgets than with beauty.
:57 POS MAG	SOF
	END CUE: " . . . the taxpayer."

The common practice of intercutting two separate interviews gives viewers the sense that a debate is taking place, because the editing is based on comments about the same topics; for example, each man's statements about pollution go next to each other, followed by their statements on the need for new schools. While this method makes their relative positions clear, the viewer should not be misled into thinking that an actual debate took place, which might lead him to conclude that one of the opponents got the better of it. The newscaster should make it plain that no argument or interchange of views took place, and the viewer is merely hearing isolated comments which have been edited together to help in understanding the positions of the two opponents.

Between two statements by the same person during an interview or news conference, the roll-thru should not show the speaker's face in close up or medium shot (a jump cut unless it is sandwiched between two cutaways). Here, the roll-thru is really a cutaway. An establishing long shot can be used. Better yet: show the back of the speaker's head or a one-quarter profile, with the speaker talking and gesturing, and the reporter, shown in the background head-on, listening. A roll-thru of cutaways which do not include the speaker is less desirable because the roll-thru copy probably sets up the speaker's next statement. In short, if the newscaster is talking about what else Mayor Smith said, let us see Mayor Smith, but let us not see a closeup of his face.

SOUND INTRO

The sound camera is often used to film a lead into a SOF statement or interview. The sound intro may be no more than an assortment of cuts which differ from a silent lead-in only by the fact that the newscaster reads over a background of natural sound. A sound film lead-in is superior to a silent film lead-in because it provides a smoother transition into the SOF and because background sound sometimes tells a story of its own (e.g., a busy street corner, a bulldozer at work, a jet landing). However, a sound camera lacks the ease of handling of a silent camera, and the gain in quality does not always offset the loss in speed and flexibility.

The sound intro may also consist of a reporter performing in the field the task the newscaster would otherwise perform in the studio. For example, here is one way of introducing an interview (everything was filmed at the interview site).

VIDEO	AUDIO
CU: DR. SMITH	REPORTER: Dr. William Smith has created a controversy among astronomers by challenging Einstein's theory of relativity.
PULL BACK TO 2-SHOT. REPORTER'S HEAD IS TURNED TO FACE THE CAMERA	Dr. Smith . . . is chairman of the Department of Astronomy here at the state university.
REPORTER TURNS TO SMITH	In words of one syllable -- or as close to that as you can manage, Dr. Smith -- can you tell us what you found.
2-SHOT. CAMERA SLOWLY ZOOMS INTO TIGHT SHOT	SMITH SOF

....

(at the end, the treatment is reversed)

TIGHT SHOT OF SMITH	SMITH SOF
TIGHT SHOT OF REPORTER, HEAD TURNED TO CAMERA	REPORTER: And so an astronomer living and working in our own city has offered a challenge to the famous theory of relativity.
ZOOM BACK TO A 2-SHOT	Dr. William Smith's theory has as yet found only a small degree of acceptance amoung his fellow scientists. But if his present research produces the results he expects, Dr. Smith's own star will shine very brightly.

The cut from the tight shot of Smith to the tight shot of the reporter at the conclusion of the interview should be overlapped (see section on *Overlap Cuts,* Chapter 13, FILM EDITING) for tighter editing of the interview.

An interesting form of double chaining (cutting or dissolving back and forth between two projectors on the air) to cover a long interview appears on several television stations, among them KGO-TV, San Francisco. The A roll carries the interview. The B roll consists of long shots and medium long shots of the reporter and the interviewee walking along, chatting. The camera never allows us to approach near enough to match mouth movements to the questions and answers we hear. The two men walk into or walk out of frame. The scene of their stroll is germane to the topic they are discussing, e.g., a campus or downtown streets.

The news clip, as it is seen on the air, might begin visually with the A roll, which shows the two men in actual conversation, dissolve into the B roll for the bulk of the clip, and return to the A roll—of the actual conversation—at the conclusion. Or the B roll might carry the entire picture. In either event, an on-camera introduction by the newscaster or the reporter in the studio should precede the film.

STANDUPPER

The term "standupper" refers to a film story which includes a reporter at the scene describing the event. He "stands up" before the camera, and what he says is his "stand up piece."

The "stand up piece" may be an "intro" and a "close" to a self-contained sound-on film segment such as a man talking, or it may be an on-camera "intro" and/or "close" to silent film in a double chain story. If the "standupper" is for a double chain, then the reporter delivers an introductory sentence or two and a closing sentence or two while looking directly at the camera, expecting that this portion of his narration will be shown to the audience. He reads the rest of the story from his notes, expecting that the "B roll" of silent or sound-under film will cover the "A roll" of him on camera. He is then reading "voice over" film. (These terms are by no means universally used in television. However, they are common enough to be widely recognized.)

In some cases, the "standupper" is simply a short statement delivered by the reporter in the field. This is the weakest kind of filmed field reporting. It is sometimes used when no other meaningful or applicable film is available, because at least it shows the audience that the television station sent a reporter to the scene of the story. If possible, the reporter should be standing near something significant to the story. Perhaps it is a building in which the action is taking place. Perhaps it is a gate, through which newsmen have been denied access. On one story, network camera crews and reporters flew to Yellowstone Park to film the killing of elk by rangers who were ordered to thin out the herd because of overgrazing. When the newsmen arrived, they were denied admittance to where the elk were being slaughtered. At least one network reporter, trying to get an early story out, did a "standupper" beside the bodies of two of the elk. There was nothing else to film.

In a memo to all network correspondents, Gary Franklin, formerly ABC News film review manager, commented on some filmed standuppers he had seen, good and bad:

1. A recent demonstration in a European capital. The immigration laws are about to be changed. Protesters marching through the streets. Many skin tones. Turbaned Indians. Robed Africans. Local gendarmes. Shouting. Chanting. Banners. Sidewalk crowds.

ABC correspondent: does standupper against nondescript wall, street sign over his head. No other activity in standup picture. Visually dull. Prognosis: if film is used at all, it will probably be voice-over only, without "picture" of the correspondent.

(Competition standupper, same story: correspondent reports from the middle of the demonstration, the participants pouring past the camera. Very effective.)

2. Vietnam. Several ABC interviews: (General) (Colonel) (VIP civilian) sitting on the folding chair, outside headquarters . . . or on Caravelle roof. Visually unexciting. Screening room reaction: "The printed press syndrome!"

(Recent competition interview in Vietnam: Correspondent with colonel-interviewee, walking through demolished district. Camera — apparently vehicle-mounted — moving backwards in front of the talking duo (forwards and *behind* them, for question reverses and cutaways). Wide-angle shot, from moving camera also shows demolished homes, burned trucks plus two outrigger GI's keeping step with the interview group — alert rifles scanning the neighborhood. Visual. Exciting. Informative. Effective.)

3. ABC correspondent in Miami opens piece on $300,000 (sic) development homes — with a wide-angle shot, showing correspondent cruising down a canal, past the huge homes, while he is talking.

As a closer, correspondent washes hands in fancy, gold-encrusted sink . . . shuts off water . . . turns to camera . . . "THIS is - - - - - -, ABC, IN A 14-THOUSAND DOLLAR BATHROOM." End. Great.

4. ABC correspondent in Rome, does story on traffic jams which are forcing city to consider tearing down the ancient wall of Rome. "Standupper" (in this case, "sitdowner") done inside car. Wide-angle shot reveals other cars outside windows . . . all stuck in middle of traffic jam. Perfect.

5. Correspondent in Paris . . . does ABC standupper, with girl in bra and stocking girdle — posing with semi-nude man for advertising photographer . . . over correspondent's left shoulder. A story on France's advertising revolution, and the media's "use" of sex. Attention-getting — to say the least.

What's the point of all this?

We want to *see* as well as hear our correspondents on the scene . . . want to *see* them in the proximity of the most important action elements of the stories they're covering.

A reporter standing against a blank wall won't be able to give us much of a substitute for track-only, voice-over.

IMPORTANT POINT: The correspondent-inside-the-scene material need not be extensive. It often requires no more than two or three sentences for the opening . . . a couple of sentences for the closing . . . and, if you really want to add an extra touch, a chunk for the middle.

For the sake of covering yourself fully — try to do the *entire* narration — including open and close — later. The duplication won't hurt — and can only help, in case the on-scene material doesn't work out.

At times it may be desirable to show the correspondent at various points within the story — in addition to, or instead of — the open and close. Therefore, *if* you can do the entire on-scene standupper/sitdowner/crouchdowner on camera, while part of the action background . . . so much the better. Everyone here realizes this isn't always possible . . . but it should be tried.

Careful, once again: make sure your pace, mood, level, background noise (as well as that certain difference between outdoor and indoor sound) will match throughout the piece. Too often, the opening sentences, recorded on the scene and in the middle of some activity, demonstrate an intensity and pitch not matched by the more relaxed track-only, recorded later, in the hotel room. It makes for some jarring audio-cutting.

In any case, a standupper recorded on an activity-filled street can never match additional narration, recorded after things have died down. Therefore, always try to provide some wild track of the action *noise* (traffic, demonstrators, water lapping against a pier, gunfire, pumps, crowds, a speaker on a podium, aircraft engines, and what have you) which can, if necessary, be *triple*-chained into your story.

To sum up:

Walk with the demonstrators (without getting hurt) . . . drive through the demolished suburb . . . sit on the rundown porch with the poverty worker and the indigents . . . stand amid the crowd of squealing youngsters . . . walk out from behind the weird statue . . . smoke the cigarette with the new controversial filter, while you intro the news conference involving the scientists . . . speak from the seat in the middle of the stadium crowd . . . let the laboratory worker and his microscope softly dominate the foreground, while you explain from — and are visible in — the background . . . intro and close from the foreground, while the VIP speaks or shakes hands behind your back . . . BE A VISUAL PART OF THE STORY!

It can make all the difference between story acceptance and (gulp) story rejection.

The copy for the introduction is essentially the same whether a reporter is at the scene doing a "standupper" or a newscaster introduces the film or gives the news from the studio, except that the reporter ought to indicate his setting: "Behind me is the courthouse where . . . ," "A biting wind is sweeping down from the mountains as these rescue workers. . . .", "From where we are located we can see . . .", "The crowbar on this table is the one used . . ." and so forth, as the camera pans up to the mountain or zooms in on the crowbar.

The close is usually just a wrap-up sentence or two, perhaps with the reporter's name and location following it: "The people of Sleepy Valley will remember this day for a long time. This is Joe Wilson, at the railroad depot in Sleepy Valley."

In addition to the standup open and the standup close, the reporter must provide voice over the accompanying (e.g., B-roll) film. Most stand-uppers are done against a background of distinctive sounds which will not always match the accompanying film. If the accompanying film is itself sound film shot at a different location or a later time, this sound is the best natural background to its own picture. Given the option, the editor would choose it instead of the background sound behind the reporter's voice. Therefore, rather than provide an unmatched audio background, the re-porter should do his voice-over narration in a relatively quiet place, such as a room or a quiet street. The voice-over narration should include the open and close, which will give the editor the option of cutting the entire film voice-over, or cutting either the open or close that way. If he chooses to have the reporter appear doing a standup open and/or a standup close, that option is also available. Sometimes the reporter does a second, on-location open and close, giving the editor even more options.

Choice of a site for voice-over narration should be made with the standup location in mind. If the standupper was done on a noisy street, the voice-over should be done on a quiet street rather than a hotel room, where the difference in acoustics will be evident. If the standupper was done *sotto voce* in the back of an auditorium where a speaker was holding forth, a quiet hallway should serve nicely for the voice over.

The body of the copy which is voice over silent film should match the film as closely as possible. It is the responsibility of the reporter and the cameraman in the field to see that suitable film is shot, and the writer and film editor in the newsroom to see that the shots are put together in the right sequence and at the right length to match the voice-over narration.

GOING TO COMMERCIAL

Going from a film directly into a commercial fails to establish the dis-tance which should exist between news and advertising. This direct method also misses an extra opportunity to confirm the newscast as an entity and the anchorman as the person in control of the newscast. Fading from a film to black, then fading into a commercial is bad enough. Cutting from a film to a commercial is unforgivable.

Here are several acceptable methods of going into a commercial:

1. The anchorman (the sports editor or weatherman, if a commercial splits his segment) says simply, "I'll be back in a moment." Or: "We'll

return after this commercial message," "More news after this announcement," etc.

2. The anchorman uses a tease: "A new effort to stop plans for the airport. The story . . . after these words." Less desirable: ". . . after these words for Sparkle Fish Bath." As a matter of policy, some stations object to any tease copy on ethical grounds; i.e., that the news, including people's misfortunes, is being used as a lure to hold people for a commercial.

3. A tease is voiced over the newscast's logo on a slide. Same objection. However, these objections are not universally held, and many stations use the news tease.

4. Similar to the tease is the billboard at the start of the newscast, with headlines of the biggest news items and the feature stories. The newscast begins after the opening commercial. A smaller billboard headlines news in the next news segment, between commercials.

5. A freeze frame of the end of a film clip is kept on the air without sound. The newscast logo and today's date are supered over it, then the director goes to black. He fades in on a commercial. This formatted end of a newscast segment gives the newscast a modern, professional appearance. It tells the viewer that someone took some pains to put this program together.

6. The director cuts to a wide shot of the news set, with several people in view. He holds it for three or four seconds, then fades to black.

FOR THE STUDENT

1. Make slides (you can paste or Scotch tape pictures to cards instead) for the three news stories and, using them as visuals, write leads into sound film (real or imagined), one still per story.
2. Now do it with two or three stills per story.
3. Write a 10-second silent film lead into sound film (real or imagined). Then write a 20-second lead into the same film. In both scripts break the silent film down by scene and time (the number of seconds for each shot). Assume that you have available to you any film shots you will need.
4. Write 15-second on-camera leads into three sound films.
5. For what kind of story and sound film might it be better to use a *photo* as intro instead of silent film? *A map? A cartoon? Newscaster on camera?*
6. When might it be more desirable for a cameraman to shoot *sound film* to lead into an SOF statement? *Silent film?*
7. Assume that you are a reporter who must do a standupper at each of these locations: outside the wall of a prison in which convicts are holding guards hostage, outside a Federal court in which an important case is being tried, on a military airfield in front of a new fighter

plane. Using your imagination (but not too much imagination), write a standupper which will sandwich around an SOF statement by someone at the scene, e.g., the prison warden. Assume that there will be no double chain silent film.

8. Compare a local newscast and a network newscast on the manner and quality of their intros to SOF statements.

9. Cite five kinds of film stories which could use a montage intro.

10. Compare the different ways to lead into commercials. Which do you prefer? Why?

10

FILMING TECHNIQUES

ACCIDENTS, FIRES and crime figure significantly in most local newscasts, for the familiar reason that people are interested in these events, particularly when they occur close at hand. It may well be argued that television news features too much crime and violence, but that opinion must be argued within the framework of defining how much is "too much." Meanwhile, some evidence that people are curious about these out-of-the-ordinary events in life's daily routine can be seen in the slow-up of cars passing an accident as drivers become gawkers even at the risk of causing their own accidents. However, the journalist must be aware that this passing curiosity may not include watching "fender-bender" footage on the nightly newscast.

If these violent events appear to dominate local television newscasts, it may be because the medium of television is uniquely adapted to showing them. The cameraman takes the viewer to the scene, usually showing him the aftermath of the event, but sometimes—when the cameraman is fortunate enough to be there when it happens—showing the event itself. The fledgling television newsman learns early how to cover fires, accidents and police business. But he may not learn to cover them well, if he has no model to rely on other than his own past experiences and the films of older members of the staff. He should study techniques used beyond the confines of his own station.

One place to learn them is the annual National Press Photographers Association TV newsfilm workshop, usually held at the University of Oklahoma in Norman each spring. The Defense Department co-sponsors the workshop, which is open to cameramen who have at least one year's experience. News directors, producers, assignment editors and film editors may also attend. For information, write to the university.

Let us consider, by actual example, some ways to cover spot news using a silent camera, with or without wild track sound from a tape recorder.

A FIRE

The cameraman got the tip by car radio telephone from his office. It took him 20 minutes to reach the site, on the other side of town. He parked his car a block away, and at that point began filming. His first shot was an establishing shot, for by the time he arrived the fire was blazing out of control. With his lens wide open, the cameraman caught only the flames themselves and the blinking red lights of the fire trucks.

He then ran toward the fire, stopping to shoot again about 30 yards away. The lens remained wide open for every shot except a few close-up cutaways of firemen, because portable lights outdoors at night are useless beyond a range of a few yards. From a distance of 30 yards, the camera-man filmed firemen at work, with flaming lumber behind them, so that the firemen were silhouetted against the flames. At that distance, a medium long shot, he filmed piles of burning lumber.

He moved still closer, shooting individual piles of burning wood. He then shot his first pan; he began with a medium shot of a fireman struggling with a hose, panned along the flow of the water, and stopped at the water's target, a pile of burning wood. The camera held steady on the fire-man for eight seconds, panned for four seconds over a sweep of 45 degrees, and held steady for 12 seconds on the fire at the end of the pan. This scene shot this way would later give the film editor the option of: a) using the entire 24 second shot; b) using any portion of the pan down to as little as six seconds (one second hold at start and finish plus four seconds of pan); c) the fireman alone; d) the flames alone.

By panning, the cameraman was also able to establish the relationship of the fireman to the fire. Under the extremely poor lighting conditions, there was no other way to establish this relationship, except to silhouette the fireman against the flames.

The cameraman took a reverse shot—nearly a 180 degree turn—of the fireman. The pan began with the camera looking at the fireman in profile. The reverse was a shot of the fireman almost head on, with the water from the hose streaking past the camera. Naturally, the cameraman did not "cross the line," the imaginary line which maintains directional continuity; if his profile shot was of the fireman's right side, the reverse was of his right front.

Operating at a distance from the story they are filming, a news film crew uses a telephoto lens with an extra long focal length and a highly directional shotgun microphone to record the action from the back of a pickup truck. Space shots and atomic blasts are obviously among news stories which must be viewed from a considerable distance.

The cameraman now began to wander around the lumberyard, getting medium and close shots of firemen, flames, spectators (one more example of public interest in such spectacle), policemen diverting traffic, fire engines, snaking hoses and signs (including street signs to identify the location and a sign identifying the lumber yard). He was also alert to any action, such as firemen battering down a door, or a structure tumbling. If a fireman had been injured, the cameraman would have given full attention to his rescue and treatment.

It did not cross the cameraman's mind to slow his camera down from the usual 24 frames per second to a fast-motion 12 frames. His film would show a fiercer fire with wildly lapping flames, but his work would be unethical.

A COLLISION

The cameraman, cruising in his car, got the tip from his police radio band. He reached the scene within moments of the arrival of the ambulance. Had he arrived ahead of the ambulance, the film he turned in would have included a shot of the ambulance arriving. Instead, his first shot was the usual establishing shot, showing both automobiles and their relationship to the street intersection. This shot was filmed as soon as the cameraman parked his own car, and took just a few seconds of his time. Had the establishing shot required more time, the cameraman would not have taken it until he filmed the focus of the story at this moment, a driver trapped inside one of the cars. The cameraman ignored all other possible shots and ran to the side of the car where firemen were trying to extricate the driver by prying open his door with crowbars.

As quickly as he could, knowing that the scene might change in a matter of seconds, the cameraman took a medium shot of the side of the car with the firemen working on the door. He then swung about for a reverse of the firemen, remembering (actually, this becomes instinctive) his camera axis ("crossing the line"). The cameraman looked carefully at the victim before photographing him. If he were covered with blood, the cameraman would not have taken a close-up, because the shot would have been too gory to use. The cameraman would have filmed nothing closer than a medium shot.

As it was, the cameraman got a single close-up with an unwavering aim for 15 seconds. One mark of a professional is his ability and willingness to hold a steady shot for what might seem to the amateur to be an interminable time. One mark of the amateur is his seeming inability to hold a camera in one position; he is forever panning, trucking, dollying, and taking a variety of short, quick shots, usually of the same subject from the same distance at almost the same angle. The professional also learns to hold his breath while he holds his camera. The amateur's camera breathes when he does.

The cameraman moved back to "re-establish" the scene, another medium long shot of both cars and the surrounding street, but from a different angle. Then he positioned himself so that when the firemen successfully pried open the car door, he would have a clear shot of the door being opened and the victim being pulled from the car.

After the ambulance took the victim away, which the cameraman recorded at several stages with cutaways of the faces of firemen, spectators, and ambulance attendants, the cameraman turned his attention to the damage done to the cars. Later he showed, again at several stages, tow trucks hauling away the wrecked cars, and again he made sure he had cutaways of spectators.

Perhaps no single element of a film story is so keenly missed as the useful, meaningful cutaway, and perhaps no single shot is so frequently neglected. Cutaways have already been mentioned, but the subject deserves repetition. A piece of wreckage is not a meaningful cutaway between two shots of a victim being loaded into an ambulance, but a spectator's face is. Actually, it does not really matter what the spectator was looking at when the cameraman took his picture, as long as it *appears* that he was watching the victim being put on a stretcher. Many experienced cameramen make it a standing practice to film some spectators on every story, including news conferences. The cameramen ask the spectators to look straight ahead, perhaps at a lamppost across the street, perhaps at a wall. Two seconds of an expressionless face looking to right or left can be a most desirable piece of film! It is important to note that a cutaway shot must be unrelated physically to the scenes immediately preceding and following it; that is, what is seen in the cutaway must not be seen in the shots which it separates except for general setting.

After the filming of any story is completed, the cameraman working alone lays aside his camera and picks up pencil and pad. From the police or other public officials on the scene the cameraman-turned-reporter gets as many details as he can. What happened? What were the names, ages, addresses of the people involved? What was the extent of their injuries? To what hospitals were they taken? How much is the estimated loss or damage? What is the name and station house of the officer giving the information (he might be needed later to suppy some overlooked details).

A Murder

The cameraman got a call from a detective friend (such friendships are not uncommon and they are professionally valuable and often mutually rewarding, provided that the television newsman does not surrender his professional standards in return for police cooperation). The tip was that two elderly women had been murdered in their home.

The cameraman arrived to find the bodies still lying on the floor, just as they had been discovered. Because the bodies were mutilated and had not been covered, the cameraman did not film them. He chose this course of action not only because the police might have objected to filming, but because gory scenes are almost never used on responsible television newscasts. Instead, he filmed the disarray in the house, the murder weapon, and policemen and detectives searching for clues to the identity of the killer. The rooms of the house afforded no space for long establishing shots, and so the cameraman panned and trucked (here, a walking shot on tiptoe to avoid jiggling the camera) in order to establish relationships between rooms and objects. Later, when the bodies were covered by sheets, the cameraman filmed them, and also took shots of the coroner's deputies lifting the bodies onto stretchers.

Shots of objects, such as the window through which the killer gained entry, are usually better if a person is in the shot; for example, a policeman inspecting the window (if they are not pressed for time, policemen are often willing to cooperate by posing for a shot).

Outside the house, the cameraman filmed a long, establishing shot showing police cars around the house and spectators (there they are again) gathered along the sidewalk. Shots were taken of the nearest street corner signs and of the house numbers, either on the house or on the mailbox. Medium shots of the spectators could provide cutaways between a shot of the bodies being carried out and the coroner's ambulance driving away.

One freelance cameraman who regularly shot crime and accident victims carried his own sheet for those occasional times when a murder victim lay uncovered and the cameraman did not have time to wait for the coroner's ambulance. He talked an obliging policeman into covering the body with the sheet just long enough for some footage. The cameraman then retrieved his sheet and went on his way. *This cameraman, once arriving after the body had been removed, talked another cameraman into posing under the sheet. Unfortunately for the wily cameraman and fortunately for the cause of ethical journalism, the "victim" was so fat that the writer who viewed the film (the author) caught the deception and chewed out the cameraman for trying to pull a fast one.*

A RIOT

The cameraman knew in advance that teenagers planned to gather for a protest meeting against what they alleged was police brutality. He showed up early, to avoid traffic congestion, and to get close to the center of action. However, he was not as early as several hundred demonstrators in their teens and twenties who quickly turned themselves into a rampaging mob, trying to turn over cars and a city bus. There was no time to plan. Disregarding any peril to himself (a man holding a movie camera is always a target in a mob), he shot quickly wherever he saw action, mixing long, medium, and close shots. Because it was evening and because he did not want to waste precious seconds taking light meter readings between shots, the cameraman—thoroughly familiar with his camera's lens capabilities—shot wide open on medium and long shots, but closed down for close-ups, guessing the proper lens opening. Here he took a calculated risk, betting his experience and intuition against the chance of losing an important shot because of poor lighting. Nor did he change lenses. Everything was shot wide angle.

There was no time for pencil-and-pad questions, no time to fool with unessentials, no time to spend on anything he might acquire later when events quieted. He moved on the run. He crouched, climbed, shot, moved, and shot again: long shots of rioters and policemen, medium shots of struggle, close-ups of emotion-charged faces. When his 100-foot spool ran out, he slapped his exposed film into a can, wrapped some tape around it, reloaded the camera, and continued filming (elapsed time for canning and reloading: about two minutes when the cameraman is in a hurry and knows what he is doing).

The total product of this unplanned collection of shots was not a mass of unrelated confusion for two reasons: a) the cameraman was astute enough to shoot a variety of shots and to follow the main action as it occurred; b) a film editor and a writer were able to thread the scenes along the story line—and to weave the story around the best film scenes.

The cameraman who filmed these scenes was a freelancer. He watched with pleasure—and growing profit—as his film was used on two local newscasts, a network newscast and, later, a network documentary.

Lost Child at Police Station

The cameraman heard on the police band of his car radio that a three-year-old girl had been found wandering along a street in her pajamas at four o'clock in the morning. A passing motorist saw her and took her to a police station.

At the station the cameraman found the child sitting quietly in the care of a policewoman summoned from downtown headquarters. He knew that the child's mother was likely to claim her soon after she woke up to find her daughter missing. If no one came by mid-morning, the little girl would be put in the care of juvenile authorities.

Knowing that a parent could arrive at any moment, the cameraman quickly shot a minute of film: a long shot showing the child appearing rather forlorn in a room of the station, a medium shot just of the child and a big close-up of most of the child's face, concentrating on her eyes. He held the close-up for a full 30 seconds. These were his "protection" shots, and with them out of the way and some cooperation from police officers, he next staged some scenes. With their help, he coaxed the child to wander around the police station, curiously poking about the desk sergeant's area. He did not, however, show the child near any guns, for this would offend viewers as being not only risky, but overly cute, obvious and stagy. One suspects that many viewers realize that scenes of a lost child in a police station are staged, but the audience enjoys the show and suspends belief. Using the same reasoning, the cameraman filmed the little girl playing with a policeman's hat, but did not place it on her head. He would have shown her licking an ice cream cone, had there been ice cream in the well-known cartoon tradition, but just before dawn there was no ice cream to be found, and if there had been, the policewoman might rightly have objected to feeding it to her. However, there was milk and there were a couple of toys lying about to entertain an occasional lost tot. The cameraman used these props to full advantage. The cameraman had no intention of waiting for a tearful mother to come rushing in, because she might not arrive for hours. However, after taking all the pictures he wanted of the child, he was not through. Why not?

The shots in his camera were all of *the child* in different situations. Now she was smiling, now she was not. Here she was holding a hat, there a toy. In this shot she was running, and in that one sitting quietly sipping milk. In one shot a policeman was holding her, in another she was squirming out of the grasp of a different policeman. In the edited film, how does the editor go from one scene to the next? Obviously, by using cutaways.

In recent years, some feature motion picture editors have broken away from the cutaway, particularly in montage editing. With this convention now established to some degree, the news film editor could adapt it to film stories like this, either with quick cuts of the child or, using a double chain, with quick dissolves. Here, the cameraman shot cutaways and the editor used them.

The cameraman proceeded to film every officer in the station, singly or in groups. He asked them to look to the left or to the right. He asked some to smile. He filmed the sergeant looking up after writing in his log and two officers arriving from patrol duty, smiling as they discovered a camera trained on them and a cameraman saying, "Why don't you smile?" Those smiles would later be cut to appear as smiles at seeing a pretty child in the station. The child herself was in none of these cutaways, for they would not have been cutaways if she had appeared. The cameraman had enough scenes of the child alone and the child with officers. As he left the police station, the cameraman turned for one last shot: the exterior of the police station.

He departed with what information was available on the police report about where the child was found and by whom. To this he added a description of the little girl. He knew that several hours later, a news writer would call the station for information that was not yet known, such as her name and address, how she managed to get out of the house, how far she traveled before she was found, and whether she had ever done this before, plus an eyewitness report from an officer of the reunion of mother and child, including any talk of a later spanking.

ON MANAGING NEWS SCENES

The cameraman who shot film of the lost child in the police station behaved a bit like a Hollywood director, asking police to look right or left, shoving toys into the child's arms, and getting everyone in sight to do

Someone off camera talks to an elderly man sitting in front of the rubble of a burned out building in Watts, near Los Angeles, while the cameraman gets his silent footage. If no one was talking to the man, he would not be engrossed and animated, and the footage might be worthless.

something. People unfamiliar with the daily realities of photographic coverage by newspaper still photographers and television newsreel cameramen might object to all this managing of events, for newsmen are supposed to record events, not stage them. If a spectator is not actually looking at the subject of a story, why ask him to look to the left or look to the right? If a child is not playing with a policeman's hat, why thrust one into her hands?

Scenes are set up for two reasons:

1. The presence of a still or motion picture photographer injects an

external element into any situation. He himself becomes a focus of attention. If a photographer could will himself to be invisible, he would do so. He cannot hold a camera four feet from a man's face without attracting that man's attention. And, because he needs that man's picture, he must instruct that man to do something, even if only to "keep looking where you were just looking" or "keep doing what you were just doing."

2. Most stories would take far too long to film and be far too dull to use if a cameraman simply waited around, camera poised, for someone to do something interesting. So the cameraman stage-directs. But he issues his stage instructions only to bring out the inherent value in a news story. He does not try to strike a false note, to make people behave in a manner contradictory to the natural story value, to their own interests or to their own values. A cameraman or any journalist who deliberately sets out to harm the people he encounters on a story would not last long in any responsible news organization. A journalist who tries to make a news event seem to be what it is not should seek another profession.

The Federal Communications Commissions agreed that some staging is within reason, provided the television newsman does not overstep the legal boundary: [1]

> In a sense, every televised press conference may be said to be "staged" to some extent; depiction of scenes in a television documentary—on how the poor live on a typical day in the ghetto, for example—also necessarily involves camera direction, lights, action instructions, etc. The "pseudo-event" describes a whole class of such activities that constitute much of what journalists treat as "news." Few would question the professional propriety of asking public officials to smile again or to repeat handshakes, while the cameras are focused upon them. . . .
>
> The licensee's newsmen should not, upon arriving late at a riot, ask one of the rioters to throw another brick through a store window for its cameras. First, if the window is already broken, it is staging a news event—one which did not in fact occur but rather is "acted out" at the request of the news personnel; the licensee could fairly present such a film only with the full disclosure of its nature. In any event, whether or not the window is broken, the licensee cannot encourage or induce the commission of a crime.

The cameraman and the reporter walk on shaky ground when they cover a news story showing people breaking the law. The camera is not an invisible presence. The law breakers know it is there, filming the action. Somehow the crime seems less a crime then. And perhaps the crime might not be committed if it were not being covered by television. For example, the FCC came down hard on WBBM-TV, the CBS Chicago station, on grounds that its newsmen "induced" Northwestern students to hold a marijuana "pot party," which it filmed. CBS News was censured by the House Investigations Subcommittee for filming a group of men in Florida planning to invade Haiti and overthrow the government. CBS spent about $170,000, some of which went to the would-be invaders, before CBS grew skittish and dropped the story, calling it "the non-adventures of a ragtag crew . . . a gang flouting U.S. law to no purpose." The House subcommittee called for a new law to "protect the public against falsification and deception in . . . news programing" and to "prohibit the practice of news media involvement in criminal activities."

As for creating news or staging news for political purposes, a television news operation should, like Caesar's wife, be above suspicion, if for no other reasons than: 1) a newscaster and/or news operation is a tempting, visible target, a scapegoat, a means by which a politician can take the heat off himself; 2) some people are politically paranoid, seeing every unpleasant news story as a lie, part of a conspiracy to discredit their side. There are, of course, many other reasons for not staging news for political purposes. They come under the heading of professional ethics. Rep. Harley O. Staggers (D., W.Va.), regarding the falsifying of a television news report to be a national disgrace, sent investigators to collect examples of distorted coverage.

Some government and military officials once claimed that CBS News faked film of the stabbing of a Vietcong soldier by a South Vietnamese soldier in the presence of an American adviser, alleging it was a "cut and paste" job involving different locales and people. As evidence that the film was not faked, CBS News reran the clip twice, once in slow motion.

The Times of London has observed, "It did not require the prophetic writings of Marshall McLuhan to uncover the fact that press and television are not passive recording instruments, with or without distortion, of the events they observe. Their presence, and still more the prospect of what they will make of their presence, may effect objective alterations in the events themselves. . . The reason is that these observers are on the lookout for 'news,' a specialized and competitive commodity, which it is to some extent within the power of the actors in the event to supply or withhold according to their judgment of their interests."

A POLITICAL REMOTE

Reporting fresh news from a city hall or state capitol is similar in many respects to what confronts a major network when it wants to present a report from a foreign correspondent before there is time for film to cross the ocean by plane. The most common approach is the combination of a telephoned report recorded on audio tape and some graphic materials, either silent film from stock or stills freshly moved by wirephoto.

Three reporters in Redding, Calif., have pilot's licenses. They fly back and forth to the state capitol in Sacramento, a round trip of more than 300 miles, to deliver their hard news and film fresh.

Carroll McGaughey, news director of WSOC-TV, Charlotte, N.C., solved his problem of reporting state capitol news in a different way: [2]

> Four years ago we decided to try to lick the problems and bring the legislature home to our viewers. We detached a man from the staff and based him in Raleigh for the duration. Those first few weeks were unadulterated hell but we learned a lot from them. Our airline schedule was even worse then, making it necessary to ship any film for a given day within a few minutes after the legislature had convened.

> The technique resorted to was simple, but effective. Our man made a daily guess as to what the lead story would be, but of course he could not foretell the action that would be taken. The reporter—who was working alone, incidentally—wrote a sort of open-ended lead and sometimes a couple of alternate closing tags, picked a legislative background, stood in front of a sound camera and delivered. Obviously neither the opening or the closing had much meat in it.

> Then, on a catch-as-catch-can basis, he clairvoyantly shot as much silent film as he could of the people he *thought* would be most involved in the day's story, with some general shots that would cover anything, and rushed it to the airport courier. Later that day, when the action was complete, he called us on a radio loop we had installed and tape recorded for us the central body of his story.

> At our end of the line, we edited up the sound-on-film opening, created a middle segment of silent film matched as best we could to the audio tape for that portion and tagged out with our reporter again sound-on-film.

> The result was that the meat of the story was up to date and usually reasonably well illustrated. The addition of advance interviews and the like improved it considerably.

> This may have been a somewhat shabby way of producing legislative news—and a seemingly pointlessly complex technique. But to our surprise it proved something, and I think this is fairly important in effective local legislative coverage. That fact is that because they *saw* our man in Raleigh daily, and *heard* him with an updated report, our audience for the most part assumed this was a live switch, with the important result that they did become identified with legislative activity. Within three weeks, our competition had their own legislative team in Raleigh. It has been that way since.

> So what are we doing now? Well, most of the time we keep two regular staffers in the legislative halls, supplemented by a young university student as handy man.

> We are allowed on the floor with cameras in the House during the session, and can shoot from a balcony position in the Senate,

where we occasionally capture some significant floor debate or an excerpt of a major formal address. But this is not the basis of our approach. We devote most of our sound coverage to committee hearings and to interpretive, condensed sound interviewing of key legislators involved in the issue. We try desperately—not always successfully—to avoid meaningless silent film. If film does not help actually illustrate the story we prefer to stick with the video of our Raleigh reporter. And we do lean heavily on issues with a high degree of local interest even if, sometimes, they are not the most important actions of the day in so far as their effect on the State is concerned.

We do consider the film an essential. It lends that vital sense of presence for the audience. But our legislative staff is made up of reporters, not a photographic team, and they are given considerably more interpretive latitude than our local reporters.

Our big twin problem remains time and distance from the legislative halls. We are not alone.

We have begun one experiment which shows, we think, a tremendous promise for the future. We have worked out a cooperative arrangement with two other TV news departments. One is with WTVD in Durham. The other is at High Point, about halfway between us and Raleigh.

For example, on a live basis during WTVD's regular newscast, the Durham air man introduces a legislative reporter with the legislative story. That reporter may actually be a WTVD man, or one of ours or one from WGHP, High Point. On a prearranged time cue, the WGHP news reporter in High Point is delivering a similar cue and so are we in Charlotte.

On the cue, WGHP picks up and rebroadcasts the air signal from WTVD—and we in turn pick up and rebroadcast the WGHP signal. It works. The result is a live switch without benefit of A.T.&T.

A Parade

The morning newspaper told the hour the parade was to begin, its staging area, its route, the location of the judging stand, a reasonably accurate listing of participants and the usual wildly optimistic guess of the number of spectators.

With the newspaper story in his pocket for reference, the cameraman drove to the staging area, timing himself so that he would arrive just as the parade was due to start, allowing a walk of several blocks if his press pass was unable to get him any closer to the route than that. He did not park at the staging area. Rather, he chose a spot near the tallest building along the parade route, because he intended to climb to the roof for his final shot, to film the parade marchers strung along the route, a segment which could be

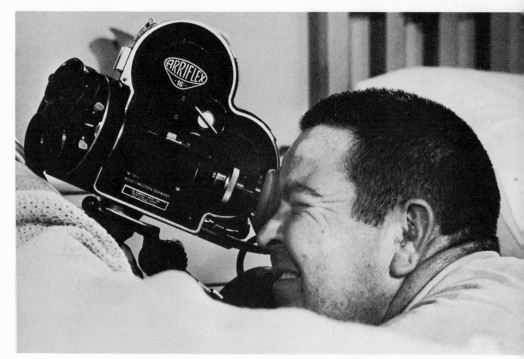

Even when he is not using a zoom lens, the cameraman steadies his camera at every opportunity. Here, a cameraman with a 16mm silent Arriflex uses his forearm for extra support even though the camera sits on a tripod.

used as either the opening or closing scene, or both. He stuffed four 100-foot rolls of color film in his pockets and loaded a fifth roll in his silent camera. He hooked his portable tape recorder and microphone to his belt. Then he walked along the parade route to the staging area, occasionally stopping to film clumps of spectators, children seated along the curb, a child perched on his father's shoulders and an infant asleep in his baby carriage. Sometimes, as he filmed these patiently waiting spectators, he balanced his camera with one hand while he waved his other hand high in the air and shouted, "Howdy" and "Hi, there." Invariably, the bored spectators perked up. Some shouted back and some waved. For all the world, it looked as if they were watching a parade.

At the staging area, the cameraman wasted no film on paraders lounging about waiting to march. Instead, he threaded his way through them, looking for groups, individuals, horses and floats he might want to film en route, to make sure he did not overlook them later. Then he walked back along the parade route and stationed himself two blocks away, estimating that the marchers needed about two blocks to straighten their formations and march in step.

Here he stayed for as much of the parade as he wanted: long shots of marching bands, medium shots of ranks of band members and marchers, close-ups of two or three musicians, medium shots of flag bearers, ranks of horsemen and floats, medium and close shots of a few of the shapliest drum majorettes. He followed a skillful drum major's baton as it flew high in the air and returned, then as an afterthought asked two spectators to look up, and filmed that as a possible reaction shot. He filmed all of the marchers head-on, approaching and coming abreast of him, never of their backs, with the single exception of two Cub Scouts who couldn't quite keep up with their fellows and were dropping behind.

The cameraman always remained on the same side of the street. Marchers moved past his camera from right to left. Had he crossed the street, the marchers would have moved across the film from left to right also, which would have been totally confusing. He always filmed movement in the same direction—a man walking, a car driving—unless he specifically wanted to show confusion of movement, such as masses of homebound traffic or pedestrians rushing to work. Showing a man going first one way, then the other, or cutting from one view of two people talking to the opposite view, is called "crossing the line" or violating the "180-degree rule" or "180 principle."

When the cameraman heard a good band, he left his position and walked along with them, at a distance far enough away to hear the band as a whole with no instruments close enough to dominate, yet not so far away that general crowd and parade noises interfered. When he saw the bandmaster prepare to begin a fresh march, he stopped filming, turned on his tape recorder and pointed his microphone at the band. He stayed with them until the final note. This "wild track" sound—sound which is not connected to a specific piece of film—could later be used with any combination of scenes. He had filmed no marching feet, except at a distance, because it is virtually impossible in the pressure and haste of a news film editing situation to match the fall of marching feet to the beat of a drum.

After he filmed his final scene, on the rooftop, he was able to reach his car in a hurry, escape the mass of people and cars which would soon cause a traffic snarl, and have his film developed, screened, edited, scripted and presented on the evening newscast just about the time the spectators, the paraders and the paraders' mothers and fathers—altogether a sizeable news audience—had wended their weary ways homeward, and had tuned in the local news, fully expecting to watch the film which they saw the cameraman take. In this expectation, they were not disappointed.

It is a capability of television news—unique among all media—to show the community to itself, to let the community see itself in tragedy and in joy, to let the community hear its own ragged music, and to present these sights and sounds either at the moment they happen, through live transmission, or very soon after, through film. In this capability of a television station to hold a mirror up to its community, television news cannot be equalled.

FOR THE STUDENT

1. What is permissible "stage managing"? What is not ethical? Discuss in class and give some examples of where the line should be drawn.
2. Interview some working reporters and cameramen on this subject. Write a brief paper.
3. Do you think CBS acted correctly in censuring a reporter who posed a wine company employee as a satisfied wine drinker, or do you think this was much ado about nothing?
4. Spend a day with a television news film crew. Report on how much "stage managing" occurred.
5. Monitor several newscasts. In how many of the films was the camera simply a passive observer of an event which would have occurred whether or not it was there?
6. List the shots which you think should be taken of a picketing demonstration in front of a courthouse, aside from any SOF statements. If the demonstration were against, say, divorce laws would you choose any other shots?
7. Assuming this was a small demonstration near the courthouse entrance on a sunny morning, with nothing blocking the cameraman's vantage points, what circumstances, if any, might lead him to pan?
8. Suppose you are covering the funeral of a well-known person and one of the mourners comes over to whisper that the presence of a camera on this solemn occasion is disrespectful. What should you reply or what should you do?
9. List the cutaways used in several newscasts, citing what each cut away from.
10. Some modern feature films intentionally jump cut. Do you think newscasts should jump cut, too, instead of using cutaways?

11

PICTURES

A FULLY-EQUIPPED sound cameraman traveling to a distant city for a story resembles in some respects a hunter on safari. His gear is likely to fill two dozen boxes, trunks and suitcases of assorted sizes.

THE SOUND CAMERA

Most television news operations use sound cameras converted to carry 400-foot magazines. A few small television station newsrooms still get by with cameras using 100-foot magazines. But 100 feet of film, going through a camera at the rate of 36 feet a minute, lasts only 2 minutes 40 seconds. It is impractical for most story situations. A 400-foot magazine lasts 11 minutes.

The most popular sound camera model for newsreel work has been the converted Auricon Cine-Voice (converted to take the 400-foot magazine) with a removable magnetic sound head so that the camera can also use optical track sound film. Bolex also manufactures a popular sound camera. So does Arriflex, but this fine camera is used more often in shooting documentaries than in daily newsreel work because it is more expensive and, some say, is not as rugged as the Auricon; however, it possesses technical advantages which lead many cameramen to prefer it for filming documentaries, where rough handling due to haste is less likely to occur.

The sound in a sound camera is created either optically or mechanically along one edge of the film. The opposite edge, of course, has the

The Bolex 16 Pro has its 400-foot magazine behind the camera. Feed and take-up reels are side by side. A pair of handles help to steady the camera. Among its features: motorized zoom lens control, remote control, and single frame filming, a technique not tried often enough in television newsrooms. Combined with a home-made animation stand, single framing can produce a high quality newsfilm from wirephotos.

sprocket holes. Film is identified as having an "A-wind" or a "B-wind," depending upon whether the film was wound clockwise or counter-clockwise. "B-wind" is most commonly used. Another term, "non-standard film," refers to film whose emulsion is on the "wrong" side of the base, compared to most commonly used film. A few small stations, some foreign cameramen and some private companies shooting public relations "handout" film, use non-standard reversal film (reversal is film which develops as a positive print). When it is used on the air, the projectionist must adjust his focusing slightly.

Along the sound edge, there will either be a brown layer of magnetic striping or one of two kinds of optical striations. The optical image is created by a hairline light from a galvanometer responsive to audio modulation. The image will be either of "variable area modulation" or "variable density modulation." Variable area modulation is generally used with reversal film, and variable density with negative film. While optical sound quality can be excellent under motion picture studio conditions, it has proved inferior to magnetic sound under the rough-and-ready conditions imposed by television news.

The sound camera, or the silent camera synchronized to a tape recorder to produce "sync sound," is the heart of television journalism, steadily pumping film for news stories, documentaries, specials, and editorials.

The Zoom Lens

On many sound cameras a zoom lens takes the place of the familiar three-lens turret mechanism. The most popular zoom, or variable focal length, lens is the Angeniux, with a range of 12 millimeters to 120 millimeters. This zoom lens enables the newsreel cameraman to expand his camera's field of vision by a 10 to 1 ratio from the extremely wide angle 12mm frame to the extreme close-up of the telephoto 120mm lens. For example, while filming a horse race, the cameraman can "zoom in" from a wide angle of the entire track to a close-up of the lead jockey at the far turn spurring his horse on.

The zoom lens is controlled by a straight rod or a crank mounted in front of the camera. For a fast zoom, the cameraman disengages the crank and turns the barrel of the lens by hand. The advantages of the zoom over the turret are:

Speed. A turret requires a cameraman to stop his camera, go around to the front of the camera, flip the turret to the lens he wants, and check his f-stop and his distance.

Ease of handling. The work in flipping a turret is a continual nuisance, compared with the simplicity of cranking a small handle controlling a zoom lens. The cameraman using a turret is tempted to take shortcuts, such as remaining on his middle, or 1-inch lens. Staying on one lens not only cheats the viewer of the best framing, but also limits the film editor who prefers a change of frame when splicing two similar scenes together.

Flexibility. The zoom lens effectively gives the cameraman a choice of seven lenses: an extreme wide angle, 12mm; a wide angle, 16mm; a normal lens equivalent to a 1-inch lens, 25mm; and four telephoto sizes, 50mm, 75mm, 100mm, 120mm.

Protection. A cameraman with a zoom lens need only stop to change film magazines. He does not fear that something important may happen or may be said while he is changing to a different lens on his turret.

Framing. Because it has a variable focus, its framing area is also variable on a continuum rather than at discrete intervals. The cameraman is able to frame for any scene precisely, rather than being limited to what a fixed lens sees.

A disadvantage of the zoom lens is that a zoom never has the quality at any given focal length of a fixed lens of that focal length, particularly in

This sound cameraman crooks his right forefinger to flip the "on" switch of his sound camera. His eye is pressed tight to the viewfinder eyepiece, seeing just what is framed by the zoom lens.

At a sports event, the motion picture cameras in the press section are equipped with zoom lenses, some of them with extra long focal length. The cameraman can zoom in from a wide shot of a playing field to a football end leaping for a pass or a baseball pitcher intently squinting to see the catcher's signals.

Looking at the business end of a zoom lens framed by a shade. The cameramen can use a straight steel rod for fast-action movement of the zoom lens, but here he prefers the more controllable hand crank.

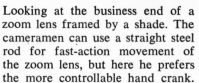

The cameraman balances his silent camera with his left hand, the arm tight to the body for added support. His right hand is used primarily to start and stop the camera, but also steadies it. A skillful cameraman can walk his camera through a scene as smoothly as if he were on wheels.

the higher focal lengths, where the picture tends to become flatter and grainier. However, this advantage is relatively small, and shrinks beside the advantages of a zoom lens. Another disadvantage is the zoom's weight.

When a plane or car goes past, there is a tendency on the cameraman's part to follow it and zoom in on the departing plane. This is a poor decision, because the plane does not appear to recede. Rather it looks as if it is standing still or even backing into the camera! The cameraman is better advised to pan and hold the shot, letting the plane grow smaller as it vanishes in the distance, or as an alternative, letting it fly out of frame.

The amateur cameraman pans too much. Most shots don't require panning, which is usually used to establish a relationship between two separated points, to encompass a wide scene, or to follow motion. It is in the last category that the experienced cameraman shows his competence. He does not pan to follow motion without a reason. Instead, he holds the camera still to let the moving object enter the camera's field of vision, move across it, then leave it. The object moves. The camera does not. And the film editor is grateful, for he will be able to splice this segment of film to other segments showing the same object in a different locale. A shot of an airplane which takes off and flies out of frame can be spliced to a shot of sky in which the airplane flies into frame, or even a shot of the plane in the sky.

Just as the cameraman should not pan unless he has a specific reason for panning, he should not zoom without a reason.

Unless done for shock effect or done with the expectation that the shot will be cut out on the editing bench, no zoom should be rapid. The "pop zoom" or "snap zoom" is disturbing to the viewer. Like the swish pan, which suddenly and blindingly moves from one scene to another, the pop zoom is a cinematic convention that says something to the viewer. The swish pan says, in effect, "Meanwhile, back at the ranch . . ." The pop zoom says, in effect, "My gosh, will you look at that!"

Most zoom lenses on news cameras are of 12mm to 120mm range; that is, from the very wide angle of a 12mm lens to the narrow cone of a 120mm lens. This is a ten-fold ratio. However, if the zoom is from 25mm, which is the standard 1-inch lens, to a tight zoom, the ratio is only five-fold.

At 120mm, a zoom lens is equivalent to a five-power pair of binoculars. At 250mm, which can only be achieved with a special and rather expensive zoom lens, the field of vision and magnification is equivalent to 10x binoculars. Obviously, a shoulder pod is useless here. The camera must be fixed on a tripod, or else the viewer will think he is being pitched in a hurricane at sea. A rule of thumb for a competent cameraman using a shoulder pod is to avoid zooming in past 50mm unless he can brace himself against a solid object such as a wall, a tree, a car, a fence or a table. At any focal length, the cameraman can keep his camera steadier if he pans than if he holds a fixed shot. He is steadier following an airplane across the sky than he is trying to hold on a balloon in the sky, because his arm tires under the camera's weight and his efforts to overcome the physical trembling accompanying fatigue are more noticeable if the camera is still.

THE SILENT CAMERA

Besides a sound camera, the cameraman usually takes along a silent camera. Lightweight, battery-powered or spring-wound, rugged, it gives the cameraman a flexibility he lacks with the sound camera.

A 16mm silent newsreel camera is usually fitted with a three-lens turret. Its lenses are: a) a wide lens, 10mm or 16mm, for getting establishing shots in confined spaces, such as rooms and hallways; b) a 1-inch lens, sometimes referred to as the "normal" or "standard" lens; c) a telephoto lens, 2-inches or 3-inches, for getting close-ups of distant action. As with the sound camera, when the telephoto lens is used on a silent camera, the camera should be braced. Otherwise, the film will be jerky. The camera man usually sets his body, his elbows or the camera itself against something solid.

At news conferences or other stationary situations, the cameraman will set his sound camera on a tripod as soon as he arrives, fix his lights and prepare everything for filming in sound. He will then use his silent camera to film establishing shots and cutaways.

The silent camera is also available on an emergency basis, in the event the sound camera malfunctions or the cameraman happens across an event occurring when he arrives, and he hasn't time to bring his sound camera into action (although a competent cameraman will not let himself get into such a fix often).

Sometimes the silent camera is used when there is no room for a sound camera or a soundman, and no need for one; for example, in a small helicopter.

Sometimes a subject will permit pictures to be taken, but forbids sound; judges occasionally set this stipulation in courtrooms during recesses.

The one-man camera crew, "the one-man band," is much better off with a single, lightweight camera and a lightweight sync-sound recorder than he is loaded with sound gear.

Combined with a tape recorder, the silent camera can shoot a sound story which does not require lip synchronization. The audio tape can perform double service in a radio newscast. The combination of a silent camera and a tape recorder is superior to a sound camera where lip sync is not needed, because it produces double system filming.

(See Chapter 13, *Film Editing.*)

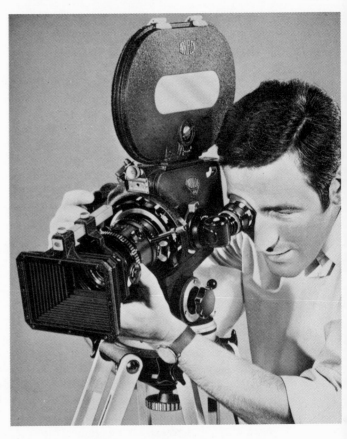

The Arriflex, a high quality (and relatively expensive) piece of equipment, is the first choice of many cameramen. Model 16 BL can run single system or double system with synchronized ¼″ tape. Among its features: quiet operation and a mirror shutter reflex system for bright, clear images through the viewfinder. The 400-foot magazine is standard equipment.

To make life simpler for the director when the newscast goes on, the cameraman loads mag stripe film in his silent camera. He also carries a tape recorder. This gives him silent film and accompanying wild track sound. After the film is edited, the sound is transferred onto the mag track from the quarter-inch tape by plugging the tape recorder into an ordinary movie projector.

Also, using two projectors, background sound from mag stripe shot in a sound camera can be transferred to mag stripe shot in a silent camera, thus eliminating the audio drop in silent cutaways.

Even lip synchronization is possible in shooting with a silent camera if the camera is equipped with a sync motor and it is hooked up to a synchronized tape recorder, like the Nagra. But allow extra time for editing.

According to Robert Rubin of CBS News,[1] "Sync sound is the key. To get sync sound of the real thing as it happens, without destroying or changing the very thing that you are trying to get on film, you need completely battery-operated equipment that is both lightweight and reliable. You need cameras that are unattached to anything else, and which are light enough to carry around for hours. The thrust toward this kind of film making has been enormous these past few years."

ACCESSORIES

1. *Body brace.* A sound cameraman carrying a power pack and a portable light in addition to his camera and a fully loaded magazine may be hauling 80 pounds of equipment. Besides the normal discomfort of handling such a weight, it is impossible to keep the camera steady without some sort of harness. A lightweight body brace, made of tubular steel or aluminum, serves this purpose. Even so, carrying up to 80 pounds of equipment and remaining steady enough to shoot film requires muscle and experience. To ease the load, cameramen are forever on the lookout for ways to lighten their pack. Considerable experimenting is being done by camera manufacturers to produce lightweight gear which will bear up under the rough handling newsreel equipment gets.

2. *Power pack.* A series of nickel cadmium batteries with a built-in inverter to keep the current flowing at 60 cycles powers a sound camera when 110-volt AC power is not available at a convenient wall socket. A power pack in satisfactory operating condition can pull up to 3,000 feet of film through a camera (about an hour and a half running time) before it needs recharging on ordinary household current.

3. *Portable light.* (See also section on lighting in this chapter). One of the handiest pieces of equipment carried by a cameraman is a small portable light. Powered by its own small nickel-cadmium battery, the portable light is either attached to the camera or held by the cameraman or the soundman. For fast-breaking, dimly lit story situations, the portable light is an absolute necessity. Cameramen often refer to their portable light as a "Frezzi" (for manufacturer Frezzolini) or Sun Gun (made by Sylvania).

4. *Tripod.* A lightweight, sturdy tripod with a fluid head to provide smooth pans is the standard sound camera base in such stationary situations as interviews and news conferences. When the tripod is placed on a marble floor, where it might slide, or on someone's rug, which it could tear, it should be supported either on grooved rubber cups or on a canvas or aluminum triangular spreader.

5. *Light meter.* This ubiquitous device is usually found dangling from a cameraman's neck on a string. One of the newest types of light meter is as highly directional as a shotgun microphone. Without leaving his camera, a cameraman can aim it and get a reading on a subject dozens of yards away, quite an advantage when he arrives late at a large news conference or at a sporting event or rally where the center of action is a long way from his camera. At least one professional silent camera, the Bolex H16 Rex 3, has a built-in electric eye, eliminating the need for a light meter.

6. *Changing bag.* This is a light-proof black bag which permits a cameraman to remove exposed film from magazines and load fresh film while he is in the field. Without a changing bag, the cameraman would

Cameraman William Spicer of Baltimore's WJZ-TV designed the "Quickie-Kart" to cut the time it takes to set up tripod, sound camera, and lights. He does it in less than 60 seconds, compared to the usual five minutes. To set up, take the already loaded camera and amplifier out of the carrying case, put the camera on the strapped-on tripod, and shoot. Breaking down is just as easy. The tripod can easily be removed if the cameraman wants to set it up conventionally. Several other stations also use Quickie-Karts.

either be required to carry a great many loaded magazines wherever he went, or forever be seeking out darkrooms.

7. *Spare magazines.* At least one, and preferably two loaded magazines should be part of a cameraman's gear.

8. *Special lenses.* Occasionally, a cameraman will take along a lens for a particular job. Extra-long telephoto lenses, for example, are useful at boxing matches.

9. *Lights.* See section on *Lighting.*

10. *A set of filters.*

11. *Spot sheets.* A pack or pad of spot sheets (also called scene sheets, breakdown sheets, white sheets, shot cards, etc.) is used to record what is on film, which reel it is on, and roughly how long it runs. When time is tight, the writer may put together a silent film story from the spot sheet and wire copy, without seeing the film, either editing the film after he hands the script in for the newscast or leaving instructions for the film editor, based on the spot sheet.

LIGHTING

Newsreel cameramen have available to them photoflood lights and quartz lights. Photoflood lights—often called scoops—are lightweight and easily transportable. Bulbs are cheaper than quartz lights. On the other hand, they are more fragile, and as they are used, their color temperature drops, so that the cameraman who shoots color film must change bulbs frequently. Photofloods burn out more frequently than the more popular quartz lights.

The lamps which hold photoflood and quartz bulbs are not interchangeable. The cameraman considering buying lights for the first time would be well advised to choose the type of lighting he intends to stay with for years.

Quartz lamps are reasonably lightweight, although not as easily hand-carried as photofloods. However, the difference in weight is not enough to matter very much. Quartz lights are also bulkier, and are difficult to use in cramped quarters, such as the cockpit of an airplane. Veteran newsreel cameramen who prefer quartz lighting often carry some photoflood lights as part of their gear for occasional shooting in tight places.

The biggest advantage of quartz lamps is that they maintain their color temperature until they burn out. A cameraman who clips in a 3200-kelvin lamp, for example, can be confident that the color of the light will remain constant for the life of the lamp, without reddening as it grows older.

Another important advantage of quartz lamps is that they can be focused. By using a lever in the back of the lamp housing, the cameraman can narrow the cone of the light beam from a floodlight's width to a spot-

Barn doors direct the light as a cameraman peers through his viewfinder while he moves the camera by adjusting the tripod head. Note the large film magazine. It holds 1,200 feet of 16 millimeter film, with a running time of slightly more than a half hour.

light. As the beam is narrowed, its intensity increases. The lever changes the relationship of the bulb to the reflector.

The quartz lamps, although expensive, have a longer life than photofloods. Still another advantage is the ease with which quartz lamps may be fitted with shades called "barn doors," scrims and other paraphernalia to block or diffuse light. Photofloods can take such adapters only with difficulty.

A newsreel cameraman might find himself carrying the following lighting equipment:

1. A *kit of quartz lights,* e.g. two 1,000 watt quartz lamps (bulbs, housing, stands, "barn doors" and light-diffusing scrims), one 650-watt quartz lamp.

2. A *kit of photoflood lights,* e.g. six 500-watt lamps (bulbs, sockets, stands, and "barn doors"). The kit would include Lowell lights, which can be clipped onto stands, or taped to walls or ceilings.

3. A *portable light kit,* including bulb, lamp housing, battery, and carrying strap (e.g., the Sun Gun or Frezzi light).

4. *Extension cords.*

5. *Sun reflectors,* for some outdoor shooting.

The art of lighting is a complex one, and goes far beyond the scope of this text. However, it might be instructive to describe briefly the basic lighting of a man at a desk. All other lighting may be considered a departure from this basic lighting situation, but even the lighting of so common a subject as a man at a desk varies from cameraman to cameraman (or gaffer to gaffer, where a "gaffer," or lighting electrician, is responsible for the lights).

The subject is lit by three lights: a key, a fill and a back light.

1. *The key* is the brightest light. The cameraman might use a 1,000-watt quartz lamp 10 to 15 feet away, depending upon such factors as the shade of wall paint, the size of the room or the color of the subject's skin complexion. The key light is often placed at a 45-degree angle from the

camera. If the light is too close to the camera, the lighting will be too flat. If it is at too great an angle, the key light will provide only side lighting. The key light is not focused narrowly. It lights the subject and the area around him.

2. *The fill light* is used to fill shadows caused by the key light. The cameraman lighting a subject at a desk might use a 1,000-watt quartz lamp widened to a flood beam with scrims to further diffuse and soften the light. This lamp might be placed close to the camera.

3. *The back light,* placed out of camera range, lights the subject's back and shoulders, gives depth to the picture, and helps separate the subject from the wall behind him. A 650-watt quartz lamp or a photoflood is common. A "barn door" on the lamp can block a portion of the light so that the camera doesn't pick up a flare from the lamp and so that the light shines only where the cameraman wants it to shine.

The cameraman may want to add other lights to remove shadows or lighten specific areas. For example, he may use a small eye light just to add sparkle to the subject's eyes.

In a memo to cameramen and correspondents Gary Franklin, formerly ABC News film review manager, made these points:

> The background to a standupper must be photographically compatible.
>
> That means doing your bit to avoid that most common photographic problem: shots of correspondents and interview subjects backgrounded by glaring sky, water, desert and beach — so that the color system finds itself unable to handle the great difference between that bright background and the lesser light, being reflected from the face (especially, a sun-tanned or black person's face). The too-often result: loss of tones and detail.
>
> Of course, the cameraman has his collection of fill-lights and reflectors — but under some conditions, even these are not enough. (That's why Hollywood location crews have trucks, to lug arc-lights and huge reflectors.)
>
> One solution which often works: making the standupper shot a slight "high angle" shot, the camera shooting downwards, to avoid sky and/or a too-bright background, Not too high, though, otherwise you'll look uncomfortable, trying to talk to that thing up there.
>
> Try to avoid being hit by near-vertical, midday sunlight. It sends dark shadows running down from eyebrows, noses and cheek-bones. (Again, even fill-lights and reflectors sometimes won't cure such visual ills.)
>
> Furthermore, beware of in-and-out-from-behind-the-clouds sunlight. Although the cameraman can and does compensate for the varying light, through manipulation of his f/stop ring, it is usually obvious, visually distracting, and much easier to move on to a shaded location.
>
> Indoors, try to avoid flat, old-fashioned newsreel lighting, when we have control over the light and/or camera position.
>
> When limited to two lights, the backlight *or* the fill can be elimi-

nated. (The fill is expendable especially when the subject is a man, whose face can stand harsher light.) The effect is then one of a strong sidelight, covering almost all of the visible face, with the backlight highlighting the right cheek and side and the hair.

Portable lights need not be kept immediately adjacent to the camera. When more than one light can be set up, don't forget the backlight for depth and separation.

Let your light do more than just move the exposure meter needle to the desired reading. Let light work for you creatively, even in straight news coverage.

FILM AND PROCESSING

News events happen under a bewildering variety of lighting and temperature conditions. Eastman Kodak and other companies which manufacture news film engage in continuous research to improve their product. The present trend toward color film has compounded the problems of manufacturing consistently high quality film. At present, no single type of film, either black and white or color, is suitable for all purposes and all conditions. Perhaps there will never be a single all-purpose film.

In choosing a film type, the cameraman must compromise between speed and graininess. Fine grain films are, unfortunately, slow, requiring plenty of light. High speed films (which record images under poor lighting condition) are, unfortunately, grainy. The cameraman must decide how much speed he is willing to sacrifice for the quality of granularity he desires; or, vice-versa, how much graininess he will put up with in order to get the speed capacity he wants.

At the time of publication of this book, the most popular newsreel color film was Eastman Kodak's EF 7242, an all-purpose film, with a range of speed ratings from ASA 20, under optimum outdoor lighting conditions, to ASA 1000, which can still provide a picture, although a grainy picture. EF 7242 is a reversal film; that is, the film comes out of the developing tank as a positive print.

The most popular black-and-white types of film for newsreel or documentary shooting were DuPont 936 A, negative film; DuPont 931 A, reversal film; and Eastman Tri-X 7278, reversal film. When negative film is televised, polarity must be changed electronically. Positive film needs no change.

Color processors have been replacing black-and-white film processors at commercial labs and television stations for several years, although the old black-and-white processor may be kept around for occasional use. Color processing requires more steps which means more tanks for chemicals, which means more cost, but the price drops as small new processors come along. Houston Fearless has offered a six-foot-long processor for

$10,000, promising an output of 15 feet per minute for 16mm film. Larger processors develop film considerably faster.

The kind of chemicals used and their temperatures also determine the speed at which film is processed or "souped." The system known as the Houston Fearless CR 100 Chemistry, used in an HF Colormaster processor, can spew 16 mm newsfilm out at 53 feet per minute after a 15-minute access time; that is, the first frame of film normally takes 15 minutes to go through the processor, although in an emergency, this can be cut to 12 minutes. With this processor and chemistry, 400 feet of film takes about 23 minutes to develop. Processors with tanks that can hold twice as much film can process that film twice as fast, after the initial 15-minutes access time.

When a cameraman brings in film he has shot at less than ASA (American Standard Association) specifications, because of poor lighting conditions, processing can be either slowed or altered by temperature change. The film is then "forced" through development. The cameraman should alert the lab technician from the field, if there is deadline pressure, so that the processor can be readied. If film is exposed at double the rated speed (tungsten, 125; daylight, 80, with a filter) the film can be forced with a small loss in quality. With a greater loss in quality, the film can be forced two f-stops, which is quadruple the rated speed.

Graininess increases if film is overexposed or overdeveloped, or if the chemicals in the development tank are heated to increase film speed ("to push it up one more stop") in order to salvage film which otherwise would be too dark. It is the cameraman's responsibility to tell the lab man when developing speed must be altered.

The relationship of poor exposure and poor development causes these results:

a) overexposure and overdevelopment: graininess.
b) overexposure and underdevelopment: washed out image.
c) underexposure and overdevelopment: contrastiness and fog.
d) underexposure and underdevelopment: fog.

Wherever possible, normal exposure coupled with normal development should be the rule.

SUPER 8

At this writing, all or almost all television stations in the nation use 16mm film exclusively. But Super 8 seems to offer potential competition. Approximately half the cost of 16mm film, it is already being used in some university film courses.

Besides several silent Super 8 cameras on the market, Leica sells a silent camera with a socket which can be used for a sync sound hookup to a tape recorder. And one company, Riker Corporation of Clark, N.J., has manufactured a Super 8 film chain for silent film.

A Super 8 camera is lighter not only on the pocketbook. Dave Hamer, of KMTV, Omaha, noted with a grin: [2]

> . . . what happened to the "cinematographer"? He discovered sound-on-film.
>
> Down with the Filmo (8 lbs) and up with the Auricon (16 lbs). Off with the fixed lens (4 oz), on with the zoom (3 lbs), and strap on an external magazine (7 lbs) and carry a crateful more.
>
> Tote that Pro-Junior (13 lbs) . . . lift that Frezzolini (13 lbs) . . . push that amplifier (5½ lbs) . . . tug that mike (2 lbs) . . . trip over those cables (7 lbs) . . . cart those Sun Guns (7 lbs each) . . . drag that Cinekad, the spare parts, tubes, bulbs, batteries, fuses, etc. Smile, be a good ambassador for the profession, and oh yes! take the Filmo (8 lbs) for a "cover shot." . . . . I don't mind. Really.
>
> But it does sort of bug me when the neighbor down the street, pops in with his Super-Eight, f 1.8, ten-to-one zoom, mag sound, ni-cads, and electric eye. He's toting it in his pocket between takes!
>
> There but for the grace of the manufacturers and suppliers go I!

Advantages of Super 8: cameras are less noticeable, a great advantage in covering demonstrations and riots; cameras and auxiliary gear are lighter; existing cameras have such built-in features as automatic exposure, power zooms, and battery power that will drive much more film past a lens aperture than the spring on a 16mm silent camera; film is cheaper; processing is faster.

Disadvantages of Super 8 (at time of publication): editing is awkward and difficult; a mag stripe, single system camera is not available; telecine equipment is not readily available; film quality is not quite up to 16mm.

Disadvantages can be at least partially overcome by either transferring the Super 8 to videotape for editing and replay, or editing the Super 8 first and then transferring it to videotape through a studio control room operation, where a director can dub A and B rolls plus an audio track, or whatever other combination of input material he has, onto videotape for replay during the newscast.

If Super 8 developing tanks could be made small enough, cheap enough, and simple enough (perhaps able to take a cassette or cartridge), a cameraman could keep a tank in his car, developing the film as he traveled from one assignment to another or returned to the studio.

FOR THE STUDENT

1. Shoot a film story with a zoom lens and another with a three-lens turret. Compare them.

2. Why does a cameraman use a silent camera?
3. Compare the advantages of a sound camera with the advantages of syncsound, using a silent camera and a synchronous tape recorder.
4. Compare the advantages of mag and optical stripe film.
5. What lights would you use for these situations: fire at night; interview in a hotel room furnished with dark drapes and a dark rug; tour of a new school?
6. Without looking back in this chapter, can you recall the effects of combinations of over- and under-exposure and development?
7. Cite three types of news stories which could be presented to advantage by single frame filming.
8. Cite three types of news stories which could use swish pans and three which could use pop zooms to advantage.
9. Estimate the amount of film you would need to cover the average automobile collision, a parade, a routine news conference. How do your estimates compare with those made by other students?
10. Suppose you worked for a station which limited a cameraman to 50 feet of film for a collision and 100 feet for a parade or a news conference. Plan each assignment.

12

SOUND

NETWORKS AND STATIONS in major cities hire a soundman to accompany a cameraman. He is the man in the background, quietly listening and monitoring his amplifer while the focus of attention is on the reporter and the cameraman. This does not diminish the soundman's importance in covering the news story, for the skills and experience he brings to the story can mean the difference between excellence and disaster.

Cameramen for most of the television news departments in the nation handle the sound along with the picture. Usually this means they set up the mike and the amplifier, check the level before they start filming, and then occasionally glance at the meter to make sure sound is being recorded on the mag track. An earpiece helps. When a reporter is not busy and a cameraman is, the reporter lends a hand with the audio.

EQUIPMENT

The basic sound equipment is:

An amplifier

A standard amplifier may weigh about three pounds. It is a "black box," maybe measuring 10″ x 8″ x 3″ with two microphone inputs, volume controls and a transmission cable leading to the sound camera. This "umbilical cord" ties the soundman to the cameraman whenever they "go portable," so that they work no more than six feet apart unless special

The soundman monitors what is recorded on film. The sound he hears has passed through the microphone(s) and the amplifier. As he listens and watches his VU meter, he adjusts the volume to compensate for such things as a speaker varying the level of his voice or shifting his position away from a microphone fixed to a podium.

cables separate them. Normally battery powered, the amplifier also uses A.C. power.

Microphones

Microphones vary according to how they vibrate, their pick-up coverage and their impedance (similar to electrical resistance).

In ribbon, or velocity, mikes, a metallic ribbon vibrates when sound waves strike it. Used mostly in studios, ribbon mikes are sensitive over a wide frequency range. They transmit the voice well and sometimes deepen it. Try an RCA 77-DX or BX-5B if you want more vocal depth and resonance, or if you have trouble with the letter *p* or the letter *s*.

In dynamic, or pressure, microphones a diaphragm attached to a coil vibrates when sound waves strike it. The dynamic mike is more rugged but less sensitive than other microphones. It does not pick up wind noise easily, which is one of several reasons why dynamic mikes are the all-purpose microphones. Hand-held mikes, lavaliers and wireless mikes are usually dynamic. So are shotgun mikes, like the Electro-Voice 642. Dynamic mikes can also be made thumb size. A disadvantage: unless you are careful, a dynamic mike will pop your *p*'s and hiss your *s*'s. Models include Electro-Voice's RE-15, RE-55, 635A, 666; RCA's BK-1A; Shure's SM-57 and SM-58.

In condenser mikes, a diaphragm attached to a backplate vibrates when sound strikes it. A condenser mike is extremely sensitive to sound, so it can be used in certain situations as a shot gun mike, like Sony's C-77 FET.

There are also crystal mikes, which depend upon a voltage change when pressure is applied to a certain kind of salt. Crystal mikes are not commonly used in television news.

In general, it is best to talk *into* a ribbon microphone and *across* dynamic and condenser microphones.

Mikes are also classified by the way they pick up sound. Unidirectional: only sound in front of the mike is transmitted. Bidirectional: sound picked up in front and back, but not to the sides. Omnidirectional: sound in any direction. Cardioid: sound picked up to the front and sides. Multidirectional: pickup patterns may be altered by turning a screw. Most hand-held microphones, lavaliers, and wireless microphones are omnidirectional.

And they are classified by impedance. Dynamic mikes and some ribbon mikes have a low impedance, which permits the reporter to stay as far away from the amplifier as he likes, perhaps with as much as 100 yards of cable. But the sensitivity of a low impedance mike is low and a transformer is needed if the mike is feeding high impedance equipment. A high impedance mike, such as a good ribbon mike, a condenser mike or a crystal mike, is quite sensitive but is limited to a cable length of, at most, 20 feet. Also, high impedance mike cables make noise if you move them.

Four kinds of microphones are used by television newsmen in the field:

1. *Hand-held mike.* With a stand, the hand-held mike becomes a desk mike. Frequently used: EV 655-C, EV 665, RCA BK-1-A. Outdoors, especially with a noisy background, the hand-held mikes should be close to the speakers. With noise all around, the reporter should hold the mike a few inches from whoever is speaking, pointed straight up so the voice crosses the mike, avoiding the problem of plosives and sibilants. During an interview in noisy surroundings he will hold the mike now in front of the interviewee's chin, now in front of his own. If the setting is not noisy, the mike should not wiggle back and forth. The reporter can hold it midway between himself and the interviewee. Or, if the interviewee has a soft voice, closer to him.

2. *Lavaliers,* with cords, are hung from the subject's neck like a necktie. The microphone reaches to the breastbone, and can be placed either in front or behind a necktie. A small amount of audio quality is lost when the "lav" goes behind a necktie, but some soundmen prefer to place it there for appearance sake. A "lav" can also be fitted beneath a jacket lapel. Popular "lavs": RCA BK-6B, EV 659-A.

3. *Shotgun mike.* This microphone picks up sound at a distance. It may be used when a camera crew goes portable or when there is neither time nor opportunity to use lavaliers or desk mikes. Being highly directional, the shotgun mike picks up sound emanating mostly from the direction in which it is pointed. Very little comes from sources outside the nar-

row cone which constitutes its receiving area. The cone is much like that of a flashlight beam.

When the distant sound comes from a wide area, such as a football cheering section or a marching band on a football field, an ordinary desk mike pointed at a small parabolic reflector gathers the sound very well. For truly sharp shotgun mike effect, use a large parabola.

4. *Wireless mike.* Also called a radio mike or an FM mike, it usually hangs like a lavalier microphone, connected by a short cable to a small transmitter worn inside a pocket or hooked to a belt, with an antenna pinned to the clothing. The sound is picked up over a range of up to 6000 feet by a receiver plugged into the amplifier. Budelman, Stevens and Sony build broadcast-quality wireless mikes, but they are expensive and lack the quality of hard-wire microphones. They also require separate FCC licenses because they are FM transmitting stations of a sort.

A tape recorder

A small, lightweight, battery-operated tape recorder of good quality is useful for catching wild track (independent) sound, which is recorded on quarter-inch tape, the same audio tape used in any tape recorder.

A charger

Amplifier batteries run down and must be recharged. The charger, another small "black box," performs this job, and this also serves as an A.C. adapter.

A supply of cables

PROBLEMS AND SOLUTIONS

1. On long establishing shots where a cable cannot be visible and—because this is news coverage—a boom mike is unavailable, the soundman may use a radio mike. The audio quality is not always satisfactory. For instance, a passing automobile in an outdoor shot will sometimes be heard on the audio track as a series of pops. The pops are caused by spark plugs. Nevertheless, the audio track produced by a radio mike is better than no track at all. Later, if the film editor finds it objectionable, he can cut out some or all of the track as desired.

2. At this point we may note a documentary technique using such sound in a unique way. Where a narrator on location is speaking in the midst of a noisy establishing shot, the sound track from the radio mike is used as a cue track in a studio to redo the sound. The narrator sits in the studio listening on earphones to the sound of his own voice, and speaks his lines again, matching his own lip movements. A track of background sound from the track of a tape recorder or camera is then added. The re-

The audio engineer in a television studio sits before a console equipped with "faders" or "pots" (short for potentiometers) to control volume. There is one for each source of sound, such as studio microphones, videotape machines, film projectors, audio tape and cassette players, and a pair of turntables usually located near the audio console. There is also a "master-gain" fader or "mixer" and an audio patchboard, which looks like a small telephone switchboard. Not all of these are visible in this photo.

sult is a reproduction of the scene with satsifactory audio quality. This process, also used in shooting feature motion pictures, is called "dialogue looping" and saves reshooting a scene which has poor audio quality.

3. Where it is necessary to join two pieces of film with sharply different audio quality in the narration, an audio bridge serves the same purpose that a cutaway serves to connect two mismatched pieces of film. A documentary often begins with a narrator on camera in an outdoor location. Such an opening keeps the narrator from being merely a disembodied voice. But this opening may be followed by a narration track done in a studio. The difference in quality is evident to all listeners, unless an audio bridge is used. For example, if the documentary is about automobiles, the narrator's on-camera introduction could be followed by an engine starting up, followed in turn by a matching engine noise in the first scene over which the studio narration track is laid. The advance planning necessary for this sound bridge produces a more professional product in the critical opening minutes of a documentary.

4. The quality difference between outdoor and indoor sound is mainly in the dispersion of sound waves outdoors because there are no walls to reflect them. To compensate for the drop in the narrator's volume a sound man outdoors must raise his audio levels, which unfortunately increases the amount of "white noise" in the signal-to-noise ratio.

5. The effect of wind is a particular outdoor problem. It is compensated for by one of two devices presently used by television soundmen. One device is a windscreen. This is a microphone cover made of a material like foam rubber. The other device is a wind bypass filter, which filters out frequencies below 100 cycles.

6. The lower frequencies add strength and resonance to voices. Almost all lavalier microphones cut off low frequencies unless the microphone is touching the speaker's chest. Lavalier microphones were designed to rest against the chest cavities. Reporters who hold lavalier mikes in their hands are often unaware that by doing so they are giving their voices a higher and slightly less masculine ring. Lavalier mikes should rest on or beneath neckties, against shirts or dresses where they can pick up the resonance of the thoracic cavity.

7. When a reporter is tired, his voice level drops. A soundman sees the drop as a movement of the needle on the meter of his amplifier. The soundman compensates by raising his gain, or volume level, especially on stories that take a full day to cover, in this way matching the reporter's fresh morning voice with his weary evening voice. A tired voice may also possess a harsh edge. Soundmen can do nothing about this. The reporter helps himself best by continuing to be relaxed, to speak slowly and to enunciate clearly.

8. A cheaply made microphone gives a voice a harsh quality. The frequency reception of a poor microphone is slightly distorted, so that listeners strain to hear. Listeners may become irritated after hearing the voices for a minute or so.

The microphone is not an ear. In some ways it is superior to the ear purely as a receptor of sound, because the human brain filters out extraneous background noises. We are familiar with the story of the veteran newspaper copy editor who sits beside a bank of teletype machines, barely conscious of their clacking. A visitor comes in and asks, "How can you work in all this noise?" The editor responds innocently, "What noise?" On the other hand, an annoying sound will be heard far out of proportion to its intensity.

The experienced soundman, aware of the difference between the microphone and the ear, tries to place his microphone where it will pick up not what the ear picks up, but what the brain filters through—in other words, what the listener thinks he would hear if he were at the scene.

9. Sometimes the soundman cheats a little to establish this perspective. For example, the the wife of Governor Ronald Reagan of California

While news analyst Howard K. Smith waits, a soundman fastens a lavalier mike underneath the jacket of the man to be interviewed. If carefully placed and pre-tested, the microphone can provide professional quality sound yet remain out of view.

was dismayed at the condition and location of the governor's mansion in Sacramento. Among the things which concerned Mrs. Reagan, mother of a young son, was the busy traffic outside. A television news camera crew filmed Mrs. Reagan inside the mansion describing its limitations. The soundman was aware that a lavalier microphone hanging from Mrs. Reagan's neck would not give listeners a true perspective of the amount of traffic outside her window. The soundman solved this problem by placing a second microphone on the window ledge. He then balanced the sound levels coming into his amplifier. When Mrs. Reagan referred to the traffic outside, the soundman briefly raised the gain of the window ledge microphone for emphasis. He was also considering the possibility that a film editor might choose to double chain film of the traffic at this point. Had he wished to, the soundman could have made the traffic on the street in Sacramento, California, sound like Times Square.

10. Riding the amplifier gain offers a soundman opportunity for editorial judgment or, if he is unethical, for blatant distortion. The unscrupulous soundman, present at a political speech to which he is hostile, can twiddle the knobs to make rousing applause seem lukewarm. Or he can suggest to a reporter he does not like that sound reception is better if a lavalier mike is hand held. More than one politician has clutched a lavalier handed to him by a politically antagonistic soundman.

At times the soundman's suggestion results in filming the one scene which gives a news story or a feature its unique character. Sound, as we know, creates moods and sparks the imagination. Critics have frequently mentioned that the belly laughs by radio audiences listening to Jack Benny's Maxwell car starting up or Benny's trips to his vault died away when the same gags were visually presented on television.

11. The greatest of all broadcast newsmen was Ed Murrow. His daily broadcasts from London during the Blitz generated in Americans a rapport with the English people which is credited with helping to change American public opinion from isolationist to interventionist. Murrow knew how to use a microphone to heighten perception. For one broadcast after a particularly nasty firebombing of London, he wanted to show how resilient Londoners were. He placed a microphone on a sidewalk to catch the footsteps of people in the city hurrying to work the next morning. For another broadcast, he wanted to illustrate the waste war brings. He did a recording in a bombed grocery store. Murrow described the ruin around him, listing some of the items which no one could now eat in the food-scarce country. Among the items was a can of peaches still on a shelf, dripping juice to the dusty floor. He placed the microphone so that well-fed Americans an ocean away would hear the drip drip drip of the juice from a broken can of peaches.

12. Each story location requires its own audio reception arrangements, just as it requires individual arrangements for optimum filming. As an example, where the people are seated at a table, a single omnidirectional microphone on a stand often provides better sound than the overlapping reception of three lavalier mikes hung around the speakers' necks. However, if the room is "boomy" with a lot of hard wall space near the mikes, lavaliers may be better adapted to the conditions because they are closer to the speakers. It may even be necessary for good sound reception to move the speakers to another part of the room if they happen to be sitting at an equidistance from two hard wall corners, which sharply reflect sound waves.

13. During news conferences or speeches covered by several stations, to get rid of the clutter of microphones and their call letters, audio bridges, or "mults," are used. The President of the United States and other top officials use them. In at least one city, Hartford, Conn., one television station WTIC, provides a bridge as a pool service. The bridge is simply a box into which tape recorders and sound camera amplifiers are plugged. The WTIC bridge, made from $250 worth of parts, connects up to 18 audio terminals with a single microphone. WTIC carries along adapters for just about every camera, tape recorder or microphone in use.

14. In a *New York Times* article,[1] Joan Walker detailed some of the audio techniques employed in news and new-related situations, including:

> . . . the lavalier microphone that Lyndon Johnson had hidden under his jacket during his press conference last November. That was

the press conference where, for the first time, Mr. Johnson left the lectern with the Presidential seal and stationary microphone on it. The long microphone cable that ran from his lavalier mike to a microphone input in the wall gave him mobility, and he used it. He walked up and down the platform, clenched his fists, raised his arms, drew curves in the air, and generally gestured away in a performance that brought to the TV screen the debut of what has been described variously as "the real Johnson," or "the new *old* Johnson." Whichever it was, it was effective use of television, and that is what wins ball games.

On their regular shows, David Brinkley and Walter Cronkite use lavalier microphones, just like the one the President used. They all hide their mikes under their buttoned jackets. When Peter Jennings had his news show, it was easy to hide his because, as the most clothes-conscious of the evening newscasters, he has very high lapels on his suits. Hugh Downs almost flaunts his, just tossing it around his neck and leaving it outside his jacket in full view of the *Today* audience. Barbara Walters, like most ladies, tries to hide hers under her dress. A lavalier mike can absolutely ruin the lines of a Donald Brooks.

Then there are the wireless microphones. They consist of a small microphone that is, depending on the sex of the wearer, clipped onto a bra or attached to a tie, shirt, or breast pocket. A cord then goes, inside the clothing, to a transmitter which is about the size of a cigarette pack and which is usually, no matter what the sex, somewhere around the hip hidden in a pouch. From the transmitter—say between the dress and the slip or down the trouser leg—dangles about 18 inches of tiny wire. It is the antenna. The wearer, thus rigged, is a walking radio station operating on an FCC-approved frequency. He is subject to interference but, under the right conditions, he has a great deal of mobility. Wireless mikes are used extensively in nightclubs and in the theater, especially in musicals. Her wireless mike is the reason Pearl Bailey can murmur "back where I belong" and IT COMES OUT LIKE THIS. The wireless mike is essential for some documentaries, especially those involving non-pros—policemen, firemen, welfare recipients, hospital patients, drug addicts. With a mike staring at him or with cables snaking all over the floor, the subject of a documentary is acutely conscious of the equipment, and becomes self-conscious. With a wireless mike, he soon forgets that every word he says is being broadcast. Thus comes verisimilitude, even television vérité.

Without a wireless mike, NBC could never have done that famous *Comedian Backstage* in which Shelly Berman blew his top. Without a wireless mike, *The Violent World of Sam Huff* would not have been as effective. With it attached to the Giants' linebacker during a game, the audience got to hear the huddles and the grunts and all the pounding thumping football noises. Without a wireless mike, Daniel Moynihan and Frank McGee would not have been anywhere near as moving as they were when they walked through the rubble of the aftermath of the Detroit riots. Cables trailing after them would have ruined the effect.

Where the wireless mike really came into its own, of course, was on *Person to Person* (1953-1961). Without it, there would have been no *Person to Person*; and Lee Bailey's *Good Company* would not have had even its short life. After all, viewers can't pretend they've been invited into a celebrity's private home for a personal tour if the celebrity, while modestly reminiscing about his trophies, is drooling cables wherever he goes. But, while the wireless mike made the show possible, it gave the *Person to Person* crew more trouble than all the celebrities put together. Men and show folk, used to the camaraderie of the locker and the dressing room, presented few problems when it came to rigging them. (Two categories of men used to be difficult: Englishmen and anyone who affected bow ties. It seems that English tailors don't provide pockets for transmitters, and that was before the day the transmitter pouch was invented. As for the bow-tie wearers, they just had to switch to four-in-hands until microphones got smaller. RCA has a microphone today that is great for a bow tie: It is one inch long and the width of a man's little finger.) The ladies presented the problems. For instance, Kathleen Winsor, although she had written *Forever Amber* and married Artie Shaw, was so shy that she refused to be wired by a strange technician. A technician had to explain the procedure to her maid, and the maid did the rigging. It worked except that the technician forgot to mention that the sensitive side of the mike should be *away* from the skin, with the result that Miss Winsor's heartbeat was audible to all throughout her stint.

In those days it took bouffant skirts to hide the transmitters, but some slim women, like Constance Bennett and Lillian Gish, were not about to hide their figures in bouffant skirts. (Miss Gish had a slim-lined Valentina, and that dress was going to be on that show.) Their transmitters had to be taped to their inside lower thighs with the same elastic bandage football players use on bum knees. That is where the transmitters still go when the dresses are tight.

As one soundman put it, 'With show folk, it's OK to hook a mike to their brassieres, but if it's a personage, like Mrs. Roosevelt or Jackie Kennedy, well, you do something else.' Mrs. Kennedy is not only a personage; she also has a voice that is so small that a boom has trouble picking it up. *Person to Person* sovled her problems by rigging the then-Senator Kennedy and having him do the walking around while she sat still and talked into a hidden, stationary, close-up mike. On other occasions, when she needed to be rigged, she agreed with alacrity, and her secretary did the rigging.

Awareness of audio problems and solutions comes with attention and experience. Considerations of sound usually take second place to considerations of picture and story. And within limits, it must be this way. The problems of the soundman, like sound itself, are a matter of perspective. But the problems exist. They should be recognized. They should be dealt with wherever possible. The best compliment a soundman can get in daily news coverage is that his product draws no attention to itself.

FOR THE STUDENT

1. For what reasons, if any, should the soundman alter sound reception?
2. In what ways can a soundman affect news coverage?
3. Record the same sound source through different types and models of microphones. Repeat this test for several sound sources; e.g., the crowd at a football game, an MOS on a busy street, a news conference, an auditorium lecture (picking up the sound at a distance).
4. What problems of sound quality may come with double chaining? How can they be solved?
5. With a short introduction and no narration, put a short news feature story on audio tape.
6. If possible, spend a day or two with a cameraman who serves as his own soundman. Ask him to teach you to use the amplifier and the mikes. If no union rules are violated, assist him on a few stories by monitoring the amplifier while he shoots film.
7. Audio tape a lecture or a public meeting. What technical difficulties did you encounter? If you did not overcome them, how *might* you do so?
8. What should a reporter who does not handle sound equipment know about sound?
9. Ed Murrow used sound dramatically in covering the London blitz for CBS Radio. What might you record to heighten radio or television coverage of a political demonstration? A high school graduation exercise? High rise construction?
10. Cite three news events during which a soundman might usefully record wild track sound.

13

FILM EDITING

"TODAY THE FILM editor's scissor wields enormous power." ABC President Elton Rule observed. "That scissor can be a deadly weapon used to sell a point of view or a constructive tool used to tell a story clearly and well."

The film editor is both artist and technician. If he fails as an artist— if he lacks experience, imagination and, occasionally, flair—his work will be usable, although pedestrian. But if he fails as a technician—if he is sloppy or slow—he sows ruin for a new operation. Film stories do not get on the air. Film breaks in the projector. Frames which should be eliminated are seen in homes everywhere in the city.

The artistic elements in film editing will not be learned from a textbook. They are instilled by practice combined with alertness. A textbook can only offer a few descriptions, some techniques, a trick of the trade here and there, and some ideas which others tried and liked.

The other elements of film editing, on the technical side, can be taught. Technical competence begins with a knowledge of the film editor's environment and tools.

THE FILM EDITING ROOM

The film editor's workshop is often a small windowless room conveniently near the newsroom. If the station does its own film processing, the room with the developing tanks may also be nearby.

The film editing room should be clean. Dust and film emulsion are not friends. Strips of film lying on the floor or left hanging on a rack or taped to the bench get in the way of an editing job, sometimes cause delays when the editor must search for a scene, and generally give evidence of a careless editing operation. If possible, the editing room should not be used for the film library as well. When film must be kept in the room, it should be stored in racks and shelves as separate from the working operation as the editor can manage. Reels of film lying on an editing bench encroach on the editor's workspace. Spare empty reels also belong on shelves and racks.

A long and wide editing bench is worth the space it takes. It should always be kept clean and free of storage. On it will go a splicer, a viewer and a sound reader. A pair of rewinds will be fastened like vises and should be perfectly aligned with each other. When the rewinds are not aligned, the film rubs the side of the reels as it is wound from one rewind to the other. Dirt or peelings accumulated on the reel transfer to the film, imbedding in the emulsion and scratching the film when it is screened in a projector.

EQUIPMENT

Splicer.

The mechanical device which bonds two pieces of film together with film cement (Ethyloid) can be either a hot splicer or a cold splicer. The latter is cheaper by far, but a splice is more difficult to make on a cold splicer, and it is more likely to break. A hot splicer, which is plugged into a wall socket, should be a standard piece of equipment in every television newsroom.

Another type of splicer uses tape to bond the film. This splicer is slower than the more commonly used overlap splicer and may put dust on the splice unless the editing room is kept antiseptically clean. On the other hand, the tape splicer, by butt-ending the film, avoids the double thickness which can cause a jiggle in a projector gate.

Viewer

This usually sits on the editing bench near the splicer and the sound reader. Like the splicer, it is brought to a part of the bench between the rewinds when it is needed, so that the film passes through it smoothly. The viewer is simply a device to magnify the film which runs through it on a sprocket wheel track. Although film can be viewed instead through a projector or merely by holding it up to the light, a film viewer is a handy and valuable piece of equipment. A projector is bothersome to thread, and may scratch the film. Too much is missed by holding a strip of 16mm film up to the light.

Sound reader

Like the viewer, the sound reader, which picks up and plays film sound tracks, enables the film editor to work at his editing bench. It usually consists of one or two sound receiving sources, an amplifier, a counter and one or more film tracking wheels. One of the most popular sound readers consists of a "mag head" (to transmit the sound of magnetic striping), a separate amplifier, a counter that counts in minutes and seconds (a footage counter is a nuisance, requiring a conversion table to translate feet to seconds), and a four-gang synchronizer. The newsfilm editor will probably never need more than two tracking wheels unless he edits a documentary requiring dissolves and double system shooting (which will be explained later in this chapter).

The four-gang synchronous sound reader can be equipped with a motor drive which runs at 16 mm projection speed. This produces normal speech, instead of the meandering or rushing pattern resulting from manual operation of the rewinds. By using the motor drive, the editor is freed from the trouble of taking his film off the editing bench and mounting it on a projector just to hear the audio track. Another type of sound reader often found in editing rooms consists of nothing but a magnetic sound head and a sprocket track, without a counter.

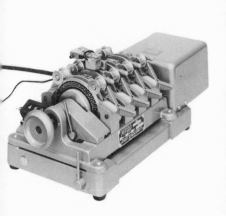 

A motor drive hooked to a synchronizer permits the editor to listen to sound as it is normally heard, without having to take the sound reel off the work bench and mount it on a projector. The motor is geared to feed 16 mm. film at its usual projection speed.

The film editor at work. His bench is kept clean of extraneous material, including old bits of film. A four-gang synchronizer centered between a pair of rewinds enables him to edit from a single reel or from a complex of three picture reels and a sound track reel.

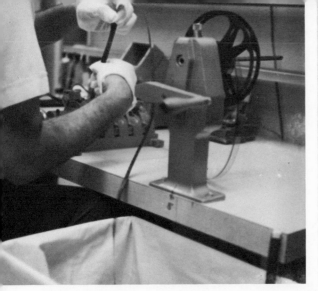

Pieces of film likely to be used in the air clip are hung by the film editor in the trim bin (or barrel) prior to splicing. He attaches them to his work bench with bits of masking tape. Unwanted film is collected on the rewind take-up reel.

The Moviola editing machine permits synchronous running of a full-coat sound track and a film reel at the regular film speed of 24 frames per second. It also permits the normal speed running of magnetic-striped or optical-striped sound film.

Another popular sound reader contains both optical and magnetic heads, plus an amplifier and a counter, all in one self-contained unit. Only one piece of film goes through at a time, however, and this model is not as convenient as the four-gang sound reader described above, but it has the advantage of two sound heads. Both kinds of sound readers provide jack outputs for headsets, which may be used instead of the built-in speakers.

Editing machine

This runs at projection speed, or at any slower speed, right down to still framing. By separating picture and sound sources, the editing machine combines some of the advantages of a projector with some of the advantages of editing table equipment. Some editors like to use a "Moviola" (the word is generally used to refer to the editing machine, but the Moviola Manufacturing Co. makes a wide range of editing equipment and other companies manufacture editing machines). Other editors prefer working at a bench with a viewer and a synchronous sound reader.

Editing barrel

Also called a "trim bin," the barrel is actually a large white cloth bag, about two feet in diameter by three feet deep, held in a frame or set in a bin. As the editor removes scenes from an unedited reel preparatory to assembling a film story, he dangles the film in the bag, keeping it from dragging onto the dusty floor, perhaps to get stepped on. The film strips hang

from a frame of some sort—such as a bar holding spring steel hooks—
or are pasted with bits of masking tape to the edge of the bench. If a frame
is used, it can consist of rows of pointed hooks over which film sprocket
holes easily slip, or the frame can consist of a row of spring clothespins.
The pointed hooks can be dangerous. Clothespins may be more trouble
than they are worth. Using bits of masking tape is the simplest method,
one which can be recommended.

Reels

The editor should keep a supply of reels of the following lengths:
100 feet (these are usually plastic); 400 feet (most useful); 1200 feet;
1,600 feet; and 2,000 feet. The 400-foot reels take 10 minutes of film, the
1,200-foot and 1,600-foot reels hold half-hour documentaries, and the
2,000-foot reels hold nearly an hour of film. For exact figures, divide the
length of the film by the film speed, 36 feet a minute. The editor should
also have a 400-foot split reel and a 1,200-foot split reel for coring film,
plus a supply of 100-foot and 200-foot cores. The cores are used for stor-
ing and shipping film.

The reels should be kept as clean as possible. When film is spun onto
a dirty reel it picks up dirt and dust which leave scratches.

Cue marker

This simple device scrapes away tiny circles of emulsion, leaving
little white spots in the corners of several frames of film. Not all film editors use cue marks, depending instead on timings and verbal end cues to
tell the director when his film is about to run out. Those who do use cue
marks may put them at two places on each film clip, say six seconds before
the end of the clip and one second before the end.

Grease pencil

A grease pencil allows the film editor to mark the place he wants to
cut, without the finality of actually cutting. For example, if the editor is
considering an overlap jump cut (matched action) which would not be
obvious on the air, he will want to roll the two pieces of film through his
viewer several times before he actually cuts the film in order to assure himself that the splice will not be obvious. Also, when the film editor is working with a reporter or writer, he should mark the places to be cut with his
grease pencil. Not only does this permit the reporter or writer to go off
sooner to write his copy but it also gives the film editor a second chance, by
himself, to consider the editing decisions they have made. A bright yellow
or white grease pencil mark is easier to locate than a black mark. Marks
and arrows drawn while the film is on a projector should be made over the
sound head, not against the film gate. All grease marks should be wiped off

before splicing. A grease pencil can also be used to mark numbers on the bits of masking tape attaching film segments to a bench, noting the order in which they will be spliced onto the reel. And it can be used to mark a piece of tape identifying each reel of arriving film.

Editing gloves

Buy white cotton gloves by the dozen from a company which sells mortician's supplies. They're cheap and they do the job, which is to protect the film from fingerprints (difficult or impossible to remove) and to protect the film editor's hands from skin irritation and film-edge cuts. Either worn or used as cloths, editing gloves wipe away mag tracks and grease pencil marks at the splices. Film cleaner removes dust and lint but won't remove grease pencil marks. Only an editing glove (not a bare finger) should do this job. Editing gloves should be worn on both hands. As for film cleaner, a velvet pad (best), a cloth or a glove soaked in cleaner should be used to wipe a reel of film clean after it is fully assembled, the last thing the film editor does before taking the film off to the projection room to be aired.

Other supplies

Needed, too, are *film cement; magnetic film cleaner* (other cleaners may take off the magnetic track); *acetone* (a good cleaning fluid for the splicer): a *degausser,* or *bar magnet,* to wipe out the sound track where it is not wanted; *a velvet pad* (on which film cleaner is sprinkled; the editor pinches the film gently with the dampened pad and runs the film through the pad using the rewind); and a roll of *masking tape.* The film editor should also have reels of academy or SMPTE leader (which contain numbers spaced to show the seconds remaining before picture appears) and at least one kind of dark leader (black or yellow opaque are common) plus, perhaps, a reel of clear or white leader.

SPLICING

Explaining how to make a splice is akin to explaining how to blow your nose. The job is more difficult to describe than to do, and the only way to learn is by doing, often.

Any piece of film—silent, mag track or optical track—may be spliced to any other, provided they both are of the same width (8mm, 16mm, 35mm) and the same polarity (positive or negative). Black-and-white film *could* be spliced to color film, but this would cause a sharp change in shading, for which a video shader could not compensate quickly enough to avoid a sloppy appearance on the home set. Such a splice is not recommended. If it is necessary to connect dissimilar pieces of film, it is better to write a "roll-thru" into the script: the director cuts back to the newscaster or to a still for enough seconds to enable the man at the video switching controls to change polarity or adjust his shading, and for the projectionist to replace a magnetic head with an optical head, in the rare event that these dissimilar types of sound film must be on the same reel.

Before splicing magnetic film, the mag track at the juncture must be wiped away. Place a drop of film cement on the mag track of the film in the right side of the splicer. Using a white glove or a clean rag, wipe away the mag track, which lies along the shiny, non-emulsion side of the film. Because the film lies in the splicer emulsion-side up, it is necessary to reach under the film to wipe away the track. The splice may now be made in the usual way, scraping the emulsion from the film lying in the left side of the splicer.

Sometimes it is necessary merely to wipe away the sound, not the entire mag track. To erase magnetic sound, use a magnet. Several styles of "degaussing" magnets are available. The only consideration in choosing and using a magnet is wiping away as much sound as you intend, and no more.

To "degauss" or "bloop" a segment of film, place the magnet on the mag track, making sure that the magnet does not dig into the film, for this might peel the track itself. Then, in one motion, move the magnet along the area of track to be erased. After erasing, run the film through the sound reader again to make sure that all the unwanted sound is gone. There may be times when a single pass of the magnet fails to get every vestige of noise on the track. If any sound still remains, a second pass of the magnet should take care of it.

When the magnet is not in use, store it in a place where it is not likely to fall or accidentally brush against film.

WHERE TO SPLICE

Because sound precedes picture, edit on the *audio* cue at the *start* of a statement. That is, if you want film of a man saying, "Boy, it sure is a hot day," cut at the start of the sound of the "B" in "Boy."

Edit on *video* at the *end* of a statement. Cut when his mouth finishes forming the "ay" sound in "day." And if the statement is the last piece of film in the film clip, leave an extra two or three seconds of film beyond that, giving the director and the TD time to cut back to the newscaster. Be sure to bloop any sound beyond "day," using the magnet *after* splicing tail leader to eliminate the possibility of a popping sound at the splice.

The film editor will cut the *end* of the statement on *audio* if he wants the last word or two to be heard over film of something else; for example, a cutaway of a reporter listening or the back of the head of the man speaking or even an outdoor scene of a hot day. Cutting the end of a statement on audio is known as an overlap cut.

Overlap Cuts

In 16mm motion picture film, the sound track precedes the picture by 26 frames on optical film and 28 frames on magnetic film. That is, the sound that belongs to any given frame of film can be found by counting 26 or 28 frames forward—frames which have already gone past the projector lens. The picture and the sound are separated so that the lens and the sound head in a 16mm projector pick up picture and sound simultaneously.

This spread between picture and sound presents some problems. The biggest problem is known as "lip flap," which occurs when someone says something the editor wants immediately after he says something the editor does not want. The sound track which begins the wanted statement lies beside the picture of the person concluding the unwanted statement. Hence, lip flap, the lips moving to form words which have been blooped. In order to pick up the wanted sound, it is necessary to use the unwanted picture adjacent to it.

Sometimes—and only sometimes—two statements by the same speaker can be overlapped to avoid lip flap. Let us say that, at a news conference, Mr. Smith makes two important statements, one at the beginning, the other near the end of his news conference, and that his second statement was immediately preceeded by a long, dull statement which will not be aired. Let us also say that Smith did not pause between the dull and the important. The way to avoid lip flap, without a cutaway or double chaining, is to overlap the two important statements. The editor cuts the first statement on sound—that is, he cuts the film a few frames past the frame of film which carries the final sound of the last word, not the picture of the lips forming that final sound. He then splices this to the start of sound on the next statement. Viewed through a projector, it appears that Mr. Smith's lip movements just before the start of the second statement from the word we hear at the end of the first statement.

Sometimes this works well. Sometimes it is botched. An experienced editor can judge, before he makes the splice, whether or not the overlap is likely to look natural.

An overlap involving the same speaker will probably not be successful if both pieces of film are close-ups or both are medium shots. Cutting from close-up to close-up of the same face would almost certainly result in an obvious jump cut. The jump cut is far less obvious if the cut is from a close-up to a medium shot or, better still, a long shot, or if it is from a long shot to a close-up. The change in framing distracts the viewers' attention from slight changes in facial expression or the angle of the head. Of course, no change in framing can hide such major differences as a head swiveled from left to right, or the sudden appearance or disappearance of a hat, a pair of glasses, or some other item on or near the head of the speaker.

16MM CONVERSION TABLE 1—Feet to Seconds

Feet	Seconds	Feet	Seconds	Feet	Seconds
1	1.7	13	21.7	25	41.7
2	3.3	14	23.3	26	43.3
3	5	15	25	27	45
4	6.7	16	26.7	28	46.7
5	8.3	17	28.3	29	48.3
6	10	18	30	30	50
7	11.7	19	31.7	31	51.7
8	13.3	20	33.3	32	53.3
9	15	21	35	33	55
10	16.7	22	36.7	34	56.7
11	18.3	23	38.3	35	58.3
12	20	24	40	36	60

16MM CONVERSION TABLE 2—Seconds to Feet

Seconds	Feet	Frames	Seconds	Feet	Frames
1	.6	24	31	18.6	744
2	1.2	48	32	19.2	768
3	1.8	72	33	19.8	792
4	2.4	96	34	20.4	816
5	3.0	120	35	21.0	840
6	3.6	144	36	21.6	864
7	4.2	168	37	22.2	888
8	4.8	192	38	22.8	912
9	5.4	216	39	23.4	936
10	6.0	240	40	24.0	960
11	6.6	264	41	24.6	984
12	7.2	288	42	25.2	1008
13	7.8	312	43	25.8	1032
14	8.4	336	44	26.4	1056
15	9.0	360	45	27.0	1080
16	9.6	384	46	27.6	1104
17	10.2	408	47	28.2	1128
18	10.8	432	48	28.8	1152
19	11.4	456	49	29.4	1176
20	12.0	480	50	30.0	1200
21	12.6	504	51	30.6	1224
22	13.2	528	52	31.2	1248
23	13.8	552	53	31.8	1272
24	14.4	576	54	32.4	1296
25	15.0	600	55	33.0	1320
26	15.6	624	56	33.6	1344
27	16.2	648	57	34.2	1368
28	16.8	672	58	34.8	1392
29	17.4	696	59	35.4	1416
30	18.0	720	60	36.0	1440

← sound

↑ direction of film

←icture →

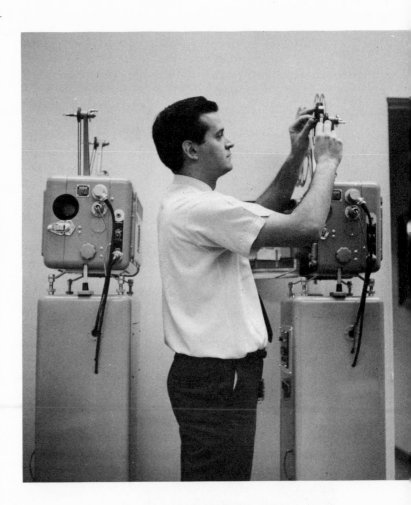

Double chain film may be screened in the film editing room by using two projectors. The film editor provides a rough but adequate approximation of what will appear on the air by "riding gain" on the sound of each projector and blocking the lenses with his hands as necessary. It helps if the projectors can run in sync, started by a single switch.

Overlapped splices produce a more tightly edited piece of film. The pause at the end of a statement, during the single second of time when a speaker's voice is not heard but his lips move with the words of the next statement, can be eliminated. Viewed through a projector, the last word or two might be heard while we are looking at a one-second or one-and-a-half second silent cutaway of the reporter appearing to listen attentively. A one-second cutaway without lip flap following it provides a smooth and natural transition.

The television program, "Dragnet," is a fine example of tight editing. Although it is filmed in double system, with film and sound on different tracks, the extremely tight cuts seem to be overlapped. The film editing of "Dragnet" is one of its distinguishing characteristics, in which its producers and film editors obviously take pride.

DOUBLE CHAINING

When a film story consists of one film clip, it is known as a single chain story, because it uses only one projector and the other mechanical, optical and electronic elements which comprise one television channel of communication. There are times when a film story should consist of two film clips fed at once from two projectors through two channels. This is a double chain story.

Before attempting to double chain, the editor must be sure two projectors will be available when he needs them. If both film clips are in color, he also needs two color channels. Should he learn he cannot get facilities to project a double chain story, the editor, or the writer, must sharply revise his organization of the story.

The editor may decide to double chain for no reason other than to mask a bad cut or lip flap. If the lip flap at the juncture of two statements is obvious, a simple cutaway cannot hide it. Instead, the cutaway should go onto a second reel, and it should be long enough to enable a director to cut to it immediately prior to the splice on the first reel and cut back immediately after the splice, without the danger of showing leader on the air.

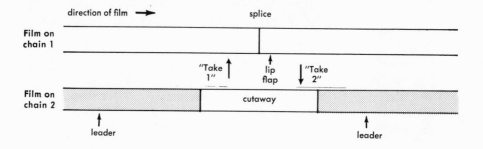

With the letters "A" and "B" representing reel 1 and reel 2, a double chain script might look like this:

VIDEO	AUDIO
COLOR POSITIVE DOUBLE CHAIN. CLIP RUNS 2:53.	
ROLL A AND B TOGETHER	
A VIDEO AND AUDIO AT START	
AFTER 12 SECS, DISSOLVE TO B VIDEO	
	AT 37 SECS IN, AFTER END CUE: " . . . . at last report." CROSSFADE TO B AUDIO
	AT 1:02 IN, TAKE A AUDIO
AT 1:47 (MAN WALKING UP STEPS), DISSOLVE TO A VIDEO	
AT 2:15, CUT TO B VIDEO FOR 5 SECS.	
AT 2:20, CUT BACK TO A VIDEO	
	ENDS: " . . . . intended to go." PLUS 8 SECS, SHOWING DIVING BELL SPLASHING INTO WATER AND DISAPPEARING

Guided either by a clock or a scene description or an audio cue, the director orders the technical director to "Take 2" just before the splice on Reel 1, then immediately prepares to return to Reel 1 with the command "Ready 1," followed after the splice by "Take 1." All three commands could occur within four seconds. If the technical director is alerted beforehand, the "Ready 1" command can be eliminated, and the length of time the cutaway actually appears on air can be shaved to three seconds, or even two seconds. However, to avert the likelihood of leader showing the editor should insert a cutaway of anywhere from five to ten seconds in length, expecting only the middle three seconds or so to appear.

Naturally, the technical director can dissolve into and out of the cutaway, instead of cutting. But a dissolve is not desirable here. For one thing, there is no aesthetic reason for a slow dissolve or even a fast dissolve. For another, a longer cutaway is aired than the story requires. Two quick and clean cuts, in and out, do the job best. And the job is to hide a bad splice.

Dissolves ought to be employed when the double chaining method is used for silent film which illustrates a sound track. For example, if Fire Chief Sam Wilson describes a blaze for two minutes, the viewer should not be made to endure the sight of the chief for the full two minutes. The viewer will be interested in what the chief says, not what he looks like. The film story should be cut to establish the chief and listen to him start his description, for perhaps 10 to 15 seconds. Then, while the chief talks away on reel 1, the technical director should dissolve to reel 2.

FIRE. DOUBLE CHAIN.
9/24. CLIP RUNS 2:00

ROLL A AND B TOGETHER
TAKE A VIDEO AT START
:12 SIL   Fire at the Suregrip tire factory north of Five Points
                                 sent a column of thick black smoke a mile into the air.
                                 It began around noon. The smoke and stinking fumes
                                 forced firemen to use gas masks.

1:40 SOF   TAKE A AUDIO

AT :15, SUPER:
SAM WILSON

AT :25, DISSOLVE TO B   HOLD B AUDIO UNDER, FOR BACKGROUND
VIDEO

                                 A AUDIO ENDS: " . . . will smell all week. "

                                 WHEN A AUDIO ENDS, AT 1:52, BRING B AUDIO UP
                                 FULL FOR REMAINING 8 SECONDS.

This script carries silent or sound film of the fire or the ruins it left behind. The writer and the editor who assemble the story retain the option of ordering a dissolve back to the chief at the conclusion of his tale, or simply staying with the silent film and going to black when the chief finishes. For an added effect, the silent film can be continued for four or five seconds beyond the conclusion of the audio, possibly followed by a fade-out. Sometimes, especially when the film is a light feature, a musical tag may be used, but this is a matter of news policy.

If the second reel is not used until the first reel has been on for some time, the film editor may choose to put an Academy leader in front of the reel 2 film, with instructions to the director to roll reel 2 at a certain time into reel 1. For example: "Roll reel 2 after reel 1 has run 45 seconds; dissolve into it when you see picture."

However, it simplifies matters for the control room if both reels are rolled at once. The film editor arranges this by beginning both clips with Academy leader, then splicing blank leader into reel 2 to fill the time until the reel 2 film is to appear.

Both reels may be carrying usable audio tracks. For example, the fire chief may be talking on reel 1, and the crackling of wood and the wail of engines may be present on reel 2. If this is the case, the audio of reel 2 should be played "under" the chief's words. Reel 2 audio might also be "established" before the chief begins talking, then brought "up full" after he is done. Where both audio tracks consist of voices, only one track should be played at a time. Otherwise, the viewers are likely to be confused.

In television newsrooms everywhere, the reels in a double chain are referred to not by number, but by the terms "A roll" and "B roll." The A

Placing a spring clamp and a spacer between two reels mounted on each shaft of a pair of rewinds maintains a steady pressure and control of both reels, preventing film from unrolling haphazardly.

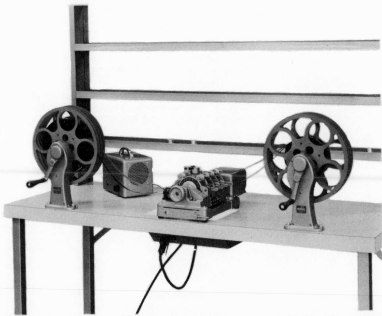

A work bench set up for double chain or double system editing. Two feed reels on the left and two take-up reels on the right are on the rewinds, with the film on adjoining sprockets. A magnetic sound head, which can be shifted from sprocket track to sprocket track, is hooked to a sound amplifier. To edit film, a viewer and a splicer are also needed.

roll may carry the main, or only, audio track, usually the interview or narration. If so, the B roll runs silent or carries only natural sound and is used as for cutaways or to illustrate what is being said on the A roll. When used to illustrate spoken words, the "B roll" scenes should match those words as closely as possible. A jumble of non-matching words and pictures creates confusion in the viewer's mind or leaves little impression. It then becomes just another news film to sit through while waiting for interesting or important information.

The following are double chain scripts used in newscasts on the Los Angeles CBS station, KNXT:

DOUBLE CHAIN FILM (TOTAL 1:39) ROLL BOTH PROJECTORS TOGETHER

> Negotiations to settle the four-day-old strike at Santa Anita collapsed once more this afternoon over the issue of fringe benefits.

TAKE A REEL VIDEO FOR TEN SECONDS SILENT

> As picketing continued, one track official warned it could be a long strike. Big News Reporter Saul Halpert visited the track and took a look behind the scenes.

AT :10 A REEL AUDIO BEGINS. At :16 SWITCH VIDEO ONLY TO B REEL.

AT :56 SWITCH VIDEO BACK TO A REEL AND HOLD A REEL AUDIO AND VIDEO TO END.

> SOUND OUT: " . . . YOU NEVER KNOW WHEN THE BREAK'S GOING TO BE. YOU'VE GOT TO BE READY."

SUPER: CUDDY

> SOUND UP: "There's a strange stillness . . .

> SOUND OUT: " . . . You never know when the break's going to be you've got to be ready."

> A flotilla of U S naval vessels steamed out of Long Beach today to join the Seventh Fleet in the Far East. Big News reporter Saul Halpert was there to watch them go:

NEG FILM (3:07) MINE-
    SWEEPERS SAIL
DOUBLE CHAIN
ROLL BOTH REELS
TAKE "A" REEL: AUDIO
AND VIDEO

> SOUND UP: "This is D-Day for . . ."

At :13, switch VIDEO TO "B"
    REEL AND TAKE NAT-
URAL SOUND IN BG
FROM "B" REEL WHILE
KEEPING NARRATION
AUDIO ON "A" REEL

At 2:01, switch AUDIO to
    "B" Reel

> (Audio cue: "Big News cameraman Doug Dare."

SUPER SLIDE: MRS. SMITH

At 2:53, SWITCH AUDIO
    BACK TO "A " REEL
Stay on "A" reel, A & V,
    to end at 3:07

> (Audio cue: "That's for sure.")

> SOUND OUT: " . . . All sailing proudly out to follow the sun."

"Sync sound," synchronous double system picture-sound recording, can be done with 16mm mag film and ¼″ mag tape. While it is a little more complex and slightly slower than single system shooting, "sync sound" gets around the "lip flap" problem and lets the film editor operate more freely.

Robert M. Brennan of CBS News has suggested double chaining speeches as a way around jump cuts, lip flap and static cutaways: [1]

The use of the second projector can make coverage of speeches much easier. You can shoot the entire speech on one close-up lens, a two or three inch, depending on your throw or whether or not you are using a zoom all the way down. Since you are using a particular part of a speech for its news impact, you should be as tight in on the speaker as you can be. I am not discussing routine speeches. Nor am I referring to an event like a civil rights rally, where you need audience as much as speaker. I do mean a situation where you are justified in using the close-up lens all the way through. You can jump cut the entire film, lay in another picture on your second projector, get reverse angles of the speaker at the rostrum and extreme long shots on a silent camera where lip sync doesn't matter. Where you have crowd shots with applause, you can even throw in a silent picture of people applauding and make it look as if they are in sync. None of this is too difficult to do. But I want to re-emphasize, get away from the 28 frame cutaway, as I did, and make your life easier and your film look better.

An example of horizontal editing benches, the Steenbeck editing table, more common in Europe than in the United States, transports film horizontally on edge. It handles 16mm and 35mm, single or double system, magnetic or optical track, or a combination of these, projecting the images on an 8″ x 10″ screen. Splicing is done without moving hardware or unthreading. If he chooses, the editor builds his air reel and his outtake reel at the same time from more than one feed reel. Film can be fed through at projector speed, 24 frames per second, for normal audio, or at either slow speed or high speed.

DOUBLE SYSTEM

Almost all television newsfilm is single system, which means the picture and the sound are carried on the same film. The sound track, either magnetic or optical, runs along one edge of the film. Sprocket holes run along the opposite edge.

However, feature motion pictures are filmed double system, and so are most pre-planned network documentaries. Double system filming, as the name implies, consists of two systems running concurrently. The film camera carries only the picture. The sound is recorded either on a sprocketed 16mm film base covered with magnetic track or—more commonly—on quarter-inch audio tape controlled by a 60-cycle sync pulse track, which is transferred later to mag film for editing. This mag film is called "full coat."

Some cameramen carry 16mm full coat for the reporter's voice-over narration, because the full coat mag film is reusable. Other cameramen load ordinary mag strip film for the voice over. In this case, it is not necessary to develop the unprocessed film carrying the narration. It can be pulled from its can and exposed to the light. The mag track is unaffected. But the cameraman had better be sure he labels his can correctly!

Single system filming can become double system editing by transferring the sound to full coat. The original reel is cut on picture. The full coat reel is cut on sound.

The sound-only reel can be used as the A roll in a double chainer. While putting sound and picture together in this manner is technically double system shooting, that term is generally reserved for the more exacting work of the film editor when he assembles a documentary, especially when he uses work prints, leaving the original film stored in a lab.

The editor lines up picture and sound on a synchronizer or a Moviola. He does so by means of (a) a clapboard, which is visible on the picture and can be heard on the sound track, or (b) a combination of a flash on the picture and a beep on the sound track, made by a light in the camera and an oscillator in the sound amplifier.

By transferring all their film and sound tracks to videotape before the newscast, many television news departments avert the danger that dealing with several tracks will result in on-air sloppiness. Using a different approach, Washington's WRC-TV put together a mixing system to combine up to five sound tracks into one. The reporter in a sound booth narrates the edited film while the editor at a console funnels the narration and other sound sources onto a 16mm full coat track.

Advantages of double system filming

1. Several film cameras may be used, offering the editor a variety of angles of the same scene.

2. Tighter editing is possible; for example, "lip flap" is no problem.

3. Audio quality is better.

4. Additional audio tracks may be added, such as: music, sound effects, narration and voice dubbing. All audio tracks are later combined in a "dubbing session."

5. Dissolves and fades can be built into the film.

6. Special visual effects may be added, such as sub-titles and cartoons.

7. Work prints, not originals, are used for the creative editing. The editor need not be afraid of scratching the film or making a splice which he might later regret.

9. A splice-free print emerges. No splice marks will be seen on the air.*

10. The soundman can operate independently of the cameraman, recording "wild track."

* This is accomplished by "checkerboard" editing. Using the finished work print as a model, and edge numbers as a guide, the editor cuts and splices the original film. But he does so on two reels, not on one, like the work print. Each scene is spliced to black leader which matches the next scene exactly in length. Thus, two reels are built of alternating scenes and leader in a checkerboard pattern. A laboratory melds the two reels together in a splice-free composite print.

When the film editor completes his work, a motion picture laboratory transfers the picture and sound elements to a composite print on a single reel. This is a positive print with an optical track.

Disadvantages of Double System Filming

1. More processing is needed than simply developing the film. Quarter-inch tape must be transferred to 16mm full-coat magnetic film if a tape recorder was used.

2. Editing is slower. The extra time required to process and edit double system film militates against its use in daily news coverage.

3. Although television film projection rooms can double chain the double system picture and sound reels, they are normally not prepared to do so and the result may be badly out of lip sync. Nor do they always have a second projector available. The separate reels are usually sent to the laboratory for transfer to a single reel. Again, delays and expense are inevitable.

4. Film and lab costs are higher.

In summary, where time is not crucial and budgets permits, double system is superior to single system filming. For normal news coverage, single system filming, perhaps with some double system single or double chain modifications, works better.

FOR THE STUDENT

1. Attend a speech or a news conference being covered by a television news crew. Compare the way you would have cut the silent and sound film with the air version. Was an important statement chosen over an interesting but unimportant statement? Vice versa?

2. Watch several newscasts for film editing. List the sloppy cuts you observed.

3. Edit a silent film clip to run 45 seconds. Then recut it to 30 seconds. Then recut it to 15 seconds. Write copy for each version.

4. Write a paper explaining your reasons for recutting your film as you did. At what point did you stop trimming "fat" and start cutting away "meat"?

5. Overlap two SOF statements so that lip flap is barely noticeable, if at all.

6. Cite all the cue marking and outcue recognition methods you can. Which do you prefer and why?

7. Practice erasing sound.

8. When should the film editor cut on sound? On picture?

9. Interview a working film editor. What was his training? What are his chief problems? His pet gripes?

10. Edit a double chainer with at least two cuts to the B roll video.

14

STILLS

PROFESSOR KARL DEUTSCH of Harvard, former president of the American Political Science Association, observed, "In television, even the best do not use the full force of the medium. TV should give you much more detail of the kind the Pentagon does with visual aids. Visual aids are hardly ever used to the maximum on TV."

In television news, still pictures and other graphics are as vital as motion pictures. There are times when only still pictures are available, and there are times when a lack of motion is preferable. For example, film can do little to increase the information of a simple map.

OUTSIDE SOURCES

Both the Associated Press and United Press International sell a photo facsimile service. Because of the large number of wire service bureaus and stringers, and because of the speed of handling and transmission, still pictures of a breaking news event reach television newsrooms around the nation much quicker than film or tape in almost every instance except where television cameras have been set up in advance for a scheduled event. The quality of these transmitted photos has steadily improved over the years, although they still leave something to be desired.

Because so many television newscasts are now in color, the Associated Press has investigated the technical feasibility of transmitting color stills by wire. According to the AP, the cost of transmission represents the major drawback.

A television station can buy 35mm color slides of major news figures from a commercial service. For instance, United Press International sells news slides not only of national and world figures, but of important people in the station's region. These "Unislides" remain on file at each station for re-use, of course. The Associated Press offers a similar color slide service.

ABC News sells slides for rear projection and Chromakey of stylized drawings of news subject areas. For example, a drawing of a dollar bill would be used as a rear projection for an on-camera story about the economy, a half-black and half-white schoolhouse would serve for stories about integration, etc. ABC News has used these graphics for its own newscasts for several years.

Library Stills

Most of the slides provided by AP and UPI show head shots of famous people. The slides are meant to be stored in television newsroom libraries. Thus, if the name of a well-known national or international figure unexpectedly appears on the teletype—often, unfortunately, by dying —newsrooms can show his face either as a rear projection (designated in a script as RP; VIZ, for Vizmo; or CHROMA, for Chromakey) over the newscaster's shoulder or fully on screen by "punching up the slide chain."

MOSCOW TRADE FAIR — Four pieces of construction paper and a title strip were pasted to cardboard to create a title card introducing a videotape. Color shades were chosen with concern for the gray scale, so that they would be distinctive on black-and-white home sets as well as color sets. Using outlines avoids the "busy" detail of a photograph. Although such cards appear for only five seconds, followed by dissolves into film or videotapes, they add a strong and imaginative touch to feature stories.

Each newsroom should keep a library of stills, as complete as possible, slides and/or cards, both head shots and news photos which have previously moved on the wire. The still library must be winnowed regularly. Otherwise, it will be inundated with stills, which is nearly as bad as having no library at all. Finding the right still in a picture file without a filing system is a frustrating task which a busy journalist soon abandons.

A library file ought to contain head shots of local and state personalities. It is a good idea to introduce the matter of head shots at a newsroom staff meeting, in order to determine whose pictures should be on file. The person placed in charge of the library can phone or write for pictures needed to complete the file and bring it up to date (so that the grizzled U.S. senator does not appear as he did when he was a freshman state legislator). A few stills of familiar places should also be filed—for example. the state capitol, the White House, a courtroom or the outside of the court-house, any of which might briefly illustrate a story where no other illustration is available. However, stills of places should be used charily. They are better suited as RP's than as full-screen pictures.

MAPS

The first rule for drawing a television news map is: *keep it simple.* The second rule is: *hold it on camera longer than a photo would be held*, giving viewers plenty of time to read place names, understand the relative distances and absorb all the information even a simply drawn map conveys. A map should contain not one place name, not one highway line, not one mark more than is absolutely necessary to locate the spot where whatever happened happened. For example, a map locating a brush fire might show nothing but the two nearest towns, or a town and a highway, plus an X to mark the fire or, better still, a drawing of flames or smoke to locate the fire.

To show movement in a map, consider the pull-tab. A pull-tab map is relatively simple to construct, and looks good on the air, telling a story clearly. The pull-tab works because of the optical illusion that makes black invisible in a television receiver when it is next to a light color. The pull-tab consists of three layers of cardboard: a top layer on which the map is drawn in white on a black card, with a strip cut out for the path of the pull-tab; a black, movable middle layer, the pull-tab itself; a white bottom layer glued to the top layer. Pulling the tab slowly exposes the white bottom layer. To the viewer at home, it seems as if an invisible hand is drawing a line. Pull-tabs can also be black-on-gray or colored. Once a television newsman gets accustomed to making such maps to show, for instance, the path of an airplane, there are few limits to what can be done with a little imagination and patience: multiple pull-tabs, perhaps showing solid,

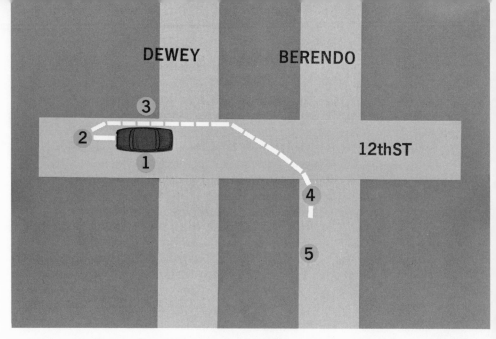

When the chronology of a news story requires a map for clarity, the map itself may be confusing. For example, an out-of-control car may carom off several objects before halting. Rather than the objects being drawn, they can be numbered. The card remains on camera while the newscaster refers to each number as he unfolds the story.

A card serving as both map and illustration gives viewers a perspective quickly and easily comprehended, when combined with the newscaster voice over. In planning a map, the first rule is simplicity. Nothing is added which is not essential to the story. If many details are essential, two or three cards are drawn. The card(s) may be used independent of film, as introduction to film, in the middle of a film story (with sound-on-film instead of narration), or at the end of the film.

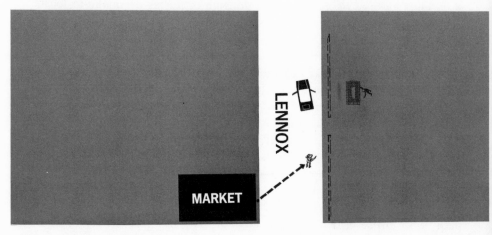

broken, or dotted lines uncovered separately or in unison; pull-tabs showing graphs or financial "pies"; even pull-tabs creating a kind of animation.

CARTOONS

As everyone who reads newspaper editorial pages knows, cartoons are not always funny. Both funny and serious cartoons have a place in television news, but they should be displayed with caution. Surprisingly, a drawing is strong medicine in a television newscast. It may be remembered long after the day's film is forgotten.

A cartoon can be used by itself, with or without a caption, with the newscaster voice over. More commonly, the cartoon—or a line drawing—with or without a caption is used as introduction to a film story. Sometimes, a story is told using a series of drawings.

Besides cartoons and line drawings, newscasts make use of collages, often several newspaper articles or headlines artfully pasted on a card to show the interest a certain matter has stirred up. (See Chapter 16, EDITORIALS.)

Because cameras are barred from courtrooms, news departments sent artists to sketch people at newsworthy trials. These quick drawings of the

The essentials of a map showing an air crash are the location of the crash by reference to a highway, a town identifiable to some or a city identifiable to all. If, in addition, the take-off point is close to the crash site, then it may be shown, along with the route and the miles traveled. Note that mountains are shown in shadowy outline, while a few hatched lines mark a city.

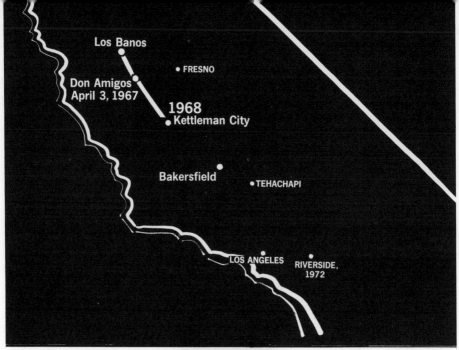

Few television graphics are as impressive as pull-tabs. The tab is sandwiched between two map layers. Pull-tabs also effectively serve in graphs and cartoons. One card often has several tabs. Attention should be given to instructing the man who pulls the tab, to make sure he does it on cue and does it slowly and smoothly. Many a carefully engineered map has been wasted by sloppiness at the critical moment.

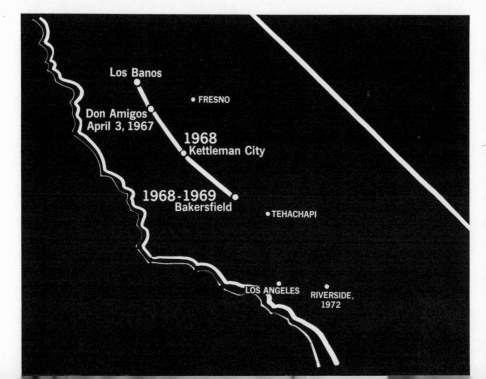

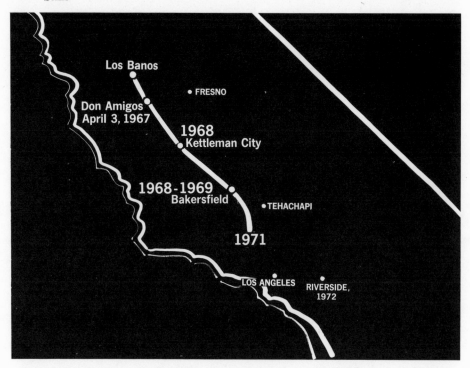

defendant(s), lawyers, the judge and witnesses are an inadequate substitute for film or videotape, but without them the public would have no visual record of a trial which may have public importance. (See section on *Canon 35,* in camera *or On Camera,* in Chapter 18, THE LAW.)

SUPERING

The super (for superimposition) card also works on the optical principle that black is invisible over a lighted image in a television receiver. White lettering on a black card shows only the white. The black shows as a neutral gray. If a television camera focusing on a super card is punched up at the same time as a television camera focusing on a person, or at the same time as a film is being shown, the result will appear as white lettering over the person or film. In practice, an identifying name of a person, place, or whatever, is "supered" over the person or place to be identified. The black card will cause the televised picture to darken slightly, but the darkening is not objectionable and, except to the accustomed eye, hardly noticeable.

A menu board, the kind seen in the window of Joe's Diner, offers the simplest and cheapest means of supering names and places, but the quality of the image is like the quality of the food served in Joe's Diner and it requires a camera and camera chain. The supers for the newscast are set up in descending order, the first name at the top of the menu board. If possible, the stage manager should dismantle or cover a line after it appears, so the cameraman can focus on the top visible line each time he breaks from the set to the menu board.

The author once created super slides using an IBM Executive typewriter and treated transparent acetate. The typewriter had very small type, Copperplate Gothic #1, which looks like printing and provides an adequate number of typed characters for a single line on a 35mm slide. The typing was done on white paper, then transferred to the acetate sheets by a Photo Rapid Matador machine which employs what is called a diffusion transfer process. A 35mm square with the impression of the name was then cut out and mounted. In the slide chain, the polarity was reversed. Electronic shading increased the sharpness.

Many stations produce super slides by setting up small art lettering on black construction paper, then shooting it with a Polaroid Land Camera loaded with positive transparency film. (See SLIDES below.)

At least four firms—CBS Laboratories, Visual Electronics Corp.,

THE DRAFT — The focus and all important information should be in the center of a card. The artist should assume that a strip one-sixth the width of the card will be lost at each side, and one-sixth the height of the card will be lost at top and bottom when the card is seen in a television monitor. Therefore, nothing should appear in the outer one-third of the card unless it is meant to run off the edge of what will be visible. The artist must also frame his card to conform to television aspect ratio of three units of height by four units of width.

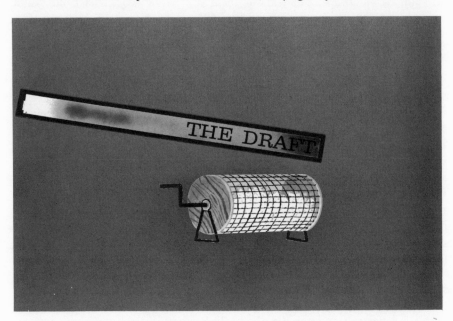

Electronic supering offers instant lettering and does away with the need for artwork to identify people. It can also serve for elections, weather reports and, above, sports coverage.

Telemation Inc., and Chiron Telesystems—manufacture electronic supering devices, which are sometimes called "titling generators." Broadcast compatible, they can super over stills, film or live action, roll vertically for credits, and crawl horizontally for bulletins and announcements. Depending upon the particular model, electronic supering devices offer such features as: 1.) flashing or blinking words to attract attention, with each word in a different color and a black border around each letter; 2.) upper and lower case printing; 3.) titles retrieved from a storage library.

Electronic supering may be used to super names on film, to identify studio guests, to show the score and standing of a ball game (*Top of the Seventh, Yankees 2, Red Sox 1*), to super titles or dates, to report election returns over movies, to announce that news follows the movie, and so on. A blinking feature can be preset in combination with a map to show where the battle is, where the cold front is centered, or where the airplane crashed.

Because it can be hooked to a memory storage unit, one device can present candidates' names in what amounts to a lot of "limbo boards" (i.e., boards viewed in limbo, not part of a set). As new returns come in during an election, each "limbo board" can be updated with the latest figures, eliminating the need for a background set with the latest returns behind the newscaster. A board is punched up on the air at the touch of a button.

TelePro Industries, which manufactures TelePrompTer, produces a non-electronic supering device which they call a "Horizontal-Vertical Color Effects Crawl." This is a translucent drum operated by a variable speed motor. It can produce supers and crawls in black-on-white, white-

The "Horizontal-Vertical Color Effects Crawl" can be used to send a bulletin crawl or an announcement crawl across the bottom of the picture screen and to create word-and-picture slides, either in black-and-white or in color.

on-black, color-on-black or black-on-color. Drawings as well as letters can be mounted on the drum.

WDBJ-TV, Roanoke, Va., designed a super crawl which cost them almost nothing. Western Union gave them an old telegraph printer which types information on quarter inch yellow tape. Western Union also donated several rolls of the yellow tape. A drive machanism was built, consisting of the motor and gears taken from a toy tank, plus a small power supply. The yellow tape is driven from right to left across an upright panel painted yellow to match the yellow tape. A television camera picks up the image of the slowly moving black printing. In the camera chain, the polarity is changed to negative, so that the letters appear white. WDBJ-TV originally designed the crawl as an aid to the deaf.

NEWS FOR THE DEAF

Deaf people do watch television. But their enjoyment—albeit restricted—of a television entertainment program can turn to helplessness or fright when the program is visually interrupted by a bulletin slide, and the news bulletin is read by an announcer. So far as they know, the news might be a warning of a tornado or an atom bomb. In Britain, the BBC provides a "News Review for the Deaf" which reviews the week's news in words and pictures, with an electrically operated roll device to supply the words. The roll device is an electric typewriter carriage, which pulls the paper from a feed roll across a "letterbox" slit. Instead of reversing polarity, the white lettering is done by using a typewriter with a silver ribbon and black paper. In the camera chain a black edge is electronically framed around the letters.

San Francisco's KRON-TV offers a daily five-minute newscast for the deaf during a break in the *Today* show. Two young people present the news in sign language. Viewers with normal hearing get the news at the same time from an off-camera newscaster or from SOF.

SLIDES

As already noted, a slide does not require a studio television camera, while a card does. Television projection rooms include slide projectors as basic equipment. Usually both 35mm and 2 x 2 inch slide projectors are present, often sharing an electronic chain with each other and with a projector, thanks to a mirror system which may be flipped around to take an image from any of them.

A slide cannot be handled as flexibly as a card; for example, it is impossible to pan across a slide without projecting it on a screen and picking up the image with a studio camera. Also, a slide takes a bit longer to make and is a bit more trouble than a card. However, using positive transparency film and a Polaroid camera mounted on a special stand designed for this purpose, 3¼ x 4 inch slides can be turned out quickly enough. Not only still photo slides but super slides can be produced. The 3¼ x 4 inch slides may be used with rear projection equipment as well as in a slide chain, which means they will appear on a television monitor either full screen or on a screen over the newscaster's shoulder.

The following script from a KNXT newscast shows how a series of slides illustrates a news story. Each slide was made from a still picture transmitted by wire photo machine.

SLIDE: POPE DOWN PLANE RAMP	Pope Paul the Sixth returned to Rome tonight from a trip to the Holy Land that made history and shattered precedent.
SLIDE: MOTORCADE IN ROME	He returned to a Roman carnival of a welcome, with hundreds of thousands lining the motorcade route from the airport, and was driven to St. Peter's Square, where he
SLIDE: POPE, HAND EXTENDED	told the multitude: "I did not want to bother anybody. I wanted to come back in a quiet way."
	Later he blessed the crowd from his apartment window.
SLIDE: POPE, ATHENA-GORAS	The jubilant homecoming capped an eventful day in which the Pope met once more with Greek Orthodox patriarch Athenagoras in Jerusalem, went to the church of the Na-
SLIDE: POPE IN CROWD	tivity in Bethlehem to say a mass on the reputed site of

SLIDE: POPE, ARMS EX-   the birthplace of Christ, was so overcome with emotion on
TENDED   leaving the church that he raised his arms and eyes to
                         heaven and called on all Christians to unite.

NEWSCASTER ON CAMERA   At home in Rome, the Pontiff told welcomers: "I bring you
                         back a blessing from Jerusalem. I bring you back the Lord's
                         peace."
                         And he repeated that he believes his three-day trip, the
                         first by a pope to the Holy Land since St. Paul, may have
                         great historical significance, may -- he said -- "mark
                         the beginning of great benefits for the church and mankind."

Illustrating Weather News

Otherwise drab newscasts may present sparkling weather forecasts. Some television stations prefer to hire weather girls instead of weathermen, the most shapely girls they can find to stand at a blackboard and talk about stationary fronts. Other television stations prefer cartoonists, who sketch not only pressure areas, but people holding umbrellas, going to the beach and so on. Some stations simply let the regular newscaster or the sports reporter handle the extra chore of predicting the high tomorrow which will follow the overnight low. And others bring in a local meteorologist, hopefully one who is not pedantic.

Weather copy frequently is humorous, maybe the only bit of lightness in a newscast filled with disasters and dire forebodings. The weatherman is introduced by the newscaster with a quip, sometimes based on a running joke shared with faithful viewers of that daily newscast. It is as if the news directors, or whoever created the format for the weather report, felt that this segment of the newscast was a chance to give the entire newscast a special bit of personality, a quality of its own, a welcome digression from the usual severe run of news.

Illustrating the weather report and the forecast add measurably to its flair. Much can be done, and done cheaply, to relieve a tedious recital of numbers and details. Here are just a few of many different ideas:

1. Maps of the United States and the local region are either painted on a blackboard or printed on big sheets of paper tacked up on a board and replaced each day. The weatherman uses chalk for the blackboard or crayon for the sheets while on camera to outline the weather pattern, with its fronts, highs, pressure areas and movements, and to write the numbers which either report today's high or predict tomorrow's.

2. A magnetic map board is a more handsome alternative to a blackboard. When designed in relief, its mountains stand out. Front movements are indicated by arrows of iron which hold fast wherever they are placed, as do the numbers. Miniature suns and rain clouds add to the display. By using a rotating polarity filter over the lens of the television camera and numbers and symbols responsive to polarized light, whatever

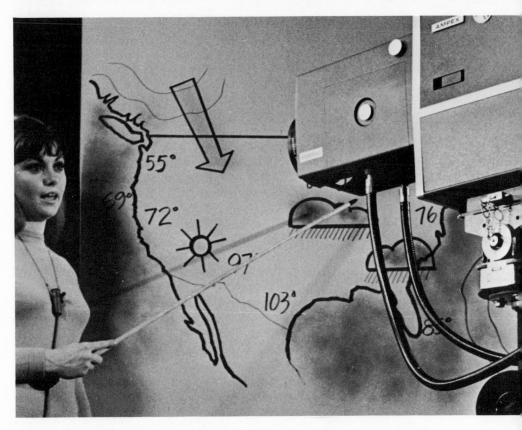

Women sometimes enter the world of television news as weather girls. A shapely girl talking about stationary fronts has definite viewer appeal.

the weatherman sticks to the board pulsates. Mystified viewers telephone the station to inquire what the trick is.

3. Another mystifying trick depends upon reversing the camera scan, which is difficult to do in a color camera and therefore would require a station to reserve one camera solely for the weather. The trick is done with a large, clear Plexiglas map. The map is placed between the weatherman and the camera. The map faces him and he sees it in its proper East-West perspective, and he writes on it normally, from left to right. The camera sees the map backward. But with the scan reversed, the audience sees the map in proper persective, the weatherman is not blocking any of the map with his body, and it appears that he is writing backwards. Of course, this could still be done without reverse scanning if the weatherman would actually learn to write backwards.[1]

4. A large pad of blank sheets is placed on an easel. The weatherman, a quick and clever cartoonist, ad libs his weather report while he draws a child in rain gear hurrying to school, a smiling sun shining down and so forth. The viewer is delighted by the rapid movements of the charcoal across the page and the effortless patter of the weatherman.

5. Stock slides are used to illustrate predictions. Because interest in tomorrow's weather is so often child-centered, the slides are pictures of children in various quantities of clothing, from thin cotton play togs through light sweaters to boots and snow mittens. The slides fill the screen, so the weatherman—or whoever reports weather news—does not appear on camera at all, unless the slides are used for rear projection.

6. A huge thermometer forecasts the weather. The weatherman makes changes on camera by means of a pull tab.

7. Each day the weather information is prepared in advance on cards. They show outline maps, names of states on a national map or towns on a local map, plus numbers.

8. A few feet of film are shot each day of scenes around town: children going to school, women shopping, a man getting in his car to drive to work, ducks in a park lake, an oil heating truck, a thermostat being turned up. Arthur S. Harris, Jr., of WRGB, Schenectady, N.Y., suggests: [2]

> Have a station's photographers bring back during the course of of their work a few feet of film which captures that day's weather. In Washington, weathercasts are enhanced with 16mm footage of children sailing boats, of joggers in Rock Creek Park. . . . . On the first day of summer vacation from school the photographer brings back a few feet of film of children playing in mid-morning; and if the next day there is a sudden summer shower with inches of rain falling in a few hours, he shoots footage showing the rain sweeping down onto the streets, rushing off into the sewers—just enough footage to capture the beauty of it all.

> The next day is a scorcher. The temperature is in the high 90's. Using his imagination, the photographer produces a series of little vignettes. Children gathered around a street corner ice cream vendor, youngsters with a Kool-Aid stand, a taxicab company installing signs on its cabs that say "Air Conditioned." These little vignettes appear on TV as the weathercaster talks about the high temperature of the day instead of having nothing more imaginative than a gigantic 97° on the screen. . .

> So we visualize turnpikes shrouded in fog, snowblowers clearing airport runways, rushing streams of springtime, splashers and swimmers and sunners at a placid country swimming hole in mid-August. We see early morning wintertime scenes of people trying to start their cars in sub-zero temperatures, overhead shots of a five o'clock downpour and workers streaming from offices with umbrellas, newspapers, magazines over their heads rushing for hard-to-get cabs and crowded buses. We get soft evening scenes of summertime haying.

The list is endless. After use, the film clips are kept in a library, but camera crews remain constantly on the lookout for new scenes to illustrate the

A picture drawn by a child delights everyone. The forecast for tomorrow promises summer showers during a sunny day. (Sketch courtesy of Daisy Fang, age 4.)

weather. The weatherman or the newscaster gives the weather report and forecast over the film, sometimes with the help of super cards or super slides containing a single number. The cards or slides, of course, are kept on file. Each time the forecast predicts a high of 51 degrees, the proper card or slide is at hand.

9. Permanent maps are built with block holes for numbers. The numbers are display digits, controlled electrically by an off-camera panel. The numbers change on camera. Display digits are also used in television news to report scores and standings, election results and stock market averages. Each number breaks vertically or horizontally in half while in view. The visual effect is like a staccato burst. It is fascinating to watch.

10. Satellite weather maps, now available, give a weather report a scientific and up-to-date appearance.

11. Children's drawings show the weather today and the outlook tomorrow. In London, the commercial channel, THAMES, came up with a delightful idea, using children's drawings. The news department contacted several elementary schools to ask if children, age 6 to 11, would draw weather pictures. The channel supplied cards, measuring 24″ x 12″, col-

Fair and. . .(6 Films)

Rain and. . .(4 Films)

Showers and. . .(6 Films)

Thundershowers and...(6 Films)

Foggy and. . .(4 Films)

Windy and. . .(6 Films)

Cloudy and. . .(6 Films)

Partly Cloudy and...(6 Films)

Freezing Rain and Cold...(1 Film)

Sleet and. . .(2 Films)

Snow and. . .(2 Films)

Snow Flurries and. . .(3 Films)

Animated cartoons showing weather conditions add sparkle to a weather report. These were designed by Animation Techniques, Inc., Skaneatles, N.Y.

ored felt drawing pens, and a list of 18 different weather conditions: light
showers, cloudy and cold, etc. Each school's drawings were used for a
week or two, and the weather reporter always mentioned the school. Two
cards appeared nightly, one illustrating today's weather and the other illustrating tomorrow's forecast.

For another delightful use of what local children produce, around
Christmas get some of their letters to Santa from the Post Office and read
them on the air, if possible over silent footage of the children who wrote
them.

12. The weatherman uses an illuminated pointer, with an on-off control, at rear projection maps.

13. Short animated films illustrate outdoor conditions. Animation Techniques, Inc. produced a series of 10-second cartoons of animals. Example: a frog under a lilypad, with the rain coming down. Fairman Productions of Milwaukee offers 16-second animations of a cartoon character called Freddy Forecast.

14. An actual radar system. The station's weatherman must be more than a television newsman who reads numbers on a board. He must either be a meteorologist or a newsman trained to read weather data on a radar scope. Several television stations now use radar systems to identify such phenomena as storm fronts. It would be hard to beat a radar-based weathercast for believability, if the weatherman knows his stuff.

FOR THE STUDENT

1. Think of one more way to illustrate weather news besides those listed.
2. Monitor a newscast, looking for stories which could have been improved by graphics, or at least by better graphics. Did you see any film stories which could have been presented as well, or better, by using maps, and/or stills instead of film?
3. From today's newspaper, clip six stories which could be illustrated on a television newscast with a chart or a drawing.
4. Is there anything in the section on illustrating weather news which can be applied to illustrating sports news?
5. Put together a three-minute news segment using stills. Be sure each still has the 3 x 4 aspect ratio. Use fairly large pictures.
6. Prepare a story using graphics you have drawn (e.g., maps, graphs, cartoons).
7. Prepare a pull-tab map and a pull-tab chart, each for a different story. Write the copy and deliver it, with someone else pulling the tabs, preferably on camera.
8. List local people and places which should be included in a local television station news picture file.
9. Visit a local television newsroom to see what is actually on file. Do they keep a slide library or a library of stills on cards?
10. Ask the man who makes the news slides at a local station to teach you his method.

15

VIDEO

MUCH OF THE technological ferment in the broadcasting industry centers around videotape and video cameras. It is technologically possible now for a single cameraman to transmit live from any spot in the world. This could mean that one day soon, a scheduled network program might be interrupted for a live report from a battlefield halfway around the world, where a correspondent at that moment is under fire.

Live coverage from many remote corners of the world is now an accepted part of broadcasting capability. A trip by the President to China or an international sports meet can be seen by hundreds of millions as it occurs, via cable, microwave transmitter and satellite. At the quadrennial political conventions, almost no corner of the convention hall and the individual candidates' headquarters escapes the ubiquitous "creepie peepie," PCP or Minicam portable cameras.

THE TELEVISION CAMERA

The word "television" derives from Greek and Latin roots meaning "to see at a distance." What the television camera sees, it makes an electronic image of. (It must be clearly understood that a *film camera,* which virtually all television news cameramen use, is not a *television camera.* The terms *television camera* and *video camera* are used interchangably.) Cables and/or a broadcast transmitter for VHF (Very High Frequency) or UHF (Ultra High Frequency) signals carry the constantly changing television image into what television people call a monitor or receiver and most people call a television set.

The "Minicam," developed by CBS and Norelco, is a Plumbicon "creepie-peepie." The camera weighs 18 lbs. and the backpack, including battery, weighs 32 lbs., making it (at the time of publication) the lightest color TV camera. The "Minicam" transmits with or without a cable to its base station. It can also be plugged into a portable videotape recorder. Among its uses: live transmission from a helicopter, live coverage of conventions, sports events, disasters.

Depending up the television tube or tubes, a television camera is referred to as a vidicon camera, a Plumbicon camera or an image-orthicon camera. In recent years new tubes have been developed, including the Isocon, the SEC vidicon, and the SIT vidicon, which was developed by the military for night operation.

All television cameras have a lens section that focuses a picture on an image section, which produces an electrical charge whose strength is determined by the light and dark elements of the picture. An electronic beam from a gun structure converts the picture into its electronic image, which is then transmitted.

The Vidicon Camera

Many television cameras, both portable and studio cameras, use vidicon tubes, which are simpler, smaller and considerably cheaper than all other kinds. The vidicon camera contains four major sections:

The lens system. As with a film camera, the lens system might consist of a single zoom lens, a powerful telescopic lens, three lenses on a turret, or any other configuration of lenses which can be fitted to the camera. For a color television camera, the lens system must feed through a prism or a mirror system which divides the incoming image into three or four separate images.

The vidicon tube. For a portable television camera, such as the "creepie peepie," the tube measures one inch in diameter by about six inches in length. Color television requires three or four tubes, for a "3-V" or "4-V" system. The 3-V system consists of tubes receiving red, blue and green pictures that have gone through the lens prism and then through a red, green or blue filter into the vidicon tubes. These red, green and blue "channels" must be in "registration"; that is, the images from each tube must fall directly on top of one another. The 4-V system adds a monochromatic (black and white) tube to improve the crispness of the picture and to eliminate a slight blur around the edges.

The scanning beam and its circuitry.

A video amplifier to strengthen the weak signal enough to send it out from the camera either by cable or by wireless transmission, usually microwave.

The Plumbicon Camera

The Plumbicon tube resembles its older sister, the vidicon tube, in most respects. Like the vidicon, the Plumbicon transmits the lens image to a photo cathode target, which is then scanned to produce the video signal.

The Plumbicon differs from the vidicon principally in that it produces a better picture at low light levels. The difference may be compared to the advantage of a faster film over a slower film. The Plumbicon has less image retention, or "burn in," than a vidicon.

The Image-Orthicon Camera

The image-orthicon, or I-O, camera remains the most widely used television studio camera. The I-O tube is much larger than a vidicon tube, so the I-O camera is seldom, if ever, used where a portable camera is required.

The image-orthicon tube has an additional electron multiplier section which produces larger video signals than do either the vidicon or Plumbicon tubes. With a larger lens, a larger target area, and greater signal output strength, the image-orthicon can give better detail and crispness than the other cameras and, consequently, a superior picture. On the other hand, the image-orthicon camera is considerably more expensive than the vidicon camera. New I-O tubes have longer life spans than vidicon or Plumbicon tubes.

A major scheduled news event, such as a presidential inauguration, brings out video camera crews ready to shoot, fair weather or foul. A microwave dish beams the signal back to the station.

Video Transmission

The picture received by the television camera is fed by cable to a camera control system, which contains additional circuitry to improve the picture, amplify the signal and add synchronous pulses to lock the picture to the television receivers (e.g., home sets, studio monitors).

Portable vidicon cameras sometimes have the camera control system as part of the portable rig. For example, the "creepie-peepie" contains not only a vidicon camera, but also a camera control unit and a small transmitter, which sends a line-of-sight or near line-of-sight signal to a nearby remote truck or fixed control station, there to be transmitted either by cable or by microwave to its destination. The "creepie-peepie" can also be directly tied to a cable.

Microwave, which must travel in a straight line, is more versatile and more flexible than cable transmission, and has a higher quality. However, it cannot be used in every situation because of terrain, and the initial cost of a microwave transmission system is higher (the cost difference between microwave and cable can be compared to the cost difference between using a walkie-talkie to send messages or using a coin telephone—buying the walkie-talkie equipment is initially more expensive than dropping coins into a telephone box, but subsequently walkie-talkie calls are cheaper).

The American Telephone and Telegraph Company at present leases broadband cables at the rate of 55¢ per mile per hour with a one-hour minimum charge, plus added charges for any loops, connections, or installation work. A film clip sent across the nation can cost a network about $1,500. For example, film from Vietnam reaches the United States by plane, landing in San Francisco. Film from Australia and New Zealand usually is landed in Los Angeles. Film being sent from China, North Vietnam or Japan often arrives in Seattle. Even if the film is immediately trans-shipped east, it would not reach Chicago or New York, for network broadcast, for at least five or six hours, usually too late for broadcasting the same day—when we add the time to get the film to a lab, process it, screen it, and edit it. Therefore, a television network will "buy a line" from "Telco" (AT&T, the "telephone company") from the West Coast to Chicago or New York if the newscast producer wants to present the story that day. It is hoped that satellite transmission will eventually sharply reduce the cost of reporting the news by television.

At present, the effort by the networks to put up their own pooled domestic communication satellite system is bogged down by political pressure exerted by A.T.&T. and Comsat (the Communications Satellite Corporation), which do not want to surrender millions of dollars of network revenue annually. If the "Open Skies" policy declared by President Nixon ever reaches fruition, the networks will orbit their own satellites. As the cost of transmitting newsfilm drops, the amount of news by satellite will rise.

VIDEOTAPE

Where a complex film story requires three or more film chains, the director would be well advised to put the story on videotape before the newscast begins. A pre-newscast dubbing session in the studio is the time to make the mistakes. During the newscast, it is easier to roll one tape than to roll three films while cueing the anchorman and swinging Camera 2 over to Easel 1.

The central piece of equipment in videotape broadcasting is the videotape machine. At present, only RCA and Ampex manufacture machines considered suitable for professional broadcasting. A videotape machine is an exceedingly complex assembly of tubes, transistors, wiring and dozens of other kinds of electronic equipment. A full explanation of its operation may be found in technical manuals, but television newsmen ought to have a basic understanding of videotape machines, because they form such an integral part of modern broadcast journalism.

Videotape itself resembles the more familiar quarter-inch audio tape, except that it is from one-half inch to two inches wide. Most videotape now used for news playback is two inches wide. Videotape carries four separate tracks: From top to bottom they are:

1) The audio track, which carries the sound.

2) The video track, taking up most of the two-inch width, which carries the picture.

3) The cue track, on which videotape engineers can record information using a microphone or a beep signal. For example, a beep might mark the start of a newsclip, such as the point in a recorded baseball game where a home run was hit with bases loaded.

4) The control track, which consists of the electronic equivalent of sprocket holes. All tracks are monitored on oscilloscopes or VU meters.

```
─────────────────────────── Audio ───────────────────────────


  ─→                         Video                         ─→


                          ── Cue ──────────────────────────────
═══════════════════════════ Control ═════════════════════════
```

THE VIDEOTAPE MACHINE

Videotape, or VTR (for Videotape Recording), machines have either a helical scan or a quadrature scan.

Helical scan machines have a video head which rotates horizontally, for recording or playback. They have two basic advantages: (1) they are relatively cheap, so they can be sold for home and hobbyist's use; (2) they can freeze frame; that is, they can be stopped at any point to show a still picture. The disadvantage of helical scan machines is the poor quality of their pictures compared with quad scanning.

Quadrature (or quad) scan machines use a video head which consists of four separate heads set in a wheel at 90 degree angles from each other.

Each of the four heads that comprise the video head is responsible for 4/16ths of the tape. Imagine the two-inch-wide tape divided into 16 bands. One of the four heads would serve bands 1, 5, 9, 13. The next would serve bands 2, 6, 10, and 14. And so on. Much of the work of the VTR engineer is the adjustment of the four heads to synchronize with one another. The video head wheel makes 240 rotations a second. A capstan drives the tape at a constant speed of 15 inches per second. As each of the four heads passes the moving tape, it lays down an electronic track. If the tape were not moving, the track would be perpendicular to the tape. But because the tape moves, the track is laid at a slight angle.

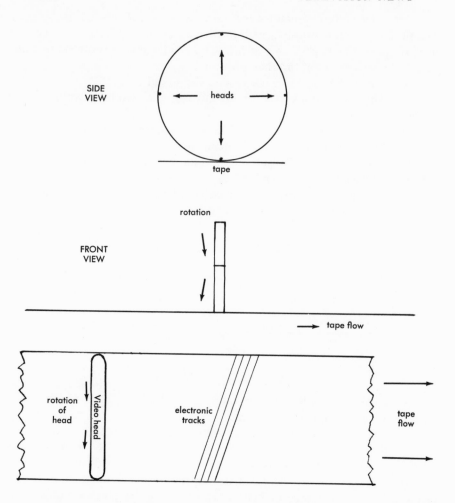

Maintaining a constant head-to-capstan relationship is another important part of the VTR engineer's job. The adjustment of this relationship or distance, is called "tracking." A tracking control knob centers the rotating video head upon the center of its "information." A guide at the video head has an air pressure vacuum which keeps the tape at an exact distance from the video head. If the head-to-guide relationship is not correct, the resulting video picture will be skewed, giving it a venetian blind effect, or it will be "scalloped," which is a rounding effect.

Besides the video head, there is an audio head consisting of several separate heads:

1) An audio record-playback head.
2) An audio erase head.
3) A cue record-playback head.

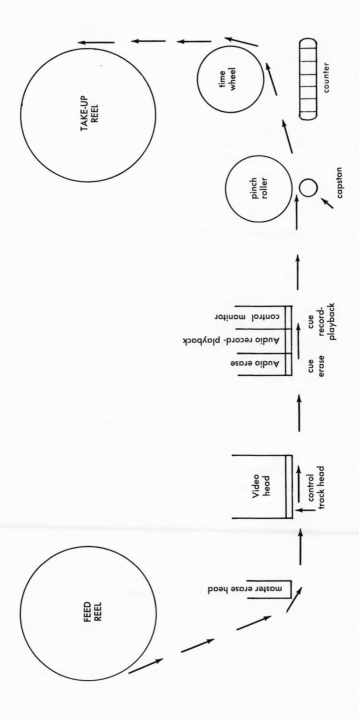

4) A cue erase head.

5) An audio and cue control monitor head.

The videotape "feed" reel is loaded on the left side or the top of the machine, depending on the model.

The take-up reel is loaded on the right side, or on the bottom. From left to right (or top to bottom) the tape passes, in turn:

1) The master erase head.

2) The video head and control track head.

3) The audio head.

4) The capstan.

5) The timer, graduated in seconds.

Some other terms used by the VTR engineer should be added to the broadcast newsman's lexicon:

High band: a frequency range of the broadcast carrier frequency used mainly for color reception and transmission. It can also be used for monochromatic (black and white) reception and transmission, but seldom is. High band frequency VTR machines are newer than *low band* receivers. They produce a better quality picture, with sharper resolution and without the distorting "noise" of low band transmission. High band transmission also suffers less deterioration in dubbing.

Modulator: an electronic device which takes the incoming carrier signal and modulates—or alters—it. The signal goes from the modulator to the recording head, and then to the videotape.

Demodulator: the reverse of the modulator, used when the videotape machine feeds a picture. It takes the modulated carrier frequency and strips the carrier signal off to leave the video picture, which is then transmitted.

The signal is modulated (some kind of carrier frequency is present) when it is on videotape, when it is being transmitted by microwave, and when it is being broadcast through the air. The signal lacks a carrier frequency when it is moving along a cable, such as its transmission from a TV camera to a videotape machine or from master control, by cable, to the transmitter.

EDITING VIDEOTAPE

Considerable progress has been made in recent years. No longer does a videotape engineer have to peer through a microscope to line up pulses on two cut pieces of videotape in order to avoid a roll bar when he makes a tape splice. The Ampex Editec and the RCA electronic splicer edit tape automatically.

Using two machines, one with a feed, or "sub-master," reel and one with a master reel (the reel which will have the finished news clip), the engineer places an "in" cue and an "out" cue on the cue track of the master reel. He backs tapes 5 or 10 seconds. This pre-roll permits the machines to get up to full speed and stabilize the picture. When the first cue is encountered the master machine automatically begins recording. When the second cue is encountered, the machine stops recording.

Using electronic editing, the news editor can dub a video-and-audio signal, video only or audio only. For example, by splicing together two statements made by a speaker and laying a video cutaway over the electronic "splice," the news editor produces the equivalent of a double-chain film, which will be played back on a single videotape machine without using studio film chains.

However, it should be noted that at present videotape editing is much slower than film editing. In the context of television news, slowness means less flexibility.

THE PORTABLE VIDEOTAPE RECORDER

Videotape has begun to challenge film in the shooting of motion pictures, but that challenge is yet in its infancy. VTR equipment at present is more expensive and bulkier than a film camera, and tape is much more difficult to edit than film. Yet videotape recording has definite advantages, too:

1. Tapes can be played back immediately.
2. No danger exists of tape being ruined in a developing tank.
3. Tape could be fed by mobile equipment, either in a remote truck or in a reporter's car equipped with a videotape playback unit and a microwave transmitter. The reporter could send the tape he had "shot" back to the studio faster than he could drive it back, and he could be on his way to his next assignment. The author knows of no reporter's rig like this now in operation, but it does not stretch the imagination much to see a reporter covering a story on the far side of town at 5 p.m., and having his tape on the air at 6 p.m., or even 5:30 p.m. It might also be possible to do some minimal editing at the scene of the story, and feed live into the newscast; in short, an edited remote while the event is just minutes old.
4. Although tape editing is slower and more cumbersome than film editing, the time saved by skipping laboratory processing makes it possible to put together many edited news stories in less time using tape than using film.
5. Present recording equipment has a 20-minute tape supply vs. 11 minutes for a film camera with a 400-foot reel. Admittedly, film cameras can be loaded with 1,000-foot reels, but they are seldom if ever carried on a shoulder pod with such big reels.
6. Although a VTR recorder is more expensive than a camera, other savings may more than compensate: a) no developing tank is needed; b)

The "scrambler," developed by ABC and Ampex, is a hand-held, color video camera, which transmits by cable (as above) or microwave. The camera, its 6-to-1 zoom lens, and its backpack of electronic gear weigh a total of 35 lbs. The "scrambler" is particularly useful in live coverage of news where large crowds have gathered.

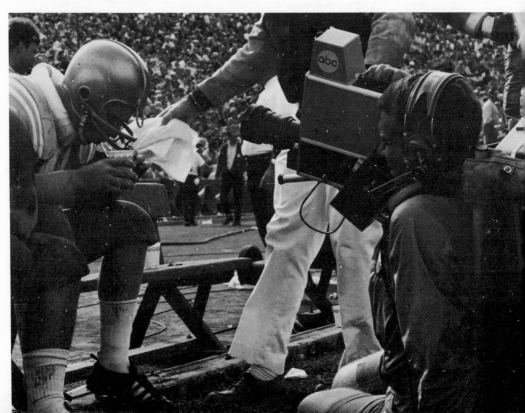

A hand-held videotape camera with a battery-operated back-pack recorder gives a video cameraman as much flexibility as a film cameraman. Both color and monochrome (black-and-white) units are available. Above, the Ampex VR 3000 consists of a monochromatic camera weighing 12 pounds and a 40-pound back-pack carrying a 20-minute reel of tape.

the considerable expense of operating a tank—technicians and chemicals —is eliminated; c) tape may be wiped clean and re-used.

7. Freeze framing is simpler using helical scan videotape or the newer magnetic disks than using film, especially if the editor wants to freeze frame in the middle or at the end of a news clip. Of course, this can also be accomplished by dubbing film onto videotape in the studio.

8. A machine with a variable slow motion control provides a news editor with unique flexibility.

9. Videotape can be copied quickly and simply.

10. Videotape can be transmitted to other stations quickly.

THE FUTURE

The first edition of this book, published in 1968, carried the prediction, "A television camera will one day accompany astronauts to the moon and to other planets, transmitting home pictures of their grand adventures." A year later, half that prediction was accomplished fact. The Apollo 11 flight, from launch to splashdown, occupied more than 230 hours of Comsat satellite time and the transmission of about 200 programs. Through a network of 20 earth stations, the television programs were seen by

Not too many years ago it could scarcely be imagined that motion picture news-film would be sent halfway around the world and be shown in most of the homes of the United States in less than 24 hours. It is possible that in a few years news events anywhere in the world will be telecast to the rest of the world as they happen.

viewers in both North and South America, Europe, North Africa, Asia and Australia. McLuhan's Global Village!

When Neil Armstrong and Edwin "Buz" Aldrin on the moon talked with President Nixon at the White House, CBS used a split screen technique to show the President and the astronauts. ABC superimposed a head shot of the President in a circle within the moon picture. Split screen is frequently used in sports coverage, but it is not common in news coverage. With special effects boards in studio control rooms and double chain projection techniques, no technical reason exists for not attempting such split screen images as showing a speaker and his audience at the same time, an interviewee and a reporter, or a parade and spectators. At present we see the audience, the reporter and the spectators only in cutaways.

Another first edition prediction, that television might one day present live reports of military battles, creeps closer to fulfillment with satellite transmission. To report live from a battlefield in Asia, for example, military clearance and considerable planning are needed. Also needed are:

1) A wireless portable television camera, like the "creepie peepie," capable of sending a microwave beam on line-of-sight or near line-of-sight to . . .

2) A repeater station a mile or so away, perhaps in a helicopter or a truck. The repeater station amplifies and re-transmits the signal to . . .

When President Richard Nixon talked to the first men on the moon, the networks showed both ends of the conversation. Superimposures (above), split screen techniques and other electronic combinations of images and sounds will become more commonplace as new equipment is developed and television journalists, directors and engineers experiment with new methods.

↓ The most impressive picture ever made! Viewers on every continent saw Neil Armstrong and "Buz" Aldrin walk upon the moon. It has been said that this live television transmission equals the feat of sending men to the moon.

3) One or more additional repeater stations. Each further boosts and moves the signal along to . . .

4) A home base station. This must be a permanent installation capable of generating enormous power, to reach . . .

5) A satellite transmitter, such as Intelsat. These transmitters are very weak relay stations, with less power output than a light bulb. But because they cover so much of the earth's surface with that output, a signal sent from Asia can be relayed across the Pacific to the West Coast, where it is picked up by . . .

6) A receiving station. This permanent installation picks up and amplifies the very weak satellite signal, which then goes to . . .

7) A telephone cable to carry the video signal on to Chicago or New York, for network transmission to television stations across the land.

Because a video picture has never been transmitted in quite this way, we cannot be sure of its quality by the time it reaches the viewer in his living room. However, previous multiple-stage transmissions, including a satellite as one of its stages, has produced marvelous pictures.

Transmission may be accomplished by using other elements than those listed above. Using two satellites instead of one, with a ground station between them, would eliminate need for a cross-country telephone line.

The superb live coverage of President Richard M. Nixon's trip to China depended upon a transportable communication satellite earth station, which relayed signals to the United States via the Intelsat IV satellite. From the United States, the pictures and sound were retransmitted to Asia. They were also sent to South America, to the score of nations belonging to the European Broadcasting Union, and to the nations of Eastern Europe served by the Eurovision network.

New equipment comes along regularly. Several competing firms manufacture electronic titling generators, which did not exist a few years ago. Videotape can be edited with a computerized device. A system created by CBS and Memorex synchronizes tape recorders, computer memory banks and magnetic disks to enable an editor to call up scenes and edit them with a light pen, with the pictures moving at regular speed, fast or slow motion, frame-by-frame, or stopped. A Japanese firm, Toho Denki, has produced the first color wirephoto transmitter and receiver. Another Japanese firm, Akai Electric, produces a ¼-inch video recorder and a 4-pound camera. The best known of the smaller video recorders is, of course, the ½-inch Sony, which has wide application for businesses, schools and CATV.

Cable television, now in about 8% of the more than 60 million television homes in the United States, promises to bring the "wired city" and even the "wired nation." CATV (community antenna television) potentionally could send news and other kinds of information into homes in several new ways. An article in *Fortune* stated: [1]

The possibilities of cable are breathtaking. If all of the homes that now have television sets were wired for cable reception, it would provide a network that could be used in countless ways. If the era of the home computer is ever to arrive, for example, it will almost certainly be via CATV, with the home television set as the information terminal. Cable capacity is great enough to make practical the facsimile reproduction of newspapers or magazines in the home, and to make TV transmitters available to almost any group with something to say. And one of the most attractive features of cable is that it uses none of the increasingly crowded radio-frequency spectrum.

Two-way CATV offers much more than a chance to shop for groceries in a new way. Conceivably, wire copy, from one or more news services, fed into a computer could be called up from telephones or keyboards and displayed on individual television sets (or computer CRT's), bringing to schools, libraries and homes more news on a· subject of interest (for instance, the economy) than any home town daily newspaper would carry. This kind of "television news" would be totally unlike a present television newscast, of course. It is mentioned here because some "think tanks" reportedly have been doing research in this area.

Also in the future, maybe not too many years away, is the use of laser light to carry messages. Unlike radio frequencies, laser light spreads very little as it travels. Its power output remains concentrated in a narrow cone, and therefore less power is required to reach a distant relay point. By aiming a laser beam from a helicopter near a ground camera directly to a satellite in stationary orbit, live transmission may one day be beamed from the remotest locations.

Water, electricity, telephone service and gas are "piped" into our homes. Broadcast signals and CATV wiring provide a kind of pipe too, bringing information and entertainment. But a few words of caution are in order, lest we become blinded by technology. It has been said that a message may take an instant to go around the world, but months to penetrate a skull. Edward P. Morgan summed it up on the air one night:

> Journalism has come quite a way, I guess. Thucydides carved some of his accounts of the Peloponnesian war on wax-covered tablets with a stylus which incidentally had a blunt end to erase errors. Quite a stretch to live TV in color and the instant sound of battle news from Saigon—with speed often seeming more important than time to correct mistakes.
>
> Some authorities maintain that the world's first reporter was Herodotus—the Greek historian of the Peloponnesian wars in the 5th century B.C. That was Thucydides' time too, but Herodotus was 25 years older.
>
> It's said Herodotus used a quill pen scratching his notes on ani-

mal skin or papyrus with ink from the vital parts of an octopus. The octopus today is the many-tentacled electronic equipment necessary to get a news show on the air.

A reporter used to begin as a cub, but in the magic media he can quickly become a lion of the headlines to unseen millions, especially if he is a ham.

Today for video purposes, a broadcast reporter has to think about the condition of his necktie more often than the condition of his typewriter ribbon.

The vital question is whether all this paraphernalia is helping to get a more understandable account of current history on your TV screen than if we scratched it out and mailed it to you on an animal skin.

I hope the answer is yes, but it won't be if we keep our mouths to the mike more than we keep our ears to the ground.

FOR THE STUDENT

1. A network news feed at 7 p.m. EST is received on the West Coast at 4 p.m. PST. If it is rebroadcast at 7 p.m. PST, what can the West Coast newsman do if a major news event occurs during the three-hour interval? What should he do if one of the reported stories changes during that interval (for example, if the network newscast reports an airliner being hijacked and, during the three-hour interval, the hijacker is shot)? (If necessary, refer to section on *Sources for Visuals* in Chapter 3.)
2. Monitor a newscast with a stopwatch, recording running time (from the top of the feed) on each item. Calculate the "item time" for each news story. How would knowing these times help the West Coast newsman (question #1)?
3. From the newscast you monitored (question #2), choose one short news item which can be covered cleanly (no "bridges" in or out). Write bulletin copy for a local newscaster which will cover that time period, allowing about two seconds pause going into and two seconds pause going out of the local cover.
4. Write a paper on how satellites affect or might affect television news.
5. Discuss the potential for television news in a CATV "wired city."
6. What drawbacks, if any, can you envision?
7. Why aren't all cameras the size of the Minicam?
8. In 1968, ABC news covered the political conventions with daily 90-minute wrap-ups, in competition with the gavel-to-gavel NBC and CBS coverage. Considering the need to "go live" on major events breaking during those 90-minutes (e.g., an important candidate's concession speech) and the need to maintain narrative continuity,

consider the problems a local station news producer might encounter trying the ABC news approach during a local election.

9. What are the advantages of videotape, compared with film? The disadvantages?

10. If you have access to videotape equipment, learn to dub a newsclip. If possible, learn to splice videotape or edit it electronically.

16

EDITORIALS

Former FCC Chairman Newton M. Minow once complained about television stations which editorialized for "canoe safety, milk for children," and causes just as daring.

IMAGINATION, GUTS—AND THEIR OPPOSITES

Some stations have more stomach for a fight. WTVJ-TV, Miami, turned its cameras on police corruption and organized crime in Dade County, forcing the county sheriff to resign. Indictments, including one with the sheriff's name on it, followed. WTVJ-TV's campaign included 85 consecutive editorials, surveillance film shot at risk, and an anti-crime telathon.

WTVJ-TV displays national awards for its editorials. In 1962, the year Minow made that crack about canoe safety, WTVJ-TV successfully fought city hall to force the rehiring of the city manager. The station editorialized that the city commissioners fired him because he was "too good for his own good."

Another oft-praised station, WDSU-TV, and its companion radio station, WDSU, of New Orleans, dared to speak out for a responsible civil rights policy at a time when local newspapers shrank back.

WDSU-TV became the first television station to use political cartoons. It has since been joined by stations in Chicago, Atlanta and Indianapolis, among others.

With musical accompaniment, WDSU-TV uses two cameras to present a John Chase cartoon. Starting with a close-up (Fig. 1), the camera pulls back and pans slightly to the right to reveal more elements of the cartoon (Figs. 2, 3, 4). The director then cuts to a second camera, a close-up of a yet unseen element (Fig. 5). The final take, using the first camera, shows the entire cartoon, adding perspective and what is, in effect, the caption.

John Chase, editorial cartoonist for WDSU-TV New Orleans, has observed: [1]

> Graphic humor belongs on a graphic medium like television . . . Response from viewers in our area has been more than enouraging, although some would like the cartoon to stay on longer. I'm more pleased that no one has written in grumbling that it stays on too long. A more general complaint is the inability of the cartoon fans to cut out a favorite cartoon to send to—well, whomever they send them to.
>
> I have many of our efforts on film. Most of them have musical accompaniment; some have narration, all have some kind of movement, and . . . all (are now) in full color. We still can't figure out how to reprint them on paper for those who write in for copies.
>
> Although my cartooning on TV has been but a few years of the number I've been a published cartoonist, I've never had so much response and so little privacy as these past few years on television.

Chase has devised several techniques to take advantage of the medium. Among them: two cameras, music, multiple panels, multi-segment overlays, and signature wipe-in. Presenting the cartoon from start to finish takes about 45 seconds. It is pre-taped.

WJZ-TV, Baltimore, campaigned against real estate "blockbusting," naming real estate agents. The U.S. Department of Justice soon investigated.

The list of stations which editorialize courageously runs longer. But the list of timid stations also runs long. A 1970 survey showed that more than a third of all television stations ran no editorials at all.[2] At least that is better than the 1958 situation when, nearly a decade after the Fairness Doctrine, only one third of the stations ever editorialized and only 5% editorialized daily. FCC Chairman John C. Doerfer wondered then if the right to editorialize was proving too much of a shock. "Ten years," he noted dryly, "is a long time to stand in stunned silence." [3]

The Radio Television News Directors Association annually awards prizes for the best television editorials. The author, who has served as a regional judge, is of the opinion that the quality of editorials has been improving but, as a category, editorials lag sadly behind spot news coverage and documentaries. In place of the sparkle and drama of documentaries, the viewer may see the station's general manager, like a schoolboy reciting "The Charge of the Light Brigade," reading from cue cards resting against the floor manager's shoe tops; the quality of writing competes unfavorably even with the quality of reading. Or, the news director will fix the camera with a baleful eye for two minutes of pointing with pride and viewing with alarm.

Editorials from many stations pop out devoid of technique or artistry, and consequently devoid of impact or charm. It seems as if all concerned, including viewers, grit their teeth, mutter "FCC", and endure the editorial. This, despite evidence that people want television stations to take editorial stands on public issues. A 1969 poll indicated that 85% favored television editorials, a 15% gain over a poll taken three years earlier.

Between "editorials" and "editorializing in news," a clear line of demarcation exists. Editorials are statements of opinion by the station management or a commentator, usually with the word "editorial" or "commentary" in plain view. Editorializing in news is a more or less covert expression of opinion through choice of words or film or subject matter or even gesture. But, like beauty, it may only be in the eye of the beholder.

A more subtle difference exists between editorializing in news, which might be sneakily intentional, and the honest reaction to a news event. In the latter case the journalist, admitting that perfect objectivity is neither possible nor desirable, tries to be fair. In the former case, he probably denies that he is not being objective, but really has no intention of being fair. (*See Why Can't You Be Objective?* in Chapter 1)

If a station speaks out courageously on local matters, almost by definition it will generate some community ill will which arrives through the diligent labors of the postman and the PBX operator. The timid station manager or news director avoids this ill will by several means: 1) dullness —a lack of wit, of bite, of impact will mitigate criticism; 2.) the "Mom's apple pie is good for you" approach—as noted, canoe safety and milk for children also work; 3.) "Afghanistanism"—say what you like about the Communist Chinese, but don't knock anything in this town; 4.) balance —"Side A has excellent arguments. So does Side B. We hope this healthy and spirited community dialogue continues"; 5.) escape—"We don't want to inflict our opinions on you. We want to reflect what our community thinks. So we have invited the people of this city to do the talking."

Washington Post columnist Nicholas von Hoffman said of broadcast editorials, "Strong points of view illuminate information, give it shape and meaning, and from the clash of many strong points of view come new understandings and validations of old ones. This is one reason for having free speech, and no amount of balanced and bland fairness can substitute for the struggle of competing advocacies."

As for #5, above, *vox populi* has strong merit, but only in addition to regular editorials, not instead of them.

Who should write the editorials? Who should deliver them? The answers depend upon station policy. For example:

> 1. The station manager writes and delivers the station's edi-
> torials. They are not aired during the newscast, but possibly adjacent
> to it.
>
> 2. An editorial writer researches and writes them. The station
> manager delivers them.

3. A news writer does the research and writing. The station manager delivers them.

4. The news director delivers them. Either he or a news writer prepares them.

5. A staff "editorialist" prepares and delivers them within the newscast. The station manager approves them.

6. A staff commentator writes and delivers opinions within the newscast. These are commentaries representing the views of the commentator, not editorials representing the views of the station.

The Fairness Doctrine requires opportunity for reply. In some cases, especially where an individual has been attacked, equal time may be demanded under the "personal attack rule" (see THE FAIRNESS DOCTRINE). Where a viewer disagrees by letter with a station's editorial viewpoint, it has been customary for the person who delivers the editorials to read from the letter a portion which gets to the heart of the viewer's disagreement. For added clarity, the station may, like CBS' *60 Minutes*, print a sentence from the letter for use as a rear projection while the letter segment is read aloud.

It has also been customary at the end of each editorial to invite viewer response.

Ralph Renick, WTVJ-TV, vice president for news, bases his daily editorials on these standards:

1. One person must be the sole, final authority.

2. The editorial should be restricted almost wholly to local and state issues.

3. The station must be able to conduct "research in depth" in a speedy manner.

4. The one who delivers the editorial must be well known and respected, and he must know his community well.

5. The editorial must be clearly defined on the air, and carefully separated from the news reporting segments.

6. Courage is important—to take a definite stand and then stick with it.

7. No editorial should be a "blast"—a course of action must be presented.

8. Editorials should be clearly on the side of righteousness and betterment. If it is necessary to delve into politics, or truly double-edged issues, then the station must be immediately prepared to air the opposing side of the issue on which it has taken a stand.[4]

A typical editorial will run two to three minutes. Whether the viewer sees only the person delivering the editorial or visuals as well depends upon the station. Of course, there is no limit to the visuals which can be used: political cartoons, stills, film, etc. Detroit's WJBK-TV neatly turned a SOF news feature, about a woman trying to raise money to run a local charity, into a fine editorial by offering to match, dollar for dollar, all money raised to reach the goal she had set.

From Carl Zimmerman, news director of WITI-TV, Milwaukee, here is still further expression of the need to dig, to go beyond the obvious, and to use the television medium fully: "If we criticize our city, county or state officials, let's show those officials in action at their meetings, at their public hearings. Let the viewer *hear* and *see* them on sound film. What better way to know the kind of men they elected? If we cry out for correction at the dangerous intersection, let's show the driver that traffic hazard, that congested bottleneck. If our expressway construction is proceding too slowly, let's take our sound cameras right there and show where and how county officials are failing to keep construction humming along. If we ask for greater speed in wiping blight from our central city, again our cameras should film the editorial right there where the problems are the greatest." [5]

THE FAIRNESS DOCTRINE

By the Mayflower Decision, in 1941, the Federal Communications Commission ruled editorials off the air, stating, "A truly free radio cannot be used to advocate the causes of the licensee. It cannot be used to support the candidacies of his friends. It cannot be devoted to the support of principles he happens to regard most favorably. In brief, the broadcaster cannot be an advocate."

The FCC gradually changed its attitude, and, in 1949, reversed itself with a report which came to be known as "The Fairness Doctrine." [6] The Commission not only said that broadcasting stations *could* editorialize, but they had a *duty* to discuss controversial issues. In all cases, they were obliged to present all sides of a controversy.

The Fairness Doctrine states:

> . . . the needs and interests of the general public with respect to programs devoted to news commentary and opinion can only be satisfied by making available to them for their consideration and acceptance or rejection, of varying and conflicting views held by responsible elements of the community. And it is in the light of these basic concepts that the problems of insuring fairness in the presentation of news and opinions and the place in such a picture of any expression of the views of the station licensee as such must be considered. . . .

> This affirmative responsibility on the part of broadcast licensees to provide a reasonable amount of time for the presentation over their facilities of programs devoted to the discussion and consideration of

public issues has been reaffirmed by this Commission in a long series of decisions. . . . This duty extends to all subjects of substantial importance to the community. . . . The licensee must operate on a basis of overall fairness, making his facilities available for the expression of the contrasting views of all responsible elements in the community on the various issues which arise. . . .

These concepts, of course, do restrict the licensee's freedom to utilize his station in whatever manner he chooses but they do so in order to make possible the maintenance of radio as a medium of freedom of speech for the general public. . . .

We do not believe, however, that the licensee's obligations to serve the public interest can be met merely through the adoption of a general policy of not refusing to broadcast opposing views where a demand is made of the station for broadcast time. . . . Broadcast licensees have an affirmative duty generally to encourage and implement the broadcast of all sides of controversial issues over their facilities. . . . . a conscious and positive role in bringing about a balanced presentation of the opposing viewpoints. . . .

The Commission believes that under the American system of broadcasting the individual licensees of radio stations have the responsibility for determining the specific program material to be broadcast over their stations. This choice, however, must be exercised in a manner consistent with the basic policy of the Congress that radio be maintained as a medium of free speech for the general public as a whole rather than as an outlet for the purely personal or private interests of the licensee. This requires that licensees devote a reasonable percentage of their broadcasting time to the discussion of public issues of interest in the community served by their stations and that such programs be designed so that the public has a reasonable opportunity to hear different opposing positions on the public issues of interest and importance in the community. The particular format best suited for the presentation of such programs in a manner consistent with the public interest must be determined by the licensee in the light of the facts of each individual situation.

A complaint to the FCC by attorney John Banzhaf asking, under the Fairness Doctrine, for anti-smoking messages to offset cigarette commercials, extended the scope of the Doctrine to commercials.

RED LION

Is The Fairness Doctrine constitutional? That question was asked many times, but was not answered until the Supreme Court ruled on a Fairness Doctrine case in 1967, *Red Lion Broadcasting Co. v. Federal Communications Commission.* We refer to it as *The Red Lion decision.* It stemmed from a radio broadcast, over a station owned by the Red Lion Broadcasting Co. of Red Lion, Pa., in which the Rev. Billy James Hargis attacked Fred Cook, author of a book, *Goldwater—Extremist of the Right*. Cook demanded equal time to reply, under an aspect of the Fairness Doctrine called the "personal attack rule," and wanted the time supplied free of charge. The station agreed on condition Cook warranted that no paid sponsorship could be found for a program carrying his reply. Cook refused. He complained to the FCC, which supported his contention. The matter went to the Supreme Court. Cook won.

Like Section 315, the personal attack rule exempts newscasts, news interviews, and on-the-spot coverage of news events, but includes editorials. It requires that the station notify the person or group attacked within a week, provide a script or tape of the attack, and offer time to reply.

In its decision on *Red Lion*, which it coupled with a decision on the *RTNDA* case concerning the FCC's rules on personal attack and political editorializing, the Supreme Court stated, "It is the right of the viewers and listeners, not the right of the broadcasters, which is paramount. . . . The First Amendment confers no right on licensees to prevent others from broadcasting on 'their' frequencies and no right to an unconditional monopoly of a scarce resource which the government has denied others the right to use."

On the question of whether a station might be able to keep silent on issues, the Court declared, "That this will occur now seems unlikely, however, since if present licensees should suddenly prove timorous, the Commission is not powerless to insist that they give adequate and fair attention to public issues."

Documentaries apparently come under the Fairness Doctrine, because they are not newscasts or on-the-spot news coverage. CBS offered equal time to medical associations which complained about two CBS-TV documentaries, "The Promise and the Practice" and "Don't Get Sick in America." Both documentaries criticized the national health care situation.

NBC and ABC changed their policies in 1970 to let the Democratic and Republican parties buy time to promote causes or ask for funds. NBC also sells time to other responsible groups. For example, a group of senators paid $70,000 for a half hour to protest the Vietnam War. CBS offered the party out of power in Washington free time to reply to presidential speeches. The offer did not include third or fourth parties, nor did it take into account major opposition within a President's own party; for example, opposition to President Lyndon Johnson's views on Vietnam came largely from his own party, as did opposition to President Nixon's approach to China.

Redefinitions of the Fairness Doctrine are likely to continue for some years, quite possibly in the direction of greater access by various segments of the public to air time. Most broadcasters oppose what amounts to a lessening of their control and any movement toward "common carrier" status for broadcasting stations. The National Association of Broadcasters has resisted efforts to widen public access under the Fairness Doctrine. Broadcasters have pointed out that if they cannot control what is said, they cannot be legally responsible for it. Conceivably, uncontrolled access to a broadcast medium could open a Pandora's Box of obscenity, libel, expressions of racial and religious hatred, and calls for riot or revolution. Of course, through recording or tape delay, such statements *could* be censored. But what *should* be censored and *who* should do the censoring are some of the problems which must be faced. Some Fairness Doctrine problems are also problems of what is widely known as Section 315. Unlike the Fairness Doctrine, which is not law, Section 315 is part of the law of the land.

SECTION 315

Section 315 of the Communications Act of 1934 states, "If any licensee shall permit any person who is a legally qualified candidate for any public office to use a broadcasting station, he shall afford equal opportunities to all other such candidates for that office . . ." Then it goes on, under a 1959 amendment ("Lar Daly Amendment") to exempt candidate appearances in newscasts, news interviews, documentaries in which the candidate's appearance is incidental, and on-the-spot news coverage such as political conventions.

The trouble with Section 315 is that, by granting equal time to every minor candidate, broadcasters would be surrendering the use of their facilities to anyone who paid the filing fee, including bigots, revolutionaries and publicity seekers. But simply repealing Section 315 might lead to the effective silencing of important third or fourth parties. Unable yet to discover a compromise, Congress knows it can suspend the equal time provisions of Section 315, so that major candidates for major offices may buy or receive free the television and radio time they want. It did so in 1960 to allow the Kennedy-Nixon debates.

At the time of publication, legislation had been introduced in Congress to repeal Section 315 for presidential and vice presidential candidates in general elections.

Over the years, the FCC ruled on some Section 315 matters relating to news. Among their decisions:

315 does not apply to political issues, which must get balanced coverage under the Fairness Doctrine.

A newscaster who becomes a candidate must leave the newscast, or else his air appearances are considered a "use" and his opponents are entitled to equal time. Anyone who broadcasts falls under this decision, a state of affairs which led comedian Pat Paulsen, a semi-serious presidential candidate, to go to court to argue that "a single class of citizens (is) required by the government to abandon their livelihoods in order to offer themselves for higher office."

315 does not apply to normal news program coverage of a candidate. It does apply if the candidate provides the film clips.

315 does not apply to regular news interview programs, such as "Issues and Answers" or "Meet the Press." It does apply if a candidate is interviewed on a talk show.

315 would not apply to a regularly scheduled "governor's news conference," but equal time provisions would apply to a special news conference program.

If a debate between two candidates is broadcast, other candidates for that office are entitled to "equal opportunities."

If an incumbent, including the President of the United States, calls a news conference while a candidate, his opponent(s) is entitled to "equal opportunities" under Section 315. If, however, the President addresses the nation on a sudden international crisis, equal time does not apply.

A station may not censor a candidate's words, but it is absolved from all liability for what the candidate says.

Because so many questions about Section 315 fall into a gray area, any news director puzzled about what constitutes a "use" should inquire directly of the FCC. KPIX-TV, San Francisco, wanted to cover state and local campaigns without risking trouble over Section 315. The FCC approved its proposal to add one hour to its nightly half hour newscast once a month for six months.

BROADCASTING AND THE FIRST AMENDMENT

Allegations that network television news is biased have sometimes been accompanied by the claim that radio and television newscasts do not share First Amendment protection with newspapers, magazines and books because the government must assign broadcast frequencies and because the Federal Communications Commission regulates broadcasting as a whole.

That is not true. The United States Supreme Court has consistently held that broadcasters are protected under the First Amendment.

Ruling on the case of the *U.S.* v. *Paramount Pictures* in 1948, the Supreme Court said, "There is no doubt that . . . moving pictures like newspapers and radio, are included in the press, whose freedom is guaranteed by the First Amendment."

In *Superior Films* v. *Department of Education,* in 1954, the Supreme Court noted, "The First Amendment draws no distinction between the various methods of communicating ideas."

In *Farmers' Education and Cooperative Union* v. *WDAY, Inc.,* in 1959, the Supreme Court said, "Expressly applying this country's tradition of free expression to the field of radio broadcasting, Congress has from the first emphatically forbidden the [Federal Communications] Commission to exercise any power of censorship over radio communications."

Some qualification was expressed in the *Red Lion* decision in 1969, "Although broadcasting is clearly a medium affected by a First Amendment interest differences in the characteristics of the news media justify differences in the First Amendment standards applied to them."

However, the Court also stated in *Red Lion,* "The people as a whole retain their interest in free speech by radio, and their collective right to have the medium function consistently with the ends and purposes of the First Amendment."

A First Amendment scholar, Professor Glenn O. Robinson, has stated, "Virtually everyone accepts the proposition that the First Amendment does apply to radio and television." [7] Another scholar, William A. Hachten, stated, "As the news and public affairs activities of the broadcasters increase in scope and importance, so has the First Amendment protection they enjoy. In fact, the FCC has encouraged broadcasters to editorialize on the air, provided they give an opportunity for opposing views to be aired later. For all intents and purposes, the broadcast journalist enjoys the same freedoms as does the pen and pencil journalist." [8]

In 1949, the FCC said "We fully recognize that freedom of the radio is included among the freedoms protected against government abridgment by the First Amendment."

Yet the FCC indicated that this freedom is not absolute: [9]

The basis for any fair consideration of public issues, and particularly those of a controversial nature, is the presentation of news and information concerning the basic facts of the controversy in as complete and impartial a manner as possible. A licensee would be abusing his position as public trustee of these important means of mass communication were he to withhold from expression over his facilities relevant news or facts concerning a controversy or to slant or distort presentation of such news.

And Congress, in 1959, included newscasts in its concern for the public interest when it amended Section 315: [10]

Nothing in the foregoing sentence shall be construed as relieving broadcasters, in connection with the presentation of newscasts, news interviews, news documentaries, and on-the-spot coverage of news events, from the obligation imposed upon them under this chapter to operate in the public interest and to afford reasonable opportunity for the discussion of conflicting views on issues of public importance.

The gist of all these statements appears to be that a broadcaster does indeed share with a newspaper, magazine or book publisher the First Amendment freedom of the press to report any news event as he chooses without fear, but unlike the publishers, who may do as they please, the broadcaster's total news and information output concerning public issues should be fair. The broadcaster is under an obligation of decency which is not demanded of a publisher. NBC News correspondent Bill Monroe remarked, "This country is already on the road, without realizing it, to a dual system of mass media: a printed press that is free but shrinking and an electronic press that is growing but unfree." [11]

As this book went to press, a congressman and a senator were moving in opposite directions in the matter of broadcast news freedom. Rep. Harley O. Staggers (D., W.Va.) was investigating evidence that television newsmen staged events in order to deceive viewers. He said, "We hope to have legislation." At the same time, Sen. Sam J. Ervin (D., N.C.) held committee hearings on broadcast news freedom, saying, "The reasons for protecting the printed press from government control apply equally to the broadcast media. If First Amendment principles are held not to apply to the broadcast media, it may be that the Constitution's guarantee of a free press is on its death bed." [12]

(See, also, section on *Subpoenas and Shield Laws,* in Chapter 18, THE LAW.)

FOR THE STUDENT

1. Interview the commentator, or editorialist, of a local station.
2. On what grounds would you judge a television news editorial?
3. If a local television station presents few editorials, what, if anything, should you do as a concerned citizen?
4. What, if anything, should you do if you feel the editorials are all strongly slanted politically and you think there is little effort to achieve either objectivity or rationality?
5. Monitor each local newscast for one week (consecutive weeks, if necessary). Write a paper comparing their presentation of editorials. Consider controversiality, quality of arguments, and willingness to gore local oxen.
6. Write and deliver an editorial on a local subject. Does your writing style or your delivery differ from the manner in which you handle news?
7. Using standards determined by the class, let each student score editorials delivered by other students. A critique should follow. Then each student should rewrite his editorial and deliver it again.
8. Should a newscast be as free of government control as a newspaper?
9. Write a paper summarizing current questions revolving around the Fairness Doctrine. (*Broadcasting* and the RTNDA *Communicator* are good sources, but consider others as well.) Should the Fairness Doctrine be extended? Curtailed? Replaced?
10. What, if anything, should be done about Section 315?

17

ELECTIONS

THE ART OF MODERN election coverage leads television journalism into unfamiliar territory: computer programming, survey research, sampling techniques and data flow. Yet the smart news director won't shrink from dealing with them, in most cases through professionals in those fields. His reasoning is simple and practical. A well-produced election night report attracts new viewers to his station's news efforts. It introduces new viewers to the anchormen and reporters. Television news viewers tend to stay with a newscast they like. But on election nights, many viewers channel-hop.

If the ratings are to be believed, there is nothing a citizen would rather do after he votes than watch television to learn if his candidates won. In fact, more people watch the three networks on election night than vote on election day. And millions who don't watch, listen.

A century ago, reporting an election was rather hit or miss. Take California's first gubernatorial election in 1849. Messengers collected the returns, but because the roads were muddy and the trails were blocked by snow and high water, a lot of polling places were not heard from for three weeks. When the returns got to the county center, there was the problem of getting them to the state capitol. The Sacramento County returns, for instance, were taken by steamer to San Francisco, where a horseback rider was waiting to jog the 120 miles to Monterey, California's first capital. The news did not reach the East Coast until the election had been over for six weeks. It arrived by steamship, along with a half million dollars worth of gold dust. Of course, today, each network spends several

Covering a major scheduled news event requires enormous expenditures, often far more than can be recovered by commercials during the event. Above, a technician prepares to set up a monitor at a remote location for a political convention.

times that half million in gold dust just to carry the election news. But in those days a dollar was worth more and they didn't have to pay for computer time.

The pony express, the telegraph, and the telephone, in their turns, improved the flow of election returns. The adding machine, the calculator, the punch card device, and the computer, in their turns, improved the figuring. And, in turn, teletype, radio, and television improved the dissemination of the news. Voting machines helped, too. Punch card voting systems should be speeding the flow of returns also, but unfortunately, a lot of debugging has been done around midnight of election night.

The single most significant factor in improving election returns—in speed, accuracy, and fullness of information—has not been mechanical or electronic, but the human factor of setting up a workable system.

The first question one asks is: why bother? Why set up a system at all? What is to be gained from the expenditure of effort and money? The answers are, firstly, that people are interested in the outcome of a major election which chooses their leaders and, by so doing, points to the policies which will affect their lives in so many ways. Secondly, even when the outcome is not vital to a viewer—say, a Cleveland viewer watching the New York mayor's race—he has his favorite, he is interested and he is curious, even more than he would be watching a baseball game being played out, because the sentiment of those New York voters may make itself felt in the next general election. Tuning in on election returns is a lot of fun. We enjoy the competition and the excitement. (And maybe because so many of us vote *"agin"* someone rather than *for* someone, there is satisfaction in watching a candidate we dislike make his concession statement.) A third reason networks and individual stations bother is that they attract viewers to the news broadcasts. If tonight's election package is interesting and informative, viewers may return tomorrow for the regular newscast. Fourthly, although networks spend millions and some stations spend thousands on election coverage, getting only a fraction of it back in commercial fees on election night, broadcast executives are aware of their public service responsibilities. There is a pride in doing a good job covering this most important of all advance-notice stories.

THE RAW VOTE

Having decided that election coverage is worthwhile, a news director next asks himself to what depth he should report an election. Before television, election night was just numbers. The returns were gathered at county seats, where stringer reporters for the Associated Press or United Press—or the county clerks themselves—periodically telephoned incoming precinct returns to a state tabulation center, where they were totted up on adding machines, and then telephoned to New York City, where Robert Trout or Elmer Davis or H. V. Kaltenborn broadcast them to a waiting America.

Such reporting of what is now called "the raw vote" contains a built-in error factor, for election returns never arrive on a purely random basis. Polls with voting machines report in first. Polls with a lot of paper ballots to count call in later than those with a few. Ghettos tend to be slower than posh suburbs. Rural precincts are often slow—sometimes because the polling place workers tuck into a good dinner after the polls close and before the long count begins. In practical terms, the result in Illinois is that the Democrats lead early in the evening, because Chicago comes in fast, while the downstate Illinois Republican vote trickles in all night long. Ditto Michigan and several other states.

If a station sets up its system only on the basis of this raw vote, it offers somewhat misleading information, and rather dull programming. Nevertheless, raw vote must be one source of information. Putting a reporter in each precinct is the ideal way to get all the returns quickly. Of course, this is expensive. Putting a reporter in each county center is much cheaper, and slower. For national elections the three networks—ABC, NBC, and CBS—and the two wire services—AP and UPI—pool their resources of men and money to create N.E.S., the News Election Service. N.E.S. gathers the raw vote, and the members agree that the only totals

Space shots, presidential election remotes, inaugurations, visits by world figures, and the funerals of world figures are handled by special events units of networks, which take turns producing a network pool operation. All three networks put men and equipment under the control of the network pool producer. *Right:* Tiered camera position at national political convention provides vantage points for still photographers, video cameramen, and film cameramen. Notice that the video cameras, second tier, are marked "TV POOL." The same signal is fed to all three networks.

they ever show on tally boards are those transmitted by N.E.S. Many newspapers, television stations, and radio stations "buy into" the N.E.S. pool for speedy top-of-the-ticket (presidential, senatorial, gubernatorial congressional) returns, and into a regional or local pool managed by the AP, a newspaper or some other organization with reporters at the polling places for speedier bottom-of-the-ticket returns.

In each state N.E.S. contracts with one or more organizations, such as a state education association or the Junior Chamber of Commerce (the Jaycees), to provide precinct reporters. The practice has been to cover half to two-thirds of the nation's precincts. Voting machine precincts usually get N.E.S. reporters. Punch card precincts do not. To report returns from uncovered precincts, and as a backup for those precincts with reporters, N.E.S. assigns a reporter to each of the nation's county centers.

The precinct reporters report their one precinct, and go home. County reporters call in cumulative returns, each higher than the last, as the precinct officials report in to the county clerks. Precinct reporters and county reporters have nothing to do with one another. These are two different systems, set up partly for speed and partly for redundancy.

Vote Flow System

The news director designing a tabulation center in or near the studio he will use to broadcast returns must concern himself with a variety of housekeeping tasks. Weeks before the election he must order special telephones, including a telephone rotary; that is, a group of phones which can be reached, one after the other, by calling a single number. Reporters' instruction sheets will carry the number, along with a note to carry some dimes and to keep trying if the signal is busy.

The report forms used by the telephone clerks must match the reporter's forms, which in their turn have to be designed to handle voting machine information or paper ballot or electronic counting returns either on a partial or complete return basis, depending upon how complex the situation is, how extensive the television coverage, and how fast the returns are wanted. The report forms should be designed for simple tabulating or key punching. On a precinct level, reports can be added up, one adding machine per candidate, or keypunched for totalling in a tabulator, like an IBM 407, or in a small computer. City level and county level returns have the added complication of cumulative votes being called in, requiring subtraction as well as addition. So instead of adding machines, the system needs tabulating machines like a Burroughs Sensimatic, with one column for each county—or better yet, a computer.

Beyond this, the system needs a politically knowledgeable editor or a political scientist who specializes in his state's politics, to cast an experienced eye over the county returns to see if any seem odd. Of course, a computer can be programmed to do this, given suitable parameters. But election veterans prefer to see an editor in this role. A basic rule for running an election system is: *don't depend only on machines.* Another rule is: *go over the paper flow a hundred times in your mind,* because of "Murphy's Law," known to every computer man: *if anything can go wrong, it will.* And when something goes wrong on election night, chaos ensues.

An election tabulation system should be designed by someone with experience. Key election night jobs should be staffed by experienced people. Such experience is surprisingly easy to acquire, because networks and stations must scrounge for competent people willing to work on such a temporary basis. University students studying to become broadcast journalists ought to apply for these jobs at every election. But disaster impends if a news director turns the task of designing a complex election tabulation system over to an inexperienced staff member. Disaster can even overtake experienced men.

The author once witnessed a pooled state tabulation center which came apart at the seams, with tallies for the candidates, yo-yo-ing all night. At one point, candidate Jones' had 10,000 and candidate Smith had 15,000 votes. Half an hour later, Smith dropped back to 10,000 and Jones had 15,000—or something like it. The manager, an editor with prior election experience, claimed someone had gotten hold of the telephone number for calling in returns, and was calling in false, wild figures. The trouble was, the system was designed with no protection feature, no redundancy.

One of the networks had an even worse system for handling returns from this pool. The system manager had arranged to look at every piece of paper himself prior to distribution. Another rule of any election operation is: *the manager should never be nailed to one position.* He should not be an integral part of the system. When vote returns start coming, they come in a blizzard of paper. This poor fellow was sometimes getting a piece of paper with fresh returns from some county or other every three seconds. He was using what can only be described as the "armpit method" of vote flow. As each piece of paper arrived, he took a frantic look at it, and shoved it under his armpit. He had quite a stack there. He was hoping for a pause so he could sort the paper out. The pause did not come until it was too late to matter. No doubt he had to explain the next day why the other networks were so much ahead of his with the same information.

KEY PRECINCTS

The news director who wants to get more out of election night numbers than growing vote totals must consider setting up a key precinct

A television camera on a crab dolly captures the bustle of an election night network operation. Behind the on-camera political reporter is a roomful of political analysts, newsmen, computer experts, statisticians and support personnel, plus an entire computer installation.

operation. Simply reporting raw vote can be misleading and certainly will be dull. How are the farmers voting? Did candidate Jones attract a large Black vote? Did candidate Smith get a backlash vote in blue collar neighborhoods? Where did the new and amorphous suburban vote go? These questions require a key precinct system. A sample of precincts is chosen which models the state. The news department gathers past voting history and demographic information about each key. On election night the sample provides analysis material of a kind and quality which used to appear in newspapers and magazines days after an election. Admittedly, only a fraction of what is available goes on the air. That is as it should be for a mass medium—having the choice of reporting which trends are most interesting, most important and most capable of being capsulized clearly.

Researching vote history consists of digging in dusty courthouse basements for old precinct voting records. Demographic surveying, which is part of key precinct research, requires a visit to the precinct and interviews with politicians or priests or school principals to estimate such things as what percentage of the voters are Negro, Mexican, Puerto Rican, American Indian, Japanese, Catholic, Jewish, Mormon. What percentage belong to labor unions, are elderly retired people, are young marrieds (or young swingers)? How many have incomes above $15,000 a year? What percentage have a bare subsistence income? Also important, has the neighborhood changed? Has it integrated in the past four years? Has a shopping center or apartment buildings or a freeway wiped out half the houses? That would make hash out of history. That, and redistricting which changes precinct boundaries.

A key precinct system also permits a station to develop a projection equation, so that the winner of a political contest may be recognized and "called" fairly early in the evening, except in close races.

The key precinct sample, which should be drawn by someone with knowledge of sampling methods, could be a pure random sample of precincts, a random sample stratified by such a basic factor as city size, a sample restricted to eliminate most late reporting precincts, or a sample consisting of "barometric" or "weathervane" precincts (the precinct's voting pattern closely matches the state pattern). Each of these methods has advantages and disadvantages. The networks themselves differ in their means of drawing samples. Trying to match the sample to the state's racial and religious proportions, which is called "quota sampling," has been discredited for many years.

So far, we have considered two sources of information—raw vote and key precinct vote—available to election analysts (sometimes called psephologists). A third source of information should be a political scientist at a university who specializes in that state's politics. His understanding of the pulls and tugs within a state is a leavening agent in any mix of computer printout and statistician's slide rules, to say nothing of how fast everyone turns to him when the computer goes down.

Television networks take particular pride in their coverage of national political conventions and national elections. These broadcasts are a public service in the fullest sense of the term. Networks spend millions of dollars to report, with the highest professional quality, the political will of the people. Solari counting boards are installed in a studio to keep track of the voting returns of individual races. In the background, computer equipment has been installed to help analyze voting trends. Viewers learn not only the "who" but the "why" of elections.

A producer and an art director plan the graphic elements which will be used in reporting an election. As much as two years of planning is devoted to a single evening's broadcast, the reporting of a presidential election.

A fourth source of information is AP and UPI, coming in by tele-type, the regular news service, with news of rain downstate, a blizzard upstate, light voting in the suburbs, or long lines in the ghettos.

<h2 style="text-align:center">Election Set</h2>

The studio election set is limited only by budget and imagination. The raw vote tally behind the anchorman can be a digital display (see section on *Illustrating Weather News*), in which electrically controlled numbers may change on camera. A number of electronic digit display devices can be installed, and so can simple, thumb controlled number wheels. A device called the Videograph (see Chapter 14, *Supering*) can produce a crawl with election figures over regular programming. Simpler and cheaper crawls can also serve.

Surprisingly, there is little attempt to match network election sets and the election sets of affiliate stations for national elections, even though the affiliates cut away from the network sets to their own sets every half hour. Nor do the networks offer the considerable expertise of their election units to the affiliates on a consulting basis. Some affiliates know what they are doing, and do it reasonably well. Others thrash around in confusion, to the detriment not only of the affiliate station but of the network, because many viewers do not differentiate between what they see and hear at 8:55 p.m. and what they see and hear at 9:05 p.m.

Well-rounded election night coverage will include live remote feeds from the headquarters of the major candidates. A caution is advised. Because a station has sent a remote truck and a reporter to a hotel ballroom, the show producer may feel some pressing need to switch to the ballroom, whether or not anything is going on. The resulting switch resembles a Wally Ballew skit on the "Bob and Ray Show." Nothing in television news is quite so pointless as watching some hapless reporter standing in the middle of an empty ballroom, saying something like, "Well, Bill, things are still pretty quiet here because the polls won't close for two hours, but there is a feeling that anything can happen. And now, over to you, Bill."

WATCHING THE VOTE COUNT

It is rumored that in one large American city, relatives of City Hall employees register Republican so they can be appointed Republican poll watchers. City Hall itself is controlled by Democrats, who appoint their own party's poll watchers. Election night in several wards of this city is a cozy affair.

Elsewhere, Republicans may be equally adroit at retaining power. Ballot box connivance is non-partisan. It is a paradox that the law, which requires legislative sessions and courtrooms to be open to public scrutiny, in many states forbids public or press to observe the counting of ballots. Admittedly, parties and candidates usually have the privilege of choosing poll watchers at the precincts, if they can find the volunteers, but charges of election fraud persist in spite of these built-in protections.

This is not to say that such hanky panky is widespread or common. The fact that it exists anywhere is cause enough for concern, especially now when many of our youngsters feel that "the system" is rigged, and the ghettos seethe in discontent.

Increasingly, the news media are sending disinterested observers into the precincts. They are there only to get the vote totals, but the very presence of the stranger sometimes proves unnerving. Most polling place officials welcome election reporters, or at least tolerate them. But some officials invoke the law to keep them outside, and a few reporters have even been threatened with harm if they tried to enter.

The polling place reporters face a bewildering variety of state laws, some of which are dimly understood or misunderstood by election officials themselves. A few states even have statutes regarding access to polling places which either contradict each other or establish different standards for paper ballot precincts, voting machine precincts and electronic tabulation centers.

The author once asked the county chairman of a political party in Indiana to help arrange to have his party's poll watchers in certain precincts hand a copy of the returns to a reporter waiting outside the door. It was a tortuous method, but strictly within the wording of the statute. "Oh, you don't have to go to all that trouble," the county chairman replied, "Reporters just walk in." When told that the reporters—all members of the League of Women Voters—wished to adhere strictly to the law, the party official obligingly offered to designate all the reporters as poll watchers for his party. This offer, too, was declined. The more complicated method was set up. After the election, it was learned that many of the reporters were invited into the precincts by the polling place officials.

Some state codes make no mention of news representatives, but limit outsiders to poll watchers chosen by candidates or by political parties. Ohio, Illinois, Washington, West Virginia, Wyoming, Utah, Tennessee, Oregon, Oklahoma, Nebraska, Missouri, Maryland, Kansas, Louisiana, Kentucky, Colorado and Arkansas have such limitations.

In some of these states, the law is either ignored at many polling places, or circumvented by news gathering agencies which acquire poll watching certificates in batches.

If many states authorize a public count, and if the practice in others is to wink at the law, the question arises, why have a law at all which forbids public observance of the canvass?

One argument for such a law is that it keeps disruptive elements away from precinct boards, whose members are often elderly men and women, weary after 12 or more hours of supervising voting, needing all their energy to concentrate on the important job of counting the ballots accurately.

The need for the "orderly conduct of elections" was cited by Illinois Governor Otto Kerner when he vetoed a bill [2] which would have permitted reporters access to returns at precincts. The thrust of the Kerner veto message was that the bill gave television networks a competitive edge. Other opponents of the bill raised the specter of television crews crowding into the precincts with their noise and hot lights. Actually, there was little likelihood of a television crew covering the count at any precinct in the state, for editorial reasons if for no other.

These scarifying arguments skirted the real issue of whether an outsider, chosen by no political party, should be permitted to observe the counting of the ballots. A more cogent argument was the use of the law as a fence which guards weary poll workers from distraction. However, the number of unpleasant incidents must be small, for no state which has permitted a publicly observed canvass has ever backed away from it, and, as already noted, the restrictive laws in many other states are often more observed in the breach. In any case, a democratic society should be able

ACCESS TO VOTE COUNTING BY STATE AND TYPE OF BALLOT

State	Public or Press Allowed	Not Public
Alabama	X[1]	X[2]
Alaska	(not specified)	
Arizona	X	
Arkansas		X
California	X	
Colorado		X
Connecticut	X	
Delaware	(at discretion of poll officials)	
Florida	X[2]	
Georgia	X	
Hawaii	X	
Idaho	X	
Illinois		X
Indiana	X[3]	
Iowa	X[4]	
Kansas		X
Kentucky		X
Louisiana		X
Maine	X	
Maryland		X
Massachusetts	X	
Michigan	X	
Minnesota	X	
Mississippi	X	
Missouri		X
Montana	X	
Nebraska		X
Nevada	X	
New Hampshire	X	
New Jersey	X	
New Mexico	X	
New York	X	
North Carolina	X	
North Dakota	X	
Ohio		X
Oklahoma		X
Oregon		X
Pennsylvania	X[1]	
Rhode Island	X	
South Carolina	X	
South Dakota	X	
Tennessee		X
Texas	(conflicting laws)	
Utah		X
Vermont	(at discretion of poll officials)	
Virginia	(at discretion of poll officials)	
Washington	X[1]	X[5]
West Virginia		X
Wisconsin	X	
Wyoming		X

[1] Voting machine precincts.
[2] Paper ballot precincts.
[3] Within sharply constrained limits.
[4] Except in a few double board precincts.
[5] Paper ballot precincts, while polls are open.

What the viewer sees on election night is the tip of the iceberg. Just below this display wall at CBS election headquarters, men operate a bank of display control consoles. News Election Service supplies the figures. The three networks, the two wire services and any news organization which "buys into" the N.E.S. feed commit themselves to reporting only what N.E.S. transmits. In the early days of election reporting, a few reporters were accused of inflating the election figures to appear ahead of the competition.

to find some recourse, other than an outright ban, to any problem created by citizen attendance.

Beyond this, there is a benefit to a democratic society in having its public officials aware that they function in public view.

It surely is plain that those who count votes perform a public duty, just as do those who administer justice, and that the public responsibility is equally great.

Another argument, sometimes voiced by polling place officials, is that how the precinct votes is none of any reporter's business. This "public-be-damned" recalcitrance was summed up by an election official who said he favored abolishing the election night unofficial tally altogether. He preferred a blackout of news about who won the election, until some days or even weeks later when the official election report was released. (It might be guessed that this official holds office in a major American city with a fragrant reputation for mishandling ballots.)

Who are the reporters? They are almost never full-time journalists. Working newsmen cannot be spared from their jobs on election night, perhaps the busiest night of the year in an editorial room. Election reporters are ordinary citizens, usually members of a statewide or nationwide organization. The organization is paid for its members' efforts by the News Election Service, by one of the networks independently (for the network sampling system), or by a local newspaper. The reporter volunteers his service to his organization. Reporters tend to be drawn from the most responsible members of the community. They may be members of the Junior Chamber of Commerce, the League of Women Voters, the Federation of Business and Professional Women, a state teachers' association, and so forth. Sometimes college students are hired individually. There have been many instances of reporters being asked by newly appointed polling place personnel for help in reading voting machines or explaining how to record write-in votes. Mutual friendliness and cooperation between precinct officials and precinct reporters is the pattern across the nation, each recognizing that he or she is spending a long and rather uncomfortable evening (and sometimes half the night) to do a job which is part of the fabric of our American election process, honestly and accurately tallying the will of the people and reporting back to the people.

A Viewpoint on Election Coverage

We hear complaints about the influence on the West of reporting Eastern votes and projecting winners based on vote samples. Complainants sometimes urge passing a law to bottle up information until every voter casts his ballot. Senate hearings on the subject were held in 1967.

Such a law would at best be distasteful to our American democracy. Bottling information to cork devils, imaginary or real, would uncork some very real devils indeed.

We may ask these questions:

1. What is new in vote reporting?
2. Is there evidence of influence on voting?
3. What would a law to hold back election news accomplish?
4. Could harm be done?
5. If change is desirable, what change?

1. What is new in vote reporting?

The mind immediately jumps to vote projection by television networks through use of computers, based on a small sample of voters in early reporting states in the East. But this is by no means all that is new.

N.E.S., the News Election Service, attempts to get reporters in most of the polling places in the United States to watch and report the counting of votes. Methods of vote counting in a few polling places have been strange, to say the least, and not all ward politicians are pleased to see such reporters present as members of the League of Women Voters.

Also new are the twin electronic giants of television and computers, which come together on election night to bring to nearly every home the results of voting in every state.

To legislate against the reporting of returns by television would also necessitate a shroud over reporting by radio, which has performed this service for nearly two generations, and by newspapers, whose early editions have been performing this service even longer.

To legislate against using computers to add totals would be just as foolish. Would we also legislate against adding machines?

And so we finally come down to passing a law against vote projection. The argument for legislative control here runs, "It's all right to report that Jones has 50,000 votes and Smith has 30,000 votes. But it should be against the law for your television news analyst to tell people that Smith has won, based on examination by statisticians and political scientists of a weighted sample of the vote."

Why should it be against the law?

According to the argument for controlling legislation, declaring that Jones has beaten Smith for the presidency before all polls close might influence voters.

2. Is there evidence of influence on voting?

Every study done to date supports the argument that such influence is negligible or non-existent. Most of the studies were commissioned by the networks and were undertaken by respected, university-connected opinion researchers.

The Opinion Research Corporation of Princeton, N.J., interviewed 1,972 voters both before the 1968 election and immediately after, a procedure common to most of the studies. This study concluded "with a high degree of confidence that television election broadcasts have no detectable influence on voting behavior." [3]

Dr. Warren E. Miller, Director of The Survey Research Center of the University of Michigan studied the voting intentions and actual votes of 1,450 registered voters in the 1964 presidential race and declared, "There is no evidence that significant exposure to predictions is associated with changes from pre-election intentions." [4] He also stated, "There are good theoretical, or social science common sense, reasons for expecting little or no influence."

Similar studies of the 1964 election done by Dr. Harold Mendelsohn of the University of Denver [5], Dr. Kurt Lang and Dr. Gladys Engel Lang of the State University of New York [6], Dr. John A. Rademaker of Willamette University, and Dr. Douglas Fuchs of the University of California at Berkeley [7] supported Dr. Miller's results. In a statement to the Subcommittee on Communications of the Senate Commerce Committee, Fuchs declared, "There was no appreciable number of voters who switched their positions . . . as a function of having known, before the polls closed of the imminent election of Mr. Johnson. Neither was there any apparent diminution of voting turnout because of this factor." [8]

Results of all these studies were presented to the Senate Subcommittee on Communications, headed by Rhode Island's Senator John O. Pastore, who concluded, "The studies submitted to this committee reveal that there is no discernible impact on the Western voting as a consequence of the projection or announcement of votes from the Eastern seaboard." And Governor John H. Chafee of Rhode Island declared, "I have seen no evidence that early predictions for computerized, analytic forecasts have in any way influenced the American voter. Why have one more restriction on the freedom of Americans?"

3. What would a law to hold back election news accomplish?

A number of bills have been introduced in both the Senate and the House, falling into four categories. They:

a) prohibit broadcasting predictions or projections before all polls are closed by amending the Communications Act.

b) prohibit releasing any election results until a specified time by amending Title 18 of the U.S. Code.

c) urge voluntary restraints upon broadcasters to keep them from predicting or projecting an outcome before all ballots in that contest are cast.

d) provide for a uniform closing time for all polling places

If a law were passed not to release any returns, or a law were passed not to make any projections, or not to hint or predict who the winners might be until everyone has voted, no information could be released under present poll closing laws until 1 a.m. EST. It must be remembered that California no longer marks our Western boundary. The state of Hawaii lies 2,000 miles further west. And after the polls close in Hawaii, American citizens are still voting in Nome, Alaska, which lives by Bering Standard Time.

A law could intentionally ignore these voters, as one House bill on the subject did,[9] by holding back information only until polls in his continental United States closed. But such a measure violates its own principles. If it is wrong to let Americans know how their fellow Americans have voted, then this is a wrong which should be remedied for all Americans. Why discriminate against Alaskans and Hawaiians?

Censoring election information until East Coast clocks strike 10 p.m. or 1 a.m. is not only injurious to our traditions, but is very likely to be unenforcible. It conjures up visions of Americans huddled around short wave radios listening to clandestine broadcasts from Canadian stations.

To snuff out even this leak of information, Congress might instead pass legislation forbidding poll workers to release results. However, even an advocate of restrictive legislation questions this approach on practical grounds: "Enforcement would involve tracing each 'leak' to a particular poll worker rather than to a more easily identified broadcaster." [10]

The FCC and the Library of Congress, asked for legal memoranda on the constitutionality of restrictive legislation on results of projections, responded, "the type of regulation involved here cuts so deeply into the right of free speech that it would probably not be upheld, particularly in view of the presence of alternative approaches." [11]

To sum up the answer to the question, what could be accomplished by a law to withhold vote information, on the face of it all one could say is that if such a law could be made to work, then Americans would be denied information about their voting until such time as the government decreed that they could have such information.

4. Could harm be done?

As free citizens we may understandably be frightened enough by the "good" such a law would do.

A law to withhold information on vote returns would be the first measure limiting the free release of news of a non-military nature. That this prior restraint—censorship—is directed against information about how Americans vote ought to cause concern, no matter how moderate the measure under consideration. For if it were permissible to decide *when* information could reach the public's eyes and ears, it might then be permissible to decide *what* could be released. Consider that city official who advocated a policy of never releasing the unofficial vote results!

Moreover, the withholding of broadcast information assumes that voters are not competent to judge the news for themselves. Such assumption is untenable in our democracy. No precedent exists for restricting the nonfraudulent dissemination of election information.

Harm of a different nature presents itself also. Newspaper reporters and carrier boys have waited at polling places perhaps as long as we have had polling places. This news presence has spread ever since Lou Harris created the Vote Profile Analysis for CBS in 1962. Besides the N.E.S. reporters, each of the three big broadcast networks field thousands of reporters to cover key precincts. Still other key precincts are staffed by reporters sent by individual newspapers, television and radio stations.

A League of Women Voters member who covered a key precinct in Arkansas later wrote "If you can ever come up with an idea of how to combat the stuffing of the absentee ballot box here, please let us know."

Another League member wrote, "The officials were not very happy to see us, since we caught them in the act of counting votes while other people were voting in the same room. Later, we decided to drive to the county seat, 20 miles away, to see if the main election official had turned in the

A video cameraman gets orders on the floor of a national political convention from a reporter who may have just gotten *his* instructions via walkie-talkie from the producer in the control room. Through a two-way headset, the cameraman can talk with the director.

ballots. One hour and a half after he left the polls, we saw him turn the ballots, in a large brown envelope, over to the clerk in the court house. He had apparently taken the ballots home with him while he ate supper . . . We saw no evidence of a locked ballot box."

Surely, such awareness and alertness should be fostered. Yet, if restrictions choke the release of information until a certain hour, there is no reason for reporters to go where votes are cast and counted. For years the news media have waged battle against entrenched political interests, particularly in the larger industrial states of the East and Midwest, who want to keep reporters out of polling places. The News Election Service, encouraged and assisted by its member broadcast networks and press associations, is supporting legislation in several states to open the polling places at counting time to reporters.

5. *Is change desirable?*

George Washington did not learn for a week that he had been elected president. More weeks went by before the entire electorate knew it. For the next century and a half, many a politician went to bed on election night with no idea about the outcome of his campaign. Occasionally a politician would fall asleep convinced he had won, then awake a loser. In 1916 the *Oregon Journal* reported the election of Charles Evans Hughes over Woodrow Wilson. In 1948, the *Chicago Tribune* printed the now famous headline that Thomas E. Dewey had won.

Today, long delays belong to the past. Mistakes occasionally occur, their incidence lessening as computer-informed analysts gain experience with each new election. Computers are used on election night by news gathering organizations, and before election night by polling organizations, political parties, and candidates themselves. Combined with electronic journalism, they provide election news of quality, speed and depth. On election night—scant hours after he has voted—an American sits before his television set with his family to discover not only the "who" and the "how much," but increasingly, the "why" of each election, from Maine and Georgia to Hawaii and Alaska. Election night is an exciting, informative experience now compressed for the most part into a single long evening. And thanks to what is learned throughout Tuesday night, Wednesday newspapers offer fuller reports and more intelligent discussions than has hitherto been available.

In future, because of wider use of voting machines and vote counting devices and because of improvements in the N.E.S. operations, returns will come in faster than ever. Indeed, it may not be long before actual votes in the East are counted and reported so quickly that winners are known even without projection techniques before polls close on the West Coast.

To force all this electronic capacity into the Procrustean bed of old poll closing statutes seems foolish and plainly wrong. Rather, the poll closing statutes should be brought up to date. We cannot disguise the fact that we live in the electronic age. If legislators are concerned that news of victory or defeat may some day significantly alter votes where polls are not yet closed, their remedy is *to close the polls everywhere at the same time*. No one flatly states that reporting of early returns will *never* affect an election, or that reporting a landslide for one party may not tip an extremely close local election somewhere. To avert this, we should seek the best way to close all polling places at once, so that counting can begin at the same time across the land.

A bill introduced by Senator Carl T. Curtis (R., Neb.) proposed a simultaneous poll closing, 9 p.m. Eastern Standard Time, 8 p.m. Central Standard Time, 7 p.m. Mountain Standard Time, 6 p.m. Pacific Standard Time, 5 p.m. Yukon Standard Time, 4 p.m. Alaska-Hawaii Standard Time, and as far back at 3 p.m. for polls in Bering Standard Time. The bill, however, does not authorize a simultaneous poll opening time, so some polls would be open fewer hours than at present.

Dr. Frank Stanton, President of CBS, and Elmer Lower, President of ABC News, proposed an expanded voting period, 24 hours with simultaneous opening and closing of polls, no matter what the time zone. The 1966 National Governors Conference endorsed a study of this proposal, but no study was undertaken.

Senator Jacob Javits (R., N.Y.) introduced a pair of bills. One called for a national election holiday, once every four years on the day a president is elected. The other called for a uniform poll closing time, running from 11 p.m. Eastern Standard Time to 5 p.m. Bering Standard Time.

Senator Pastore, Chairman of the Subcommittee on Communications, has said, "I don't think we are going to take all this science and sweep it under the carpet. I think we have to live with it."

The question is how.

FOR THE STUDENT

1. What aspects of election coverage can television handle better than other media? What can radio handle best? Where do newspapers do the best job?
2. If you, as news director for a small station, received a $1,000 election night budget, how would you spend it? Assume that, heretofore, you had no special set, no remotes and no source of information except the regular AP news wire.
3. Add $5,000 to question #2. Keep spending.
4. Design a vote tally pool for your city, a miniature N.E.S.
5. Design an election set.
6. Suppose that you, as a news director, had four remote units on election night and the following races: a tight, nationally important Senate race; a one-sided Governor's race; and four House races, of which two were expected to be close and a third was the expected re-election of a nationally famous congressman. All the candidates would be at their headquarters in town. Assign the remote units. You can, within reason, shift them as the night wears on.
7. How can raw vote be put into better perspective for viewers?
8. In class discuss alternative ways to eliminate any possibility that reporting of voting in the East might affect an election in the West.
9. Should states permit reporters to enter polling places during the balloting? During the counting? Should state legislatures retain the power to decide these matters, or should the Congress legislate here?
10. Work for a television or radio station on election night. Write a brief paper describing what you saw and heard.

18

THE LAW

A TELEVISION JOURNALIST who totes a camera into a court-room is likely to be hustled out by the bailiff. If he tries next at a com-mittee hearing, the door may be slammed in his face.

City council meeting? "No!"

Public records? "You can't look!"

School board meeting? "Sorry. Executive session."

He's not sure he can run this film without running into obscenity laws. He's not sure he can use that quote without running into libel laws. What if his outtakes are subpoenaed? And can he get some private information without fearing he will be forced to testify and name the man who gave it to him?

Fenced by laws, judicial decisions, rulings, recommendations, and some legal question marks, the television journalist who wants to perform his duty to inform the public of matters they ought to know, and to per-form that duty professionally, honestly and ethically, must at times agree with Dickens' Mr. Bumble. "If the law supposes that," said Mr. Bumble, "the law is a ass, a idiot."

But some things are improving.

LIBEL

Until recent years, a person who felt he had been libeled in print or on the air expected, if he proved his case, to collect a lot of money in actual and punitive damages. But in 1964, the Supreme Court ruled that a public official had to prove actual malice, which means knowing a statement is false, or having reckless disregard for the truth. This landmark decision in reporting news was based on a suit brought by City Commissioner L. B. Sullivan of Montgomery, Alabama, against *The New York Times* over an advertisement paid for by a civil rights group. Subsequent extensions of *The New York Times* decision included public figures as well as public officials.

Then, in the *Rosenbloom* decision of 1971, the Supreme Court further broadened the freedom of the media to report. Now, not even a private citizen, a "little man," may successfully sue unless he proves actual malice or reckless disregard for truth. George A. Rosenbloom, a Philadelphia magazine distributor arrested on charges of criminal obscenity, was described in a WIP radio newscast as a "smut distributor" and "girlie book peddler." Rosenbloom was acquitted. He sued WIP and was awarded damages in a lower court. A court of appeals reversed this decision. The Supreme Court agreed, 5 to 3, holding for WIP.

The majority decision stated, "If a matter is a subject of public or general interest, it cannot suddenly become less so merely because a private citizen is involved, or because in some sense the individual did not voluntarily choose to become involved."

In an oblique reference to the *Red Lion* decision (Chapter 16, *Red Lion*), the Supreme Court added, "If the states fear that private citizens will not be able to respond adequately to publicity involving them, the solution lies in the direction of insuring their ability to respond, rather than in stifling public discussion of matters of public concern."

In another 1971 decision, the Supreme Court ruled that the private lives of public officials are also exempt from libel suits, because their private activities often give clues to their qualifications to hold public office.

However, this protection does not cover defamatory news about the private lives of private citizens, including well-known persons. It is one thing to accuse a man, in error, of being a lawbreaker. It is quite another to accuse him of being, say, an adulterer. (See also THE RIGHT OF PRIVACY)

The Supreme Court has defined "actual malice" as knowing that a statement is false or having reckless disregard for whether it was false or true. In a classic of libel law the Iowa Supreme Court at the turn of the century decreed that the Cherry Sisters vaudeville team could not collect from the *Des Moines Leader*. The court decided that the following passage from a review was fair comment and criticism:

> Effie is an old jade of 50 summers, Jessie is a frisky filly of 40, and Addie, the flower of the family, a capering monstrosity of 35. Their long skiny arms, equipped with talons at the extremities, swung mechanically, and anon waved frantically at the suffering audience. The mouths of their rancid features opened like caverns, and sounds

like the wailings of damned souls issued therefrom. They pranced around the stage with a motion that suggested a cross between the *danse du ventre* (belly dance) and fox trot—strange creatures with painted faces and hideous mien. Effie is spavined, Addie is stringhalt, and Jessie, the only one who showed her stockings, has legs with calves as classic in their outlines as the curves of a broom handle.

And Drew Pearson learned that he was a public figure when he sued the *Fairbanks Daily News-Miner* for calling him the "garbage man of the fourth estate."

Athletic Director Wallace Butts of the University of Georgia won a judgment of nearly a half million dollars from *The Saturday Evening Post* because the *Post* failed to check the facts in an "expose." A case of "reckless disregard" for truth or falsity!

Truth and fair comment on public matters are defenses against libel. Where a libel is committed, a full and prompt retraction and apology will lessen the severity of the damages awarded.

Section 315 of the Communications Act, requiring "equal opportunities" for all candidates, also prevents a station from censoring a candidate's remarks. What if such remarks are libelous? In *Farmers Union v. WDAY*, the Supreme Court ruled that a broadcasting station, barred from tampering with a candidate's speech, cannot be held responsible for what he says.

Before *Rosenbloom* UPI attorneys drew up a list of "red flag words." UPI staffers were warned that the improper use of these words could lead to libel charges.[1] They included:

> Atheist, Communist, Red, Fascist, Ku Klux Klan, Nazi, or any organization which may be held in ill-repute.
> Seducer, bigamist, moral delinquent, illicit relations, unmarried mother, illegitimate.
> Deadbeat, rascal, suicide or attempted suicide.
> Unsound mind, incompetent, intemperate.
> Any loathesome disease, acute mental illness, narcotics addict.
> Bankrupt, blackmail, fraud, bribery.
> Swindle, sharp practice, corrupt, adulteration of products.

Whether or not *Rosenbloom* now removes fears of using some of them, the working journalist should use these words with care.

Libel is written defamation. Slander is oral defamation. Broadcast defamation if it stems from a written script, is libel, writing-read-aloud. If the defamation is ad-libbed, the law tends to regard it as slander. A legal gray area exists here, but the difference is important because libel victims can collect more than slander victims can.

Laws of defamation protect the individual's good name. A communication libels or slanders someone if it exposes him to "contempt, aversion, disgrace, or induces an evil opinion of him or deprives him of friendly intercourse in society."

A broadcaster (or newspaper, etc.) can offer three main defenses: truth, qualified privilege (a news medium may publish a fair report of public proceedings), and fair comment (it is a subject which invites public controversy).

THE RIGHT OF PRIVACY

Surprisingly, not every state recognizes a law of privacy. But 35 do, although there are sharp differences from state to state, and even from court jurisdiction to court jurisdiction. The differences represent the results of the conflict from place to place between the individual's right to be let alone and the public's right to know. The right to be let alone includes not only publication of material, but physical intrusion. Television newsmen who use telephoto lenses and shotgun mikes to enter forbidden areas could be inviting a lawsuit.

Much remains to be clarified. When in doubt, consult a lawyer who has some experience in privacy matters. Here are seven general guidelines: [7]

1) News of legitimate public interest is privileged (it may be published).

2) A story about a person involved in the news is privileged, as long as what is published deals with the news event.

3) News about a public figure is generally privileged.

4) Matter taken from a public record is privileged.

5) Fictional accounts of real events may not be privileged. The James Hill family of Whitemarsh, Pa., sued *Life* for connecting them with a novel and play (later a movie), *The Desperate Hours,* about a family which, like the Hills, was held prisoner in their home by three escaped convicts. (The Supreme Court narrowly—5 to 4—supported *Life,* but left questions unanswered. The losing attorney was Richard Milhous Nixon.)

6) It is unsafe to show pictures of individuals in stories not involving them; for example, using "stock footage" as a substitute for a story the cameraman missed. One Miami, Florida newscast showed an innocent bystander being questioned during a police raid on a hotel cigar shop. The bystander sued the station and lost. The judge ruled that the film clip was not an unreasonable invasion of privacy. Yet he said newsmen should "make a reasonable effort to portray persons who are thrust into an event of public interest in a manner which will not subject the person to false and harmful inferences."

7) Truth is no defense if a story is not newsworthy.

SUBPOENAS AND SHIELD LAWS

Television journalists have been bothered and angered by a growing practice by law officials and attorneys, the use of subpoenas to lay their hands on film, including outtakes, and written information, including notebooks. Newsmen have also been forced into court by subpoenas to give eyewitness testimony, under threat of contempt proceedings. Walter Cronkite wryly commented, "Advice for a modern lawman: let the reporters do it for you." Because judges issue subpoenas to extract information about demonstrations and militant groups, political questions arise which need Constitutional clarification. Richard Salant, president of CBS News, said, "The whole question of subpoenas in the news field lies in this area. . . This is the time for legal innovation, for redefinition of basic tenets of the First Amendment." Between January, 1969, and July, 1971, NBC and CBS received 123 subpoenas for films and tapes.

CBS News has been the principal target of government attempts to secure information and outtakes. A 1967 report of a soldier trying to cut off the ear of a dead Viet Cong soldier, a 1969 film report of the stabbing of a Viet Cong prisoner in the presence of a U.S. officer, and a 1970 film showing South Vietnamese soldiers nearly suffocating a Viet Cong prisoner during interrogation, all brought efforts by the Defense Department to acquire additional information and outtakes. In each case, CBS News refused. To disprove charges that the stabbing incident was a "cut and paste" job, CBS News replayed it twice, once in slow motion.

Other examples: The Justice Department acquired from CBS News some film which was never broadcast of Mike Wallace interviewing Eldridge Cleaver and other Black Panthers in Algiers. CBS News also handed over film of a planned, then abandoned, documentary on preparations to invade Haiti.

Matters grew considerably more serious when a House investigation subcommittee chaired by Rep. Harley O. Staggers (D., W. Va.) subpoenaed the outtakes and notes used in the documentary, "The Selling of the Pentagon," which alleged that millions of dollars were being spent annually on propaganda in support of the Vietnam War and the military services. CBS refused to surrender the material and was supported in its refusal by broadcast and press journalists and journalistic organizations throughout the nation, including a few, notably *The Chicago Tribune,* which argued that the documentary itself was distorted. On the other hand, Barron's, the financial weekly, editorialized that CBS should lose its O & O licenses.

The FCC took the position that it would consider the "fairness" of the CBS documentary in terms of the Fairness Doctrine, but it refused to consider the matter of distortion, stating: [2]

    . . . action by this Commission would be inappropriate—and not because the issues involved are insubstantial. Precisely to the contrary, they are so substantial that they reach to the bedrock principles upon which our free and democratic society is founded . . .

Lacking extrinsic evidence or documents that on their face reflect deliberate distortion, we believe that this government licensing agency cannot properly intervene. It would be unwise and probably impossible for the Commission to lay down some precise line of factual accuracy—dependent always on journalistic judgment—across which broadcasters must not stray . . .

What we urge—because we believe it will markedly serve the public interest—is an open, eager and self-critical attitude on the part of broadcast journalists. We urge them . . . to examine their own processes, to subject them to the kind of hard critical analysis that is characteristic of the best traditions of the journalistic profession . . .

The position of many members of the journalism profession is that no government or individual has the right, where controversial news is presented, to demand anything beyond what is presented, for this amounts to harassment and violates the rights of free speech and free press.

In the case of broadcast journalism, the principal counter argument, as stated by Rep. Fletcher Thompson (R.-Ga.) is that, since television is licensed, Congress has a responsibility to be certain the American public is shown "a balanced news coverage." This cannot be determined unless there is an opportunity "to see what is the unedited picture as related to the edited picture . . . because it gives us, supposedly an impartial body, the right to determine whether or not there is any slanting of the TV coverage through editing and deletions of items." [3]

"The Selling of the Pentagon" involved no court trial, a crucial point. Broadcast journalists have surrendered outtakes many times upon being handed a subpoena signed by a judge.

Like all citizens, journalists have an obligation to serve the needs of justice through testimony. The public has a right to everyman's evidence. But some journalists have protested that judges, issuing subpoenas indiscriminately, have abused the obligation, with the result that some sources of news information dry up because the newsman willy-nilly has been transformed into a legman for the authorities. He can no longer be considered a friend or trusted confidant.

The Newsman's Privilege Act has been introduced in Congress to stop government bodies from forcing newsmen to disclose information, except where foreign aggression, grand jury proceedings or libel proceedings are involved. And a federal court in San Francisco has ruled that a reporter cannot be forced to reveal confidential information unless the government proves compelling need—that this is the only way it can learn matters of national interest. In the case of New York Times reporter Earl Caldwell, the court ruled against fishing expeditions for unspecified information, arguing that a reporter would become an investigative agent of the government.

At the time of publication, the Supreme Court agreed to rule on a Massachusetts Supreme Court decision that newsmen do not have the privilege of keeping their information confidential. The case involved reporter Paul Pappas of WTEV-TV, Providence, R.I., and New Bedford, Mass., who refused to testify before a grand jury about what he had learned on a visit to a Black Panthers headquarters a few hours before police raided it. Pappas said he had entered the headquarters on the promise that he would not disclose what he saw and heard.*

Eric Sevareid opposed subpoenas of journalists because they limited his sources of information: [4]

> I regularly talk with government officials, former officials, military people and a wide spectrum of others who possess special information or expertise on public issues.
>
> A great deal of this talk is of the "off the record" or "not for attribution" kind. It is for my own information. Many people feel free to discuss sensitive matters with me in the knowledge that I can use it with no necessity of attributing it to anyone.
>
> Should a widespread impression develop that my information or notes on these conversations is subject to claim by government investigators, this traditional relationship, essential to my kind of work, would be most seriously jeopardized. I would be less well-informed myself, and of less use to the general public as an interpreter or analyst of public affairs.

In seeking protective laws, journalists argue that the journalist-source communication deserves the same legal umbrella, absolute privilege, given to attorney-client, doctor-patient, priest-penitent, and husband-wife communications. Opponents point out that in all these other communications, the source of the information is known and the information is confidential. Only in the journalist-source relationship is the source confidential, while the information is made public. Therefore, they argue, this particular analogy breaks down.

Laws to protect newsmen from being forced to disclose sources of information are called shield laws. Seventeen states have them: Alabama, Arizona, Arkansas, California, Illinois, Indiana, Kentucky, Maryland, Louisiana, Michigan, Montana, New Jersey, New Mexico, New York, Ohio, Pennsylvania, and Nevada.[5] The New York law protects the journalist from disclosing information as well as sources.

RESTRICTIONS ON INFORMATION

The U.S. Department of Justice has instructed its personnel to limit what they tell reporters about defendants awaiting federal trial to the following: name, age, address, employment, marital status and similar back-

---

* In summer, 1972, the Supreme Court ruled, 5 to 4, that journalists must testify before grand juries as other citizens do. (However, state law can grant immunity.)

STATE	YEAR ENACTED	PERSONS COVERED	MEDIA INCLUDED	ABSOLUTE	QUALIFIED	WHERE ASSERTED	WHAT COVERED	PUBLICATION REQUIRED
Alabama	1935	Engaged, employed, connected with newspaper, radio or television	Newspaper, radio, television	Yes		Anywhere	Source	Yes
Arizona	1937	Engaged in newspaper, radio or television reportorial work	Newspaper, radio, television	Yes		Anywhere	Source	Yes
Arkansas	1936	Editor, reporter, writer for any newspaper, or periodical or radio station or publisher of any newspaper or periodical or manager or owner of any radio station	Newspaper, periodical, radio	No	Must have written, published, or broadcast in good faith, without malice, and in the public interest		Source	
California	1965	Publisher, editor, or other person connected with or employed	Newspaper, press association, wire service, radio, television	Yes		Anywhere (*cannot be adjudged in contempt)	Source	Yes
Indiana	1941	Any person connected with; bonafide owner, editorial or reportorial employee who receives principal income from legitimate gathering, writing, editing, and interpretation of news. Any person connected with commercially licensed radio or television station as owner, official or as an editorial or reportorial employee who receives principal income from gathering, writing, editing, interpreting, announcing or broadcasting news	Weekly, semiweekly, triweekly, daily newspaper which shall have been published for 5 consecutive years and which has a paid circulation of 2% of the population in which it published; Press assoc., commercially licensed radio or television	Yes		Anywhere	Source	No

STATE	YEAR ENACTED	PERSONS COVERED	MEDIA INCLUDED	ABSOLUTE	QUALIFIED	WHERE ASSERTED	WHAT COVERED	PUBLICATION REQUIRED
Illinois	1971			No	All other sources must be exhausted. Disclosure must be essential to public interest		Source	Yes
Kentucky	1936	**Any person engaged, connected, employed**	**Newspaper, radio, television**	**Yes**		**Anywhere**	**Source**	
Louisiana	1964	Reporter (one regularly engaged in collecting, writing, editing news for publication)	Newspaper, periodical (issued at regular intervals and having paid general circulation) Press assoc. wire service radio, television, news reels	No	Can be revoked in the public interest upon application	Anywhere	Source or identity of any informant	No
Maryland	1896	**Any person engaged, connected, employed**	**Newspaper, journal, radio, television**			**Anywhere**	**Source**	Yes
Michigan	1949	Reporters	Newspaper or other periodical	Yes		Only criminal investigations	Source	No
Montana	1943	Person engaged, connected, or employed for the purpose of gathering, procuring, compiling, editing, disseminating, publishing, broadcasting, television news	Newspaper, press assoc. radio or television	Yes		Anywhere	Source	No
Nevada	1969	Reporters & editorial employees	Newspaper, periodical, press assoc., radio.	Yes		Anywhere	Source	No

State	Year	Engaged, connected with, or employed by	Newspaper	(Yes/No)	Disclosure	Anywhere	Source, author means, agency or persons from or through whom any information was procured, supplied obtained, furnished or delivered	(Yes/No)
New Jersey	1933	Engaged, connected with, or employed by	Newspaper	Yes		Anywhere		Yes
New Mexico	1967	Reporter (one regularly engaged in collecting, writing, or editing news)	Newspaper, periodical issued at regular intervals and having a paid general circulation; press assoc., wire service, radio station, television station	No	Disclosure required when essential to prevent injustice	Anywhere	Source	No
New York [6]	1970	Professional journalist, newscaster	Newspaper, magazine, news agency, press association, wire service, radio, television	Yes		Anywhere	Source, or information of public concern or public interest or affecting the public welfare	No
Ohio	1941	Person engaged in work of, connected with, employed by; in order to gather, procure, disseminate, publish, compile, edit news	Newspaper, press assoc.	Yes		Anywhere	Source	No
Pennsylvania	1937	Engaged in, connected with, employed by; in order to gather, procure, compile, edit, publish news	Newspaper of general circulation, press assoc., radio or television	Yes	Radio or television must keep transcription or recording of broadcast	Anywhere	Source	No

ground information; the charge; the federal agency involved, the length of the investigation and the circumstances of the arrest. They are to make no comments about the defendant's character, any statements or confessions, lie detector or laboratory tests, witnesses, evidence, or arguments. They are to do nothing to encourage picture taking.

Even broader restrictions have been recommended for all police officers, all defense and prosecuting attorneys and all judges by the Reardon Report, approved in 1968 by the American Bar Association. The Reardon Report's guidelines have been adopted in whole or in part by several states, including Colorado, Massachusetts, Minnesota, Oregon, Washington, and Wisconsin.

The Reardon Report (named for a committee headed by Massachusetts Supreme Court Justice Paul Reardon) recommends withholding all information about prior criminal record, confessions or statements, examinations or refusal to submit to examinations, witnesses, possibility of guilty pleas, opinions about guilt or innocence or the merits of the case or evidence. It also recommends that lawyers say nothing about a case after the verdict is in, if there is any chance the sentencing might be affected. Lawyers who break the silence would face punishment ranging from a judge's reprimand to disbarment, if Reardon's recommendations become law, and media publishing such information would face contempt charges.

Journalists have reacted angrily to the Reardon Report. At present, the right to comment freely upon pending cases is still solidly established. The Reardon Report throws one bone to journalists, however. It turns police blotters, in effect, into public records.

CBS News has declared:

Unless there are overriding public policy considerations, henceforth we will refrain from reporting such confessions and prior records until they have been admitted in evidence at the trial. However, it will still be possible (if in the judgment of a news director it is necessary to do so) simply to declare that a confession has been reported—but to go no further and give no details. (In this respect, we do not go as far as the recent guidelines by the Attorney General that in Federal criminal proceedings 'no such confessions—or even the fact that a confession has been made—should be provided by the Justice Department.' But, in any case, we will not give details of a confession.)

Several U.S. Supreme Court decisions in recent years have extended the protection of people accused of crimes. *Gideon v. Wainwright* established the right of every accused person to have an attorney. *Escobedo v. Illinois* established the right of an accused person to have his attorney present whenever he is questioned. *Miranda v. Arizona* determined that an accused person must be informed of his right to have an attorney present and to remain silent during questioning. The *Jencks* rule gives the accused the right to inspect prosecution evidence.

These decisions have nothing to do with what a reporter may publish, but because they concern pre-trial statements, they have made police much more cautious about what they will tell the reporters. Sometimes police tell too much for everyone's good. After a shoot-out raid at a Black Panther's apartment in Chicago, killing two members, the police re-enacted the raid for the cameras. WBBM-TV ran the re-creation for 28 minutes and thought well enough of it to enter the film in RTNDA competition. A federal grand jury later criticized the showing of this film in a report denouncing all Chicago media handling of the story and, especially, slapping the fingers of the police and the Cook County state's attorney's office. Moral: television journalists must be cautious about pre-trial publicity, even when police are not.

The famous San Francisco attorney, J.W. (Jake) Ehrlich, suggested ten rules for reporting trial news: [8]

1. You may publish or refer at any time to the wording of the complaint and the indictment.

2. You may publish at any time evidence which is admissible at the trial.

3. Do not publish news about a case until it is verified.

4. Be prepared to rebuff charges of malice or prejudice.

5. Be aware of information by the holier-than-thou citizen who is for strict law enforcement. He sees only one side of the coin.

6. Beware the friendly district attorney or judge or lawyer or policeman who, because he likes you, has a piece of confidential news. It can be, and most often is, a deliberate plant.

7. As a group, do not enter into any agreement which provides that you first secure consent or clearance from some authority before using the news.

8. Do not agree to limit yourself to court or police handouts.

9. Do not agree to any set of so-called "guidelines" or cooperative work rules; such rules may be changed without notice.

10. Demand maximum freedom in carrying on the important functions of informing the people of public events and court proceedings. But exercise that freedom with absolute fairness.

Joseph L. Brechner, general manager of WFTV, Orlando, Florida, has challenged all withholding of information: [9]

> Let us assume for the moment that you are the innocent defendant, a victim of false accusation or suspicion, or mistaken identity, or whatever. Do you wish absolute secrecy before your trial? Limited information? Should your lawyer or husband or wife, or any other person be permitted to speak out in your defense prior to your

trial and inform the widest group of citizens? As an innocent defendant would you prefer a complete blackout and secrecy about your arrest until trial is held—a trial which restricts information? Is justice best served when information is released after the verdict? Who should determine what should be released and what is prejudicial?

The following declaration is offered for consideration and endorsement by members of the bench, the bar, and the media:

Joint Declaration Regarding
News Coverage of Criminal
Proceedings in California*

I
STATEMENT OF PRINCIPLES

The bench, bar, and news media of California recognize that freedom of the press and the right to fair trial, as guaranteed by the First and Sixth Amendments to the Constitution of the United States, sometimes appear to be in conflict. They believe, however, that if the principles of fair trial and free press are applied responsibly in accord with high professional ethics, our society can have fair trials without limiting freedom of the press.

Accordingly, the following principles are recommended to all members of the bar and the press in California.

1. The news media have the right and responsibility to gather and disseminate the news, so that the public will be informed. Free and responsible news media enhance the administration of justice. Members of the bench, the bar, and the news media should cooperate, consistent with their respective ethical principles, in accomplishing the foregoing.

2. All parties to litigation, including the state, have the right to have their causes tried fairly by impartial tribunals. Defendants in criminal cases are guaranteed this right by the Constitutions of the United States and the State of California.

3. Lawyers and journalists share with the court responsibility for maintaining an atmosphere conducive to fair trial.

4. The news media and the bar recognize the responsibility of the judge to preserve order in court and to conduct proceedings in such a manner as will serve the ends of justice.

5. Editors in deciding what news to publish should remember that:

(a) *An accused person is presumed innocent until proved guilty.*

(b) *Readers, listeners, and viewers are potential jurors or witnesses.*

(c) *No person's reputation should be injured needlessly.*

* Endorsed by the State Bar of California, California Freedom of Information Committee, California Newspaper Publishers Association, California Broadcasters Association, Radio and TV News Directors, and the Executive Board of the Conference of California Judges.

6. No lawyer should use publicity to promote his version of a pending case. The public prosecutor should not take unfair advantage of his position as an important source of news. These cautions shall not be construed to limit a lawyer's making available information to which the public is entitled. Editors should be cautious about publishing information received from lawyers who seek to try their cases in the press.

7. The public is entitled to know how justice is being administered, and it is the responsibility of the press to give the public the necessary information. A properly conducted trial maintains the confidence of the community as to the honesty of its institutions, the competence of its public officers, the impartiality of its judges, and the capacity of its criminal law to do justice.

8. Journalistic and legal training should include instruction in the meaning of constitutional rights to a fair trial, freedom of the press, and the role of both journalist and lawyer in guarding these rights.

9. A committee of representatives of the bar, the bench, and the news media, aided when appropriate by representatives of law enforcement agencies and other interested parties, should meet from time to time to review problems and to promote understanding of the principles of fair trial and free press. Its purpose may include giving advisory opinions concerning the interpretations and application of these principles.

These principles are recommended for adoption to the bar and to the media of California.

II
STATEMENT OF POLICY

To give concrete expression to these principles in newsmen's language the following statement of policy is recommended for voluntary adoption by California newspapers and news broadcasters.

Our objective is to report the news and at the same time cooperate with the courts to assure the accused a fair trial.

Protection of the rights of an accused person or a suspect does not require restraint in publication or broadcast of the following information:

—*His or her name, address, age, residence, employment, marital status, and similar background information.*
—*The substance or text of the charge, such as complaint, indictment, information and, where appropriate, the identity of the complainant.*
—*The identity of the investigating and arresting agency, and the length of investigation where appropriate.*
—*The circumstances surrounding an arrest, including the time and place, resistance, pursuit, possession and use of weapons, and a description of items seized.*

Accuracy, good conscience, and an informed approach can provide non-prejudicial reporting of crime news. We commend to our fellow newsmen the following:

Avoid deliberate editorialization, even when a crime seems solved beyond reasonable doubt. Save the characterizations of the accused until the trial ends and guilt or innocence is determined.

Avoid editorialization by observing these rules:

—Don't call a person brought in for questioning a suspect.
—Don't call a slaying a murder until there's a formal charge.
—Don't say solution when it's just a police accusation or theory.
—Don't let prosecutors, police or defense attorneys use us as a sounding board for public opinion or personal publicity.

Exercise care in regard to publication or broadcast of purported confessions. An accused person may repudiate and thereby invalidate a confession, claiming undue pressure, lack of counsel, or some other interference with his rights. The confession then may not be presented as evidence and yet have been read by the jurors, raising the question whether they can separate the confession from evidence presented in court. If you do use a "confession" call it a statement and let the jury decide whether the accused really confessed.

In some circumstances, as when a previous offense is not linked in a pattern with the case in question, the press should not publish or broadcast the previous criminal record of a person accused of a felony. Terms like "a long record" should generally be avoided. There are, however, other circumstances—as when parole is violated—in which reference to a previous conviction is in the public interest.

Records of convictions and prior criminal charges which are matters of public record are available to the news media through police agencies or court clerks. Law enforcement agencies should make such information available to the news media upon appropriate inquiry. The public disclosure of this information by the news media could be prejudicial without any significant contribution toward meeting the public need to be informed. The publication or broadcast of such information should be carefully considered.

In summary:

This Statement of Policy is not all-inclusive; it does not purport to cover every subject on which a question may arise with respect to whether particular information should be published or broadcast. Our objective is to report the news and at the same time cooperate with the courts to help assure the accused a fair trial. Caution should therefore be exercised in publishing or broadcasting information which might result in denial of a fair trial.

Judge George C. Edwards Jr., a member of the United States Court of Appeals for the Sixth Circuit has drawn up a set of rules for press and bar worth the most serious consideration by members of both:

"1. Let us insist that our trial judges make full use of the tools which legal tradition has given them to guarantee a fair trial.

"2. When these are inadequately employed, let us accept the fact that due process may require an occasional retrial of a highly newsworthy case because of prejudicial influences.

"3. Let us seek the voluntary cooperation of the press in withholding publication of material directly related to a criminal trial in progress which is not offered or admitted in the trial until after the verdict has been rendered.

"4. Let us use the administrative sanctions advocated by the American Bar Association to control press statements by lawyers, prosecutors or law enforcement officials *during the trial period.* . . .

"5. Let us not attempt to muzzle prosecutors, defense lawyers or police by amending current law or Canons of Ethics as to any time prior to the trial period.

"6. Let us leave the First Amendment unabridged."

ACCESS

In what may be a historic statement on prior restraint, the freedom of the press and the public's right to know, U.S. District Judge Murray L. Gurfein declared, *"A cantankerous press, an obstinate press, a ubiquitous press must be suffered by those in authority in order to preserve the even greater values of freedom of expression."*

In mid-1971, in *U.S.A. v. The New York Times*, Judge Gurfein considered the publication of Pentagon-classified papers on how the United States became deeply involved in the Vietnam War. He added, "These are troubled times. There is no greater safety valve for discontent and cynicism about the affairs of government than freedom of expression in any form."

Yet all times are troubled. Some degree of discontent and cynicism always stalks the land. And, although he may not be confronted as *The Times'* reporter was with the "Top Secret" stamp, the journalist will meet public servants who would prefer to have certain things kept from the public.

The right of a journalist to inspect public records or attend public meetings varies from state to state, depending upon what are known as "access laws." The laws not only differ from state to state, but they are often interpreted differently within a state from one public body to another, and from one public office to another. For example, a city council may welcome coverage, while the school board resists at every opportunity, holding executive sessions and private meetings to transact its real business and holding public meetings for little more than show. A full discussion of access laws lies beyond the scope of this text.[10] Concern here is with broadcast news access to public meetings.

Cameras and microphones transmit, live, sessions of the United Nations during crisis. Millions of people hear the debates. But debates in Congress remain barred, except to the handful who can squeeze into the gallery. At the time of publication, a bill to open House committee hearings was creeping through. Some Senate committee hearings are broadcast. Most famous of them were the Kefauver Crime Subcommittee investigations; the historic Army-McCarthy hearings, which are said to have turned

The presidential press conference has received a lot of criticism over the years, including the complaint that the presence of so many reporters tends to prohibit coherent discussion of a single issue or follow-up questions. President Richard Nixon tried some new approaches, including (above) a televised news conference with one representative from each network. From left, Howard K. Smith, ABC; Eric Sevareid, CBS; John Chancellor, NBC.

the national mood against Sen. Joseph McCarthy; and the Fulbright Foreign Relations Committee hearings on the Vietnam War. Urging the opening of all Senate, House and Supreme Court sessions to television and radio, CBS President Frank Stanton said, "There is no reason why we cannot do it with regard to critical sessions of the highest legislative and judicial bodies in the land—bodies whose actions and determinations influence our lives, our pocketbooks, our present, and our future." [11]

Television and radio journalists enter few legislative and committee sessions with microphones and cameras. More than state laws are involved. Personal attitudes of committee chairmen and speakers of the legislative houses go a long way toward determining what will be permitted. Sometimes the laws are not clear. Sometimes they are non-existent. Sometimes the chairman gives ground grudgingly. And sometimes he is willing, maybe eager, but he has never been asked!

This last condition needs remedy. Broadcast coverage of meetings will not come about by itself. Newsmen ought to approach the official in charge of each public body which meets regularly. Is live television or radio coverage of meetings or hearings permitted? Audio tape? Film?

Where these questions have been asked in the past, some officials like the members of the Altoona, Pa., City Council welcomed live coverage but objected to edited segments.[12] In Chicago, it was suggested that tape and film coverage only be permitted at City Council sessions provided a council committee got editing power. The suggestion was rejected. In Galveston, Tex., the Board of City Commissioners agreed to taping on condition that each commissioner had his own microphone. And so it goes.

Among states permitting broadcast coverage of general sessions of the legislatures: Colorado, Idaho, Indiana, Kentucky, Maine, Minnesota, Nebraska, New Hampshire, New Mexico, North Carolina, Oregon, Rhode Island, South Carolina, Tennessee, Texas, Utah, and Wisconsin. Florida, Mississippi, and Missouri leave the matter up to presiding officers. Vermont and California occasionally waive their prohibitions. The New York State Assembly permits television cameras, but no taping.

What are the advantages of broadcast coverage of public meetings? Thomas L. Ray, state legislator in Kentucky, which permits microphones and cameras in both state houses, drew these conclusions: [13]

1. People get to "really know" their elected officials when they hear and see them.

2. People get a new perspective of legislative action when they hear and see what actually happens in legislative chambers.

3. People are angrier than ever over legislative tomfoolery.

4. People react more violently to legislative trickery when they can hear and see the maneuvers as they actually took place.

5. People are more interested and more aware of the State Legislature.

These comments came after Louisville radio-TV stations WHAS and WHAS-TV sent a news crew daily to Frankfort, covered each session, then fed, shipped or carried the film and tape back for their evening newscasts, a round trip of 110 miles. Rep. Ray added:

> There were occasional whispered comments that some of our colleagues were "showing off," playing for attention. There was some evidence of this and, of course, in such cases the camera and microphones were performing a disservice, a distraction from normal legislative routine. On the other hand, responsible editing by the broadcast newsmen managed to eliminate most, if not all, of this "grandstanding."

> I feel that what the Louisville broadcast newsmen have done is something that could—and should—be repeated in every state in the union. Having been on the "receiving" end as a member of the Legislature, I feel that I can recommend the experience. . . .

The coverage was not without its light moments. One TV newscast featured film of Senator C. W. A. McCann, apparently sound asleep in his chair. The next day he rose as a point of personal privilege and told the Kentucky Senate, "My wife called last night and said if that's the best I could do, she would come down and replace me. I want it known, Mr. President, that I wasn't asleep. I just had my eyes closed, thinking about the next bill."

I can't say it's comfortable to know that microphones and cameras are always nearby as you conduct the business of the state. But as one interested in democracy, I *can* say it is invaluable: the legislator's right to privacy in the public's legislative chambers must always come second to the public's right to know.

After live coverage in Missouri, a reporter wrote, "Instead of some dozens of gallery spectators and a gaggle of newsmen as the only auditors, the legislators' pros and cons were heard over the air by hundreds of thousands of Missouri citizens. It is a fact that many of the lawmakers stated they had never before had so much reaction from their constituents."

Reporters, cameramen and soundmen should wear jackets and ties, conservative colors. Rubber-soled shoes are useful.

The crew should survey the meeting place in advance to locate power outlets, camera and microphone positions. Lights should be used only if they cannot be avoided (use high speed film). If possible, equipment should be set up before anyone arrives. Electrically powered cameras should be used instead of noisier spring-wound cameras; a sound camera on a tripod can shoot cutaways, too. The sound camera should be mounted on a tripod, not a shoulder pod. A zoom lens is less distracting than a three turret lens. The largest magazine in the newsroom should be mounted on the camera to cut down on reloading, and pre-loaded spares should be at hand.

With the exception of an almost whispered statement at the rear of a large legislative hall, the reporter should never do a standupper or an interview in a meeting room while the meeting is going on. If he can't wait for a recess, there is always the corridor outside. Waiting for the recess is the better choice, because camera and people can stay where they are.

The Texas House of Representatives got rid of annoying clusters of cameras, lights and microphones by doing some redecorating, with the advice of a television station engineer. Floodlights went into the ceiling. AC plugs and audio jacks were fitted against the columns. Cameras went onto carpeted platforms.

Television journalists have argued for years that modern techniques and modern equipment make their coverage unobtrusive. It would be foolish to destroy that argument by carelessness or haste.

What is true of meeting rooms is true of courtrooms, when the broadcast newsman can go in.

Just a word about access to public records, or at least federal records.

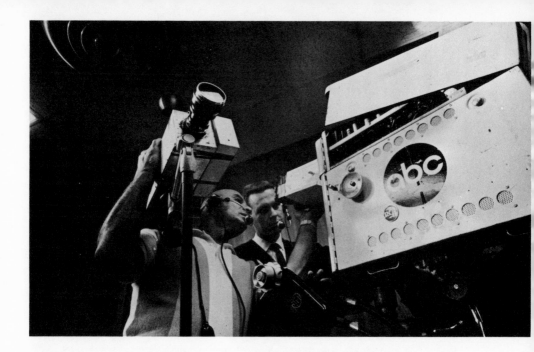

A television cameraman with a "creepie-peepie" mounted on his shoulder pauses to peer through the viewfinder of a full-size television camera, which is mounted on a dolly. Over the years, the trend has been toward smaller, lighter cameras, but the requirements of color television have compounded the difficulties of shrinking the cameras.

For $5 you can buy an eight-section "kit of tools" for using the freedom of information law to gain access to federal government records. Seller is the Freedom of Information Center of the University of Missouri's School of Journalism. The reporter will learn what the Federal Public Records Law allows, how to locate federal records, how to ask for them, how to appeal a refusal, what kinds of records may be withheld, what government agencies control public records, and what court actions were taken soon after the law went into effect.

(See section on *A Political Remote* in Chapter 10.)

CANON 35: *in camera* OR ON CAMERA

Los Angeles County has constructed a new Criminal Courts Building wired for television. At present, a California Judicial Council ruling blocks use of courtroom television, but if this ruling is discarded, silent and unobtrusive television cameras and microphones will permit broadcasting from any of the 60 courtrooms, with two camera outlets in each courtroom:

1.) . . . to a remote truck, then to a dish antenna on the roof for beaming to a transmitter for public broadcasting.

2.) . . . to auxiliary courtrooms to handle an overflow of reporters for a major trial, as was done in the Sirhan case.

3.) . . . to a room where a disruptive defendant is kept, perhaps solving some of the legal implications of preventing a defendant from witnessing his own trial and hearing his accusers.

4.) . . . to classrooms where law students and other students watch actual cases and discuss them while the trial is in progress, as medical students discuss surgery they watch on closed circuit television.

5.) . . . to the offices of the district attorney and the public defender, who want to observe a trial deputy in court.

6.) . . . to the presiding judge, so he can see what is going on in any courtroom.

7.) . . . to the sheriff for security reasons.

8.) . . . to videotape and audiotape machines, replacing or supplementing stenographic records.

That these possibilities exist is due to the perseverance and imagination of a broadcast journalist, KNXT editorial director Howard S. Williams, who designed the installation with the cooperation of some of the criminal court judges.[14]

Not all the judges are convinced that television belongs in courtrooms, and full use of the facilities may be a long time coming. The history of trial broadcasting is spotty and marked by some bitterness between journalists on one side and many attorneys and judges on the other.

The first broadcast of a trial of national significance was by *The Chicago Tribune* radio station, WGN, in 1925. It leased lines to Dayton, Tennessee, for the Scopes "monkey" trial on the teaching of evolution. WGN broadcast the trial proceedings and photographers were permitted in the courtroom. Apparently, no one complained.

In 1935, Bruno Hauptmann was tried in the Flemington, New Jersey, courthouse for the kidnap-murder of the Lindbergh baby. Tourists took snapshots of each other on the judge's bench. Guides ran sightseeing trips. Hawkers peddled little wooden ladders, souvenir reminders of the ladder the kidnaper used to climb to the second story nursery. Reporters and photographers crammed into the tiny courtroom each day. Their stories heaped contempt upon Hauptmann. The lawyers told reporters who the witnesses would be, what evidence was coming up, what was wrong with the other lawyers' tactics and how guilty—or innocent—Bruno Hauptmann really was, all of which the reporters eagerly printed or aired. The judge finally barred cameras, but one photographer in the balcony used some special equipment to snap dramatic photographs surreptitiously at the end of the trial. His pictures were published coast to coast. If all this weren't enough, it was rumored that the Hauptmann jury was seriously considering an offer to go into vaudeville.

Two years later, the American Bar Association adopted Canon 35 of its Judicial Ethics:

> Proceedings in court should be conducted with fitting dignity and decorum. The taking of photographs in the courtroom during sessions of the court or recesses between sessions, and the broadcasting of court proceedings are calculated to detract from the essential dignity of the proceedings, degrade the court and create misconceptions with respect thereto in the mind of the public and should not be permitted.

The A.B.A. amended Canon 35 in 1952 to include television.

It may be argued that nothing in the U.S. Constitution provides for "dignity and decorum" in the courtroom, while it does provide, in the Sixth Amendment, for "a speedy *public* trial before an impartial jury." It may also be argued that the members of the bar give lip service to "dignity and decorum" while flouting them during jury trials, and some of the most flamboyant lawyers are among the best known and best paid. Famed criminal lawyer Percy Foreman has said, "It is the object of the defense to prejudice the minds of all persons possible. My clients want freedom, not justice." He also said, "The best defense in a murder case is the fact that the deceased should have been killed, regardless of how it happened."

No responsible television journalist would argue against "dignity and decorum." Yet in a trial with important political implications, such as the Billie Sol Estes and Chicago Seven trials, other considerations must be weighed.

"Dignity and decorum" have been severely challenged by militants in the trials of the Chicago Seven and the Black Panthers in New York. Both trials had political overtones. Here, it seemed, were the spearpoints of a revolutionary attempt to overthrow the entire judicial system. The defendants appeared all sweetness and light and reason and logic in televised news conferences, yet they turned the courtroom air blue with profanity, blasphemy and scatalogical humor, insulting the judge with those totems of language we find so offensive that broadcast newsmen cannot bring themselves to report them to the public. One result may have been that a segment of the public developed a sympathy for the Chicago Seven and the Panthers they might not have felt if cameras and recorders had observed the unpleasant antics. Accusations of bias against the Chicago Seven judge, Julius Hoffman, might have been intelligently examined by a mass eyewitness citizenry. As it is, the public reached its conclusions based on hearsay.

The Chicago Seven's discovery of a way to present one face to a judge and another to the public will surely be exploited by others intent on disturbing the judicial system. Removal of Canon 35 might eliminate this particular means of disruption. There may be other problems which journalists and lawyers could face together to assure dignified courtroom proceedings.

Television newsmen should start by wearing jackets and ties whenever they enter a courthouse. Reporters usually wear dress shirts, jackets and ties. Cameramen and soundmen often do not. They should, despite the gear they haul around.

USIA general counsel Richard Schmidt Jr. stated, "You know the cameraman who walks in with no tie, no coat, and barrels right across in front of the judge. The lawyers are aghast, so is the judge and everyone else. The judge raps for order and the cameraman looks at him like, 'Well, what did I do?' . . . This is the thing that lawyers see, and . . . they say keep the newsmen and cameramen out." [15]

Broadcast journalists have vigorously opposed Canon 35, arguing that the presence of modern television equipment does not detract from the dignity of courtroom procedure or necessarily distract participants, as long as journalists themselves work discreetly.

If trials are public and are open to news coverage, it should not matter whether the reporter has pencil and paper, tape recorder or camera, if neither he nor his equipment obtrude.

A case in point was the filming of a trial in Denver, Colorado, in 1969. It was shown in 1970 over the National Educational Television net-

At the bench: a delicate legal point is weighed by (l–r) Assistant City Attorney Wright Morgan, Judge Zita Weinshienk, and defense attorney Leonard Davies, three of the principals in NET's six-hour study of "Trial — The City and County of Denver vs. Lauren R. Watson."

work on four consecutive evenings. Colorado permits cameras in court if judge and defendant assent. Lauren Watson, a member of the Black Panthers, had been arrested by Police Officer Robert Cantwell in a gas station. The charges: "resisting a police officer in the discharge of his duty" and "interfering with a police officer in the discharge of his duty." Watson, in his turn, claimed that Cantwell had been harassing him with shouts of "white power."

A woman judge, Zita Weinshienk, presided at the trial, the first documentary study on American television of an entire courtroom trial. A Harvard Law School professor commented on each day's events. Selection of a jury came during the first day of "Trial—The City and County of Denver vs. Lauren R. Watson." On the second day, Officer Cantwell took the stand. On the third day, defendant Watson was on the stand. On the fourth day came the verdict.

Judge Weinshienk later said she felt the trial brought out deep feelings blacks have toward the police, and their mutual fears and distrust. She also felt it was an excellent way to show viewers, many of whom have never been inside a real courtroom, how an actual trial is conducted. Her only concern was that a more experienced judge should have had the honor of presiding for this television first.

In an era when American citizens see men walk upon the moon, it seems quizzical and arbitrary that their television sets may not also take them inside an American courtroom.

"The old assumption that a newspaper reporter was in effect the representative of the unseen multitude no longer can be narrowly applied," noted Jack Gould in *The New York Times.* "The camera now enables the public to see for itself in full attainment of the democratic principles of an open court."

Justice Oliver Wendell Holmes, in an often quoted opinion, stated: [16]

It is desirable that the trial of causes should take place under the public eye, not because the controversies of one citizen with another are of public concern, but because it is of the highest moment that those who administer justice should always act under the sense of public responsibility, and that every citizen should be able to satisfy himself with his own eyes as to the mode in which a public duty is performed.

In 1956 a judge permitted radio station KLPM in Minot, North Dakota, to broadcast a murder trial in an effort to end some slanderous talk against one of the principals. After the trial, the judge praised the station for its coverage. Two years later, a three judge panel in Oklahoma ruled that there was no basis for distinction among various types of news media, including radio and TV.[17]

In 1957 a judge permitted KOMU-TV, Columbia, Missouri, to cover a murder trial in Tuscumbia. Silent film was shot of testimony, on the grounds that SOF would add weight to any testimony aired. Sound-on-film was shot of the judge's instructions to the jury, the summation by attorneys, and the delivery of the verdict. Afterwards, Circuit Judge Sam C. Blair told news director Phil Berk, "Hardly anyone knew you were there. . . I hope you come back again." [18]

A 17-year-old Wichita, Kan., girl was charged in 1971 with incorrigibility, shoplifting and being a runaway. KAKE-TV reporter Charles Duncan and cameraman Larry Hatteberg got permission from the judge, the girl and her parents to film the juvenile court hearing for a documentary. Said Judge Michael Corrigan, "We must be smart enough to be able to establish a system whereby the public can be informed and the judicial decorum maintained . . . We had a message in the approach that the court takes and in the type of young people that come before the court."

But such exceptions to the general ban are few and far between.

NBC-TV quietly televised a meeting of the District of Columbia Bar Association while members debated the merits of Canon 35, some arguing that television coverage disrupts and degrades. No one present realized that the entire meeting was being recorded.

It has been argued that a hidden camera is less disruptive than a visible reporter who sporadically scribbles testimony. It has also been argued that taping a trial would produce a much better record of testimony than a court stenographer can manage. The argument that witnesses may be disconcerted if they know that they are being televised has been countered by the argument that witnesses may also be disconcerted by knowing that court stenographers are, and that reporters may be, taking down their words, and the further argument that public testimony is less likely to be false testimony.

For an injury claims case in Sandusky, Ohio, in 1971, Judge James McCrystal ordered all testimony videotaped, then permitted the opposing lawyers to present the testimony in any order they wished. One lawyer moved a physician's testimony from lead-off witness to closing witness position. The judge was absent during the questioning. He watched the tape afterward in chambers, considered objections while being free of courtroom pressures, and erased everything he regarded as objectionable.

Only then was the testimony, via television, presented to the jury. Afterwards, the jury heard the lawyers' summations live, then retired to consider a verdict. Among other advantages, this method shortcircuited the lawyer's well-known trick of saying something they know will be overruled, but saying it in hopes that jurors will remember it.

Wisconsin, Iowa, Colorado, and Illinois are among states in which videotape of drivers arrested for drunkenness may be introduced as evidence in court.

Few recent trials have stirred so much world interest as the Los Angeles trial of Sirhan Sirhan for the assassination of Robert F. Kennedy. More than 100 reporters and correspondents applied for credentials to enter a courtroom in which 40 seats were set aside for newsmen. Judge Herbert Walker, over some objection from his colleagues, set up a closed circuit television system. Planned by KNXT technicians, a camera hidden in a dummy courtroom air conditioner fed three monitors in another room assigned to the overflow of reporters. The quality of the picture was rather poor, but the system worked without disrupting the proceedings. Although news about the hidden camera was widely reported, people in the courtroom seemed unaware of its presence. A standard Norelco black-and-white vidicon camera about the size of a cigar box, noiseless, using normal interior lighting, was placed behind the air conditioner grill. The fixed lens got its image through the louvers at first. Later, the louvers were removed. Sound was transmitted separately, utilizing the courtroom's regular amplification system.

One of Sirhan's defense attorneys said the public, as well as accredited reporters, should have been permitted to view the trial in the television room. *From the public in a room to the public at home is just a step. From a hidden remote camera with an immovable lens to a hidden remote camera with a zoom lens is another step.*

In fact, in the course of the Sirhan trial, several changes were made in sound transmission. Five microphones were spaced along the counsel table. Lavalier mikes later replaced witness and bench table microphones. When attorneys began to question prospective jurors, the jurors could not be heard, so they were asked to hold a table microphone. Later, a lavalier mike was used. In future, with more time to prepare, less obtrusive sound arrangements would surely be available, such as a remotely controlled highly directional shotgun mike hidden from sight.

Proponents of Canon 35 have argued that the presence of television cameras disrupts judicial proceedings too much to be permitted. As an example, they point to the 1963 preliminary hearing for Billie Sol Estes, the Texas wheeler-dealer, on charges of swindling. According to *The New York Times,* "a television motor van, big as an intercontinental bus, was parked outside the courthouse and the second floor courtroom was a forest of equipment. Two television cameras had been set up inside the bar and four marked cameras were aligned just outside the gates. A microphone stuck its 12-inch snout inside the jury box, now occupied by an overflow of reporters from the press table, and three microphones confronted Judge Dunagan on his bench. Cables and wires snaked over the floor."

A 1965 survey by the New York Bar Association showed that these states had *not* adopted Canon 35 or some modification of it by statute or statewide court rule: Alabama, Colorado, Georgia, Idaho, Indiana, Louisiana, Maryland, Minnesota, Mississippi, Missouri, New Hampshire, North Carolina, Oregon, Rhode Island, Texas, Vermont, Virginia, Wisconsin, and Wyoming. Some of these states may have done so since then, and in several of these states, local courts have adopted Canon 35. In others, custom keeps electronic recording instruments out. Even where Canon 35 prevails, permission is usually given for televising naturalization proceedings and judicial ceremonies inside the courtroom. Adoption proceedings have also been filmed.

Texas and Colorado are the two states with most experience in broadcast coverage of trials. Texas, which tried Estes, requires the judge's consent. Colorado also requires the consent of the defendant; additionally, a witness may refuse to be photographed or recorded.

Cameras are barred from *federal* courtrooms by Rule 53 of the Federal Rules of Criminal Procedure. Federal judges have been known to bar television cameramen not only from the courtroom, but from the entire courthouse and even from the sidewalk outside. A federal circuit court of appeals in Illinois said *that* was going too far, and shrank the area of the judge's jurisdiction.

These rules, canons and statutes are battlefield markers in a lengthy combat between supporters of a defendant's right to a fair trial and supporters of the public's right to know, between supporters of the Fourteenth Amendment's "Due Process" clause and supporters of the First Amendment. Other battlefield markers:

Bruno Hauptmann was convicted and electrocuted. Billie Sol Estes, who had objected to the televised hearings, was convicted. He appealed —in part on grounds of TV coverage—and the Supreme Court voted 5 to 4 to reverse his conviction, holding that "the activities of the television crews and news photographers led to considerable disruption of the hearings." Estes was tried again. Television was kept at arm's length. Again, Estes was convicted.

Some opinions delivered by Supreme Court justices on both sides of the *Estes* decision bear upon television news coverage:

> Justice Clark: "The heightened public clamor resulting from radio and television coverage will inevitably result in prejudice. Trial by television is, therefore, foreign to our system. Furthermore, telecasting may also deprive an accused of effective counsel. The distractions, intrusions into confidential attorney-client relationships and the temptation offered by television to play to the public audience might often have a direct effect not only upon the lawyers, but the judge, the jury and the witnesses."

> Chief Justice Warren: "So long as the television media, like the other communications media, is free to send representatives to trials and to report on those trials to its viewers, there is no abridgment of the freedom of the press. The right of the communications media to comment on court proceedings does not bring with it the right to inject themselves into the fabric of the trial process to alter the purpose of that process . . . On entering that hallowed sanctuary,

where the lives, liberty and property of people are in jeopardy, television representatives have only the rights of the general public, namely to be present to observe the proceedings, and thereafter, if they choose, to report them."

Justice Stewart: "The suggestion that there are limits upon the public's right to know what goes on in the courts causes me deep concern. The idea of imposing upon any medium of communications the burden of justifying its presence is contrary to where I had always thought the presumption must lie in the area of First Amendment freedoms."

Finally, Justice Brennan said *Estes* was "not a blanket constitutional prohibition against the televising of state criminal trials."

Someone dryly noted that the *Estes* decision doesn't kill television in the courtroom, but it leaves it in a critical condition. Until the Supreme Court chooses to speak again on the subject, the *Estes* decision, decrying broadcast coverage, will have the force of law for judges in state after state.

A few years before the Estes case in Texas, Dr. Sam Sheppard, an osteopath, was brought to trial in Ohio on charges of bludgeoning his wife Marilyn to death. After he was sentenced to life imprisonment, he appealed, charging that newspapers attacked him so viciously that he could not get a fair trial. As for broadcast news he charged, among other things: [19]

> On the evening before the trial began, journalists from *The Cleveland Press* and *The Cleveland Plain Dealer* debated over radio station WHK on the question of which paper deserved more credit for indicting him.
>
> One day on the courthouse steps, while jurors were arriving, there was a television interview with the judge, the prosecutor, a city detective, and Inspector Fabian of Scotland Yard, then retired and working as a Scripps-Howard stringer.
>
> All available rooms on the courthouse floor were taken over by television, radio and newspaper journalists, who filled the rooms with equipment.
>
> In the halls outside, television lights and photographers were constantly present.
>
> Sheppard's objections to being photographed were ignored.
>
> One juror and her family were interviewed for television in their home.
>
> Bob Considine, in a radio broadcast, compared the Sheppard trial to the Alger Hiss trial.
>
> Walter Winchell, in a radio broadcast, quoted a woman as declaring she was Sheppard's mistress.

Sheppard's conviction was reversed by a U.S. District Court, reversed again by the U.S. Court of Appeals, and finally, in 1966, was reversed again by the U.S. Supreme Court, setting Sam Sheppard free. But the Supreme Court's majority decision stated:

> The principle that justice cannot survive behind walls of silence has long been reflected in the Anglo-American distrust for secret trials. A responsible press has always been regarded as the handmaiden of effective judicial administration, especially in the criminal field . . . The press does not simply publish information about trials but guards against the miscarriage of justice by subjecting the police, prosecutors, and judicial processes to extensive public scrutiny and criticism.

The Chicago Tribune, supporting Canon 35, editorialized, "The purpose of the courts is not to provide the populace with entertainment or even with instruction. The purpose is to do justice."

The real question at issue in the battle over Canon 35 is simply: "How can justice best be served?" The answer has not proved so simple. It probably lies half way between absolute license and absolute proscription in that useful realm called compromise. Preserving courtroom decorum while filming trial proceedings should not prove insuperable as the new Los Angeles County Criminal Courts Building may show. Where a trial has relevance, especially political relevance, to the public, ample justification exists for using cameras and tape recorders to widen the courtroom walls.

OBSCENITY

During a WINS, New York, radio newscast in 1970, newscaster Lee Murphy quoted former Soviet Premier Nikita Khrushchev as calling President Richard M. Nixon "a son of a bitch." On another newscast sometime earlier, Murphy quoted California Governor Ronald Reagan as referring to a political opponent by the same epithet. As a result of the Reagan quote, nothing happened. As a result of the Khrushchev quote, Murphy was fired and so was the news editor. Murphy fought to get his job back. Through arbitration, he was reinstated, but the news editor chose to take another job.

If this example seems to prove nothing, it may be because obscenity exists in a kind of legal fog.

Section 326 of the Communications Act of 1934 forbids government censorship of broadcast content. But it also says "No person within the jurisdiction of the United States shall utter any obscene, indecent, or profane language by means of radio communication." And Section 1464 of the Criminal Code states, "Whoever utters any obscene, indecent, or profane language by means of radio communication shall be fined not more than $10,000 or imprisoned not more than two years, or both."

Legally, obscenity over the air is as elusive as obscenity in print. And that's pretty elusive these days. In practice, broadcasters must be more careful than printers. The FCC maintains a vigil of sorts. Frank J. Kahn wrote: [20]

> On occasion a commissioner's speech or a proposed (but not enacted) FCC rule will stimulate program decisions in the industry. This phenomenon is known as "regulation by raised eyebrow," and is often as imprecise as it is subtle.
>
> Nor are governmental pressures the only ones that affect the output of radio and television stations. Audience ratings, sponsor needs, and the temper of the times all exert their influences on what is broadcast.

In the Pacifica case, concerning non-news programs, the FCC declared, "We recognize that as shown by the complaints here, such provocative programing as here involved may offend some listeners. But this does not mean that those offended have the right, through the Commission's licensing power, to rule such programing off the airwaves. Were this the case, only the wholly inoffensive, the bland, could gain access to the radio microphone or TV camera. No such drastic curtailment can be countenanced under the Constitution, the Communications Act, or the Commission's policy, which has consistently sought to insure "the maintenance of radio and television as a medium of freedom of speech and freedom of expression for the people of the nation as a whole."

In the FCC's view, freedom of expression does not extend to songs which overtly or covertly sanction the use of drugs. The FCC generated considerable heat with a notice in 1971 warning licensees of their responsibility to be aware of the music they play. While drug lyrics are not obscene in the more restricted sense of that troublesome word, they might be regarded as indecent.

The outer limits on what is obscene were vaguely defined by the Supreme Court's *Roth* decision as to whether the material as a whole, by contemporary community standards, appeals to prurient interests.

Broadcast material stops far short of these outer limits. Most newsrooms follow the rule, "When in doubt, don't." (Or, to state the actual practice more precisely, "When in doubt, splice it to the stag reel instead." Material considered blasphemous, obscene, or on the borderline of obscenity almost always reaches the television newsroom on film.)

Yet, "When in doubt, don't" is too easy an answer today. It is simplistic in a complex time when some extremists wield obscenities like weapons, at times speaking softly, at other times letting fly in all directions. To report, "A policeman hit a demonstrator who cursed him," is a guarded truth which may be only a half truth. In a day when breasts and buttocks, bare or barely draped, fill our newspaper and magazine ads, our billboards, and even—with only slightly more cloth—our television commercials, television newscasts retain a modesty resembling prudery.

On British television, films of American demonstrations appear without the sound track blooped or the expletives edited out. News viewers learn what the demonstrators say.

Contemporary journalistic standards reflect "the temper of the times." Remember when journalists could barely bring themselves to write the words "social disease"? When nobody was "pregnant"? Today, television newscasts and documentaries tell the community about drugs and venereal disease and divorce and unwed mothers and the pill and ex-priests and abortion and pornography and a dozen other matters of community interest and concern that a generation ago would have been left in the closet.

A survey of RTNDA members showed considerable agreement that "hell" and "damn" in filmed actualities should be left alone, but there were strong reservations about "God damn." All the respondents said they bleeped it.[21] Some background or wild sound had been left alone although it contained shouts or chants, like "Screw the Fuzz," which would have been cut out had the words been spoken directly on camera.

When a speaker, usually a militant, uses an obscenity as part of his speech, the usual decision is to bleep it out. Some differences were indicated in the survey as to whether the single word would be bleeped (one example: a speaker was put on a newscast saying the poverty program officials could shove their poverty funds "up their ———"), leaving no doubt about the missing word. Some news directors said the phrase would be bleeped; some said the entire passage would be edited out.

One news editor in North Carolina reported that standards for the 6 p.m. newscast were tighter than standards at 11 p.m. An editor in Georgia said he was convinced that listeners were understanding about profanity on film but would resent the same words coming from newscasters, even as quotations.

A television news director in the Midwest was faced with a decision about obscene language and gestures in a filmed story. His cameraman had shot a police raid at a roadhouse. As a prostitute caught in the raid was being led away, she addressed some choice language to the camera, accompanied by some equally choice gestures. What was on film was clearly obscene by contemporary standards, by what might be called the standards of Middle America or the Silent Majority. Of course, he did not use the film. But as he later described the film during a panel discussion on obscenity, he sounded most upset that the girl's words and gestures forced him to kill what would otherwise have been a most desirable segment of film, a lewd girl being taken away by the police. This is hypocrisy. If a television news director wants to uphold standards of community morality—and there is no reason he should not want to do so—those standards begin at the assignment desk. The assignment editor should not have sent the cameraman on a roadhouse raid in the first place.

No area of news judgment is as touchy as determining what is too obscene to be aired. The news director and all the journalists involved must summon up the best that is within them, that intelligence and skill and experience which from time to time elevate the craft of journalism to the level of professionalism.

Some examples illustrate the need to *judge* whether an obscenity should appear in a newscast, rather than to follow the rule that any obscenity must be banned.

An ABC network news reporter went to a West Virginia farm to interview the father of a soldier who was sentenced to life imprisonment for killing Vietnamese civilians. In the farmyard stood a tall flagpole. The father, a World War II veteran, admitted that he once flew the American flag daily, but no longer flies it. Angry at the nation (or the government) for its treatment of his son, the father, his voice breaking, told the reporter, "If they send my boy home in a casket, they'd better not put a flag on it, because I'll tear the son of a bitch off." [22] Not only did the man utter an obscenity, but he expressed a disrespect for the flag in doing so. Yet, here was an honest, deeply felt emotion, the grievance of a father and an embittered patriot stated plainly. In its way it was, in fact, a political statement, an objection to a government whose policies would permit his son to be condemned on such a charge. The sentence was meaningful, and ABC News used it.

The second example also deals with an aspect of the Vietnam war. The government of North Vietnam once released a newsfilm clip showing the Viet Cong capturing South Vietnamese soldiers and their American adviser. It was exciting newsreel footage. But the most exciting scene of all, the scene which provoked the most comment, was of the tall, handsome American prisoner making several obscene gestures. As he was being marched along a jungle road to an uncertain fate, flanked by his smaller captors and mindful of the camera grinding away for enemy propaganda, the American suddenly made a gesture familiar to boys who grew up in "ethnic" neighborhoods. He slammed his left fist into the crook of his right elbow, a gesture which a bowdlerized translation might give as "Go to Hell." He followed this gesture by placing his right hand against his cheek and surreptitiously making three different finger gestures, one after the other. One television newsroom staff watching the scene intently again and again before reaching an editing decision decided that the American was repeating his "Go to Hell' message in non-verbal language which would be understood, in turn, by Englishmen, Frenchmen and Americans.

What does a news producer do? The gestures are obscene. No doubt about it. But consider the circumstances. The American prisoner took his life literally into his hands. If the Viet Cong understood what he was doing, they might have killed him on the spot. Chances are those in North Vietnam responsible for the news clip mistook the gestures for scratching or swatting at mosquitoes. The American risked his life to make a powerful statement. Should not a newscast risk censure to present that statement?

After conferring by long distance phone, the producers of at least two of the three networks (the third network may have used it, too), left the first gesture in. One producer did not call attention to it in copy. The other did with the following words, after deciding to eliminate the finger gestures as being "too much":

AMERICAN SEARCHED	The American adviser was not cowed by his captors . . . or by the Viet Cong cameraman.
LED DOWN ROAD	And in the tough and silent language of a soldier,
MAKES GESTURE	he lets the world know . . . . (SILENCE FOR THE LAST 5 SECS.)

The point here is circumstance and intent. Had the gesture been made by a drunk as he was being arrested by city police, it would certainly have been cut. The gesture would probably have been cut out of most newscasts if it had been made by an unidentified political extremist, or if the captured American had leered at the camera as he gestured. But he was unsmiling and ramrod straight. He breathed pure defiance, pure courage.

In a similar case, a UPI wirephoto of four captured U.S.S. Pueblo sailors showed them all making obscene finger gestures. Again, the captured men risked their lives to make a political statement. Many U.S. newspapers ran the photo. The men of the Peublo were beaten for it later.

The student may ask, how do I decide what to use? Indeed, he should ask it. He is either a fool or a Solomon if he does not, and our universities turn out few Solomons. To answer the student's question, one is tempted to say, don't decide, because you are too young and too green. Give the problem to someone older and more experienced in news editing. But this answer is not really an answer at all. It is an evasion of the question, although it shall serve as one of the guidelines set down here concerning judgment in matters of propriety:

1. Remember that editing is art, and not science. Outside the legal strictures, few absolutes prevail.

2. When in doubt, seek counsel and, if possible, consensus.

3. Consider the intent of the questionable word or act. Consider its possible effect. If either is prurient, do not broadcast it.

4. At the same time, do not guide your decisions according to the imagined response of every little old lady in tennis shoes. You are reporting the news of a real world. The sight of blood, the sound of pain, and the gesture of defiance are part of the real world.

5. Don't overdo it. A four-second shot of the victim of a fatal accident is usually acceptable in a long shot, or covered with a sheet. Fifteen seconds of the same footage, or a four-second close-up is not acceptable.

6. Be cautious about intruding into private lives of citizens thrust into the news, especially when publication would distress them. For example, never name or show film of a rape victim. For such news coverage, live by the Golden Rule.

7. Learn by observing, and don't forget. Sensible decisions are based upon common sense and experience. As you grow older, experience is the best commodity you provide in return for a paycheck. The experience of the veteran is worth more than the energy of the beginner. Their comparative paychecks reflect it.

GAMBLING

The FCC has spoken more clearly about another problem area, the broadcasting of lottery information. Even if it is treated as a news item, a station may not report the winning numbers in a public lottery. It does not matter if the lottery is conducted by the state government, as in New York or New Jersey. The FCC also cracked down on a California radio station which ran a commercial promoting a musical show at which a $25 door prize was given away to a ticket holder, but commercials for *Reader's Digest* sweepstakes, in which no purchase was necessary, were permitted.

FOR THE STUDENT

1. What useful purposes could camera coverage of a trial serve? What harm could be done?
2. Would you recommend a law in your state permitting some compromise in broadcast trial coverage; e.g., the type of trial which might be covered (or forbidden), the kind of equipment which could be used, the extent of coverage (e.g., live or film), or the approval of certain persons? What compromises do you recommend?
3. In a class discussion compare the trial coverage bill you would prefer with the bills other students would prefer.
4. Discuss the soundness of the rule-of-thumb, "When in doubt, don't," as regards obscenity or other matters which might offend some people in the community.
5. Have community standards of morality broadened in the past decade?

Should broadcast news standards move from their present position? If yes, how and how far?

6. Draw some guidelines on good taste and common sense in newscasts. Consider not only sex and obscenity, but also violence, carnage and graphic descriptions of crime (e.g., a filmed description of how easy it is to break into a car).

7. Interview a working reporter (any medium) about restrictions he has encountered in getting information which he regards to be in the public sector.

8. Should there be a federal law which gives a journalist the right to keep his source of information confidential? Why?

9. Should a television journalist have the legal right to withhold out-takes? Under all circumstances?

10. Where should "the right of the public to know" end? Where should "the right of privacy" end? Give some examples of how you would like to see the laws framed.

19

THE PROFESSION

ANYBODY CAN BE a journalist. All he needs is a job. Although he may be in a position to *inform* millions of his fellow citizens, no law requires that he have so much as a fourth grade education. He may be in a position to *influence* millions of his fellow citizens, who can vote governments into and out of office, yet if he is incompetent, unscrupulous, or even provably unethical, no law can remove him and no body of his fellow practitioners can deny his right to practice, unless his employer chooses to fire him.

STANDARDS

Groups such as Sigma Delta Chi and the Radio Television News Directors Association set ethical standards, but they cannot enforce them because of the First Amendment to the Constitution. Freedom of speech and press may not be abridged. Journalists might wish standards existed, but not at the expense of freedom of expression. We cannot cheerfully contemplate the licensing of journalists, even for such a laudable reason as enforcing the standard of a trifle of education or skill. We may envy physicians and attorneys for being able to set up standards of competence, but we cannot agree on a way to emulate them.

In 1966, the Professional Development Committee of Sigma Delta Chi reported to the national convention:

> Sincere concern over professional development inevitably will bring any newsman or other journalist around to the problem of pro-

fessional standards. Related to the problem of professional standards, of course, are those of adequate training for the profession and enforcement of its code of ethics—both in training and in actual practice by a member of the profession.

It is the opinion of many newsmen, although perhaps not shared by all members of our society, that the time has arrived—it is long overdue, in fact—for the profession of journalism to establish its minimum standards, announce them to the public, and begin enforcing them.

This idea has not been adopted.

When Dr. W. Walter Menninger of the Menninger Foundation proposed certification for journalists perhaps by a board of their professional peers, he received little support and considerable opposition. He said: [1]

> Freedom of the press is the only guarantee of the Bill of Rights which cannot be exercised by each individual citizen. Practically speaking, this privilege can be exercised only by those in the journalistic profession. Thus journalists and broadcasters hold an important trust as guardians of democracy. How does the public have any guarantee of the quality and integrity of these guardians?
>
> In other professions with a public trust—medicine, law, education—laws for licensure and certification assure the public that the practitioner has fulfilled minimum standards, met certain requirements for training and demonstrated competence in the profession. The public is entitled to similar safeguards in the quality of the practitioners of this most important cornerstone of our democratic society, the news media.

Peter Hackes of NBC News declared: [2]

> Journalism to become one of the true professions must set minimum standards with which its adherents must comply. Journalism, for example, has yet to specify uniform educational and professional requirements for all of its would-be professionals. In the meantime, misfits, ill-fits and don't-fits daily bring down whatever nebulous standards we set for ourselves. And the business of journalism—which it is—continues to be just that, having great difficulty emerging into the profession it should be.
>
> One of the worst offenders in this area, I feel, is my own field of broadcast journalism. Why shouldn't someone who is giving the news over radio or television be required to have as much of a news background as the average cub reporters on a newspaper? Why should a young fellow whose major qualification is a resonant voice be given the responsibility of relating events to thousands of people—as if he

knows what he's talking about—often without a shred of preparation, either in covering news events or in pre-professional schooling?

Instead of statute law, the law of supply and demand works more or less, and it can work to the benefit or the detriment of the journalist. Some television station owners care little about news coverage or community affairs. To them, news is a dead loss. They will hire almost anyone who agrees to work for a depressed wage. On these stations, television reporters with university degrees earn little more than clerk-typists. Congress or the FCC could give these station owners the motivation to upgrade their news operations, but have not yet done so.

Other station owners relish their news department's position in the community. Television journalists on the staff receive salaries reflecting their education and experience, salaries matching those of pharmacists, accountants and engineers in the community, professions which compare with journalism in the years of needed education and the dependence for employment upon a businessman whose training may lie in other fields and whose present interests are basically business-oriented. The skilled journalist is valued and sought after. The beginner is expected to get his training elsewhere. On the network level, top news salaries are quite handsome.

The young journalist will learn more on a small television or radio station than he cares to know. But learn it he must. The small radio station newsman "not only gathers the raw material for a story, but he writes the copy and broadcasts it. He must edit and rewrite wire copy, make telephone checks, answer the telephone, change ribbons on teletype machines and keep the machines supplied with paper. The newsman must record telephone reports, edit audio tape, monitor police and fire receivers, file news scripts, keep stringer and tipster logs, and do a host of other chores." [3]

ETHICS

A journalist takes no Hippocratic Oath in order to work at a newspaper, a radio or television station, or anywhere else. To perform his functions he never promises objectivity or even honesty. He does not swear that he will not prostitute his art. Indeed, the history of journalism finds its roots not in reporting events as they happened but in the burning desire to express points of view.

Edward R. Murrow once said, "A communications system is totally neutral. It has no conscience, no principle, no morality. It has only a history. It will broadcast filth or inspiration with equal facility. It will speak the truth as loudly as it will speak a falsehood. It is, in sum, no more or no less than the men and women who use it."

The American journalist is, by and large, an honorable man. He is often fiercely honest, and sometimes so objective that he will lose his job rather than play a story in a way he thinks is not right. His pen is not for

Sometimes television newsmen are more welcome than reporters for other media in the misguided belief that a filmed report cannot be slanted as can a written report because motion pictures *show* what is really happening. Such a naive notion not only overlooks the editing controls of cameraman, soundman, film editor and writer, but ignores the real fact that any news coverage is as honest and ethical as the newsmen assigned to it. Above, a television film crew covers a Ku Klux Klan rally, sharing the speakers' platform, the bed of a truck trailer.

hire, although outside the major cities he is often badly underpaid for a man with his education, experience and responsibility, to say nothing of the hours he is asked to work and the risks he must sometimes take.

Not all newsmen are so scrupulous. Not all newspaper publishers or broadcast license holders are objective and aboveboard. But the overwhelming majority of them are decent men with a strong sense of ethics.

Objectivity never comes easily to a responsible journalist. It comes because he wills it so, although he personally has developed strong political views on many subjects, based on an intelligent appraisal of news events daily and even hourly during all of his professional years. He forces these views to the background. If he lets them take over, he becomes nothing more than a hack, a flack or a propaganda mouthpiece.

Sometimes a well-meaning journalist will compromise his independence a little in order to acquire or present the story he wants. The NBC network was given a demonstration of such a compromise when an outside producer brought in a documentary he had made about American missiles. Robert E. Kintner, then NBC president, related what followed: [4]

> It was a good job. The producer assured us that it was ready to run, that he had already made the changes demanded by the Department of Defense.
> "Oh," said Bill McAndrew. "Security?"
> "No," said the producer. "Editorial."
> We turned down the program.

A scandal involving ethics at WPIX, owned by *The New York Daily News*, threatened to cost the station a license valued at up to $50 million. A journalist employed at the station charged, among other things, that the news broadcasts passed two- and three-day-old film clips along as current news; used some old film from Romania as being current film of the Soviet invasion of Czechoslovakia; and pretended old film of German student riots was new film of Paris student riots.

In another matter involving ethics, a cameraman for a San Diego television station moonlighted for the FBI in covering news about radical organizations. *Time* quoted him as saying, "It's just that I'm in the wrong occupation. If I had been a construction worker or a ditch digger, none of this would have mattered." *Time* added, acidly, "Precisely." [5]

There is a movement among some journalists and journalism professors to establish press councils, which would investigate complaints against journalists, much as bar and medical associations consider complaints against members of their professions. One all-media press council has now been established in Minnesota. But nothing in the United States matches the BBC's three-man commission to evaluate BBC handling of viewer complaints about news reporting and editing. The commission considers grievances against the BBC action on complaints; it does not deal directly with the original complaints, serving instead as a kind of appellate court. Such a commission, if it existed in the United States, might have been called upon to examine network response to the arguments raised by Vice President Spiro Agnew, or to CBS response to the criticism of the documentary, "The Selling of the Pentagon." (It should be noted that Great Britain is by no means to be universally admired for journalistic professionalism. Its first university-level journalism curriculum was not established until 1970. The ITA network was sharply criticized for banning a documentary about troubles in Ireland. And the enormous payments by newpapers for sensational first-person exclusives is a running sore.)

(Also see *On Managing News Scenes,* Chapter 10.)

EDUCATION

Journalism has been called a "with it" major. It is attracting a lot of students.

Some 38,000 students in 1971 majored in all fields of journalism at the 175 colleges offering journalism and communications programs.

A journalist is a translator, not of language but of complexity. He writes for laymen, and we are all laymen in fields outside our own.

At 10 a.m., reporter Bill Jones talks to a local heart surgeon for an explanation of a transplant technique announced yesterday in Houston. At 11 a.m., Jones talks to an architect about plans for a bridge. At noon, Jones learns from an economics professor what the latest Federal Reserve Board action is all about.

If Jones works for a newspaper, he must write his stories so that they are not only accurate, but clear to everyone. The surgeon and the economist must be able to understand what the architect is talking about. Experts in their own fields, they know nothing about architecture. If Jones works for a radio station or a television station, his concern for clarity is even greater because his audience has only one chance to understand the ideas rushing by. And if reporter Jones is filming or taping interviews with the surgeon, the architect and the economist, he must guide these men into explaining their complex information themselves in a few simple words.

Jones cannot expect his audience to understand what he himself cannot understand. Words and ideas are not hot potatoes to be passed quickly to the audience. Rule: *If you don't understand something, don't expect anyone else to understand it. Insist on an explanation until you can understand it without any nagging doubts.*

What kind of an education should Bill Jones seek in college if he intends to become a television reporter or news writer?

Many of the stories he covers—maybe a majority—will deal with government in some form. Should he take political science courses? Covering what areas?

It is easy to bog down in the jargon of the stock market, international trade, and banking. Should he study basic economics?

Urban and racial crises could be the most important news of the coming decades. Fools see simple cause-effect relationships. Reporter Jones does not want to be a fool. Should he delve deeper through some sociology classes?

Pollution remains major news. So does space. Breakthroughs in physics, medicine, and biology make headlines. Should Jones take some basic science courses? Which ones?

Even on a local station, Jones cannot escape international news. Should he study geography?

With what other fields should he have familiarity? Law? Psychology? Music? Sports? Meteorology?

Surely, young Jones cannot go through a university catalog and take every course, or even every introductory course. And if he tries to become a modern version of a Renaissance man, he must still consider how much he should learn about techniques.

Should he learn how to write? Information writing is an art, taught and learned. Should he be taught to edit film and to write copy to film? Should he learn to use a camera? Should he learn to speak clearly and comfortably? Should he know anything about sound? optics? broadcast electronics? Should he learn anything about communications research? After all, motivation studies, public opinion polling methods, and propaganda techniques are all used in television. Finally, what should he know about mass communications law, in addition to knowing that too much enthusiasm in getting a story can result in a million dollar invasion of privacy suit?

Student Bill Jones will not learn all this in the four years it takes him to get a B.A. or the five years or even six years it takes to get an M.A.

Ideally, he will prepare himself with a broad education in the liberal arts. He will certainly take some political science and history courses, plus electives in other social sciences, in the physical sciences and the behavioral sciences. In areas where he does not take formal class work, he should retain enough curiosity to read magazine articles and an occasional well written book. He need not plow through thick textbooks to acquire a rudimentary grasp of a subject.

Television newsmen sometimes find themselves in strange places. An ABC cameraman shooting "Comrade Soldier," a documentary about the Soviet Army, went aloft in the Russian version of a "cherry picker."

Besides his general knowledge, he should take classes in broadcasting which teach him techniques. The most useful technique is learning how to write. Classes in speech fundamentals, reporting, film editing, motion picture photography, and television production will teach him other techniques.

At the university, a professor may tell him that learning techniques is time wasting, because he will learn them on the job. Quite true, he can learn techniques on the job. But Jones may not get the job in the first place if he is not prepared to hold it from the day he walks in. Let's say an employer who must hire a newsman to start Monday is faced with a choice between a college graduate who has never held a piece of film or heard his voice on a tape recorder and a high school graduate who spent two years as a reporter at another television station. It is the author's guess that the employer will hire that high school graduate as surely as a flush beats a pair of sixes. Now let's say the college graduate submits a videotape of an in-class newscast plus a half-hour radio documentary. Depending upon how skillfully the newscast and the documentary were prepared, the job should go to the college graduate, and will go to him if the employer recognizes his potential.

The news director of a New York City radio station wrote:

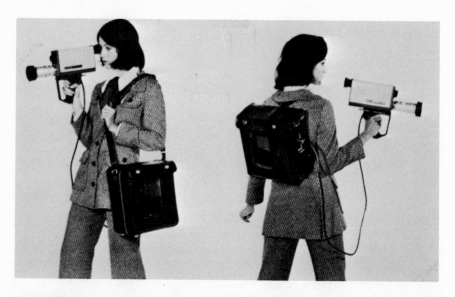

Sony manufactures a small, lightweight videotape recorder. With adapters, the ½" videotape is compatible with a television broadcast system, but the picture, although good, is not top-notch broadcast quality. However, the unit makes a versatile teaching tool for broadcast classes. Not only can students shoot with it, but the videotape gives students an immediate replay of their news delivery techniques in a classroom, without the need for a television studio on or off campus.

I am reduced to running my own school of journalism. The students coming out of the schools of journalism sometimes have a few basic tools, but they lack a conception of what a radio newsman is or what he does. They have had virtually no involvement with tape during a four-year college curriculum. Most college radio stations, it seems, give the students a microphone, tell them not to cuss over it, and let them delight in the sounds of their own, usually ill-trained voices.

I have talked to scores of students who have come out of our better schools of journalism with the honest notion that radio news is nothing more than ripping and reading the UPI radio wire. I once pilloried a professor in Florida over this allegation, and invited him to stop by our radio newsroom and see what really went on. He refused on the ground that his job as a pedagogue was to teach ivy-covered theory, not cruddy reality. I therefore answer the criticism of radio news (including the many valid ones) with a challenge. Train and send us better people, and the medium will improve.

A number of fine universities offer undergraduate and/or graduate training in broadcast journalism, with emphasis on developing practical skills to accompany a broad liberal arts background. The National Association of Broadcasters issues a biennial report, edited by Dr. Harold Niven, of *Radio-Television Programs in American Colleges and Universities,* listing degree programs, facilities, scholarships available and faculty members. The NAB is located at 1771 N Street, N.W., Washington, D.C. 20036.

At least one television station, WCBS-TV, New York, began its own systematic internship program, although it did not necessarily later hire these interns, just as a hospital does not necessarily add to its staff those interns it trains. The WCBS-TV News Workshop declared that it wanted "to bring the fledgling journalist into the television newsroom and the journalism professor closer to the television news director." As initially established, five interns were selected each semester, one from each of five New York area universities, to spend several hours one day each week in some part of the news operation. The workshop included a day each with the assignment editor, a reporter, a cameraman, a film editor, a writer, a director, and the documentary unit. They also spent a day each with the specialist reporters in arts, finance, business and labor, politics and city government, education, health and science, and weather. Students also received assignments to rewrite AP and UPI wire copy. Their rewritten copy was later compared with the work of staff news writers.

During his college career, our mythical student, Bill Jones, will develop a respect for news in a democracy. Mitchell Charnley, an esteemed journalism professor, considers this paramount in the student's education. He said: [6]

I believe that the attack on the sins of the rip-and-read stations—almost certainly a majority among American radio stations, and a considerable segment in attitude if not in fact among TV stations—has to be made by newsmen, working from within. I believe that the hope of driving out bad news with good is going to come from the personnel in the newsroom if it comes at all; for there is today no appreciable force at work, beyond this, to persuade ownership that news is a social and professional responsibility.

I believe that the young men and women going into broadcast news must see this problem clearly, and be prepared to fight the good fight. And they'll be prepared for this not by learning all about tape recorders, image orthicons, and the best way of setting up crews for covering football games, but by gaining a respect for the social importance of news, a passion for public service, and a deep knowledge of what genuinely meaningful news service is.

RESEARCH

Sadly, it must be admitted that the gap between the university and the practitioner is wider in journalism than in most professions. Unlike so many architects, engineers, pharmacists, economists, lawyers, systems analysts and so many professionals in other fields, journalists generally do not look to the universities for new advances in their profession. A university department of journalism or school of mass communication is regarded firstly as a source of manpower, secondly as a place to give occasional speeches, and thirdly as a pleasant, ivy covered substitute for the daily rat race late in the working newsman's career. Journalism professors are sometimes regarded by working journalists as people who really don't know what they're doing or even (without thinking the matter through) as people who teach because they cannot hold jobs as working journalists.

Journalism itself is sometimes downgraded by those engaged in it. Some of the people who earn their living as journalists scoff or bridle at the term, preferring to call themselves newsmen or newspapermen. They identify what they do as a trade, craft or occupation, not as a profession. Lack of enforceable standards and generally low wages outside the large cities buttress their self-defeating attitudes.

Along with everything else, research suffers. In broadcasting, almost no journalism research is done outside the university, and what is done within the university appears to have no effect outside the university.

Networks and large television stations maintain sales research departments. The networks and some large stations also do some election coverage research, with the help of university experts. This research includes writing and programming probability equations, drawing up samples and preparing information flow systems. As a result of this use of research,

Shifting sands hold no terrors for a video cameraman who uses a tilt wedge on the tripod pan head to increase the camera's vertical tilt. This camera is on location at Cape Kennedy for live coverage of a space shot. The rig looks awkward, but the camera will tilt smoothly to follow a rocket's path in the sky.

coupled with journalistic skill, television election coverage has become so *efficient* that people complain about its efficiency: "You've taken all the fun out of sitting up all night listening to elections." Networks also work with polling firms to explore the opinions of the American people, resulting in some interesting reports ranging from newscast inserts to hour-long programs. At least one network, ABC, does content analyses of its newscasts to examine its overall degree of fairness and balance. Beyond this, at the present writing, there is little to report.

Vanderbilt University videotapes newscasts of all three networks, the only library of its sort in the United States.

Networks and large stations ought to engage in basic and applied mass communications research, using university facilities where needed. And the results of their research should influence their work. Other professions benefit from their own research. So should journalism. Harry J. Skornia has contended that broadcasting can no more exist without real research than can medicine or science.[7]

Millions of dollars have been spent in the United States on research into "market" effects of the mass media. But little has been done to develop significant research by the broadcast industry into learning theory, and the many kinds of effects which broadcasting has on different kinds of individuals, under different circumstances. A great profession would conduct such research, and would develop information theorists who would guide operators of these media in their wisest and soundest uses. . . .

Better criteria for the measurement of broadcasting effects need to be developed, so broadcasters may know how viewers and listeners are really affected by them, emotionally and subconsciously, rather than merely in their purchasing habits.

As an example, very little research (probably none outside the universities) has been done on the effect of visual images on auditory news information. Television stations and networks spend millions of dollars each year to shoot silent and sound-under film to go with news which must be spoken, yet it is quite possible that this money is being wasted so far as information is concerned. The effort may even run athwart the intent; that is, much of the film may actually detract from the information a viewer absorbs and may help to "turn him off" the news. From that attitude to turning the newscast off is just a step. For instance, a news director seeing some important news on the wire about federal aid to education may send a cameraman out to shoot silent film of children at school. The viewer, *hearing* the news and *seeing* the children, may actually get less out of the story than if he just *heard* the news. Some non-news research in this area indicates that this is what happens. On the other hand, just watching the newscaster talking is boring. This does not take advantage of the television medium. Some combination of word and picture will be best, but what combination? Research is needed to find out. Meanwhile, news directors continue sending cameramen out to shoot silent film to go with news copy, and money that might be better applied may be going down the drain.

A few other areas of television news which could benefit from systematic research include:

1) ways to put violent or dramatic events, particularly filmed events, into context for the viewer (not necessarily for the reporter or the newscaster, who presumably already see such events in their proper perspective);

2) the concerns about reporting "good news" versus the concerns about reporting the mostly tragic changes from normal occurrences;

3) how demagogues should be reported, a question which Vice President Spiro Agnew raised in his famous Des Moines speech criticizing network television news practices;

4) how reporters perceive their responsibilities, and what should be proposed if researchers conclude that internal conflicts exist;

5) the fairness of newscasts and other news and public service programming in dealing with candidates, issues, the national Administration's policies, etc.

It would not be too difficult a task, particularly for an experienced television newsman, to add to this list.

Fred Friendly has noted another problem, sometimes described as "herd journalism": [8]

> That television news suffers from overexposure and underdevelopment is certainly not due to any professional inadequacy. It is due to an awkward and often archaic system of news gathering that favors bulk footage and costly duplication, frequently at the expense of interpretive and investigative reporting. Overkill in journalism, as in war, is counterproductive. The spectacle of a half dozen camera crews and a dozen microphones, several from the same organization, standing tripod to tripod at Andrews Air Force Base to witness the Secretary of Defense's routine departure for a NATO meeting, or to cover S.I. Hayakawa's, Abbie Hoffman's or George Wallace's latest news conference, often says more about the news gatherers than it does about the news makers.

THE LIBRARY

Every newsroom should have a reference bookshelf. At a minimum, it should contain:

1. Dictionary, preferably of recent vintage. An unabridged dictionary is not necessary.
2. Almanac, no earlier than last year's model.
3. World atlas.
4. U.S. state-by-state road guide, if the atlas does not have it.
5. Thesaurus.
6. Telephone directories of all cities in your broadcast area, plus the state capital.
7. City street map. Those you pay for, to carry in the glove compartment or hang on the newsroom wall, are better, but the maps the gas stations hand out are good enough unless the city is growing rapidly. Keep a few handy. They tend to stray.
8. Pronunciation guide.

If the man with the purse strings will loosen them for *these* books, you should thank him:

1. Pronouncing gazetteer.
2. Biographical dictionary or *Who's Who in America*.
3. Cross-listed phone directory (by street addresses) or current city directory.
4. Book of famous quotations.
5. State government manual ("Blue Book") (who has charge of what, and how you reach him).
6. County maps of nearby counties.

7. *Congressional Directory.*

8. *Statistical Abstract of the United States,* fairly current.

9. *U.S. Code.* (Note: each congressman and senator gets four sets a year to give away free.)

10. Style guide, or book of modern English usage.

11. One or more practical texts in the field of television news and its sub-disciplines, not only as a reference for present employees, but also as a guide for less experienced newcomers.

Besides a bookshelf, you should also keep:

1. All scripts.

2. Films used on air.

3. Outtakes, for at least 30 days.

4. Notes, handouts and wire copy used as the basis for scripts. File them for 30 days.

5. Stills which might be used another day, especially head shots and well-known public places (e.g., the city hall, the airport, the New York skyline).

Your newsroom should subscribe to:

1. All local city newspapers.

2. At least the larger suburban and small town dailies in your broadcast area.

3. At least one national news magazine.

4. *Congressional Quarterly.*

5. *Broadcasting.*

6. *RTNDA Communicator.*

7. *Quill.*

8. *Journal of Broadcasting.*

These last named publications are concerned, at least in part, with our profession. The techniques, standards, research and news developments of broadcast journalism are reported and discussed for your benefit. Take advantage of them.

A Word From Our Sponsor

Simply put, broadcasters are in the business of delivering audiences to advertisers. While newscasts also exist to serve the public interest, which broadcasters are required to do, the newscasts are expected to attract audiences in sufficient numbers to attract advertisers. The two goals, although often in harmony, sometimes conflict.

An advertiser may be put off by the grimness of news. Said one agency man, "In terms of the commercial's effectiveness we do wonder to what degree we are inhibiting its ability to sell when placing it in an atmosphere of horror or grief." One news director has even admitted surrounding commercial breaks with lighter news stories when possible: "I can't watch a Marine being killed in Vietnam and go into a Dr. Pepper commercial."

(The agency news man and the news director could be wrong. Their instinct may be leading them astray, for the factor of attention also operates. Grim and startling news may sell *more* soda pop, sad as that thought is to contemplate.)

The networks and many, if not all, large stations have a policy of keeping the advertising department out of the newsroom. A policy of advertising department directives to the newsroom should be bitterly resisted. Advertising department "requests" should be received courteously and should be given the weight of any outside requests for coverage. No more. No less.

A few television station managers insist that the "word from our sponsor" be delivered by the newscaster. If he wants to hold his job, the newscaster, after he has informed the community about the horrors of a disaster, must smilingly inform them about the delights at the local furniture store. If his gorge does not rise every time, he can be sure that some members of his audience are not so lucky. The practice is self-destructive, because the newsman's credibility wanes. He becomes a huckster who also happens to read news.

Walter Cronkite expressed the feeling of many journalists in these angry words: [9]

> It is beyond me to understand how anyone can believe in, foster, support or force a newsman to read commercials.
>
> This is blasphemy of the worst form. A newsman is nothing if not believable. And how can he be believed when he delivers a news item, if in the next breath he lends his face, his voice and his name to extolling a product or service that the public knows he probably has never tested?
>
> . . . It is difficult if not impossible for the individual newsman who wants to feed his family to stand up to a management that demands that he indulge in this infamous, degrading and destructive practice. But I fail to understand why our professional organizations . . . should not take a firm stand and help enforce an ethic that should be fundamental to our craft.

FOR THE STUDENT

1. Should a news department be independent of station management except for budget and the hiring of the news director?
2. If your answer is "yes," write an argument to convince a station manager. If "no," write an argument to convince a news director.
3. How independent of station management are each of the news departments in your city? (This can be the topic of a term paper.)

4. Write a term paper on how labor unions are aiding, or retarding, professionalism in television journalism.
5. Ask a young television newsman to speak to your class about his problems in "learning the ropes."
6. List 10 occupations, including either "television newscaster" or "television reporter." Then take a straw poll, asking people to rank them according to desirability.
7. If you could buy only six books for a television news library, which six would you choose?
8. Should there be professional standards for a journalist or, specifically, for a television journalist? If so, what should they be? Should they be enforced? If so, how?
9. Someone once described journalism as a "para-profession." What do you think he meant? Do you agree with him?
10. What is the biggest block to professionalism in broadcast journalism?

20

OPPORTUNITIES AND SALARIES

PERHAPS NOTHING EXCITES curiosity so much as how much the other fellow is earning. For television journalists, as for many others, this curiosity is buttressed by some practical considerations.

If the journalist is a news director, he will want to know how much he must pay to get and retain good men. If he must depend to any extent upon what applicants tell him, he may be getting a warped picture. If he mentally subtracts 10% or 25% from the requested salary, his arbitrary adjustment may lead him still further astray.

If the journalist is a working newsman who feels he is underpaid, his salary information may be restricted to the feedback he gets when he asks the boss for a raise, the response to his applications for employment elsewhere, and the information fed to him from colleagues who are willing to provide such information, in truth or exaggeration.

Other questions arise concerning employment practices, such as chances for raises, staff sizes and turnover, opportunities for women in television news, and the preferences of news directors as to the backgrounds of the journalists they hire.

A national survey of employment opportunities and salaries was undertaken by the author and a student, Frank W. Gerval, who in late 1970 mailed a single-page questionnaire to the news directors of 680 VHF and UHF commercial television stations in the United States, as listed for 1970 by *Television Digest*.[1] Of the 364 forms returned (53.5%), all except 14 were usable and were included in the tabulation.[2] Most of the remaining 350 stations, but not all of them, responded to each of the nine questions that were asked:

1. Do you have a combined TV-radio news department?
2. Approximately how many full-time employees?
3. How many were hired in the past 12 months?
4. What is the average weekly salary for a beginning newsman?
5. Average salary after 5 years?
6. Any women reporters?
7. Would you hire a woman as a reporter?
8. Given the following choices, who would you hire as a reporter?

　——Local youth, junior college graduate, no experience
　——College graduate in broadcast journalism, no experience
　——College graduate, major in ——————, no experience
　——Broadcasting trade school graduate, no experience
　——Reporter with 2 years experience, no college education

9. What skills or qualities do you look for most when you interview an applicant for a job as a reporter or writer?

The stations were divided by network affiliation, by city size, and by region. The nation was divided into four regions: East, South, Midwest, and West.[3]

SALARIES

A total of 324 television news departments [4] reported their average weekly starting salaries for reporters.[5] Because the questionnaire did not specify *base* salaries, some news directors may have reported total average salaries including average overtime. Nationwide, the mean starting salary was $139; the median, $130. Regional levels were:

> East: mean, $152; median, $150.
> South: mean, $122; median, $125.
> Midwest: mean, $140; median, $135.
> West: mean, $148; median, $142.

Fewer stations, a total of 249, reported average weekly salaries for reporters after five years. No distinction was made between journalists who had worked for the same station for five years and those who had received all or part of that experience on other stations. For reporters with five years experience, the mean salary nationwide was $194 in late fall, 1970; the median, $185. By region:

> East: mean, $218; median, $200.
> South: mean, $169; median, $167.
> Midwest: mean, $196; median, $180.
> West: mean, $205; median, $200.

About half of the television newsmen at stations in the East and West started out at salaries below $150. In the Midwest, about 7 out of 10 newsmen did; in the South, nearly 9 out of 10 did. Nationwide, a journalist with five years experience was earning $250 or more at 1 station out of 8.

A fairly direct relationship existed between salaries for both starting and experienced reporters and the size of the cities where their television stations are located. It was almost exclusively the metropolitan television stations which paid $300+ salaries to experienced reporters—about one station in four. Salaries also correlated strongly with size of news staffs, which itself correlated strongly with city size; i.e., the bigger the city, the more likely it is that TV news staffs will be larger and salaries will be higher, which is hardly a surprise. The average by city size:

City Size	Starting		After 5 years	
	mean	median	mean	median
Over 1,000,000	$189	$175	$259	$245
500,000 to 1,000,000	$143	$145	$207	$200
250,000 to 500,000	$126	$125	$173	$174
50,000 to 250,000	$125	$125	$180	$180 [6]
Under 50,000	$121	$120	$168	$161

A station's network affiliation bore little if any relationship to the salaries the station paid to its local reporters. VHF stations generally paid higher salaries than UHF stations and had larger staffs.

SIZE OF STAFFS

Based upon 348 responses, the mean average television news staff nationwide in late 1970 was comprised of 12.9 employees. In the East: 17.9; South: 10.8; Midwest: 12.1; West: 13.1. Nationwide, an average of 2.7 employees was hired in a year. In the East: 3.3; South: 2.9; Midwest: 2.3; West: 2.5.

There was a consistency from region to region in both size of staffs and number hired. More than four out of five stations had fewer than 20 full-time employees, presumably including on-air staff, news editors, field reporters, writers, cameramen, film editors, secretaries, and dispatchers. Many stations do not have all these job classifications, hire people part-time, assign them to other departments, contract with outsiders, or divide the work differently, while a few large stations have additional job classifications, such as producers, assignment editors, soundmen and even gaffers, or electricians (who set up the cameraman's lights and help haul gear).

As might be expected, the larger the home city,[7] the larger the television news staff is likely to be. More than two-thirds of the news staffs in cities above 1,000,000 population consisted of more than 20 employees.

The networks and many television stations employ women as reporters, and their numbers grow year by year. Some women seem content to be a newsroom's "girl reporter," chasing after light features. Other women will not accept such limitations. They prove daily that they can cover any story, anywhere, any time. At left, Marlene Sanders talks to welfare demonstrators in Chicago. Below, Marie Torre anchors a newscast for KDKA-TV, Pittsburgh. Lower left: Reporter Belva Davis for KPIX, San Francisco.

Nearly one-third of these staffs exceeded 35 employees. The largest station news operation in the United States in late 1970 had 132 full-time employees. Seventeen stations reported having only one full-time newsman, and three stations reported that they had no full-time newsmen on staff, yet were fully operating stations, not simply satellites.

City Size	Staff Size	Hired in Past Year
Over 1,000,000	32.0	5.2
500,000 to 1,000,000	13.9	2.5
250,000 to 500,000	8.8	2.3
50,000 to 250,000	8.0	2.3
Under 50,000	5.2	1.5

Once again, network affiliation did not appear to be a determining factor. On the average nationally, ABC affiliates, CBS affiliates, NBC affiliates, and independent stations were fairly consistent in the size of their staffs. and number hired.

The greatest percentage of combined television and radio news operations was found in the South, among NBC and CBS affiliates, and in cities of less than 50,000 population. The smallest percentage of combined operations was found in metropolitan areas.

Minority Hiring

Year by year opportunities have increased in television news for blacks and members of other minorities. Blacks appear in front of the cameras as anchormen and reporters, and behind the cameras in technical jobs. Minority student scholarships and special programs speed the movement of men and women from minority groups into television news. Memory is still bright of angry blacks who refused to permit all-white camera crews and reporters to move freely in ghettos, arguing that black newsmen should be sent in, because blacks would better understand the less visible causes which created the all-too-visible wreckage, and also because simple justice required that blacks be hired.

Some television news and public affairs programs specifically seek black audiences; among them: "Black News," "Black News Conference" and "Ebony Beat." These also attract white viewers.

Women Reporters

On a national average, 45% of all television stations responding to the questionnaire had at least one woman working as a reporter. Regionally, the South led the rest of the nation by a small margin, despite their smaller average staffs. Independent stations, again by a small percentage, showed a greater readiness to hire women as reporters than did stations with network affiliations.

As might be expected, there were direct correlations between the employment of women as reporters and both total news staff sizes and city sizes: i.e., the bigger the news staff and the larger the city, the more likely you are to find a woman working as a reporter. Three out of four major metropolitan television stations employed women reporters. So did three out of five stations in cities between 500,000 and 1,000,000 in population. At the other end of the scale, news directors in very small cities were less likely to hire women. More than one news director explained that reporters were required to tote heavy camera gear, and they would not hire a woman for this reason.

But overwhelmingly, news directors said they would hire a woman as a reporter. No question drew such uniform response as "Would you hire a woman as a reporter?" Nationally, 94% of the news directors replied "Yes," and in no category was the response less than 91% affirmative.

EDUCATIONAL PREFERENCES

News directors were asked to choose among five kinds of preparation for a job as a reporter, and it was hoped that a degree of equality existed among the choices. There were 425 first choice responses to the question, "Given the following choices, who would you hire as a reporter?" [8]

Here were the results: [9]

> Reporter with 2 years experience, no college education: 176
> College graduate in broadcast journalism, no experience: 165.
> College graduate with another major; no experience: 50.
> Local youth, junior college graduate, no experience: 24.
> Broadcasting trade school graduate, no experience: 10.

Of the 50 responses favoring a major other than broadcast journalism, the most often mentioned majors were: political science (14), English (11), liberal arts (9), history (6), general journalism (4), telecommunications (3), speech (1), humanities (1), social science (1).[10]

DESIRED SKILLS AND QUALITIES

The only open-ended question in the survey brought a rich variety of replies: What skills or qualities do you look for most when you interview an applicant for a job as a reporter or writer?

160 mentions: writing ability, use of the English language, writing skill, must know how to write, etc.

90 mentions: on-air ability, voice, poise, good looks and delivery, potential for on-air work, etc.

60 mentions: photographic skills, use of camera equipment, potential for learning photography, etc.

22 mentions: film editing skills, film editing judgment, etc.

12 mentions: reporting skills, nose for news, news sense, able to get a story, etc.

12 mentions: typing.

10 mentions: knows how to use sound equipment and tape recorders, etc.

An effort was also made to categorize the nouns and adjectives used to identify desirable personal qualities, and tally the number of times each was mentioned:

90 mentions: energy, desire, eagerness, self-starter, enthusiasm, drive, guts, motivation, aggressiveness, ambition.

53 mentions: positive attitudes, good manners, maturity, stable personality.

22 mentions: hard worker, not afraid to work long hours, a real work horse.

20 mentions: imagination, creativity, ingenuity, expressiveness.

17 mentions: good habits, clean and neat, clean cut, no personal hangups.

16 mentions: ability to work with others, congenial, cooperative.

14 mentions: objective, open minded, clear headed.

13 mentions: dependable, reliable, dedicated.

What follows are two lists of attributes a radio journalist should have. They apply to television newsmen, too. The first list was issued by the American Council on Education for Journalism:

1. Ability to write radio news copy.
2. Judgment and good taste in selecting news items for broadcast.
3. Ability to edit copy of others, including wire copy.
4. Knowledge of the law especially applicable to broadcasting.
5. Knowledge of general station operation.
6. Understanding of the mechanical problems of broadcasting.
7. Appreciation of broadcasting's responsibility to the public, particularly in its handling of news.
8. Ability to work under pressure.
9. Ability to make decisions quickly.
10. Speed in production.
11. Familiarity with the various techniques of news broadcasting (including first-person reporting, tape recordings, interviews, remotes).
12. Knowledge of newscast production (including timing or back-timing of script, opens and closes, placement of commercials, production-newsroom coordination).
13. Ability to gather news for radio/tv.

14. Ability to read news copy with acceptable voice quality, diction, etc.
15. Ability to find local angles in national or other stories.
16. Quickness to see feature angles in routine assignments.
17. Ability to simplify complex matters and make them meaningful to the listener or viewer.

The second list was written by James Bormann of WCCO, Minneapolis.

The successful applicant would:
1. Know how to write an easy, lucid narrative style.
2. Know how to write rapidly, particularly under pressure.
3. Have more than normal skill as a typist.
4. Possess a liberal educational background.
5. Have a basic understanding of people, their desires and their motivations.
6. Know how to get along well with others—particularly with his own associates.
7. Be first a good reporter; other journalism skills will flow from that.
8. Feel an absolute affection for news reporting as a career.
9. Possess unassailable integrity and an effective determination to resist pressures.
10. Have a lively interest in the affairs of the world.
11. Have the ability to remain objective in his observations—to feel deeply the emotions of people and the significance of events without becoming personally involved.
12. Be unafraid of hard work.

Some Conclusions and Suggestions

The range of salaries for both beginning television reporters and experienced reporters is wide indeed. As of late 1970, starting salaries ranged from less than $4,000 a year to more than $16,000, the top starting salary being considerably higher than most of the salaries being paid to veteran reporters.

Advice to the television reporter looking for higher earnings would be: Go North, go East or West, go to the big cities, and don't pay attention to whether television and radio news operations are combined, or to affiliation labels. Of course, this last conclusion overlooks the advantages of making contacts through affiliate relationships and stringer work.

At the same time, the correlation of staff size and city size tends to support the advice given to many a novice journalist: Start your career in a smaller city so that you will be forced to do a variety of jobs (and really learn what television news is all about). Of course, a novice journalist may spurn such advice, preferring to start in a large city and move quickly to a specialization.

Opportunities for women in television news appear to be strong. Half the stations now employ a woman as a reporter, and most of the others express a willingness to do so.

News directors by a very wide margin seem to want employees who can do the job from the day they walk in, either graduates in broadcast journalism or experienced reporters even though they lack a college education. Relatively few would prefer, instead, an untrained man or woman whose background consisted of a university education in one of the more traditional fields. They also state a preference for writing ability, followed by on-air ability and ability to work with film.

Some graduates ask themselves, "Shall I go to a small town as a reporter or to a large city as a copy boy?" The author tried both and unhesitatingly recommends the former route. The young reporter in a small town observes how all the jobs are done which mesh together to produce a program, learns to do many of them himself and, most important of all, develops a "sense of self" as a craftsman. Self-confidence and self respect are the best of the resources he will eventually carry to the big city, if that is where he is headed. He knows he can do the job. He will look a news director straight in the eye and tell him so, without varnishing the truth. On the other hand, it has been the author's observation that graduates who go the copy boy route are more prone to irritation and pugnacity, seeking friends who might help them emerge from their serfdom, and pulling what strings they can. Walter Cronkite remarked, "We have some bright young men and women in CBS News who came up through the copy boy (or girl) route, but it takes exceptional people to do that successfully, because the truth is we don't yet have the means to train them from scratch." [11]

As for a social life and good times, it has also been the author's experience that life for a reporter in a small city can be as varied, exciting, and mentally stimulating as he chooses to make it. The life of an underpaid copy boy in an overpriced metropolis compares poorly.

EMPLOYMENT SERVICES

The weekly magazine *Broadcasting* runs classified ads, both Help Wanted and Situations Wanted, with separate sections for television and for radio.

The Radio Television News Directors Association runs a placement service. Journalists seeking employment and stations seeking journalists should write to the RTNDA Placement Service. The present address is 6016 Fallbrook Avenue, Woodland Hills, California 91364. Journalists pay a small fee. Stations are not charged.

University departments of journalism usually offer a placement service for their graduating students. Quite often a professor will recommend competent students to news directors who call.

FOR THE STUDENT

1. This chapter is based on the author's research. How could it be improved?
2. What should have been added to the questionnaire?
3. Design a second questionnaire for news directors. Choose any topics you like, as long as you think a statistical tally of the answers will prove interesting or useful.
4. Write a term paper on job opportunities for blacks and other minorities in television news.
5. Draw up a four-year curriculum for a student who wants to become a television journalist.
6. If the student takes 45 courses during those four years, how many should be technical, "how-to" courses? What should he learn in them?
7. Write a job resumé, anticipating the day you graduate. (Save it.)
8. Plan a job-hunting campaign. (Save it, too.)
9. Spend a couple of days with a local television newsman who has a job you would like to have one day. Tell him so and talk to him about it.
10. Within five years, get his job. Or a better one. (Maybe he will have a better job himself by then.)

APPENDICES

January 14, 1972, was a "typical" news day, in that a few events were generally significant but no single event stood out.

Here are the scripts used in the 11 p.m. local newscasts of the three network O & O stations in Los Angeles: KABC-TV's *Eyewitness News,* *KNBC News,* and KNXT's *The 11 O'Clock Report.*

Preceding them is a portion of the AP broadcast wire which was sent to Southern California subscribers that evening before the 11 p.m. newscasts.

(Note: pages containing only references to commercials or listings of visuals have been removed. Actual script pages have been reset in type and combined to save space. Shorthand abbreviations were left unchanged.)

APPENDIX A

Associated Press Broadcast Wire (AP)

AP440
018
--SECOND FIVE-MINUTE SUMMARY--

HERE IS THE LATEST NEWS FROM THE ASSOCIATED PRESS:

(WASHINGTON)--THE STATE DEPARTMENT DISCLOSED FRIDAY THAT
A U-S AIR FORCE ATTACHE WAS PHYSICALLY ASSAULTED IN THE SOVIET
UNION JANUARY FIFTH. IT ALSO SAYS THE SOVIETS HAVE REJECTED A
STRONG U-S PROTEST OVER THE AFFAIR.
    A SPOKESMAN SAYS AIR FORCE CAPTAIN ELMER ALDERFER WAS
THROWN TO THE GROUND, MANHANDLED AND GRILLED FOR 30 MINUTES.
THE INCIDENT IS SAID TO HAVE TAKEN PLACE AT RIGA AIRPORT WHERE
THE DEPARTMENT SAYS HE WAS FALSELY ACCUSED OF TAKING PIC-
TURES. THE STATE DEPARTMENT ACCOUNT OF THE INCIDENT SAYS
ALDERFER FLEW TO RIGA ON A TRIP PREVIOUSLY CLEARED WITH
SOVIET AUTHORITIES. HE WAS REPORTEDLY ATTACKED BY FOUR TO
SIX PERSONS AT THE AIRPORT. THEN ANOTHER DOZEN OR SO JOINED
THE ASSAULT. HE WAS RELEASED AFTER QUESTIONING.

(WASHINGTON)--THE PRESIDENTS OF THE TEAMSTERS AND WEST
COAST LONGSHOREMEN'S UNIONS REPORTEDLY HAVE SIGNED A LETTER
OF INTENT TO MERGE THEIR ORGANIZATIONS. THE "WASHINGTON POST"
SAYS IN ITS SATURDAY EDITIONS THAT TEAMSTER CHIEF FRANK FITZ-
SIMMONS AND PRESIDENT HARRY BRIDGES OF THE LONGSHOREMEN'S
UNION SIGNED THE LETTER DURING A MEETING IN WASHINGTON FRI-
DAY. BRIDGES HAD NO COMMENT ON THE REPORT.
    THE TWO UNIONS HAVE BEEN ENGAGED IN A JURISDICTIONAL DIS-
PUTE OVER HANDLING OF CONTAINERIZED CARGO IN WEST COAST
PORTS. THE DISPUTE HAS BLOCKED EFFORTS TOWARD A CONTRACT
SETTLEMENT BETWEEN THE LONGSHOREMEN AND SHIPPERS. THE

MERGER--IF APPROVED BY DOCKWORKERS--WOULD END THE DISPUTE. MEANWHILE NEW TALKS AIMED AT AVERTING RESUMPTION OF THE WEST COAST DOCK STRIKE ARE SCHEDULED IN SAN FRANCISCO SATURDAY.

(NEW YORK)--A FORMER F-B-I AGENT SAYS HIS ASSIGNMENTS INCLUDED MONITORING TELEPHONE CONVERSATIONS TO AND FROM THE ISRAELI EMBASSY DURING THE SIX-DAY WAR OF 1967. ROBERT WALL SAYS IN A NEW YORK INTERVIEW HE RECEIVED THE ASSIGNMENT AFTER A YEAR'S TRAINING IN THE NATIONAL SECURITY AGENCY AT FORT MEADE, MARYLAND.
WALL SAYS BOTH ISRAELI AND ARAB EMBASSY PHONE CALLS WERE MONITORED AT THE TIME AND HE CLAIMS CONVERSATIONS HE OVERHEARD WERE "SO TRITE" HE CAN'T REMEMBER ANYTHING ABOUT THEM. WALL SERVED IN THE F-B-I FOR FIVE YEARS UNTIL RESIGNING IN 1970. HE MADE THE DISCLOSURE IN CONNECTION WITH AN ARTICLE PUBLISHED IN THE "NEW YORK REVIEW OF BOOKS."
10:13PPS   01-14-72

AP441
   021
   N-B-A
GOLDEN STATE 115 NEW YORK 111
10:13PPS   01-14-72

AP442
   610
U R G E N T
(SPORTS)
   (LOS ANGELES)--TOP-RANKED UCLA OVERWHELMED STANFORD 118-TO-79 TONIGHT AS BILL WALTON SCORED 32 POINTS AND HENRY BIBBY ADDED 22. IN A GAME ACROSS TOWN IN LOS ANGELES, U-S-C DOWNED CALIFORNIA 102-TO-69.///C611
   R 20 21 22 23

--22ND CALIFORNIA SPOT SUMMARY--

(WASHINGTON)--THE WASHINGTON POST REPORTS THAT THE TEAMSTERS UNION AND THE INTERNATIONAL LONGSHOREMEN'S AND WAREHOUSEMEN'S UNIONS HAVE AGREED TO MERGE. LONGSHORE PRESIDENT HARRY BRIDGES SAYS IN SAN FRANCISCO HE HAS NO COMMENT ON THE REPORT. A DISPUTE BETWEEN THE TWO UNIONS HAS BLOCKED A CONTRACT SETTLEMENT OF THE WEST COAST DOCK DISPUTE.

(SAN FRANCISCO)--THE CHIEF FEDERAL MEDIATOR HAS CALLED A MEETING IN THE DOCK DISPUTE TOMORROW IN SAN FRANCISCO. HE IS ATTEMPTING TO AVERT A RESUMPTION OF THE STRIKE ON MONDAY.

(SAN FRANCISCO)--COMMUNIST PARTY LEADER GUS HALL SAYS THE STATE SHOULD PAY FOR THE DEFENSE OF ANGELA DAVIS IN HER KID-

NAP, MURDER AND CONSPIRACY TRIAL. IN ANOTHER DEVELOPMENT,
HER REQUEST FOR RELEASE ON BAIL HAS BEEN DENIED BY A FEDERAL
JUDGE.

(TURLOCK)--THE MOTHER OF A MAN ACCUSED OF PLANTING BOMBS
IN BANKS ACROSS THE COUNTRY SAYS SHE CAN'T BELIEVE HER SON DID
IT. THE COMMENT CAME FROM SONIA KAUFMAN, WHOSE SON, 33-YEAR-
OLD RONALD KAUFMAN, HAS BEEN CHARGED BY THE F-B-I WITH PLANT-
ING DELAYED FUSE BOMBS IN NINE BANKS.
    10:17PPS   01-14-72

AP443
    019
    SECOND FIVE--TAKE 2

(SAIGON)--THE FIVE COMMUNIST ATTACKS LAUNCHED SATURDAY
IN SOUTH VIETNAM'S COASTAL LOWLANDS BRINGS THE FIVE-DAY TOTAL
THERE TO 115 INCIDENTS. THAT'S THE LARGEST FIVE-DAY TOTAL IN
MORE THAN THREE MONTHS.
    IN ONE ASSAULT, A MINE EXPLODED UNDER A BUS, KILLING FOUR-
TEEN CIVILIAN MOURNERS IN A FUNERAL PROCESSION. THE INCIDENT
OCCURRED IN A TOWN ABOUT 15 MILES SOUTH OF DA NANG.

(QUITO, ECUADOR)--ASSISTANT SECRETARY OF STATE CHARLES
MEYER HAS ENDED A THIRD ROUND OF TALKS WITH ECUADORIAN OF-
FICIALS IN QUITO (KEE'-TOH). THE NEGOTIATIONS ARE AIMED AT SOLV-
ING A FISHING CONFLICT THAT HAS STRAINED RELATIONS BETWEEN
THE U-S AND ECUADOR.
    THE DISPUTE GREW OUT OF ECUADORIAN SEIZURE AND FINING OF
AMERICAN TUNA BOATS WHICH HAVE REFUSED TO BUY LICENSES TO
FISH WITHIN THE NATION'S CLAIMED 200-MILE TERRITORIAL SEA
LIMIT. THE U-S RECOGNIZES ONLY A 12-MILE LIMIT. MEYER SAYS A
POSSIBLE SOLUTION MIGHT BE THE PURCHASE OF LICENSES "UNDER
PROTEST." ECUADOR SEIZED 50 U-S TUNA BOATS LAST YEAR AND
THREE SO FAR THIS YEAR.

(MEXICO CITY)--MEXICO'S DEFENSE MINISTER SAYS HIS NATION'S
ARMS AND AMMUNITION INDUSTRY WILL BE NATIONALIZED. HE SAYS
MOST OF THE 26 ARMAMENTS FACTORIES WILL BE SHUT DOWN.
    THE ACTION FOLLOWS LAST YEAR'S PASSAGE BY THE MEXICAN
CONGRESS OF A STRINGENT ARMS LAW. IT DRASTICALLY CHANGED
LAWS REGULATING POSSESSION OF WEAPONS.

(SAN FRANCISCO)--THE LEADER OF AMERICA'S COMMUNIST PARTY
VISITED BLACK REVOLUTIONARY ANGELA DAVIS IN JAIL FRIDAY. GUS
HALL SAYS THE STATE OF CALIFORNIA SHOULD PAY FOR HER DEFENSE
TO PROVE -- IN HIS WORDS -- "THAT NOT ONLY THE RICH CAN GET A
FAIR TRIAL." HALL SAYS HIS PARTY HAS BEEN AND WILL CONTINUE TO
RAISE ALL THE MONEY IT CAN FOR HER TRIAL ON MURDER, KIDNAP
AND CONSPIRACY CHARGES.
    10:22PPS   01-14-72

AP444
    023
    N-H-L
CALIFORNIA 5 VANCOUVER 3
10:22PPS   01-14-72

AP445
    020

    SECOND FIVE--TAKE 3

    (CONCORD, NEW HAMPSHIRE)--DEMOCRATIC PRESIDENTIAL HOPE-
FUL EDMUND MUSKIE SAYS HE'S AGAINST ANY ATTEMPT TO ALLEVIATE
PROPERTY TAX BURDENS THROUGH A NATIONAL SALES TAX. THE
MAINE SENATOR WOUND UP A TWO-DAY CAMPAIGN SWING IN NEW
HAMPSHIRE FRIDAY CLAIMING THE SALES TAX WOULD "SUBSTITUTE
A NEW REGRESSIVE FORM OF TAXATION FOR AN OLD ONE."

    IN OTHER POLITICAL DEVELOPMENTS . . . MAYOR CHARLES EVERS
OF FAYETTE, MISSISSIPPI SAYS HE'LL SUPPORT NEW YORK MAYOR
JOHN LINDSAY'S BID FOR THE DEMOCRATIC PRESIDENTIAL NOMINATION.

    AND LIEUTENANT GOVERNOR LESTER MADDOX OF GEORGIA SAYS
HE WON'T SEEK THE DEMOCRATIC PRESIDENTIAL NOMINATION.

    (JAKARTA)--PRESIDENT SUHARTO OF INDONESIA CLAIMS NIGHT
CLUBS AND STEAM BATHS ARE "NEGATIVE INSTRUSIONS OF UNHEALTHY
WESTERN CULTURE." AND HE CLAIMS THEY WERE BROUGHT TO HIS
NATION BY HIPPIES.

    --DASH--

SUMMARY BY WES RICHARDS
10:25PPS   01-14-72

AP446
    612
    (SPORTS)

    (SAN DIEGO)--NATE THURMOND SCORED 17 POINTS IN THE SECOND
HALF TO LEAD THE GOLDEN STATE WARRIORS TO THEIR EIGHTH
STRAIGHT VICTORY. THE WARRIORS DEFEATED THE SLUMPING NEW
YORK KNICKS 115-TO-111 IN SAN DIEGO.
10:26PPS   01-14-72

AP447
    611

--22ND CALIFORNIA SPOT SUMMARY--

(WASHINGTON)--THE WASHINGTON POST REPORTS THAT THE TEAM-
STERS UNION AND THE INTERNATIONAL LONGSHOREMEN'S AND WARE-
HOUSEMEN'S UNIONS HAVE AGREED TO MERGE. LONGSHORE PRESIDENT
HARRY BRIDGES SAYS IN SAN FRANCISCO HE HAS NO COMMENT ON THE
REPORT. A DISPUTE BETWEEN THE TWO UNIONS HAS BLOCKED A CON-
TRACT SETTLEMENT OF THE WEST COAST DOCK DISPUTE.

(SAN FRANCISCO)--THE CHIEF FEDERAL MEDIATOR HAS CALLED
A MEETING IN THE DOCK DISPUTE TOMORROW IN SAN FRANCISCO. HE
IS ATTEMPTING TO AVERT A RESUMPTION OF THE STRIKE ON MONDAY.

(SAN FRANCISCO)--COMMUNIST PARTY LEADER GUS HALL SAYS
THE STATE SHOULD PAY FOR THE DEFENSE OF ANGELA DAVIS IN HER
KIDNAP, MURDER AND CONSPIRACY TRIAL. IN ANOTHER DEVELOPMENT,
HER REQUEST FOR RELEASE ON BAIL HAS BEEN DENIED BY A FEDERAL
JUDGE.

(TURLOCK)--THE MOTHER OF A MAN ACCUSED OF PLANTING BOMBS
IN BANKS ACROSS THE COUNTRY SAYS SHE CAN'T BELIEVE HER SON DID
IT. THE COMMENT CAME FROM SONIA KAUFMAN, WHOSE SON, 33-YEAR-
OLD RONALD KAUFMAN, HAS BEEN CHARGED BY THE F-B-I WITH PLANT-
ING DELAYED FUSE BOMBS IN NINE BANKS.
10:29PPS   01-14-72

AP448
    613
    (SPORTS)

(OAKLAND)--THE CALIFORNIA GOLDEN SEALS RALLIED FOR FOUR
GOALS IN THE THIRD PERIOD TO TURN BACK THE VANCOUVER CANUCKS
5-TO-3 IN THE ONLY NATIONAL HOCKEY LEAGUE GAME TONIGHT.
10:30PPS   01-14-72

AP449
    022

--A SPOT SUMMARY--

HERE IS THE LATEST NEWS FROM THE ASSOCIATED PRESS:

(WASHINGTON)--THE STATE DEPARTMENT DISCLOSED FRIDAY THAT
A U-S AIR FORCE ATTACHE WAS PHYSICALLY ASSAULTED IN THE SOVIET
UNION JANUARY FIFTH AND THAT THE SOVIETS HAVE REJECTED A
STRONG PROTEST OVER THE AFFAIR.

(WASHINGTON)--THE PRESIDENTS OF THE TEAMSTERS AND WEST
COAST LONGSHOREMEN'S UNIONS REPORTEDLY HAVE SIGNED A LETTER
OF INTENT TO MERGE THEIR ORGANIZATIONS.

(NEW YORK)--A FORMER F-B-I AGENT SAYS HIS ASSIGNMENTS IN-

CLUDED MONITORING TELEPHONE CONVERSATIONS TO AND FROM THE
ISRAELI U-N EMBASSY DURING THE SIX-DAY WAR OF 1967.

(SAIGON)--THE FIVE COMMUNIST ATTACKS LAUNCHED SATURDAY
IN SOUTH VIETNAM'S COASTAL LOWLANDS BRINGS THE FIVE-DAY TOTAL
THERE TO 115 INCIDENTS.

(QUITO, ECUADOR)--ASSISTANT SECRETARY OF STATE CHARLES
MEYER HAS ENDED A THIRD ROUND OF TALKS WITH ECUADORIAN OF-
FICIALS AIMED AT RESOLUTION OF A FISHING CONFLICT.
10:34PPS   01-14-72

AP450
    614
    (SPORTS)

(LONG BEACH)--JANET LYNN OF ROCKFORD, ILLINOIS, HAS WON THE
WOMEN'S FIGURE SKATING CHAMPIONSHIP FOR THE FOURTH STRAIGHT
YEAR, ASSURING HERSELF OF AN INVITATION TO COMPETE IN THE WIN-
TER OLYMPICS NEXT MONTH.
10:42PPS   01-14-72

AP453
    028

COLLEGE BASKETBALL

WASHINGTON 91 CINCINNATI 81
PACIFIC LUTHERAN 86 PACIFIC U. 62
EASTERN OREGON 95 OREGON TECH 77
WESTERN WASHINGTON 81 CENTRAL WASHINGTON 73
CHICO ST. 83 SONOMA ST. 55
HUMBOLDT ST. 77 UC-DAVIS 57
U.S. INTERNATIONAL 72 PASADENA 65
UC-RIVERSIDE 109 CAL STATE FULLERTON 92
VIOLA 69 FRESNO PACIFIC 41
RACELAND, IOWA 92 MISSOURI VALLEY 76
ST. MARY OF THE PLAINS KAN. 92, KANSAS WESLEYAN 73
JOHN BROWN, ARK. 73 SCHOOL OF THE OZARKS, MO. 72
BAKER, KAN. 84 WILLIAM JEWELL, MO. 83, (OVERTIME)
10:52PPS   01-14-72

APPENDIX B
ABC Evening News (KABC)

LIVE ON BENTI

Good evening ...
According to reports from Washington, it's going to be almost impossible to tell the difference between teamsters and west coast dockworkers ...

TOTAL: 17 secs
SIL FILM...06 secs...
v/o

On a street in East Los Angeles, there's no problem seeing the street for the trees--the trees are gone ...

LIVE ON SCHU (FILM
ROLLING 05 SECONDS)

Bail has been refused for Angela Davis and she is asking the state to pay for her legal fees.

SIL FILM...06 secs...
v/o

Up north they turned the water on for Southern California.

LIVE ON BENTI

Alan Sloane will have the weather and the silver haired tout will size up the weekend next on eyewitness news.

TEAMSTER MERGER,
BENTI
A REEL

LIVE ON BENTI

West Coast longshoremen apparently have turned to the old philosophy, if you can't beat em, join em to solve the major roadblock to a settlement of the West Coast dock dispute ...

SIL FILM...15 secs...
v/o

That roadblock is an argument between the longshore union and the Teamsters over which union should load and unload containerized cargo like this.

Tonight, the Washington Post reports that Long-shore President Harry Bridges signed a letter of intent with Teamster President Frank Fitz-simmons to merge the dockworkers with the teamsters.

LIVE ON BENTI

If the report is accurate, and the longshore union member's approve such a merger in a secret ballot, there may not be a resumption of the strike. Negotiations between the shippers and the dockworkers resume tomorrow and the contract extension expires on Monday.

WHOLESALE PRICES

VTR
TOTAL TIME 1:15
JOE OVER KEY CD.
(WHOLESALE PRICES)

The government announced today that wholesale prices shot up eight-tenths of one per cent last month after the price freeze. But the chairman of President Nixon's Council of Economic Advisers ... Dr. Herbert Stein ... didn't seem too concerned:::

VTR/SOT :59

IN.. "Stein was far from gloomy.."
ENDS.. "Matney, ABC News, Washington.."

TREE PROTEST

LIVE/SOF A & B
FILM TIME: 1:59
STORY TIME: 2:20

SCHU ON CAMERA

Protests by homeowners in an East Los Angeles community were drowned out by bulldozers today when the county moved in to rip out trees lining Hoefner Avenue.

The residents have been fighting to keep the majestic shade trees where they stand--the county says they must go to widen the street.::

SOF 1:59

IN: "When the tree-cutters arrived ..."

MATTES: EE-21; AN-
DERSON (use twice)
EWN/EAST L.A.
dickerson
hixon

OUT: "... Channel 7 Eyewitness news, East Los Angeles"

BRANT (TEASE)

JOHN ON CAM

Willie Brandt had a close call but at the time probably never realized it. We'll have that story in a moment.

BRANDT'S PLANE

JOHN ON CAM

A spokesman for the Federal Aviation Agency says tonight that an earlier report was false... that the plane carrying Chancellor Willie Brant home from Florida last week, came close to colliding with another plane.

The FAA says the incident did occur outside of Jacksonville. That Brandt's plane was flying at 33-thousand feet and that an Eastern airlines jet was climbing toward it.

A spokesman for the Air Traffic Controllers said that only quick thinking and expertise by one of its members . . . averted disaster.

FAA says that planes were 2 miles apart... that the Eastern jet had spotted Brandt's jet and asked to change altitude.

ANGELA DAVIS

LIVE
TTL TIME :25
SCHU

A federal judge in San Francisco has denied bail for Angela Davis. Judge William Sweigert ruled that her rights are not being violated by keeping her in jail, where she's been for the past 15 months pending her trial on charges of murder, kidnap and conspiracy. The trial is set to begin January 31st in San Jose .. but the defense has another court motion pending for a change of venue.

In another development ... Miss Davis says she's broke and wants the state to pay for her defense.

YOUNGER/BROWN

LIVE/SOF A & B ROLLS
FILM TIME 1:18
STORY TIME:
JOE ON CAMERA

More than four and a half years have elapsed since a death sentence has been carried out in the United States. Next week, the Supreme Court will decide whether the moratorium

should continue indefinitely--or if capital punishment should be reinstated. California's
Attorney General, Evelle Younger says he'll
fight to retain the death penalty:::

SOF 1:18   IN: "We argue that . . ."

MATTE YOUNGER/
BROWN   OUT: ". . . went to their death"

JOE LIVE/ON CAMERA
TOTAL TIME 1:50   The American Civil Liberties Union has already
                            filed a suit in California Supreme Court to have
                            the death penalty declared unconstitutional. After
                            an hour long hearing today, the court took the
                            arguments under submission for ruling at a
                            later date.

KING FREDERIK

LIVE
TOTAL TIME :20
JOE ON CAM   A humorous and modern young mother of two
                            children is the new queen of Denmark.

                            31-year-old Princess Margrethe (MARGRAY'TUH)
                            became Queen Margrethe the second upon the
FULL CARD (King   death of her 72-year-old father . . . King Fred-
Frederik)   erik. The king died today as a result of a heart
                            attack two weeks ago.

                            He had ruled Denmark for 25 years.

CALIF WATER PROJECT

A ROLL
TOTAL TIME :55
SCHU ON CAMERA   The first Northern California water flowed today
                            into Castaic Lake . . . a key terminal reservoir
FILM SU/VO (:49)   in the state water project located 45 miles to
                            the North of Los Angeles. The 475 mile waterway
MATTE: Calif Water   is a joint project of the state and the Los Angeles
Project   Department of Water and Power. As water began
                            filling the reservoir site . . . state water resources
                            director William Gianelli said today shares in
                            significance in project history with the first de-
                            liveries of water in the San Francisco Bay area
                            nearly 10-years ago. It will be several months
                            before deliveries can be made from Castaic Lake
                            to local agencies. In addition to conveying water
                            to Southern California . . . the two-Billion 800-
                            million dollar project will generate one-and-a-

half million kilowatts of power at five hydroelec-
tric plants by 19-91. The beginning of operations
at Castaic also brings closer the day when Southern Californians will be able to avoid those long
drives and enjoy fresh water recreation close to
home.

VETS FACILITY/EARTH-
QUAKE

LIVE/SOF A & B ROLLS
FILM TIME: 1:24
STORY TIME: 1:40
SCHU ON CAMERA

A special committee has determined that last
year's earthquake has made three Veterans
Administration Hospitals structurally unsafe.
The V-A plans to relocate patients to other
facilities--including the new 811-bed hospital
scheduled to open in San Diego next month:::

SOF 1:24   IN: "Of the 236 ... "

MATTE: EE-15; WIMAN
(use twice)
VETERANS HOSPITAL
FRED RHODES   OUT: "Veterans Hospital, west Los Angeles"

SPORTS

NBA
JOE LIVE

Wilt Chamberlains all around brilliance plus a
part-time peacemakers role helped the Lakers
to a 135-121 victory over Philadelphia in the
Lakers last game before Tuesday nites NBA
all-star game at the Forum. Wilt put in 23 pts,
grabbed 20 rebounds, blocked 7 shots, and interrupted a fourth period scuffle between Gail Goodrich and Philadelphias Kevin Loughery. West

SLIDE KR 295
SUPER NBA 1

put in 30 .. Goodrich 29 .. Mil broke 2 gm losing
streak .. and Cincy made it 3 in row with win
over Atlanta

SUPER NBA 2

Boston over Detroit ..
Portland took Buffalo ..
Phoenix beat Cleveland ..
and ... Golden State ... NY ...

LIVE - STU

Kings wind up current 7 game road trip with games in Drt and Philly over the weekend.

SLIDE KR 144
NHL 1

One NHL game tonight ...
Vancouver ... Calif ...

SUPER BOWL

LIVE

48 hours before the Super Bowl begins ... both teams report no serious injuries aside from the Cowboys Calvin Hill who def will not start.

Dallas remains a 6 pt favorite in their second Super Bowl appearance.

UCLA
LIVE/KEY CARD
UCLA-STANF

At Pauly Pavilion in Westwood, Bill Walton and Henry Bibby combined for 54 pts as the UCLA Bruins def Stanford 118-79. The victory was the Bruins 11th straight this year, 26th in a row over the past 2 years and gave them a Pac 8 Conf record of 3-0. It was Stanfords 1st Conf loss after 2 straight wins.

USC-CAL.

SU/VO
TOTAL FILM TIME
LIVE/KEY CARD
USC-CAL

At the sports arena ... USC piled up a 23 pt lead in the 1st hlf, then coasted to a 102-69 win over Univ of Calif ...

SU/VO USC
SUPER USC VS CAL

Paul Westphal put on quite a shooting demonstration, getting 18 pts, his season avg is 20 .. 15 of those points plus 8 assts came in the first half.

Sophomore center Mike Westra from Fresno was strong on the boards ... Joe Mackey led the Trojans scorers with 19 pts. The victory gives USC a 3-0 conf record ... their overall seasonal mark is now 10-2 ...

GOLF
LIVE/KEY CARD
NICKLAUS

Jack Nicklaus bounced back after a disastrous first nine by shooting a 2 over par 74 to share the second round lead in the Bing Crosby Pro Am Up at Pebble Beach.

Nicklaus took a five over par 4 on the back nine of the spyglass course ... came back strong to

KEY CARD
GOLF SCORES

tie Tony Jacklin for the lead . . . The former US and British Open champ shot his second straight 2 under par 70 for his 140. One stroke back is an unknown Herb Hooper whose 68 today gave him a 141.

Trevino had a 74 to bunch him and 6 others at 143 . . . Three strokes back of the leaders . . .

FIGHT

VTR SOT
TOTAL TAPE TIME
52 SECS
LIVE/KEY CARD
BOXING GLOVES

For the first time since he defeated Muhammad Ali last March, heavyweight champ Joe Frazier will step into the ring tomorrow night in New Orlns to do battle with little known Terry Daniels in what has to be the worst mismatch in recent years.

ABCS Bill Frink reports from the fighters training camps . . .

52 SECS VTR SOT

End cue--ABC News Reporting--

PATULSKI
LIVE/KEY CARD
PATULSKI

Notre Dames all-American def end Walt Patulski tonight won the second annual Vince Lombardi trophy as the outstanding college lineman in 1971.

The 6-6 230 pound Patulski started every game for Notre Dame in his 3 year varsity career . . . winning this coveted honor over three other nominees Larry Jacobson and Rich Glover of Nebraska and Ron Estay of LSU.

WELLS
LIVE/KEY CARD
WELLS

Warren Wells the former Oakland Raiders wide receiver who has been serving a prison sentence for a 1969 attempted rape conviction, had that sentence suspended today and was placed on 3 years probation, also ordered to enter Synanon, the rehabilitation center.

Wells was also ordered to refrain from liquor, have nothing to do with firearms, and sell his car. Wells has been confined to the Vacaville Medical facility for 3 months, missing the Raiders 1971 season.

LONG HAIR

A & B REELS

LIVE ON BENTI   Finally, if Stu Nahan or the rest of us suddenly
                             find ourselves out of work, and sometimes that
                             prospect doesn't seem too far away, we can al-
                             ways get in line at the unemployment office . . .
                             but for men with long hair, that may be a problem:

SOF . . . 1:25 . . .   INCUE: "According . . ."

MATTES: EE-50 HENRY
(use twice)
BRENNER   OUTCUE: ". . .channel seven eyewitness news."

APPENDIX C
CBS Evening News (KNXT)

Dunphy:

From the desert to the sea, to all of southern California, a good evening ...

Lead to Dunn

Both UCLA and USC opened their Pac-8 <u>home</u> schedules tonight ... They're rated the two teams in the always-tough league...and here's Bob Dunn to tell us if they lived up to their billing ... Bob ...

SPORTS

CU Dunn

Yes they did Jerry, and judging from the way they both played tonight, we won't really know about the strength of the Pacific 8 conference until the Bruins and the Trojans meet February 5th at Pauley Pavilion ...

UCLA beat Stanford by 39 points and SC trounced Cal by 33 ...

the Lakers beat Philadelphia by 14 to wind up their road trip on a winning note ...

color film 1:22
sof BG
w/v.o.

The UCLA rout was as usual decided early; and the pattern the same, Walton rebounds, triggers the fast break and zap, the Bruins have scored again. .Henry Bibby gets 2 of his 22 points..

then the Bruins steal the ball, as the result of their pressing defense and again it's 2 for Henry Bibby ...

426

Bill Walton had another fine night, scoring 32
points, on 15 field goals and 2 for 5 from the
free throw line ...

The Bruins defense completely befuddled the
Indians, causing numerous turnovers, most resulting in an easy Basket for the Bruins, this
time it's forward Kieth Wilkes

then Greg Lee feeds Larry Farmer underneath
for an easy basket ...

the Bruins fast break worked like a machine as
they kept right on pounding the Bears defense,
this time it's Greg Lee taking it all the way

crowd shot ...   meanwhile across town at the sports Arena a
crowd of over 7,000 watched the Trojans destroy
the Cal Bears

SC had 6 starters in double figures led by
Mackey's 19 Westphal had 18 and Dan Anderson
had 10 mostly from the outside ...

forward Ron Riley had 14, as the Trojans won
in a walk ...

they confused the Bears with a tight zone defense at the outset, and a full court zone press...

film ends 1:22

slide BG Basketball
super: UCLQ -   the finals: UCLA 118 Stanford 79 ...
        USC   SC 102 California 69 ...
                           the two teams swap opponents for more of the
                           same tomorrow afternoon ...

super: LA..   the Lakers got back on the winning track with
                           a 14 point win over Philadelphia ...

                           that win streak of one will stand for at least a
                           week, because they don't play again until next
                           Friday night at the Forum ...

                           I'll be back with more sports later ...

Anncr: The 11 O'clock report.

Super: Dunphy   With Jerry Dunphy.

Super: Keene   Bill Keene with the weather.

Super: Dunn	And Bob Dunn with sports.
Drop Effects	Once again, Jerry Dunphy.
Transport Bassett	From mothballs to a pollution problem along the Washington seacoast. .all in less than a week.
	That's the story tonight of the General W. C. Meigs.
	The Meigs was taken out of mothballs at Bremerton, Washington, on Sunday ...
	And, while being towed to Long Beach, the troop transport broke up on the rocks of Cape Flattery in northwest Washington.
	High seas have made it impossible for anyone to reach the broken hulk ... and all that can be done, is stand and watch while oil pours from the broken transport
	Here's a report from Dave Marriott from Seattle television station K-I-R-O.
VTR (1:22)	IN CUE: "So far, it's estimated ...
	OUT CUE: ... indicate it's not possible to do this.
	The Meigs was to have been outfitted and re-commissioned at Long Beach ... a sad end for a troop ship.
Lead to 1st Break	Industrial safety in California ... is it everybody's business?
	Some say no.
	That story after this.
1st Commercial Break	
INDUSTRIAL SAFETY	California's industrial safety chief is still on the job tonight ... whether or not he wants to be.
	Governor Reagan refused to accept Jack Hatton's resignation until the safety department is investigated. An assembly committee is hearing charges that the department failed to prosecute contractors who endangered their workers'

safety. But some officials say that's not the committee's job. KNXT correspondent Warren Olney reports.

FILM 2:27 col mag   SOUND UP: "California's safety experts...
DOUBLE SYSTEM
Roll both together
   Take "A" video
     "A" audio full

SUPER: XT/SACTO   At 1:11 Dissolve to "B" video
                                          Sneak "B" audio under
                                               on cue: ...to develop safe
                                                   habits on the job."

SUPER: YESTERDAY   At 1:31 Take "B" audio full
                                          "A" audio out
                                               on cue: ...what kind of a job
                                                   he's doing."

SUPER: KNAPP   At 1:59 Dissolve to "A" video
                                          Take "A" audio full
                                          "B" audio out
                                               on cue: ...an inadequate
                                                   job...all right."

At 2:27 FILM ENDS   SOUND OUT: ...Warren Olney, KNXT News, Sacramento."

MISSION PAK   Send a Mission Pak...and it's on its Merry way.. sooner or later.

                                     This year the bright packages of fruits and nuts didn't get to their destinations in time for the holidays.. it seems the company couldn't overcome a series of handicaps.

                                     But there's hope for those awaiting mission paks.. as KNXT's Bob Navarro reports.

MISSION PAK CUES

FILM 1:03 col mag   (SOUND UP: FOR MORE THAN)

DBL SYSTEM
ROLL BOTH TOGETHER
TAKE A VIDEO
    B AUDIO
    A AUDIO UNDER

SUPER COMPTON AT
TOP

AT :32 SUPER:

FILM ENDS 1:03

MISSION PAK TAG

LIVE TAG

Lead to 2nd Break

2nd Commercial Break

POVERTY FUNERAL

FILM: COL MAG POS
    (1:53)
DOUBLE SYSTEM,
ROLL BOTH
    TAKE "A" VIDEO
        "A" AUDIO
           FULL

AT :09 TAKE "B" AUDIO
        FULL
    "A" AUDIO
        UNDER

AT :37 DISSOLVE TO
    "B" VIDEO

AND SUPER: CRANDLE

("A" AUDIO CONTINUES
    UNDER)

AT 1:14 SUPER: MARTIN

AT 1:37 DISSOLVE TO
    "A" VIDEO
  TAKE "A" AUDIO FULL
  ("B" Audio Out)

NAVARRO REPORTING

(SOUND OUT: BOB NAVARRO, KNXT NEWS, COMPTON.)

An investigation by the Los Angeles District Attorney has disclosed NO fraud ... and investigators believe the candy and fruit firm is trying to live up to its commitments.

More news and Bill Keene with the weather ... when the 11 O'clock Report continues ...

Generosity ... we are told ... is rare.

But it exists at Washington High School in Los Angeles.

The students generosity made possible a simple farewell ceremony today. KNXT's Jim Brown was there.

SOUND UP: NATURAL SOUND MUSIC

(MUSIC)

(..."turned to her fellow students at Washington High School.")

(..."they came forward without question.")

AT 1:47 SLOW DISSOLVE
   TO "B" VIDEO

FILM ENDS AT 1:53   SOUND OUT: <u>MUSIC ENDS</u>

POVERTY FUNERAL/
TAG   Mrs. Rebenel Crandle was buried at Evergreen
                           Cemetary in Boyle Heights.

KING   The world's only known tattooed king died today.
                           He was Frederik the 9th of Denmark, who ruled
                           Europe's oldest monarchy for nearly 25 years.

STILL: FREDERIK   Frederik was tattooed--dragons on his chest
                           and upper arms--during his many years in the
                           navy.

                           He was a staunch believer in the Democratic
                           government, and was genuinely loved by his
                           people.

                           The King suffered a heart attack January 3rd--
                           his condition complicated by flu and pneumonia.

OFF STILL   He was 72-years-old. His eldest daughter--
                           31 year old Margrethe--takes the throne as
(mar-GRAY-the)   Denmark's second ruling queen.

Lead to weather   Dunphy ad lib to Keene

                          Keene Leads to Break

3rd Commercial Break

VIET ACTION   The North Vietnamese are developing a new. . .
                          and far more aggressive technique to counter
                          American air strikes on their country and
                          neighboring Laos.

STILL: INDO   The Communists are setting up mobile ground-
(OPEN WIDE, THEN   to-air missile sites just north of the demilitarized
ZOOM TO QUANG TRI)   zone. .using them to take pot-shots at U.S.car-
                          rier-based planes crossing northern South Viet-
                          nam enroute to Laotian targets.

                          Just south of the DMZ, Quang Tri Province is
                          bracing for an expected enemy Thet offensive
                          next month, and CBS Correspondent Phil Jones
                          reports on the preparations.

VTR (1:30 SOT)
Note this is :08 shorter   IN CUE: "Americans are working during every
than original   break. . .

OUT CUE: ...heavy tanks west of here near Khe Sanh and the Laotian border."

STILL: ABRAMS

Ready or not, the U.S. is moving out of South Vietnam.

The American commander--General Creighton Abrams--is expected to leave before June... his giant headquarters complex destined for

OFF STILL

downgrading to the status of an advisory group. ... And that's the same title it held in 1965, when the big American troop build-up began.

Lead to Sports

As we've seen. . .It was hu-ray and hallelujeh for the local basketball teams tonight. . .Here's Bob Dunn once again. . .to fill us in on the rest of today's sports action. Bob. . .

CU Dunn

As we reported earlier Jerry, UCLA, USC and the Lakers all won tonight by a wide margin. . in other NBA action:

slide Basketball
super: Mil-Chi-
           Bost-

The Milwaukee Bucks held the Chicago Bulls to fewer than 20 points in each of the 1st 3 quarters, and went on to a 104-77 rout, which is a record low point total for Chicago. . .

Dave Cowens, Eastern all-star Center scored 26 points and pulled down a career high of 28 rebounds in leading the Boston Celtics to an easy win over Detroit . . .

super: Cincy
          Port

Cincinnati beat Atlanta and Portland edged the Buffalo Braves . . .

super: Phoenix
          Golden St.
(off slides)

the Phoenix suns won from Cleveland and the Golden State Warriors beat the New York Knicks

CU Dunn

the Lakers have a full week off now before they meet the New York Knicks at the Forum next Friday night, with the exception of Jerry West, Gail Goodrich, and Wilt Chamberlain who'll be playing in Tuesday night's All star game at the Forum . . .

hockey slide:
super: Calif-

There was only one game in the National Hockey League tonight: The California Golden Seals beat Vancouver . . .

CU Dunn

for the 2nd day in a row, the weather was beautiful on the Monterey Penninsula and for the second straight day Jack Nicklaus is in the lead; but not with the same style and grace he displayed yesterday with his opening round of 66 ...

color still
Nicklaus

Jack played the tougher spyglass hill today, was 4 over par on the first 9 with a 40 then shot two under par golf on the back for a two over par 74 and a share of the lead

color slide Golf
super: scores

with Britain's Tony Jacklin who shot his second straight 70...

off slides ...

Herb Hooper is all alone at 143, and Lee Trevino is tied with 6 other pros two shots back at 143... Trevino slipped to a 74 today at Spyglass ...

CU Dunn

Dallas is favored in the Super Bowl by 5 points, even tho Calvin Hill, will not be in the starting line-up ...

the game will be seen here on KNXT at 11:30 with the pre-game show starting at 11 ... AM

and that's sports--the 11 o'clock report continues after this ...

Lead to 4th Break

Dunn Leads to Break

4th Commercial Break

ECONOMY

...A mixed bag of economic news tonight...like tea leaves...read it the way you see it.

Two major New York banks today lowered their prime interest rate from five, to four-and-three-quarters percent...an 11-year low. The sales of all retail items--including cars--are up...and the Commerce Department predicted that industrial plant expansion will skyrocket this year.

But in almost the same breath, the Commerce Department admitted it had widely overestimated last year's Gross National Product.

Last month, the wholesale price index leaped eight-tenths-of-one-percent, and consumer prices are expected to follow within weeks.

Meanwhile, the latest federal figures show a new high of 14-and-a-half million welfare recipients, but a 10 million dollar savings in their maintenance...I warned you it was a mixed bag!

RED DOG

The Red Baron may be long gone from the skies of the Western Front but Baron Red Dog is up to his muzzle in legal trouble. The Baron--a German shepherd--and his master, John Miller were busted when they were cruising down the San Bernardino Freeway on a motorcycle. The judge said the Baron was an unsafe load. Miller says the pooch is a dandy co-pilot and he wants an appeals court to allow the Baron back on the wild concrete yonder.

SUPERBOWL

If you plan to attend the Superbowl game in New Orleans this Sunday, better think it over. The city is up to here in fans ... and the only ones assured of winning are the city's businessmen, and CBS Correspondent Jed Duvall, who reports from the Queen of the Delta.

VTR:COLSOT (1:58)

SOUND UP: New Orleans' arms are open to the Superbowl, however the hotel rooms ...

at 1:58 VTR ENDS

FAST OUT

SOUND OUT: ... say the city is making a real effort to curb it. Jed Duvall, CBS News, New Orleans.

CLOSE

The fans...
And their antics...
Almost as much fun as the game itself...

That's tonight's news.

Clete Roberts will be back tomorrow evening at six, with the Big News.

Jerry Dunphy saying good night.

APPENDIX D

NBC Nightly Report (KNBC)

GOOD EVENING. There is still a chance the western dock strike will start up all over again-- even though negotiations continue.

The trees will stay along Highland in the Wilshire district.

And guess who's been visiting pals at the Lom- poke federal jail. Mayor Yorty--that's who.

Details next on KNBC News.

TOM/HARD WALL:

Good Evening . . .
The newspaper . . . the Wash Post . . . reported tonight that the Teamsters and west coast long- shoremens unions have agreed to merge. The Post said a letter to that intent was signed in Washington today by Frank Fitzsimmons of the Teamsters, and President Harry Bridges of the dock worker's union.

The two unions have been engaged in a jurisdic- tional dispute over the handling of containerized cargo in the west . . . A merger could help to settle that point.

TOM & VIZ:
"SHIP BACKGROUND"

New negotiations aimed at preventing resumption

435

SUPER: of the West Coast dock <u>strike begin</u> tomorrow in
"DOCK STRIKE?"   San Francisco. The longshore labor dispute be-
                                gan early last year, and has outlasted a one-
                                hundred day-strike and an 80-day Taft-Hartley
                                back-to-work injunction. The possibility of a
                                new strike is affecting work in western ports,
                                and Channel 4 reporter Bill Windsor has more
                                on why.

                                        (FILM NEXT) (SOT)

LONGSHOREMEN

16 CLR POS
INTERLOCK
SOT 2:06   SOT 2:06

MATTES: 4 L.A. HAR-
BOR (U/3)
(at top of SOT)

KNBC REPORTER
BILL WINDSOR
(at :10 into SOT)   END: "... Bill Windsor, KNBC News, Los
                                Angeles Harbor"

HARD WALL
LIVE TOM   Economists tidied up their books for 1971 today. .
                                and some of the figures for the final months of
                                the year are not encouraging.

                                But bureaucrats ... in their own special way ...
                                can find some good in everything ... even in a
                                rise in the Wholesale Price Index.

                                        (TO VTR-SOUND)

PRICES
VTR-SOUND   VTR SOUND for 1:27
                                ENDS: "... NBC News, Washington."

HARD WALL
LIVE TOM   And next on the Newservice ... that interesting
                                guest book at Lompoc.

                                        (TO COMM'L)

"LOMPOC"
TOM/VIZ MAP: That investigation into alleged special treatment
                                given certain inmates at the federal prison at
SUPER: LOMPOC   Lompoc has resulted in the suspension of two
                                employees at the facility. Two prominent pris-

oners are said to be involved in the investigation. .
John Allesio and Maurice Friedman. Allesio ...
the former head of the Caliente Race-track in
Tijuana . . . is in jail for income-tax evasion.

Friedman was sentenced in the Friars Club gin
rummy cheating case.

The investigation at the Lompoc prison involves
unauthorized leaves for prisoners ... in exchange
for gifts to the employees.

(FILM NEXT) (BG-v/o)

16 CLR POS
INTERLOCK
BG :26 v/o
SOT :55

MATTE: 4 LOMPOC
(U/3)
(at top of BG)

There are two parts to the Lompoc institution.
The main prison is a high security facility ...
with guard towers, barbed wire and bars. It
contains longer-term prisoners. There is a
separate prison camp at Lompoc. It has no
bars . . . very liberal visitation rules . . . and is
in general, less of a prison. It is in this camp
where the irregularities occurred. Warden F.F.
Kenton admitted that much to reporter Warren
Wilson ... but he would not comment further.

SOT :55

MATTE: F.F. KENTON
(at top of SOT)

END: "... the answer is no comment."

TOM/HARD WALL:

MATTE:
"SNYDER"

A source said today that inmate Allesio had been
visited by Mayor Sam Yorty, San Diego millionaire C. Arnholt Smith and others during his in-
carceration.

Mayor Sam admitted he had visited Allesio in
Lompoc last May 28th. Yorty said the two are
long-time friends, and that the visit had nothing
to do with politics.

VIZ CHROME
"A. Davis"
LIVE TOM

Two developments in the Angela Davis case
today. A U.S. district court judge in San Francisco denied Miss Davis' appeal for bail in her
murder-kidnap case.

About the same time in San Jose, Miss Davis'

chief attorney announced that the Angela Davis
Defense Fund is penniless ... and that the state
ought to pay for her defense.

TOM & HARD WALL

Conservationists on Highland Avenue in the
Wilshire District won a reprieve this week when
the city delayed a plan to cut-down some stately
palm trees there. However, the tree lovers in
East Los Angeles have not been so fortunate.
The story from Channel 4 reporter Joe Ramirez.

(FILM NEXT, SOT)

TREE PROTEST

16 CLR/POS
INTERLOCK

SOT for 1:53

MATTES:

4 EAST LOS ANGELES
(TOP)

REPORTER JOE
RAMIREZ
(:21 IN)

ALEXANDER MANN
(:40 IN)

ENDS: "... KNBC NEWS, EAST LOS ANGELES."

HARD
WALL
TOM

The Los Angeles Harbor Department closed the
Wilmington Marina today because owners had
fallen behind in rent payments to the city. The
closure had been anticipated by boat owners,
but still many were left without any place to
moor their boats.

3-SHOT
LIVE TOM

Ross Porter and the sports report anon; Kelly
Lange and the weather a little later on.

(TO COMM'L)

LEDE SPORTS

2-SHOT
LIVE TOM for :10 (Ad Lib)

ROSS LIVE

Los Angeles' Big Three of basketball registered impressive victories on the second Friday night of the year.

(TURN. .VIZ-CHART. .USC-Cal score/VIZ)

VIZ-CHART
USC-Cal
score/VIZ
Basketball

Southern Cal returned home after seven straight road games ... and blasted Cal to make its Pacific Eight mark 3 and 0.

USC hit 67% from the field in the first half, built a 60-37 bulge, and coasted. Six men were in double figures, topped by Joe Mackey's 19 and 18 for Paul Westphal.

The Trojans have copped 10 of 12 so far.

VIZ-CHART
UCLA-Stanford
score/VIZ

UCLA posted its 11th consecutive win this season and 26th in a row since last year, fracturing Stanford's five-game win string. The Bruins connected on 17 of their first 25 shots and went on to deal the Indians their first league defeat.

Bill Walton and Henry Bibby tallied 24 of UCLA's initial 28 points ... scoring 12 apiece.

TO FILM

UCLA
16 POS OLR
BG

With two minutes gone. .Walton's lay-in put the Bruins ahead to stay, 6-4. He also hit UCLA's next six points.

Bibby then warmed up. .sinking five baskets in four minutes.

By halftime. .Bibby had made six of seven from the field ...

The 6-11 Walton, only a sophmore, took 12 shots in the decisive first half. .and missed only two.

During the first half. .UCLA sank 28 of 41 tries for a blistering 68 percent and at one time, Walton had outscored the Indians, 18-17 ... It was 59-35 at intermission.

ROSS LIVE

Walton wound up with 32 in only 28 minutes and Bibby had 22. The Bruins and Cal play here at 2:40 tomorrow before the Trojans and Stanford at 8.

UC Riverside's Sam Cash set a school record
with 28 rebounds ... in a 109-92 win over Cal
State Fullerton ...

Washington downed Cincinnati, 91-81.

The Lakers have now won 41 of 46 games.

VIZ-CHART
Lakers-76ers/
VIZ-H/T Laker Action

After trailing early by 13 in Philadelphia, Los
Angeles stormed back and the starters had at
least 8 field goals each. Wilt Chamberlain did
everything but take tickets. .He scored 23 points,
grabbed 20 rebounds, blocked 7 shots and lifted
Kevin Lockery off the court when he had a fight
with Gail Goodrich.

(TURN. .back to Ross)

ROSS LIVE

Milwaukee held Chicago to 33 points in the first
half, 77 in the game, and won by 27. Golden
State nipped New York by 4. .Phoenix drilled
Cleveland by 10. .Boston tripped Detroit by 14. .
Cincinnati clubbed Atlanta by 24. .and Portland
nudged Buffalo by 2.

Compton's Reynaldo Brown tonight became the
first American high jumper to clear 7-feet 4
inches indoors. .He beat world record-holder
Pat Matzdorf, who leaped 7-1 at College Park,
Maryland. Kip Keino won the mile in 3:59/4.

Tony Jacklin of England is tied with Jack Nicklaus after 36 holes at the Crosby pro-am golf
tourney.

(TURN. .VIZ-CHART. .Crosby/VIZ-Golf)

VIZ-CHART
Crosby/VIZ
Golf

Jacklin shot a 70 at Spyglass Hill today while
Nicklaus took a 74 on the same course, 40 on
his first nine. Jacklin had two three-putt greens
and Nicklaus birdied four of the par five holes
to make it close. .Herb Hooper of Richmond,
Virginia is one back after firing a course record
68 at Spyglass. Lee Trevino is one of seven at
143, while Al Geiberger leads the Southern
California contingent with a 144. Dave Stockton
has 146.

VIZ-CHART
Tomorrow on KNBC

You can see the third round of the Crosby tomorrow at 1:30 on channel 4, immediately following our KNBC High school Game of the Week between unbeaten Jefferson and Manual Arts.

(TURN..back to Ross)

ROSS LIVE

On the ice tonight ... California beat Vancouver, 5 to 3 in the NHL ...

Terry Kubicka of Cypress has captured his second consecutive junior mens' title in the U.S. figure skating championships at Long Beach ... Wendy Burge of Tarzana is the leader in junior girls.. and Janet Lynn of Rockford, Illinois has just won her 4th straight womens title.

A graduate of Los Angeles Roosevelt high school, A-TOY Wilson, is the first black man to be featured in pro skating. Wilson, who is performing at the Forum, told KNBC sports reporter Tom Hawkins it's not an ego trip for him.

TO FILM

ICE SKATING
16 POS CLR
MATTE Atoy
Wilson at :03

SOT: :53

ENDS.."takes a little money to train.."

ROSS LIVE (VIZ-CHROME..Super Bowl Trophy)

VIZ-CHROME
Super Bowl Trophy

It's 36 hours and 15 minutes until the Super Bowl ... Although Calvin Hill won't start in the backfield..I like the Cowboys over the Dolphins, either 14-10 or 17-10 ... Dallas' defensive line may be the difference.

VIZ-CHROME
Pepper
Rodgers

UCLA football coach Pepper Rodgers has visited the Oklahoma coaches in Norman and plans to install the Wishbone T next fall ...

(TURN..back to Ross)

ROSS LIVE

NCAA tennis champion Jimmy Connors of UCLA has turned pro

STREET DANCER paid 7.20 in the Santa Anita feature

and Joe Frazier should maul Terry Daniels to-

morrow night in their heavyweight mismatch..
That's sports..have a nice weekend ... Tom?

WALL
LIVE TOM

Thanks Ross.
Still to come ... Kelly Lange and the weekend
weather outlook.

(TO COMM'L)

KELLY
VIZ
LOCAL
MAP:
REVEAL

Tom, the weekend's going to be absolutely trop-
ical for mid January ... Today's hi was 69 downtown ... tmrw and Sun. we expect 80. Orange
county cities'll get up around 78 tmrw. The
valleys should reach 80. Beach highs'll be 70
in the air & 54 in the water with gusty winds off
shore ... small craft warnings are up from
Ventura County to Malibu. Even the mountains'll
be warm ... the snow's melting fast ... it'll
get up near 60 at mountain resorts. The desert
highs'll range from 67 in Plmdale to 77 in the
low deserts & Palm Springs.

VIZ
DESERTS:
WIPE

If you're going to the deserts, there's a couple
of things going on you don't want to miss. On top
of the Palm Springs Tramway, they're having
the annual dog sled races tmrw..24 dog teams
will race along a one-mile course..It starts at
noon..they've got a foot of snow up there, and
it'll be about 40 degrees at race time. And to
show you we have a little something for everybody here in So. Calif ... if you happen to be a
nut for barbed wire ... Up in Ridgecrest tmrw..
the Calif. Barbed Wire Collectors Assoc. is
having a show..all day tmrw from 9 to 5, they'll
exhibit antique barbed wire. It's at Burrough's
Hi School in Ridgecrest ... it'll be sunny up there
with a high of 66 tmrw.

VIZ
NAT'L
MAP:
REVEAL

In contrast to our warm wx, one of the severest
artic cold waves in many yrs hit most of the
country today. In N. Dakota & Minnesota, the
highs today were mostly 20 below zero or colder,
and they got highs below 10 degrees as far south
as the Texas Panhandle. The cold caused a
really freak wx phenomenon in Lake Mich ...
As the below zero air passed over the warm
water in the lake ... 12 giant waterspouts sprang
up. The coldest spot in the country was Int'l
Falls, Minnesota, with a low of 42 below zero.
In the west & south it was warm..the hot spot

was Orlando, Fla with a high of 86. Tmrw will
be pretty much the same ... bitter cold in most
of the country and very warm in the south and
west.

FORECAST:
WIPE
And we fall in the warm zone I'm pleased to say..
as high as 80 degrees expected downtown and in
the valleys over the weekend. We'll have more
fog at nite, burning off by mid mornings, then
sunshine all day both Sat. & Sun. We're into a
mild Santa Ana condition ... we've got winds to
35 mph below the cyns thru tmrw, & a moderate
buildup of smog in the basin.

TOM & HARD
WALL
Thanks Kelly--
The United States is prepared to launch its first
space probe of the planet Jupiter. We get the
story from NBC News correspondent Roy Neal.

(FILM NEXT, SOT)

JUPITER
SOT for 1:59

16 CLR POS
INTERLOCK

MATTES:
4 REDONDO BEACH
(TOP)

REPORTER ROY NEAL
(:22 IN)

CHARLES HALL
PROJECT MANAGER
(1:19 IN)
ENDS: "... ROY NEAL, NBC NEWS."

(To Com'l)

TOM & HARD WALL
A blind boy, who was allowed to inspect a sculpture exhibit by touching it, has suggested a similar experience be made available to people who
have sight.

(FILM NEXT, V/O)

BLINDFOLDS

16 CLR/POS
INTERLOCK
V/O BG :19
MATTE: (TOP)
4 SACRAMENTO
This week, a special exhibit in Crocker Art
Gallery in Sacramento afforded normal youngsters a chance to personally inspect works-of-
sculpture. Recorded messages explained how
sculpture reflects man's changing image of himself. Then, instead of saying "hands off," the
gallery allowed visitors free rein.

SOT for :57

ENDS: "...the last one, the last one here, you see."

3-SHOT
LIVE TOM

That's the news. Tom Snyder for Ross Porter, Kelly Lange and all the people at KNBC News: Have a nice weekend.

(TO VIZ CRAWL)
& THEME

GLOSSARY

A ROLL: One of two film clips in a double chain. The A roll may carry narration while the B roll carries most of the picture, or vice versa.

A-WIRE. The AP and UPI teletype services which emphasize world and national news; the primary news wire.

ACADEMY LEADER: Film numbered in reverse from 10 to 1 or 5 to 1, used at the start of a film clip, or in a roll-thru of 10 seconds or longer. The numbers guide the projectionist and the director.

ADD: An addition to a story.

AD LIB: Unscripted, spur-of-the-moment comment.

AFFILIATE: A station, not owned by a network, which contracts to take the network's programs.

AIR CHECK: The videotape recording of a television program or one performer's work, or the audio taping of a radio program.

AIR TIME: The time scheduled for a broadcast to start.

AMTEC: See PIXLOCK.

ANALYST: One who explains the meaning of a news event and considers its consequences.

ANGLE: In news writing, the approach to a story.

AUDIO: Sound; the sound portion of a broadcast.

BG: (abbr.) Background.

B ROLL: See A ROLL.

B & W: (abbr.) Black and white; that is, not in color.

B-WIRE: The AP and UPI services emphasizing features and reports in depth; a supplementary service to the A-wire.

BACK-TIMING: Timing to a closing segment whose length is known. A script is back-timed to give it a strong, clean ending. Weaknesses of filling and stretching occur in the middle of the newscast, where they are less obvious.

BARN DOORS: Metal shades used to block light emission.

BEAT: (noun)
1. The reporting of a story ahead of the competition.
2. The list of places a reporter is assigned to cover, usually daily.

BEEPER: A telephone interview recorded on audio tape. The interview usually comes over a special telephone circuit which emits a regular beep sound to inform the parties to the conversation that they are being recorded.

BILLBOARD: In broadcast news, all the headlines at the start of a newscast.

BLACK: A blank screen (which actually appears mid-gray on a receiver).

BLOOP: Erase, or "wipe" sound from a magnetic track with a magnet.

BLURB: A publicity release (derogatory).

BOOTH ANNOUNCER: A television announcer who speaks from a small booth, heard but not seen.

BREAK: In reporting, a new development in a running (continuing) story.

BRIDGE: In a newscast, a few words tying one element of news to another. (In broadcasting generally, the musical bridge is better known.)

BRITE: See KICKER.

BROADCAST WIRE: See RADIO WIRE.

BUDGET: (noun)
1. The sum allocated for running a news department, for covering a special news event, or for producing a special program.
2. A listing of news stories a wire service plans to transmit.

BULLETIN: Important late news.
1. Teletype copy introduced by the word "bulletin."
2. News read on the air over a bulletin slide.

BUSY: Crammed with detail.

BUTT END: (verb) To splice one piece of film directly to another; the term often refers to the splicing of film of one speaker directly after another.

CAMERA CHAIN: A television camera, its camera control unit and its power supply.

CHROMA: (abbr.) Chromakey, a process which places an electronic image on a screen behind the newscaster. The image may be a live remote, a still, film or videotape.

CLIP (or FILM CLIP): An edited film story.

CLOSE-UP: Framing which, roughly speaking, includes just the head, or head and shoulders, or an object seen at close range.

CLOSING (or CLOSE): The standard concluding segment of a newscast according to format.

COLLAGE: In a newscast, several photos, newspaper headlines or printed stories pasted onto a card.

COMMENTATOR: One who gives his own views of news events, especially political and international news events. See ANALYST, EDITORIALIST.

CONTINUITY: Non-news copy; e.g., commercial, promo, or station break copy.

COPY: News printed or typed. WIRE COPY is teletype news. HARD COPY refers to complete news items on paper, as distinct from LEAD-IN COPY or FILM COPY, both written for use with other elements.

COVER SHOT: See ESTABLISHING SHOT.

CRAWL: A display of words in a single line moving horizontally across a screen without interrupting regular programming. Also, the mechanical device which moves the display either horizontally (for a "crawl") or vertically (for a "roll.")

CREEPIE PEEPIE: A portable black and white video camera. (See HAND-HELD).

CROPPING: Trimming a still to a ratio of 3 units of height by 4 units of width to match the aspect ratio of a television screen.

CROSSFADE: To change sources of sound by steadily lowering the volume of the outgoing sound while raising the volume of the incoming sound.

CROSSING THE LINE: Changing directional relationship on film.

CU (abbr.): Close-up.

CUE: In a newscast, a hand signal by the stage manager to the newscaster. Common cues are those to begin, slow down, speed up, or conclude in a certain number of seconds; e.g., one index finger upraised means one minute left, both index fingers crossed in a "t" means 30 seconds, a fist means 15 seconds, all 10 fingers held up means 10 seconds left.

CUE PUNCH: A spot mechanically scraped onto each corner of several frames of film as a warning that the film is about to end.

CUT: 1. (noun) A recorded segment of a record or an audio tape.
2. (verb) To end sharply, usually at a precise time or at the conclusion of a news item. In a studio the cut signal is a finger drawn across the throat, meaning "End it right now."

CUTAWAY: A short piece of film placed between two scenes of the same person or locale. The cutaway shows something other than the persons or places in either scene.

DEAD AIR: Silence, due to error, in a broadcast.

DEADLINE: That moment before each newscast when all copy and film should be prepared. The copy deadline and the film deadline may come at different times. Deadlines are ignored for bulletins.

DEGAUSS: Demagnetize. See BLOOP.

DISSOLVE: A smooth exchange of one image for another.

DOLLY: 1. A movable camera platform.

2. A shot taken from such a platform, or its equivalent, while moving to or from the subject.

DOPE SHEET: The paper on which a cameraman writes story and film information; e.g., names of crew members, story location, total film footage, developing instructions, etc. Also called POOP SHEET, SPOT SHEET, SHOT CARD, etc.

DOUBLE CHAIN: 1. (noun) A film story using two reels of film (designated A Roll and B Roll) going through two projectors simultaneously. The studio's switching equipment, controlled by the technical director, determines which picture and which sound is fed at any moment.

2. (verb) Use two film chains.

DOUBLE SYSTEM: Separation of sound and picture in filming, using a camera synchronized to a recording device.

DUB: 1. (noun) A duplicate of film, videotape, or audio tape.

2. (verb) Make such a transfer; re-record.

EDITEC: The Ampex electronic editor.

EDITORIALIST: One who expresses opinions, usually those of station management, about news events, local conditions and pending legislation. See COMMENTATOR.

END CUE: See OUT CUE.

ESTABLISH SOUND: An instruction to play a sound track at full volume (usually for about 5 seconds) before lowering the volume, often to the level of background sound.

ESTABLISHING SHOT: A camera view of the entire scene.

ET: (abbr.) Electrical transcription, meaning a phonograph record.

ETA: (abbr.) Estimated time of arrival.

FADE (or FADE TO BLACK): The electronic equivalent of a film fade out. A dissolve from a picture to darkness, which is a mid-gray rather than black.

FCC: (abbr.) The Federal Communications Commission. Among other responsibilities, it issues and renews television and radio station licenses.

FEATURE: A human interest story whose news value is not necessarily limited to the day of its occurrence, as distinct from HARD NEWS.

FEED: 1. (noun) A news story or an entire program electronically transmitted to other stations or broadcast to the public.

2. (verb) Broadcast or transmit.

FEEDBACK: The whine caused by loudspeaker output being picked up by a microphone feeding the loudspeaker. This sound circle is broken by separating mike and loudspeaker.

FILL: 1. (noun) A light used to fill shadows.

2. (verb) Read pad copy to fill a time gap.

FILM CLIP: See CLIP.

FLOP: A card, placed on a stand, to be viewed through a studio camera.

FLUFF: An on-air verbal error, such as a mispronunciation.

FORMAT: In television, the framework of a program (independent of content).

FREEZE FRAME: A frame of film or videotape, to or from which action flows; arrested motion.

FREZZI: A type of portable light.

FUTURE FILE: Also called FUTURE(S) BOOK, DATEBOOK, AD-VANCE FOLDER, etc. A file of upcoming events, divided into 31 days.

GAFFER: A member of some film crews who is responsible for lighting.

GAIN: Audio volume. To RIDE GAIN is to adjust volume as needed during recording.

GOOF: An on-air technical error. Also referred to in less polite terms.

GRAPHICS: Any fixed, two-dimensional representations such as photos, maps, graphs, cartoons and super cards. A subset of the term "visuals" (film, videotape and props are considered visuals, but not graphics).

HAND-HELD: A portable color video camera.

HANDOUT: Free film or copy (a printed news release) mailed or hand delivered, issued by a private company, an organization, a government agency, a political candidate, etc., or a public relations agency or film company acting as agent.

HARD NEWS: Reports of current events which are of interest because of their timeliness and general importance or violence (as in crimes and accidents). Feature stories are not hard news.

HEAD SHOT: A still photo of a person's head or head and shoulders.

HEADLINE: In broadcast news, a phrase or short sentence at the start of a newscast summarizing a story.

HIGH ANGLE SHOT: An above-eye-level view, often filmed by standing on a ladder or furniture.

HIGH BAND: A frequency range used mainly for color transmission.

IN CUE: The place where a newsfilm segment is to start, a start cue. Sometimes, the first words of a statement.

INTEGRATED FORMAT: The inter-relating of newscaster(s), weatherman, sports reporter, commentator, and field reporters doing studio reports. The studio set, the introductions, and occasional chatter give the newscast a mood of relaxed informality.

INTRO: 1. (noun) Introduction; introductory copy to film or tape.
2. (verb) Introduce.

JIGGLE: Derogatory term for activity shown on the screen instead of a newscaster reading the news.

JUMP CUT: A direct cut on film to the same person or scene.

KEY LIGHT: The main light.

KICKER: A short, humorous news item at the end of the newscast. Also called a TAG, a BRITE, or a ZIPPER.

LEAD: A fresh introduction to a story, as in NEW LEAD. Also, the first sentence or two of a news story.

LEAD STORY: The first story in the newscast.

LEADER: Film placed at the head or tail of a film clip for threading through a projector, or in the middle of a film clip where a roll-thru is needed. Leader may be numbered, clear or blank, black or yellow.

LIMBO BOARD: A graphics display (e.g., showing election returns in a particular race) which is not part of the set. It exists "in limbo." To show it, the director usually "breaks" a camera from the set.

LINE-UP: Arrangement of items in a newscast.

LIP FLAP: The result of cutting a film of a speaker to begin in mid-speech, so that his lips are seen moving before he is heard.

LIP SYNC: Synchronized speech, with picture and sound matching frame for frame.

LIVE: 1. On-the-air. A live mike is broadcasting sound.
2. In transmission, immediate, as contrasted with the delay of film and tape.

LOCAL NEWS: News of the city in which the television station lies, and its environs; sometimes, by definition, anything covered by the station's own news staff, or any news occurring within the station's reception range is considered "local."

LOGO: The identifying symbol of the newscast, usually on a slide.

LONG LENS: See TELEPHOTO LENS.

LONG SHOT: Framing which takes in the scene of an event.

LOOSE SHOT: A view which leaves lots of space, or "air," around the subject.

LOW ANGLE SHOT: A below-eye-level view, often filmed from a crouching position.

LS: (abbr.) Long shot.

MAG: (abbr.) Magnetic sound track film; a magnetic stripe on the base side of film, used to carry the sound. Also called MAG STRIPE or MAGNETIC STRIPE.

MAG HEAD: The device on a projector, a sound reader or an editing machine which plays back or "reads" the sound track of magnetic striped film.

MAGAZINE FORMAT: Development of a newscast with several long stories each day, instead of many short news items. Also distinguished from the segmented format, in which local news, sports, etc. are totally separated and sometimes individually sponsored.

MEDIA: The plural form of medium, or means, of transmitting information. Media include television, radio, motion pictures, newspapers, magazines and books.

MEDIUM SHOT: Framing which roughly encompasses anything from head to waist of one or two persons to the framing of three or four people seated at a table, or the equivalent.

MONITOR: 1. (noun) A television or radio receiver.

               2. (verb) In radio, to listen, and in television, to watch and listen, taking notes, often of subject matter and running times.

MONTAGE: In television news, a rapid succession of moving or still pictures assembled to create an overall effect.

MOS: (abbr.) Man-on-street. The interviewing of average citizens for short responses to a question; the interviews can take place any-where. By extension, "MOS" is sometimes also used to define the editing of a film to get several very brief comments on a subject, no matter what the sources of the film are.

MOVE: Transmit copy or pictures by wire.

MS: (abbr.) Medium shot.

NEG: (abbr.) Negative image film.

N.E.S.: (abbr.) News Election Service, the pool which gathers election returns.

NETWORK: Any interlinked group of stations; usually refers to CBS, NBC, ABC, or, in radio only, Mutual, which are corporations providing programming for O & O and affiliate stations.

NEWS WIRE: A news-by-teletype service.

NON-EXCLUSIVE: Refers to identical film clips, prints offered equally to competing newscasts.

NON-STANDARD FILM: Film having the emulsion on the reverse side of the base, compared with the most commonly used film.

O & O: (abbr.) Owned-and-operated; refers to stations owned and operated by networks.

O/C: (abbr.) On camera; a symbol typed in a script to indicate when the newscaster should be seen. The newscaster's name often replaces this symbol.

OPENING (or OPEN used as a noun): The elements which begin a newscast; by definition, the opening may refer to the standard daily announcement with music, film, sound effects, etc., but not head-lines or tease, if any.

OPTICAL: Optical track sound film; sometimes abbreviated in a script as OPT or OP.

OUT CUE: The place where a newsfilm segment is to end; the last words to be included in a statement.

OVERLAP: A splice which causes the sound track at the end of one seg-ment of film to appear with the start of the following segment's picture.

PAD COPY: News stories not expected to be aired, but available if needed. Pad is usually "pinned up" (i.e., stapled to 8½" x 11" sheets for ease of handling) wire copy. The stories are unrelated to other items in the newscast.

PAN: 1. (verb) Camera movement horizontally or vertically (tilting) from a fixed position.

2. (noun) Film resulting from such a movement.

PATCH: A connection between two pieces of electronic equipment, directly or by means of a patch board.

PHOTOFAX: The Associated Press picture-by-wire service.

PIC: (abbr.) Still picture.

PIXLOCK: A feature on some RCA videotape machine which permits dissolves into and out of tape (e.g., from a still to tape, then tape to film). AMTEC, sometimes referred to as "fully automatic," is a similar feature on Ampex machines.

PLUG: Free advertisement; e.g., mentioning a product or a new motion picture in a news story.

POLARITY CHANGE: Electronic reversal of negative and positive images.

POOL: The combination of competing news media to achieve a particular result; e.g., several television stations in the same city agreeing to dub and share a single videotape, or the three major networks sharing cameras and personnel to cover the presidential inauguration.

POP ZOOM: A fast zoom in from a long shot to a close-up.

POS: (abbr.) Positive film image. Dark objects appear dark on film, etc.

POT: (abbr.) Potentiometer; the volume control dial.

PROMO: A "house" commercial, advertising an upcoming program.

PROP: In news, a three-dimensional object which is part of a story or gives credence to a locale.

PROTECTION SHOT: A filmed scene of a changing news event. The cameraman shoots this scene when he arrives to be sure he has something "in the camera."

PUBLIC SERVICE ANNOUNCEMENT: PSA. An unpaid "commercial" for a non-profit cause; e.g., the anti-smoking spots.

PULL-TAB: A drawing, usually a map, with a movable portion which is physically pulled on camera to expose what lies beneath it.

PUNCH (or PUNCH UP): To cut to, electronically, in the studio.

QUARTER-INCH TAPE: Audio tape.

RADIO WIRE: A teletype service largely of news summaries written in broadcast style.

READY: A warning the director gives to the technical director and other studio personnel that a command is imminent; e.g., "Ready camera one" warns that the next command for a camera change will be a cut or dissolve to number one camera.

REAR PROJECTION: A slide process which places a visual on a screen behind the newscaster. The rear projection, or RP, slide may be a still photo, map, graph, cartoon, or a film, if proper equipment has been installed.

RECAP: 1. (noun) A news summary in headline form at the end of the newscast, or the summary of the main elements of a long story.

2. (verb) To summarize news.

REGIONAL SPLIT: A specified period (e.g., 10 minutes each hour on the half hour) set aside by wire services for regional news. Usually, the New York offices of the wire services relinquish control to their bureaus in the major cities. Only specified teletype lines are permitted splits from the trunk service.

REVERSAL FILM: Motion picture film which develops as a positive print. Most news color film is reversal.

REVERSE: A camera shot approximately 180 degrees from the preceding shot; an opposite angle shot; e.g., each of two people talking face to face.

RIP AND READ: A somewhat derogatory term describing the practice on some newscasts, especially radio newscasts, of simply reading the latest news summary torn from the radio wire, without rewriting or incorporating local stories.

ROLL: 1. (verb) To film, or tape; an order to start a camera or tape machine.

2. (noun) A spool of film; a reel.

ROLL-THRU: Film not meant to be aired, spliced into a film clip so that the clip may continue rolling through a projector at a known speed. Blank or black leader is often used. Just before the roll-thru goes past the projector film gate, the director "takes" another film chain, a camera on the newscaster, etc.

ROUGH CUT: A preliminary editing of film.

RTNDA: (abbr.) The Radio and Television News Directors Association.

RP: (abbr.) Rear projection.

RUNNING STORY: A story of continuing interest as new developments occur day after day.

RUNNING TIME: The time, in minutes and seconds, from the start of a program or segment. Monitoring normally includes a log of running time.

SCOOP: 1. A photoflood, used as a main light source.

2. (noun) A story reported before the competition reports it. Also called a "beat."

3. (verb) To report a story first.

SCREEN: To view film or videotape.

SCRIPT: In television news, the arranged collection of news stories, together with open, close and leads to commercials.

SECS: (abbr.) Seconds.

SEGUE: See CROSSFADE.

SHOOT: To film.

SHOT: A film scene.

SHOW: A newscast.

SIL: (abbr.) Silent.

SINGLE SYSTEM: Filming sound and picture on the same film using a sound camera. Most television news sound film is single system.

SLANT: The approach to a story, usually (but not always) from a political standpoint. See also ANGLE. A slanted news story is one written from a political bias.

SLIDE: A transparency shown with a slide projector, either through a film chain, a separate projector chain, or as a rear projection.

SLOT: 1. (verb) Place in a newscast; e.g., "slotting" a story to follow a commercial.

    2. (noun) The position of a story or commercial.

    3. (noun) The position of the chief desk editor (more common to newspapers than to broadcast newsrooms).

SLUG: 1. (noun) A length of leader film serving as a spacer in a double chain film clip.

    2. (noun) An identifying name for a news story.

    3. (verb) Label.

SOF: (abbr.) Sound-on-film.

SOT: (abbr.) Sound-on-tape.

SOUND BITE: A sound-on-film statement.

SOUND CREW: Basically, a cameraman and a soundman. In some union jurisdictions a lighting man (called an electrician or a gaffer) and/or an assistant cameraman are part of the crew. A reporter and/or a producer may accompany them, but are not considered part of the crew. See also TEAM.

SOUND-ON-FILM: Film carrying its own sound track.

SOUND UNDER: An audio level which permits background sounds to be heard, but not so loudly that they interfere with the newscaster or reporter.

SOUP: 1. (verb) To develop film.

    2. (noun) Developing chemicals in the tank.

SPLICE: 1. (verb) To connect two pieces of film or tape.

    2. (noun) The connection.

SPLIT SCREEN: Two images, not superimposed, sharing the screen.

SPOT: A commercial. DOUBLE SPOTTING and TRIPLE SPOTTING are the assigning of two or three commercials back-to-back.

SPOT SHEET: Record of what was filmed.

STANDUPPER: A report at the scene of an event, with the camera focused on the reporter.

STILL: A photograph; may also refer to a map or drawing.

STRETCHING: Reading slowly to fill a time gap.

STRINGER: In television news, a free lance cameraman.

STUDIO CARD: A still that is shot with a studio camera, not transmitted through a projector.

SUPER (or SUPER CARD): (abbr.) Superimposition. White lettering on a black card. A television camera picks up only the white. When this image is combined electronically with another image on film or tape, or a live scene, the lettering identifies person, place or time.

SUSTAINING: Unsponsored.

SWISH PAN: A very rapid, blurred pan indicating a change of scene.

SYNC: (abbr.) Synchronous, synchronize or synchronization. The frame-for-frame matching of sound and picture. OUT OF SYNC: Inexact union of sound and picture, often due to the length of a film loop in a projector.

TAG: See KICKER.

TAKE: 1. (noun) A film or taped scene.
2. (verb) An order from the director to the technical director to cut to a certain camera or film chain. The take is an immediate cut, not a dissolve.

TEAM: Loosely, all personnel sent to cover a story.

TEASE: A headline or bit of news before the station break preceding the newscast. Also, an announcement of an upcoming news item.

TELEPHOTO LENS: A long lens, with a narrow angle of view and a long focal length.

TELOP: A device to project the image of an opaque still into a television chain.

THEME: Identifying music at the start and/or finish of a program.

THROWAWAY PHRASE: A few words delivered quickly and casually in an offhand manner.

TIGHT SHOT: Framing with little or no space around the central figure(s) or feature(s); usually a close-up.

TIMING: Noting the length of time of each story or segment and its running time (how far into the newscast each story begins and ends).

TITLE CARD: A card naming a story, sometimes used to begin a feature. Besides a title, the card may be illustrated with a design, a cartoon or a photograph.

TRACKING: Adjusting the head-to-capstan distance of a videotape machine.

TRUCK: In television news, to film while walking or riding. Also, camera movement parallel to the subject.

TWO SHOT: Camera framing of two persons.

UHF: Ultra High Frequency, the range in which a small but growing number of commercial and educational television stations transmit.

UNIFAX: The United Press International picture-by-wire service.

UP-CUT: A loss of words at the start of film or tape. A newscaster's delivery is also up-cut if his microphone is cut in after he begins a sentence.

UPDATE: A new version of a story, requiring a change in script or, if a network newscast has been received on tape for later playback, a fresh story exactly timed to lay over the old story on the playback.

"UP ON ONE" (or TWO, etc.): An order by the director to the technical director to fade into the scene on number one camera.

VHF: Very High Frequency, the range in which most commercial television stations broadcast.

VIDEO: 1. Television.

2. The pictorial portion of a broadcast.

VISUAL: Anything seen on the television screen.

VIZ: (abbr.) Vizmo, a rear projection process.

VO: (abbr.) Voice over.

VOICE OVER: Speech by a newscaster or announcer over film or cards.

VTR: (abbr.) Videotape recording.

WAYBILL: A freight ticket with an identifying number, address and statement of contents. When film is shipped (by plane) the sender must phone or wire the receiver to tell him the waybill number, the flight number and the estimated time of arrival (ETA).

WHITE NOISE: (sometimes called just NOISE) Undifferentiated background sound of all frequencies; static.

WIDE-ANGLE LENS: A lens with a wide angle of view and a short focal length.

WILD TRACK: Background sound recorded at the scene of an event by tape recorder or sound camera. The sound is not recorded to match any particular scene or to provide lip sync.

WIRE: See NEWS WIRE.

WRAP (or WRAP-UP): 1. (noun) Conclusion.

2. (verb) Finish.

WRAPAROUND: Copy with a lead into SOF and a tag or further copy after the SOF.

WOODSHED: To practice reading copy before the newscast.

ZIPPER: See KICKER.

ZOOM: 1. (noun) A variable focus lens.

2. (verb) Alter framing while filming by means of a zoom lens.

REFERENCE NOTES

PREFACE

1 Address to Midwest Regional Republican Committee, November 13, 1969.
2 Survey by Prof. Walter DeVries, University of Michigan, reported in *RTNDA Communicator,* January, 1971, p. 6.
3 Survey taken January, 1971, by The Roper Organization, Inc.
4 Research by Andrew A. Stern, University of California, Berkeley, 1971.
5 Lecture, Memphis State University, April 23, 1969.
6 *Broadcasting and the News.* New York: Harper & Row, 1965, pp. 46-47.

CHAPTER 1: THE TROUBLES WE'VE SEEN

1 "Troubled Reflections of a TV Journalist," *Encounter,* May, 1970.
2 *Look,* November 17, 1970.
3 Robert Ardrey, "The Violent Way," *Life,* Sept. 11, 1970.
4 Speech, reported in *RTNDA Bulletin,* February, 1970.
5 Neil Hickey, *Television and the Troubled Campus,* Triangle Publications, 1971.
6 Richard Graf, "Dear Sir: You cur . . . " *TV Guide,* April 11, 1970.
7 *Newsweek,* January 19, 1970.
8 Frank, op. cit.
9 PBL interview, December 22, 1968.
10 *News Is What We Make It,* 1953.
11 Speech, November 25, 1969.
12 *Broadcasting,* July 13, 1970.
13 Reported in *RTNDA Bulletin,* December, 1969.
14 Triangle Publications, Inc., 1971.
15 "Heat and Light Through the TV Tube," in *Race and the News Media,* ed. by Paul L. Fisher and Ralph L. Lowenstein. New York: Frederick A. Praeger, 1967, p. 73-4.
16 "Television: The Chosen Instrument of the Revolution," in *Race and the News Media,* op. cit., p. 90.
17 Address to American Society of Newspaper Editors, Washington, April 16, 1971.
18 Ibid., p. 83-4.
19 *The Quill,* May, 1968.

CHAPTER 2: THE DAY

CHAPTER 3: PUTTING IT TOGETHER

[1] February 10, 1972, p. 1. (Reprinted with permission of *The Wall Street Journal.*)

CHAPTER 4: REPORTING

[1] Time, January 5, 1968, p. 13.
[2] RTNDA, "Television Newsfilm Standards Manual," New York: Time-Life Broadcast, Inc., 1964, p. 75.
[3] July 17, 1961.
[4] RTNDA, "The Newsroom and the Newscast," New York: Time-Life Broadcast Inc., 1966, p. 78.
[5] CBS News, June 17, 1965.
[6] Related by Merrill M. Ash in "Radio Programming in Action," ed. by Sherril W. Taylor, New York: Hastings House, 1967, p. 16.
[7] RTNDA, "Television Newsfilm Standards Manual," pp. 75-76.
[8] *Newsday,* August 14, 1967, p. 2A.
[9] RTNDA, "Television Newsfilm: Content," p. 86.
[10] "The Roles and Decision Making of Three Television Beat Reporters," paper delivered at 1971 convention of the Association for Education in Journalism, Columbia, S.C.
[11] RTNDA, "Television Newsfilm: Content," p. 30.
[12] *The Quill,* November, 1962, pp. 16-17.
[13] Paper delivered at 1971 meeting of American Orthopsychiatric Association, Washington, D.C.

CHAPTER 5: TELEVISION NEWS AS NEWS

[1] April 29, 1971.
[2] New York: The Macmillan Company, 1922, pp. 38-39.
[3] Ibid. p. 65.
[4] See Wendell Johnson, *People in Quandries.* New York: Harper & Brothers, 1946.
[5] James Bormann, "Radio News Strives for New Format." *Quill,* January, 1959, p. 15.
[6] May 3, 1971.
[7] *RTNDA Bulletin,* May, 1970.

CHAPTER 6: RADIO NEWS

[1] Robert Lewis Shayon, *Saturday Review,* April 25, 1970.
[2] Hastings House, 1971.

CHAPTER 7: WRITING

[1] New York: Harcourt, Brace and World, Inc., Second Edition, 1964, pp. 176-179.
[2] Quoted in UPI's *Broadcast Stylebook,* 1969, p. 10.

CHAPTER 8: THE FILM STORY

[1] March 11, 1967.

[2] RTNDA, *Television Newsfilm Standards Manual,* New York: Time-Life Broadcast, Inc., 1964, p. 88.
[3] NBC-TV, September 3, 1965.
[4] RTNDA, *Television Newsfilm Standards Manual,* p. 81.

CHAPTER 9: THE LEAD-IN

CHAPTER 10: FILMING TECHNIQUES

[1] Inquiry into WBBM-TV broadcast, Nov. 1 and 2, 1967, of a report on a marijuana party.
[2] RTNDA, *Television Newsfilm: Content.* New York: Time-Life Broadcast, Inc., 1965, pp. 57-58.

CHAPTER 11: PICTURES

[1] RTNDA, *Television Newsfilm Standards Manual.* New York: Time-Life Broadcast, Inc., 1964, p. 33.
[2] "Range Finder," NPPA Newsletter.

CHAPTER 12: SOUND

[1] "Of Mikes and Men—The Hidden Story," *The New York Times,* Jan. 21, 1968, Sec. D, p. 19. © 1968 by The New York Times Company. Reprinted by permission.

CHAPTER 13: FILM EDITING

[1] RTNDA, *Television Newsfilm Standards Manual.* New York: Time-Life Broadcast, Inc., 1964, p. 86.

CHAPTER 14: STILLS

[1] "Those Dull TV Weathercasts," *The Quill,* December, 1970.
[2] Method described in *Television and Radio Announcing,* second edition, by Stuart W. Hyde. Boston: Houghton Mifflin Co., 1971.

CHAPTER 15: VIDEO

[1] "The Coming Shake-up in Telecommunications," by Dan Cordtz, *Fortune,* April, 1970.

CHAPTER 16: EDITORIALS

[1] RTNDA, *Television Newsfilm: Content.* New York: Time-Life Broadcast, Inc., 1965, p. 47; plus a private letter to the author.
[2] *Television/Radio Age,* September 21, 1970.
[3] Sammy R. Danna, "Broadcast Editorializing," Freedom of Information Center publication no. 141, p. 5.
[4] Ralph Renick, "News is Not a By-Product at WTVJ," Wometco Enterprises Inc., pamphlet.

[5] RTNDA, "Television Newsfilm: Content," New York: Time-Life Broadcast, Inc., 1965.
[6] *In the Matter of Editorializing by Broadcast Licensees.* 13 FCC 1246, June 1, 1949.
[7] Minnesota Law Review, Vol. 52, 1967.
[8] *The Supreme Court on Freedom of the Press,* Iowa State University Press, 1968.
[9] *In the Matter of Editorializing by Broadcast Licensees.*
[10] 48 Statute 1062, as amended (1959).
[11] Statement to Sen. Ervin's Constitutional Rights Subcommittee, *Broadcasting,* February 7, 1972, p. 81.
[12] *RTNDA Communicator,* February, 1972, p. 2.

CHAPTER 17: ELECTIONS

[1] From "Watching the Votes Being Counted," *Journalism Quarterly,* Winter, 1969, pp. 803-07.
[2] Senate Bill 43, vetoed in September, 1967.
[3] *Broadcasting,* May 19, 1969.
[4] "Analysis of the Effect of Election Night Predictions on Voting Behavior," Mimeographed report. May 3, 1965.
[5] "Ballots and Broadcast: Exposure to Election Broadcasts and Terminal Voting Decisions." Paper presented at the 1965 annual conference of the American Association for Public Opinion Research.
[6] "Ballots and Broadcasts: The Impact of Expectations and Election Day Perceptions on Voting Behavior." Paper presented at the 1965 annual conference of the American Association for Public Opinion Research.
[7] "Election Day Radio-Television and Western Voting." *Public Opinion Quarterly.* 30:212-34. Summer, 1966.
[8] Statement to the U.S. Senate Subcommittee on Communications, July 20, 1967. On July 18, 19 and 20, the Subcommittee held hearings on projections of elections results.
[9] House Bill 11648, introduced by Rep. Charles S. Gubser of California.
[10] Kevin W. Carey, "Tom Swift and His Electric Electorate: Legislation to Restrict Election Coverage," *Notre Dame Lawyer.* 40:191-202. February, 1965.
[11] Transcript of Proceedings of Hearings on Projects of Election Results, Volume 6, July 18, 1967, p. 7.

CHAPTER 18: THE LAW

[1] UPI *Broadcast Stylebook,* 1969, p. 18.
[2] Letter, April 28, 1971.
[3] *Broadcasting,* May 17, 1971, p. 10.
[4] *Broadcasting,* April 20, 1970, p. 50.
[5] Table from *RTNDA Bulletin,* May 1970, and *Harvard Journal of Legislation,* VI:307, 1969.
[6] L. 1970, c. 615, the "Freedom of Information Bill for Newsmen."
[7] See Don. R. Pember, "Privacy and the Press: The Defense of Newsworthiness," *Journalism Quarterly* 45:1 (Spring, 1968), pp. 14-24.
[8] RTNDA Bulletin, September/October, 1968, p. 12.
[9] *News Media and the Courts,* Freedom of Information Center Report no. 004, School of Journalism, University of Missouri, Columbia, Mo.
[10] Sources of information include. *The People's Right to Know* by Harold L. Cross, New York: Columbia University Press, 1953; Freedom of Information Center reports on access laws, School of Journalism, University of Missouri.
[11] Speech to the Advertising Council, December 15, 1969.
[12] Electronic Access to Public Meetings," Freedom of Information Center Publication no. 114. School of Journalism, University of Missouri.
[13] Rep. Thomas L. Ray, "Television and Radio Provide a New Perspective to Legislative Coverage," *Quill,* May, 1958; pp. 8-10.

14 See "Television's Courthouse" by Howard S. Williams, *The Quill*, January, 1971.

15 *RTNDA Bulletin*, October, 1967.

16 *Cowley v. Pulsifer*, Supreme Judicial Court of Massachusetts, 1884.

17 See *TV's Fight for Courtroom Access*, Freedom of Information Center Report No. 200, School of Journalism, University of Missouri, Columbia, Mo.

18 "A Judge Favors TV Cameras," Freedom of Information Center Publication No. 2, School of Journalism, University of Missouri.

19 See Gillmor and Barron, *Mass Communication Law*. St. Paul: West Publishing Co., 1969, pp. 350ff.

20 *Documents of American Broadcasting*. New York: Appleton-Century-Crofts, 1968, pp. 111-112.

21 " 'Modern' Language Makes Reporting Problems for Speeches, Actualities," by Sam Kuczun, *RTNDA Bulletin*, March, 1970.

22 ABC Evening News, June 22, 1970.

CHAPTER 19: THE PROFESSION

1 Speech to National Press Club, February 4, 1970.

2 Speech to Georgia Radio and Television Institute, January 24, 1968.

3 David Dary, *Radio News Handbook*. Thurmont, Md.: TAB Books, 1967.

4 Robert E. Kintner, *Broadcasting and the News*. New York: Harper & Row, 1965, pp. 17-18.

5 November 14, 1969, p. 69.

6 *Static*, AEJ publication, December 15, 1960.

7 *Television and the News*. Palo Alto: Pacific Books, 1968, pp. 210-211.

8 Speech at University of Michigan, Ann Arbor, 1971.

9 RTNDA address, September 25, 1970.

CHAPTER 20: OPPORTUNITIES AND SALARIES

1 Handy Pocket Directory of Television Stations in Operation, 1970.

2 Six stations reported being satellites of nearby stations, 1 station was off the air, 5 stations had no news departments, 1 station provided insufficient information, and 1 station responded from Canada and was excluded.

3 East (12 states): Connecticut, Delaware, Maine, Maryland, Massachusetts, New Hampshire, New Jersey, New York, Pennsylvania, Rhode Island, Vermont, West Virginia.

South (12 states): Alabama, Arkansas, Florida, Georgia, Kentucky, Louisiana, Mississippi, North Carolina, South Carolina, Tennessee, Texas, Virginia.

Midwest (13 states): Illinois, Indiana, Iowa, Kansas, Michigan, Minnesota, Missouri, Nebraska, North Dakota, Ohio, Oklahoma, South Dakota, Wisconsin.

West (13 states): Alaska, Arizona, California, Colorado, Hawaii, Idaho, Montana, Nevada, New Mexico, Oregon, Utah, Washington, Wyoming.

4 Of a possible 666, subtracting the 14 responding stations which were excluded.

5 Where news directors distinguished between salaries for reporters and salaries for writers, the former figures were used.

6 The author cannot explain why these figures run counter to the general pattern.

7 City size based on 1970 World Almanac metro region and city populations.

8 Where news directors checked more than one choice, and gave no order of preference, both choices were counted, which explains why there are more responses tallied than questionaires returned.

9 Several news directors wrote that they would accept none of the choices offered. A few others expressed dissatisfaction with the range of choices, or preferred some variation of the given choices.

10 Where more than one field was listed, only the first was counted.

11 *Quill*, November, 1962, p. 17.

A SELECTED
BIBLIOGRAPHY

(This is by no means a comprehensive list of books concerned in whole or part with the broadcasting of news. Recent books have been given preference. In some cases a book is listed because of a single, excellent chapter on the subject.)

DELIVERY

Bender, James F., *NBC Handbook of Pronunciation,* Thomas Y. Crowell Co., 1951.
Hyde, Stuart W., *Television and Radio Announcing,* Second Edition, Houghton Mifflin Co., 1971.
Kenyon, John S., and Thomas A. Knott, *A Pronouncing Dictionary of American English,* G. & C. Merriam Co., 1953.
Lewis, Bruce, *The Technique of Television Announcing,* Hastings House, 1966.
Noory, Samuel, *Dictionary of Pronunciation,* Second Edition, A. S. Barnes & Co., 1971.

FILM AND FILM EDITING

Atkins, Jim and Leo Willette, *Filming TV News and Documentaries,* Amphoto, 1965.
Baddeley, W. Hugh, *The Technique of Documentary Film Production.* Second Edition, Hastings House, 1969.
Bobker, Lee R., *Elements of Film,* Harcourt, Brace & World, Inc., 1969.
Fielding, Raymond, *The Technique of Special Effects Cinematography,* Third Revised Edition, Hastings House, 1972.
Jacobs, Lewis, *The Movies as a Medium,* Farrar, Straus & Giroux, 1970.
Kuhns, Robert and Stanley, *Exploring the Film,* Pflaum, 1970.
Mascelli, Joseph V., editor, *American Cinematographer Manual,* American Society of Cinematographers, 1971.

Mascelli, Joseph V., *The Five C's of Cinematography*, Cine/Graphic Publications, 1965.
Mercer, John, *An Introduction to Cinematography*, Stipes Publishing Co., 1967.
Pincus, Edward, *Guide to Filmmaking*, Signet Books, 1969.
Reisz, Karel, and Gavin Millar, *The Technique of Film Editing*, Revised and Enlarged Edition, Hastings House, 1968.
RTNDA, *Television Newsfilm Standards Manual*, Time Life Broadcast, Inc., 1964.
RTNDA, *Television Newsfilm, Content*, Time Life Broadcast, Inc., 1965.
Smallman, Kirk, *Creative Film-making*, Collier Books, 1970.
Souto, H. Mario Raimondo, *The Technique of the Motion Picture Camera*, Revised and Enlarged Edition, Hastings House, 1969.
Walter, Ernest, *The Technique of the Film Cutting Room*, Revised Edition, Hastings House, 1972.

GRAPHICS

Ballinger, Raymond A., *Layout and Graphic Design*, Van Nostrand Reinhold Co., 1970.
Halas, John, and Roger Manvell, *The Technique of Film Animation*, Revised Edition, Hastings House, 1968.
Laughton, Roy, *TV Graphics*, Reinhold Publishing Corporation, 1966.

LEGAL MATTERS

American Bar Association, *The Rights of Fair Trial and Free Press*, American Bar Association, 1969.
Ashley, Paul, *Say It Safely, Legal Limits in Publishing, Radio, and Television*, Fourth Edition, University of Washington Press, 1969.
Chernoff, George, and Hershel Sarbin, *Photography and the Law*, Chilton Books, 1965.
Devol, Kenneth S., editor, *Mass Media and the Supreme Court*, Hastings House, 1971.
Federal Communications Commission, *Rules and Regulations*, 1963.
Friendly, Alfred, and Ronald L. Goldfarb, *Crime and Publicity, the Impact of News on the Administration of Justice*, The Twentieth Century Fund, 1967.
Gillmor, Donald M., and Jerome A. Barron, *Mass Communications Law*, West Publishing Co., 1969.
Kittross, John M., and Kenneth Harwood, *Free and Fair: Courtroom Access and the Fairness Doctrine*. Association for Professional Broadcasting Education, 1970.
National Commission on the Causes and Prevention of Violence, *Rights in Conflict*, New American Library, 1968.
Nelson, Harold L., and Dwight L. Teeter, Jr., *Law of Mass Communication*, The Foundation Press, 1969.
New York Bar Association, *Radio, Television and the Administration of Justice*, Columbia University Press, 1965.
Phelps, Robert H., and E. Douglas Hamilton, *Libel*, Macmillan, 1966.

MASS MEDIA

Emery, Edwin, Phillip Ault, and Warren K. Agee, *Introduction to Mass Communications*, Third Edition, Dodd, Mead, and Company, 1970.
Kirschner, Allen, and Linda Kirschner, *Radio and Television, Readings in the Mass Media*, The Odyssey Press, 1971.

Kirschner, Allen, and Linda Kirschner, *Journalism, Readings in the Mass Media,* The Odyssey Press, 1971.

Rivers, William I., Theodore Peterson, and Jay W. Jensen, *The Mass Media and Modern Society,* Rinehart Press, 1971.

Rivers, William L., and Wilber Schramm, *Responsibility in Mass Communication,* Harper & Row, 1969.

Steinberg, Charles S., editor, *Mass Media and Communication,* Revised and Enlarged Edition, Hastings House, 1972.

REPORTING

Bingham, Walter Van Dyke, and Bruce Vistor Moore, *How to Interview,* Fourth Edition, Harper & Brothers, 1959.

Bush, Charles R., *Newswriting and Reporting Public Affairs,* Chilton Book Company, 1965.

Campbell, Laurence R., and Roland E. Wolseley, *How to Report and Write the News,* Prentice-Hall, Inc., 1961.

Charnley, Mitchell V., *Reporting,* Second Edition, Holt, Rinehart and Winston, Inc., 1966.

Dunn, Delmer D., *Public Officials and the Press,* Addison-Wesley Publishing Company, 1969.

Hohenberg, John, *The Professional Journalist, A Guide to the Practices and Principles of the News Media,* Second Edition, Holt, Rinehart and Winston, Inc., 1966.

SOUND

Cushman, George W., *Sound for Your Color Movies,* Camera Craft Publishing Company, 1958.

Nisbett, Alec, *The Technique of the Sound Studio,* Revised Third Edition, Hastings House, 1972.

Oringel, Robert S., *Audio Control Handbook,* Fourth Edition, Hastings House, 1972.

TELEVISION, GENERAL

Bleum, A. William, *Religious Television Programs, A Study of Relevance,* Hastings House, 1969.

Bleum, A. William, John F. Cox, and Gene McPherson, *Television in the Public Interest,* Hastings House, 1961.

Brown, Les, *Televi$ion,* Harcourt Brace, Jovanovich, 1971.

Cole, Barry G., editor, *Television,* The Free Press, 1970.

Dizard, Wilson P., *Television, A New World,* Syracuse University Press, 1966.

Glick, Ira O., and Sidney J. Levy, *Living With Television,* Aldine Publishing Co., 1962.

Quaal, Ward L., and Leo A. Martin, *Broadcast Management,* Hastings House, 1968.

Roe, Yale, editor, *Television Station Management,* Hastings House, 1964.

Skornia, Harry J., *Television and Society,* McGraw-Hill Book Company, 1965.

Skornia, Harry J., and Jack William Kitson, *Problems and Controversies in Television and Radio,* Pacific Book, Publishers, 1968.

Spottiswoode, Raymond, editor, *The Focal Encyclopedia of Film and Television: Techniques,* Hastings House, 1969.

TELEVISION NEWS: HISTORY AND COMMENT

Barnouw, Erik, *A Tower in Babel, A History of Broadcasting in the United States,* Vol. I; to 1933, Oxford University Press, 1966.

Barnouw, Erik, *The Golden Web, A History of Broadcasting in the United States,* Vol. II; 1933-1953. Oxford University Press, 1968.

Barnouw, Erik, *The Image Empire, A History of Broadcasting in the United States,* Vol. III; 1953-present. Oxford University Press, 1970.

du Pont, Alfred I., *Survey of Broadcast Journalism, 1968–69,* Gosset & Dunlap, Inc., 1969.

du Pont, Alfred I., *Survey of Broadcast Journalism, 1969–70,* Gosset & Dunlap, Inc., 1970.

du Pont, Alfred I., *Survey of Broadcast Journalism, 1970–71,* Gosset & Dunlap, Inc., 1971.

Fielding, Raymond, editor, *A Technological History of Motion Pictures and Television,* University of California Press, 1967.

Friendly, Fred, *Due to Circumstances Beyond Our Control,* Random House, 1967.

Gordon, George N. and Irving A. Falk, *On the Spot Reporting, Radio Records History,* Julian Messner, 1967.

Keeley, Joseph, *The Left Leaning Antenna,* Arlington House, 1971.

Kendrick, Alexander, *Prime Time, the Life of Edward R. Murrow,* Little, Brown & Co., 1969.

Lang, Kurt, and Gladys Engel Lang, *Politics and Television,* Quadrangle, 1968.

MacNeil, Robert, *The People Machine,* Harper & Row, Publishers, 1968.

McGinniss, Joe, *The Selling of the President, 1968.* Trident Press, 1969.

Mendelsohn, Harold and Irving Crespi, *Polls, Television and the New Politics,* Chandler Publishing, 1970.

NBC, *The Longest Night,* National Broadcasting Company, 1963.

National Advisory Commission on Civil Disorders, *Report,* E. P. Dutton & Co., 1968.

Skornia, Harry J., *Television and the News,* Pacific Book Publishers, 1968.

Small, William, *To Kill A Messenger,* Hastings House, 1970.

Wood, William A., *Electronic Journalism,* Columbia University Press, 1967.

TELEVISION AND RADIO NEWS: METHODS

CBS News, *Television News Reporting,* McGraw-Hill Book Company, 1958.

Dary, David, *Radio News Handbook,* TAB Books, 1967.

Dary, David, *Television News Handbook,* TAB Books, 1971.

Green, Maury, *Television News, Anatomy and Process,* Wadsworth Publishing Company, Inc., 1969.

Hilliard, Robert L., editor, *Radio Broadcasting,* Hastings House, 1967.

RTNDA, *The Newsroom and the Newscast,* Time Life Broadcast Inc., 1966.

Siller, Bob, Ted White, and Hal Terkel, *Television and Radio News,* Macmillan, 1960.

Swallow, Norman, *Factual Television,* Hastings House, 1966.

Taylor, Sherril W., editor, *Radio Programming in Action, Realities and Opportunities,* Hastings House, 1967.

TELEVISION PRODUCTION

Bretz, Rudy, *Techniques of Television Production,* McGraw-Hill Book Company, Inc., 1953.

Chinn, Howard A., *Television Broadcasting,* McGraw-Hill Book Company, Inc., 1953.

Lewis, Colby, *The TV Director/Interpreter,* Hastings House, 1968.

Millerson, Gerald, *The Technique of Television Production,* Ninth Revised Edition, Hastings House, 1972.

Zettl, Herbert, *Television Production Handbook,* Wadsworth Publishing Company, Inc., 1961.

WRITING, GENERAL

Flesch, Rudolf, *The Art of Clear Thinking,* Harper & Row, 1951.

Flesch, Ruolph, *The Art of Plain Talk,* Harper & Row, 1946.

Flesch, Rudolph, *The Art of Readable Writing,* Harper & Row, 1949.

Gunning, Robert, *The Technique of Clear Writing,* Revised Edition, McGraw-Hill Book Company, 1968.

Hayakawa, S. I., *Language in Thought and Action,* Second Edition, Harcourt, Brace, & World, Inc., 1964.

Strunk, William, Jr., and E. B. White, *The Elements of Style,* Macmillan Paperbacks, 1959.

WRITING, NEWS AND DOCUMENTARY

Bliss, Edward Jr., and John M. Peterson, *Writing News for Broadcast,* Colorado University Press, 1971.

Bluem, A. William, *Documentary in American Television,* Hastings House, 1965.

Brown, Donald E., and John P. Jones, *Radio and Television News,* Rinehart & Co., Inc., 1953.

Hall, Mark, *Broadcast Journalism, An Introduction to News Writing,* Hastings House, 1971.

Hilliard, Robert L., *Writing for Television and Radio,* Hastings House, 1968.

Parker, Norton S., *Audiovisual Script Writing,* Rutgers University Press, 1968.

Wimer, Arthur, and Donald Brix, *Workbook for Radio and TV News Editing and Writing,* Third Edition, Wm. C. Brown Company Publishers, 1966.

INDEX